James

James

by mark tonra

**Andrews McMeel
Publishing**

Kansas City

www.JamesFans.com

www.ucomics.com

ISBN: 0-7407-2196-8

Library of Congress Control Number: 2001095891

02 03 04 05 06 BAH 10 9 8 7 6 5 4 3 2 1

──────── ATTENTION: SCHOOLS AND BUSINESSES ────────

Andrews McMeel books are available at quantity discounts with bulk purchase for educational, business, or sales promotional use. For information, please write to: Special Sales Department, Andrews McMeel Publishing, 4520 Main Street, Kansas City, Missouri 64111.

Foreword

I used to sleep. I have very distant memories of an uninterrupted horizontal posture that was as restoring as it was unconscious. I may even have done it for hours at a stretch. With my eyes closed. That's how good I was. I had talent. Dreams had a beginning, a middle, and an end. Sometimes there were cats involved (I was inclusive). Not infrequently, I would open my eyes, shift my weight, and go right back out again. Flashy, I know—but such is youth. Or is it? Time has a way of sweetening one's memory and mine may be the perfect illusion.

James moved in with us almost two years ago. He is thirty-two inches tall, bald, and a great dancer. He loves, in no specific order, Latin jazz, Gene Kelly, and the potted ficus tree in our living room. We clicked right away. The master bedroom is his favorite, so we gave it to him. He still lets us use the Jacuzzi from time to time, and I think that speaks *volumes* about the relationship. He doesn't pay rent, but I figure the money we're saving on alarm clocks makes it a wash— which brings us back to my original topic:

"sleep."

James is an early riser. He makes Ben Franklin look like Rip Van Winkle on muscle relaxants. If we haven't watched *Singing In The Rain* at least ten times before Katie Couric gets in the shower, say your prayers, the world is coming to an end.

The first "knock," courtesy of the ever-present baby monitor, happens around midnight:

"Five hours till show time, Daddy" (my translation).

Three o'clock: "Two hours till show time, Daddy."

And finally: "Show time!"

As any proud parent will concur, these are golden moments. Take it from me, one who knows. You would have to be without a heartbeat not to think—after hearing your own child's voice before the dawn—"There must be *some* way to exploit this short stranger for personal profit."

And so I did.

On November 13, 2000, *James* was introduced by Universal Press Syndicate to comic strip readers worldwide. What you're browsing now is the first in a series of *James* anthologies being published by Andrews McMeel. The official James Web site (www.JamesFans.com) is up and running; come visit.

As always, I feel deeply honored—and humbled—to be sharing a job title with the great Charles Schulz, E. C. Segar, George Herriman, and Percy Crosby. If I didn't know better, I'd think I was dreaming. But alas, as everyone knows, that requires sleep.

Mark Tonra
January 2001

For James

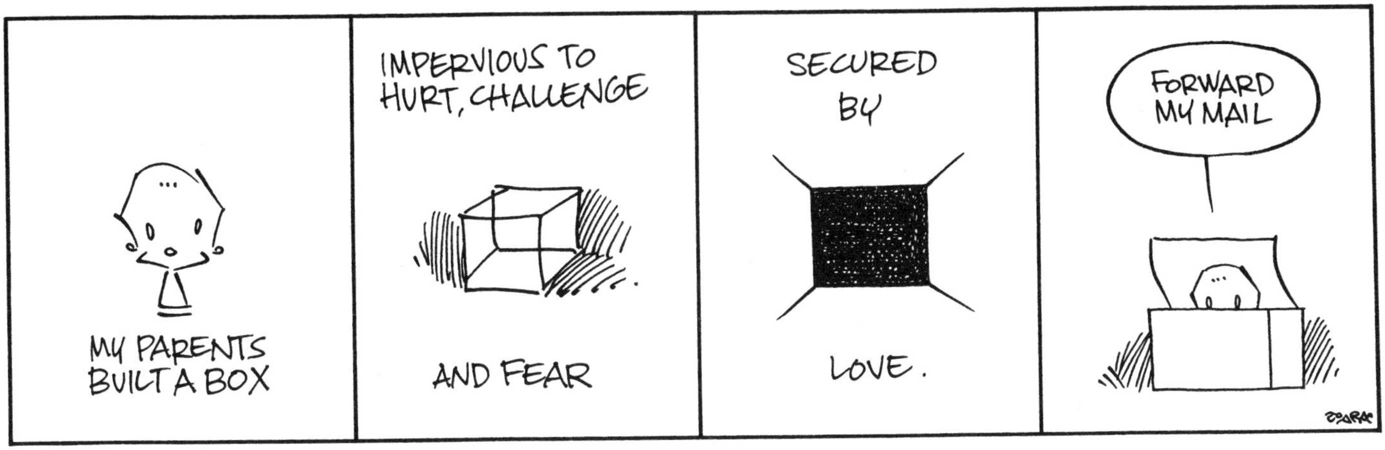
MY PARENTS BUILT A BOX
IMPERVIOUS TO HURT, CHALLENGE
AND FEAR
SECURED BY
LOVE.
FORWARD MY MAIL

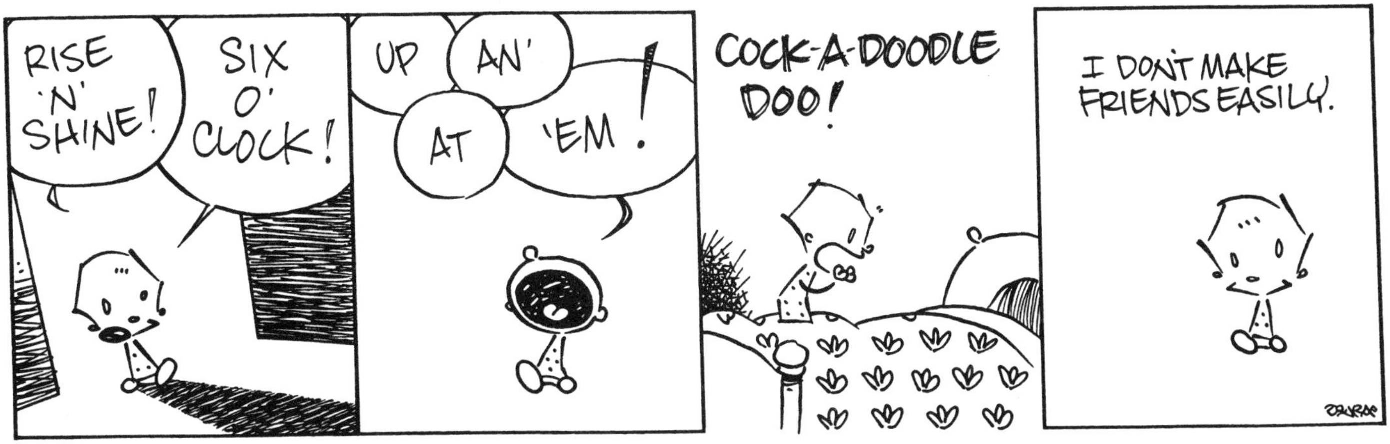
RISE 'N' SHINE!
SIX O' CLOCK!
UP
AN'
AT
'EM!
COCK-A-DOODLE DOO!
I DON'T MAKE FRIENDS EASILY.

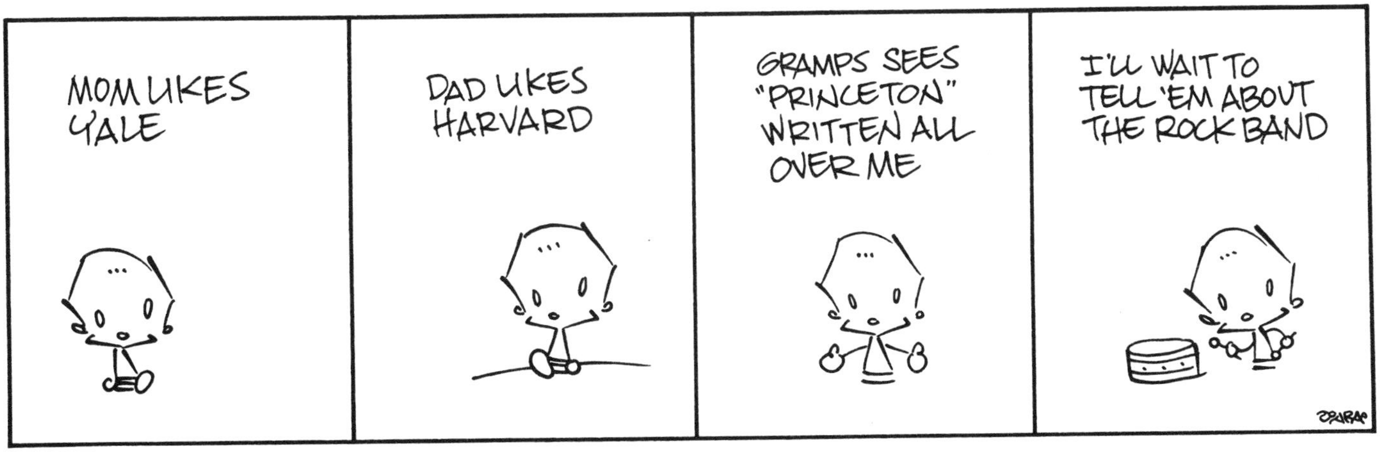
MOM LIKES YALE
DAD LIKES HARVARD
GRAMPS SEES "PRINCETON" WRITTEN ALL OVER ME
I'LL WAIT TO TELL 'EM ABOUT THE ROCK BAND

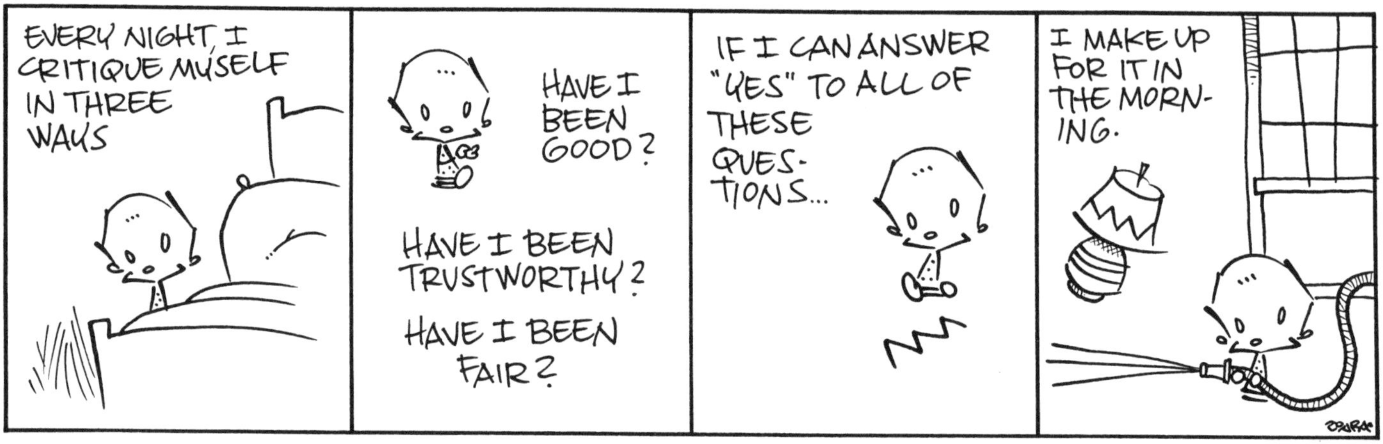
EVERY NIGHT, I CRITIQUE MYSELF IN THREE WAYS
HAVE I BEEN GOOD?
HAVE I BEEN TRUSTWORTHY?
HAVE I BEEN FAIR?
IF I CAN ANSWER "YES" TO ALL OF THESE QUES-TIONS...
I MAKE UP FOR IT IN THE MORN-ING.

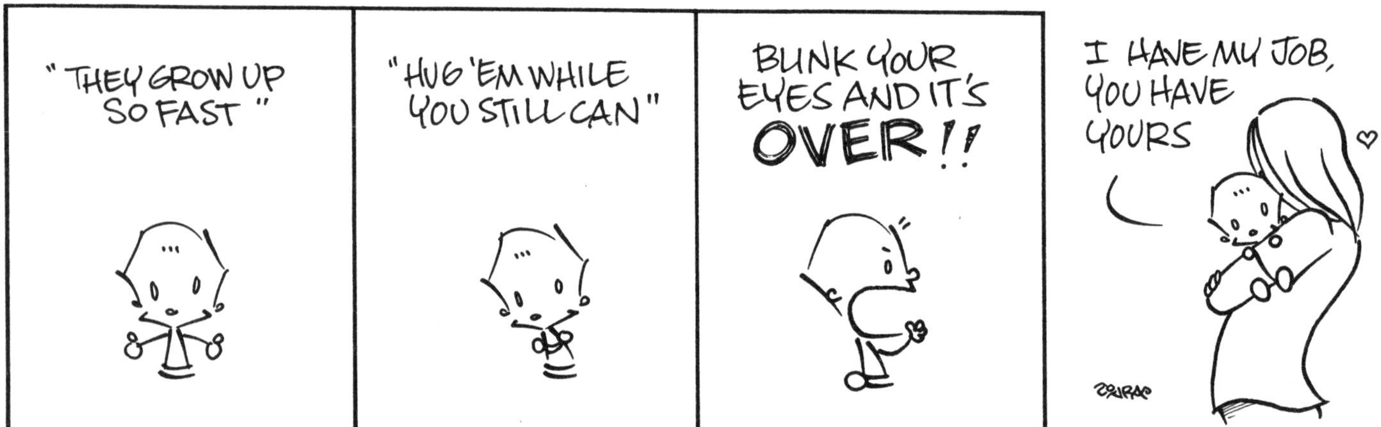
"THEY GROW UP SO FAST"
"HUG 'EM WHILE YOU STILL CAN"
BLINK YOUR EYES AND IT'S OVER!!
I HAVE MY JOB, YOU HAVE YOURS

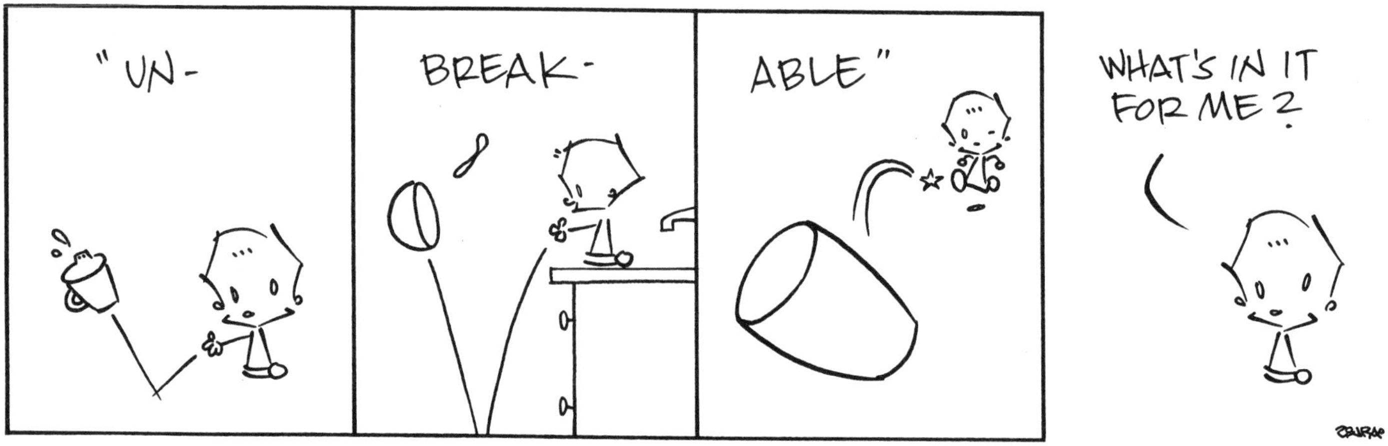
"UN-
BREAK-
ABLE"
WHAT'S IN IT FOR ME?

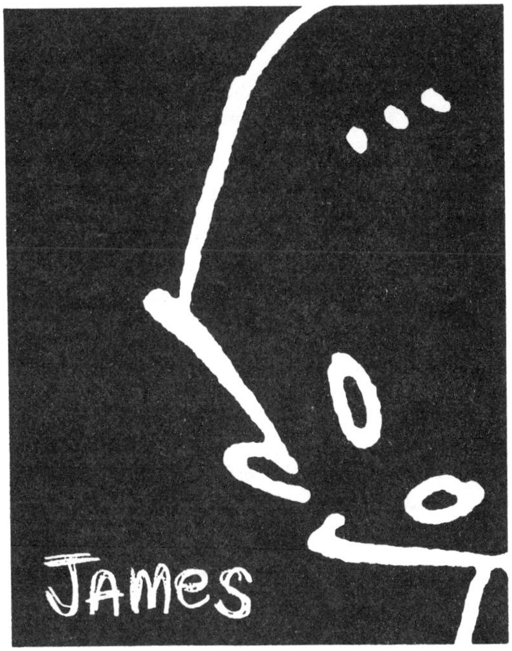
JAMES

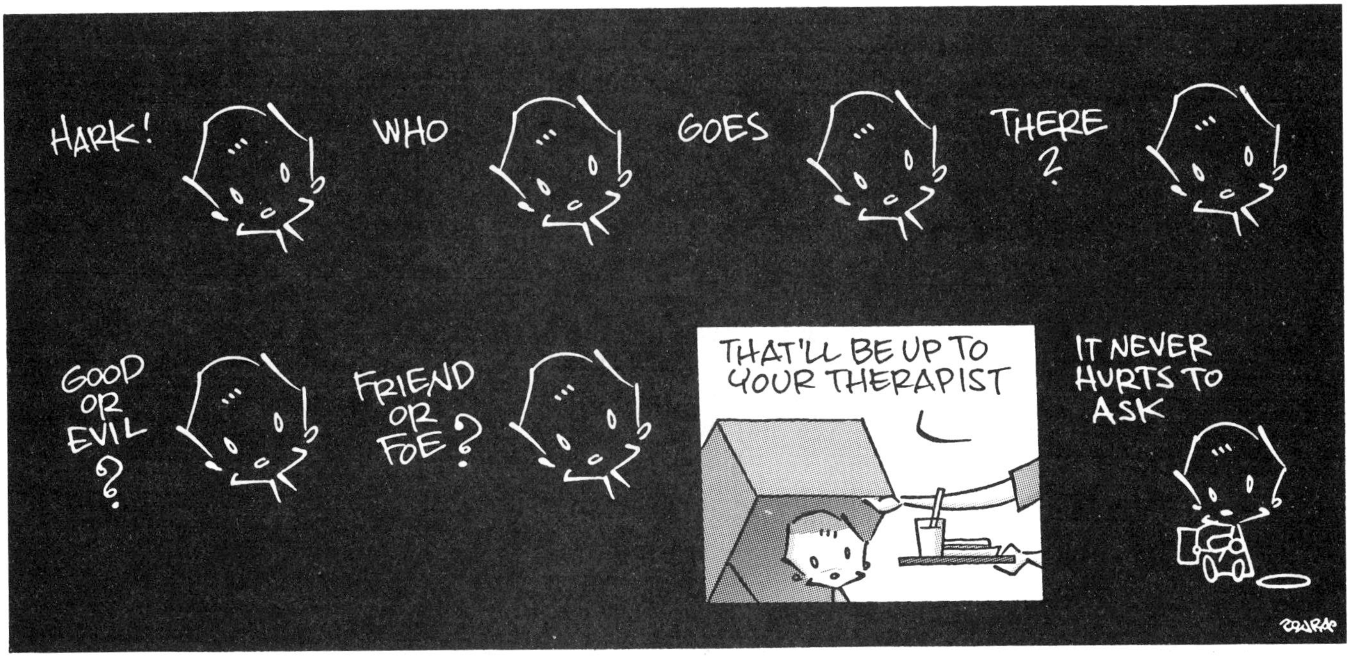
HARK!
WHO
GOES
THERE ?
GOOD OR EVIL ?
FRIEND OR FOE ?
THAT'LL BE UP TO YOUR THERAPIST
IT NEVER HURTS TO ASK

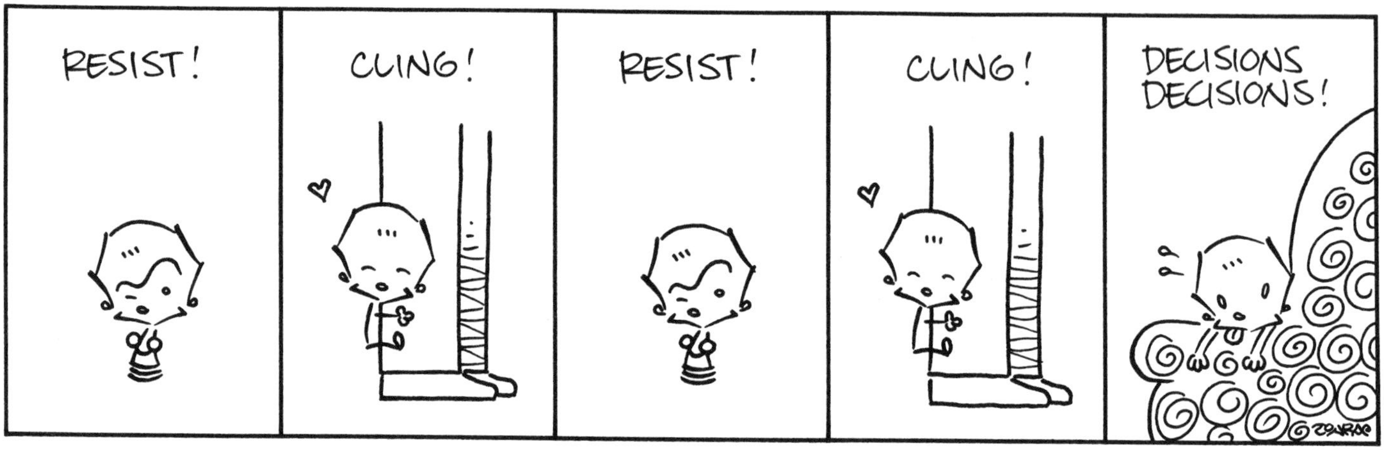
RESIST!
CLING!
RESIST!
CLING!
DECISIONS DECISIONS!

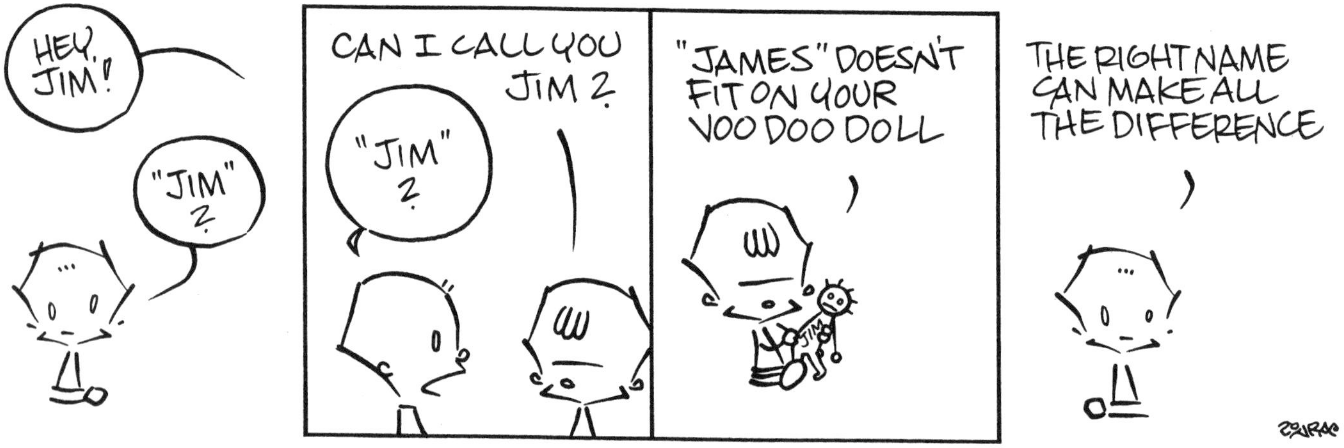
HEY, JIM!
"JIM" ?
CAN I CALL YOU JIM ?
"JIM" ?
"JAMES" DOESN'T FIT ON YOUR VOO DOO DOLL
JIM
THE RIGHT NAME CAN MAKE ALL THE DIFFERENCE

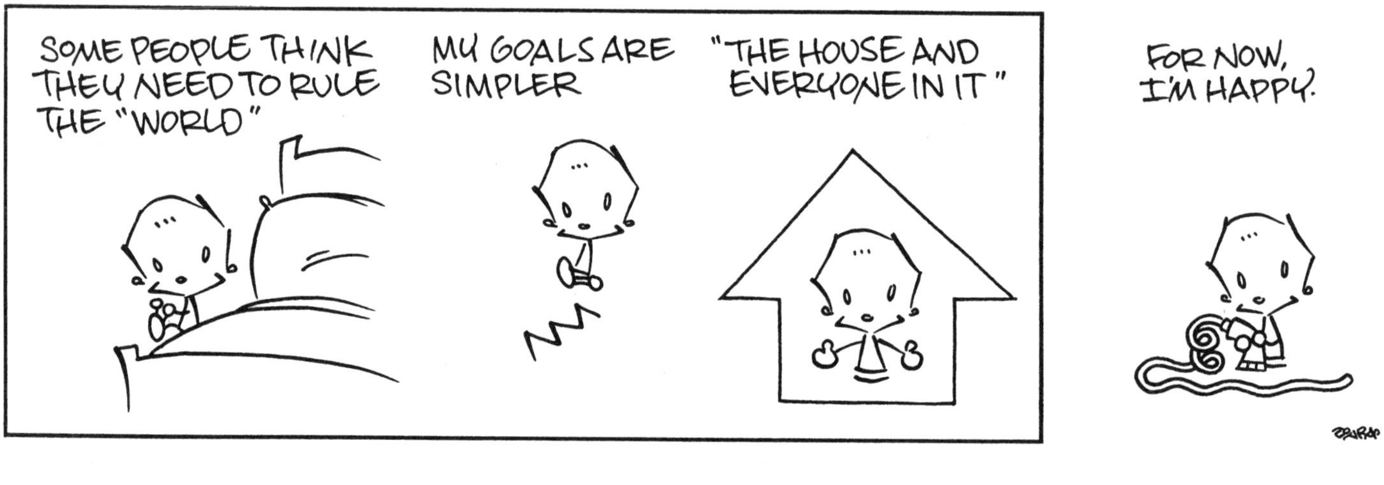
SOME PEOPLE THINK THEY NEED TO RULE THE "WORLD"
MY GOALS ARE SIMPLER
"THE HOUSE AND EVERYONE IN IT"
FOR NOW, I'M HAPPY.

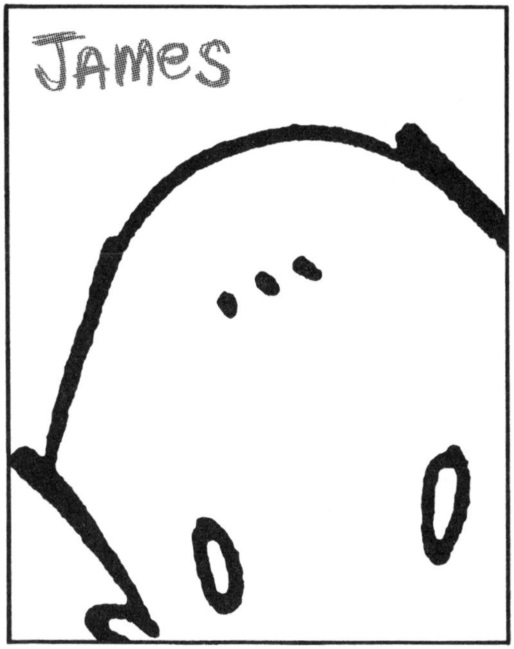
JAMES

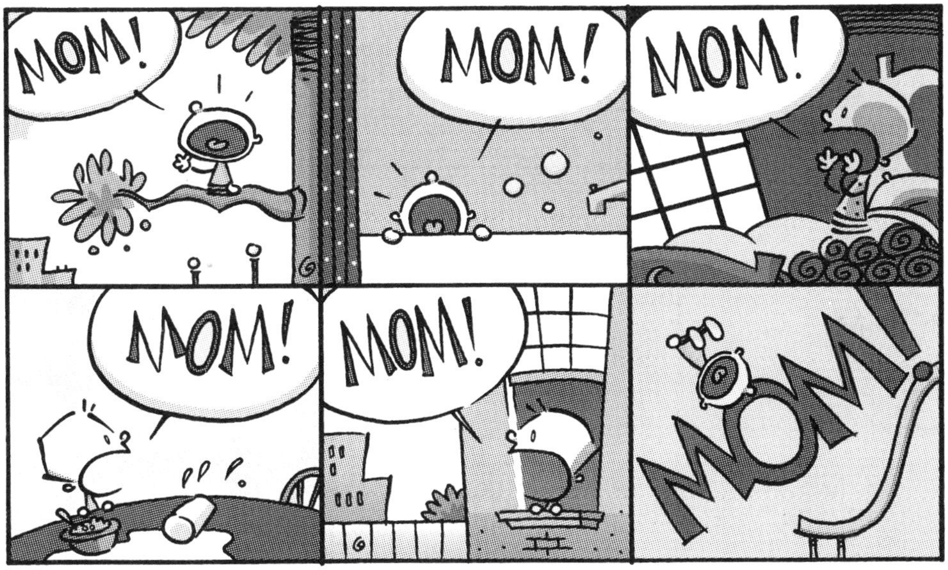
MOM!
MOM!
MOM!
MOM!
MOM!
MOM!

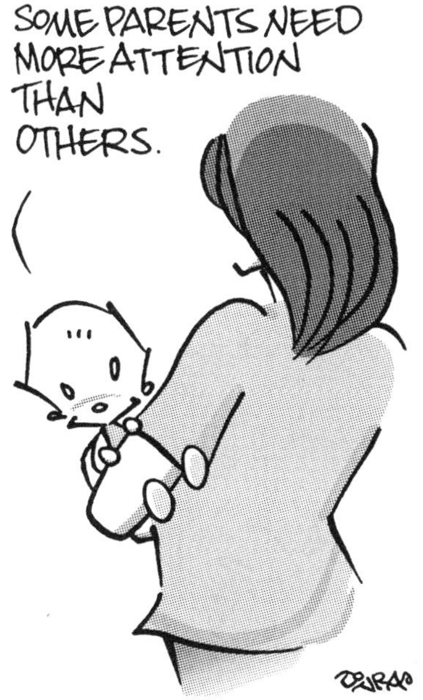
SOME PARENTS NEED MORE ATTENTION THAN OTHERS.

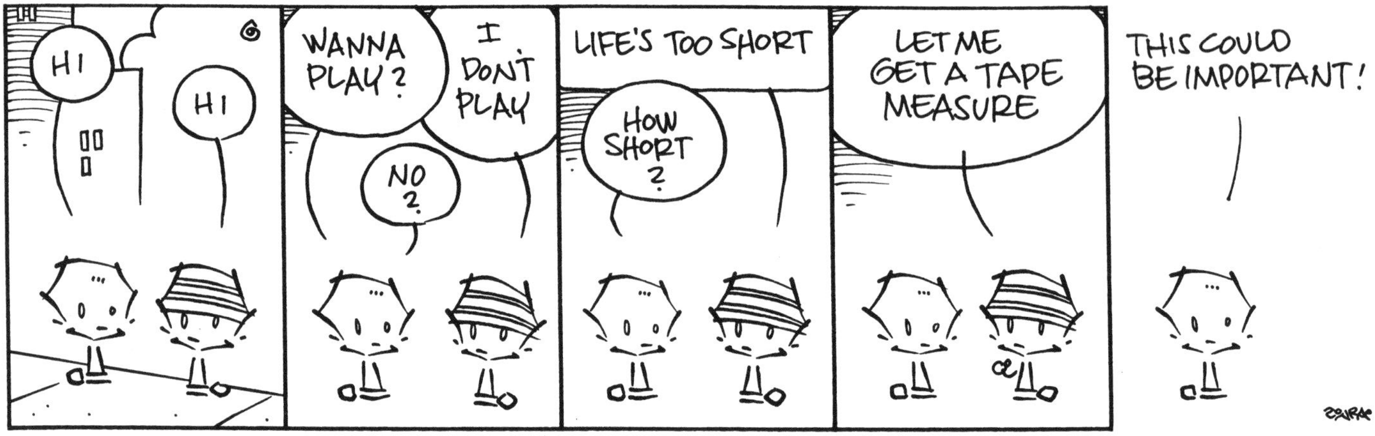
HI
HI
WANNA PLAY?
I DON'T PLAY
NO?
LIFE'S TOO SHORT
HOW SHORT?
LET ME GET A TAPE MEASURE
THIS COULD BE IMPORTANT!

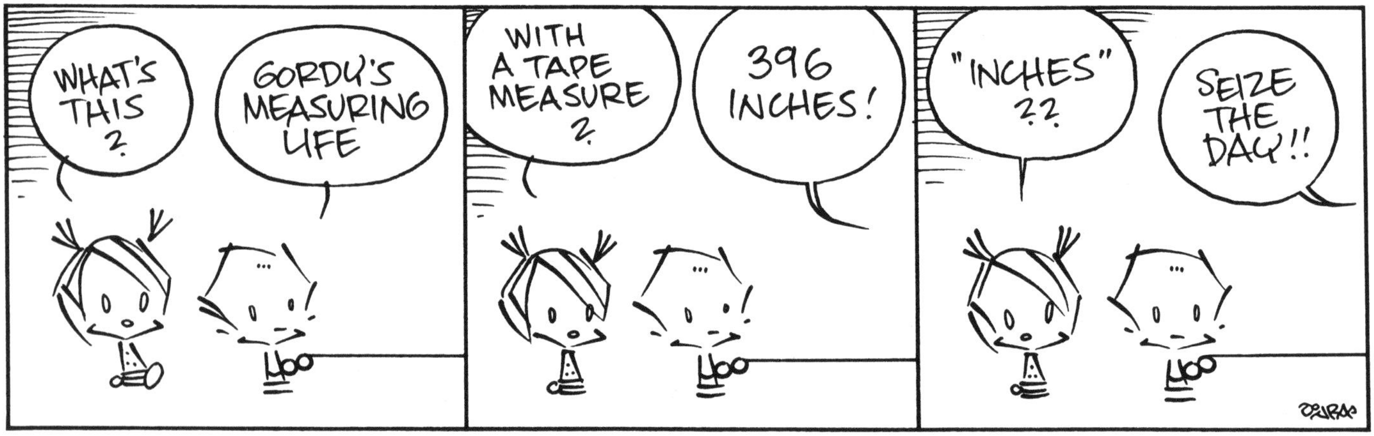
WHAT'S THIS?
GORDY'S MEASURING LIFE
WITH A TAPE MEASURE?
396 INCHES!
"INCHES"??
SEIZE THE DAY!!

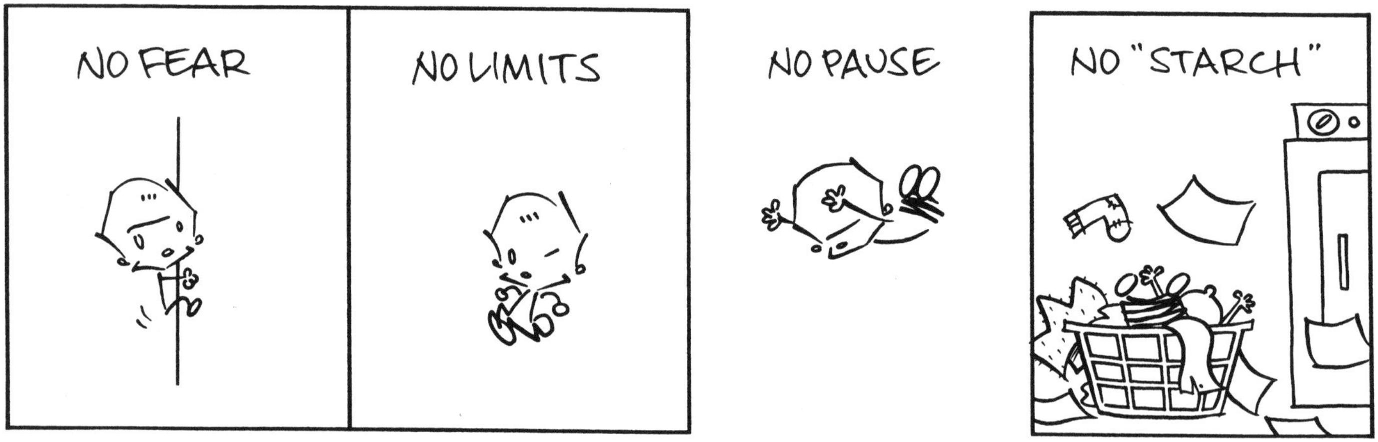
NO FEAR
NO LIMITS
NO PAUSE
NO "STARCH"

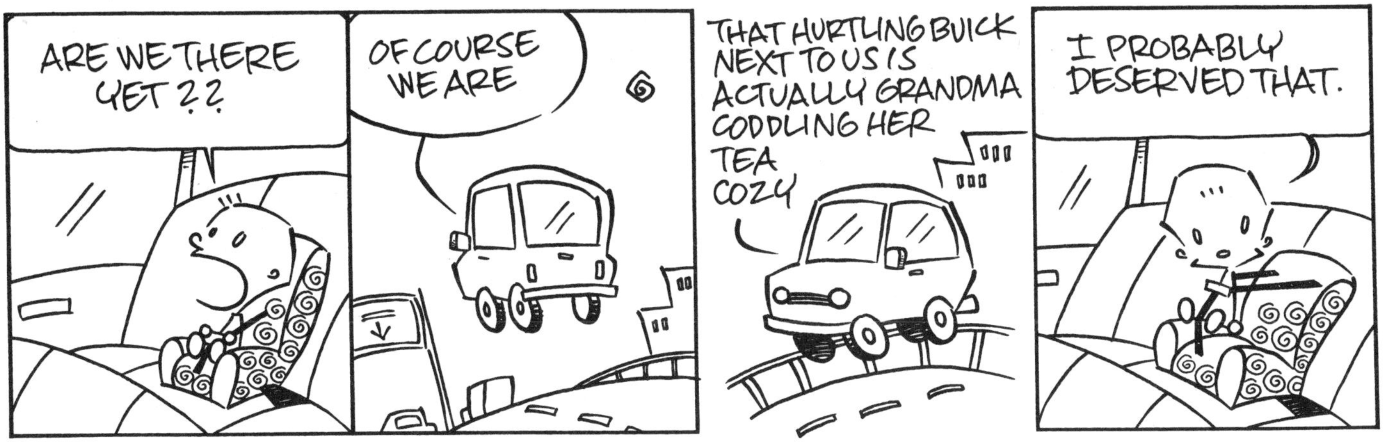
ARE WE THERE YET ??
OF COURSE WE ARE
THAT HURTLING BUICK NEXT TO US IS ACTUALLY GRANDMA CODDLING HER TEA COZY
I PROBABLY DESERVED THAT.

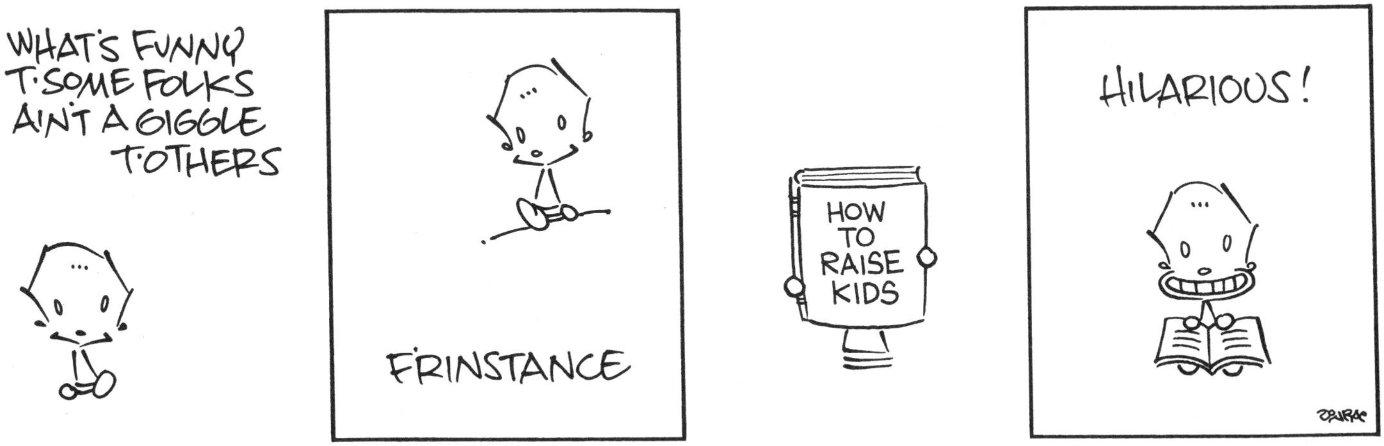
WHAT'S FUNNY T'SOME FOLKS AIN'T A GIGGLE T'OTHERS
FRINSTANCE
HOW TO RAISE KIDS
HILARIOUS!

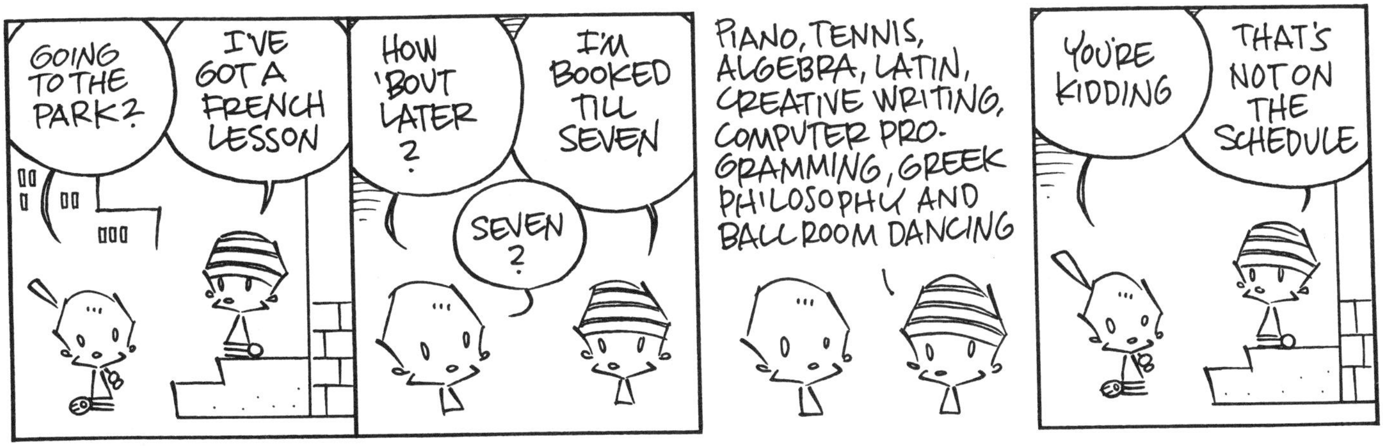
GOING TO THE PARK?
I'VE GOT A FRENCH LESSON
HOW 'BOUT LATER ?
I'M BOOKED TILL SEVEN
SEVEN ?
PIANO, TENNIS, ALGEBRA, LATIN, CREATIVE WRITING, COMPUTER PRO-GRAMMING, GREEK PHILOSOPHY AND BALLROOM DANCING
YOU'RE KIDDING
THAT'S NOT ON THE SCHEDULE

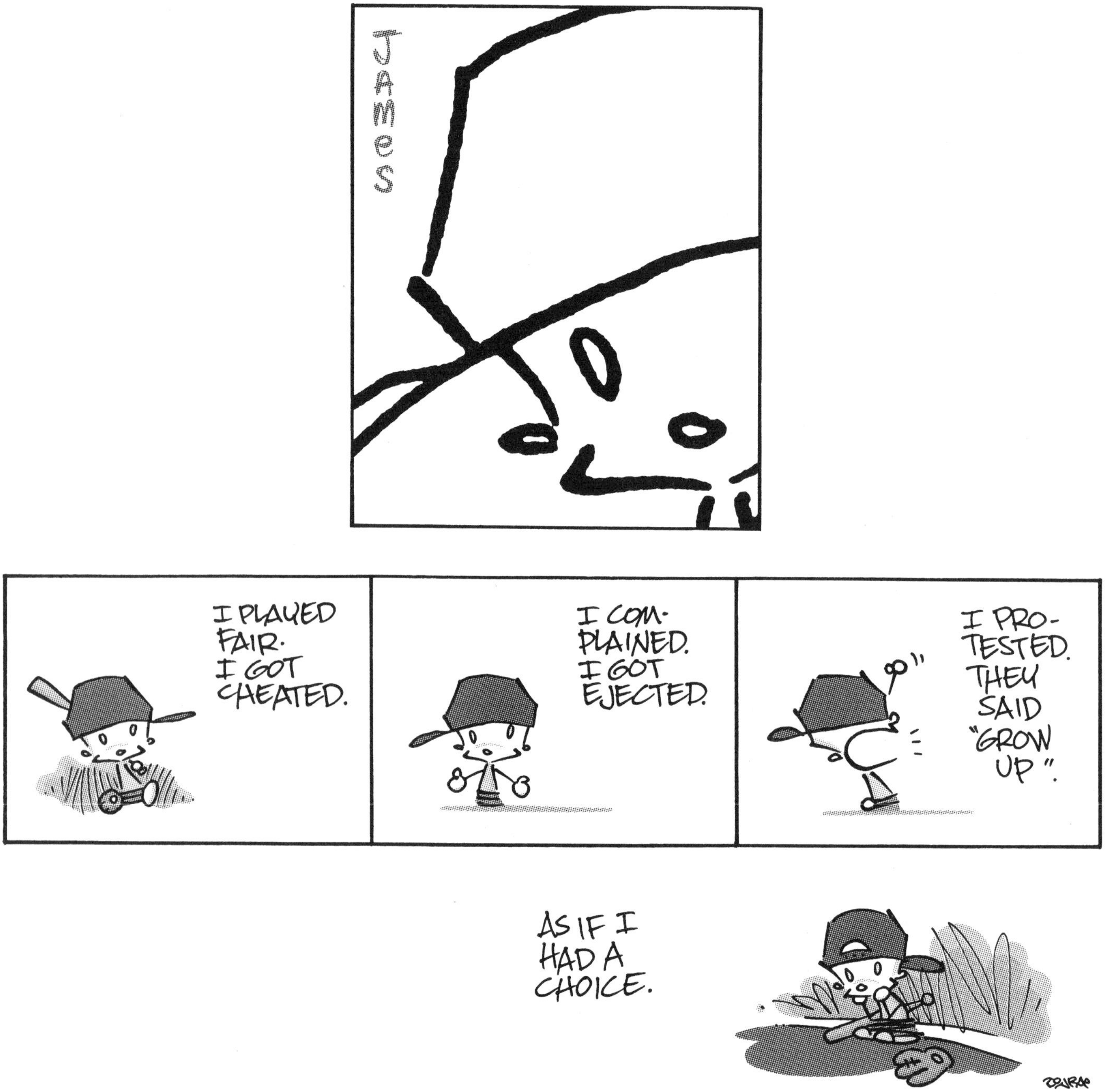
JAMES
I PLAYED FAIR. I GOT CHEATED.
I COMPLAINED. I GOT EJECTED.
I PROTESTED. THEY SAID "GROW UP".
AS IF I HAD A CHOICE.

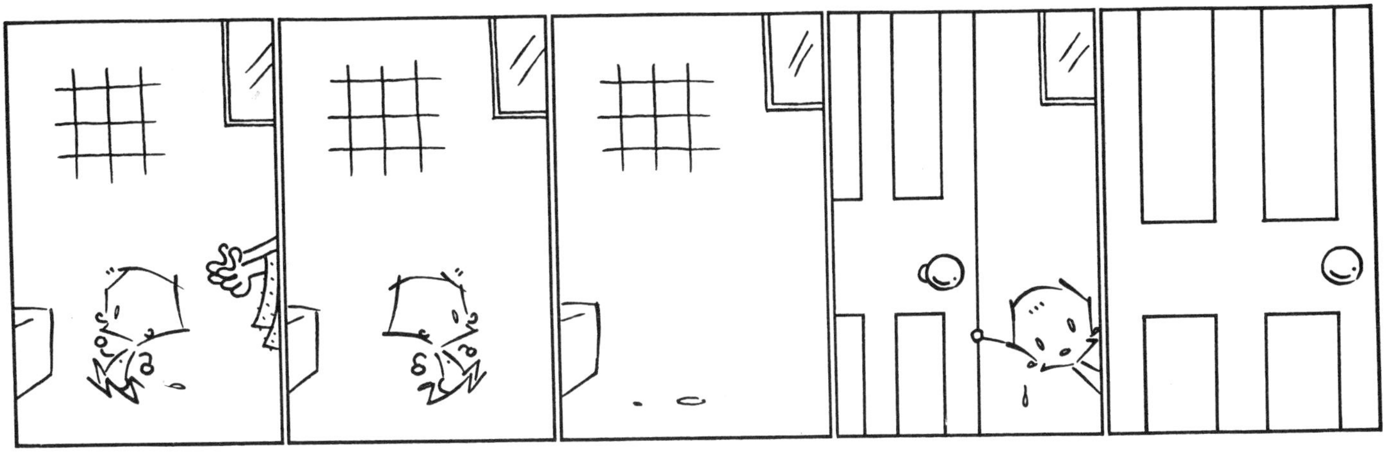

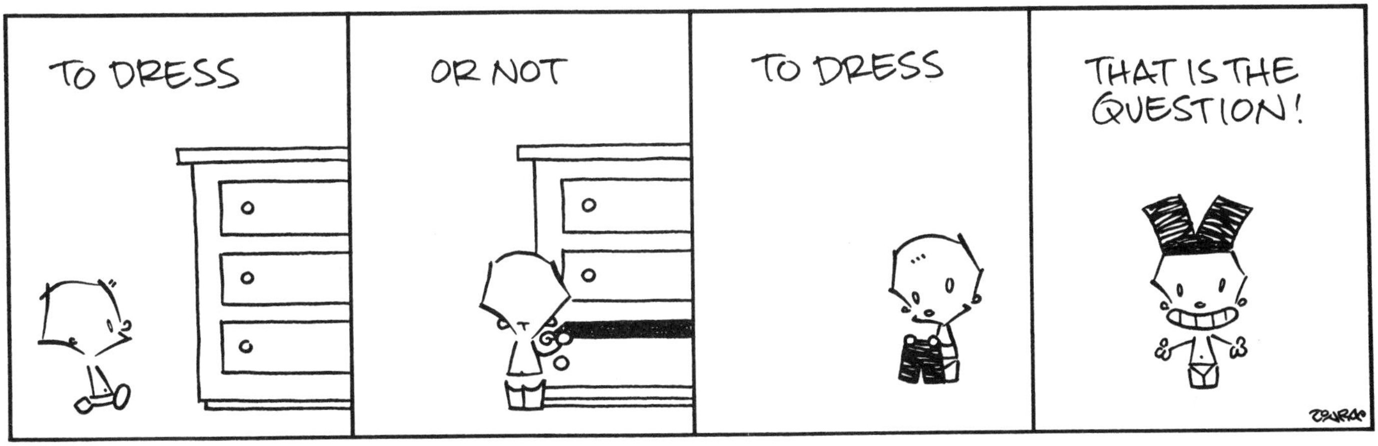
TO DRESS
OR NOT
TO DRESS
THAT IS THE QUESTION!

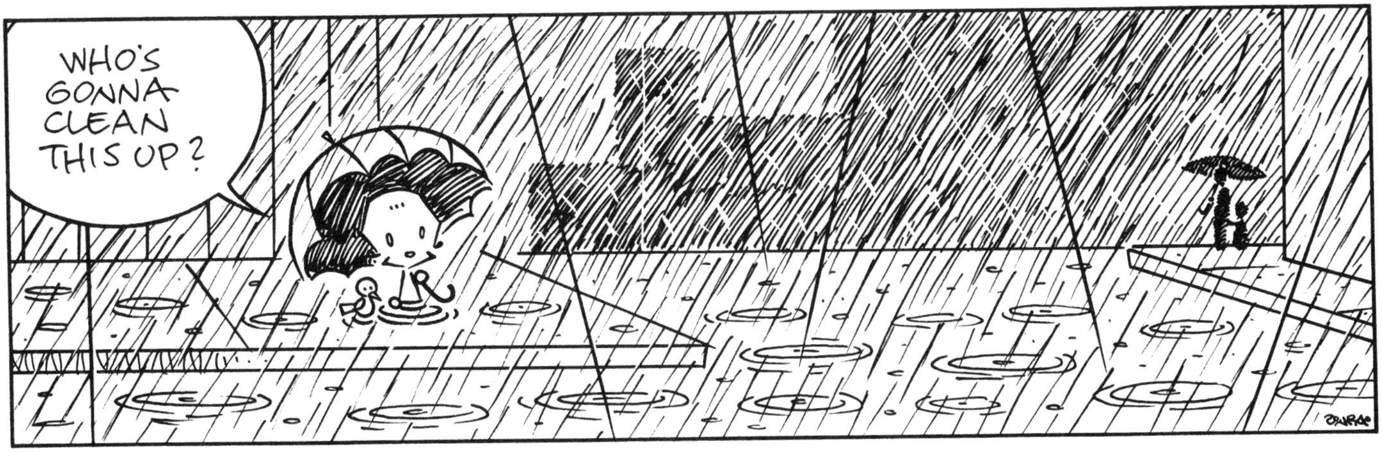
WHO'S GONNA CLEAN THIS UP?

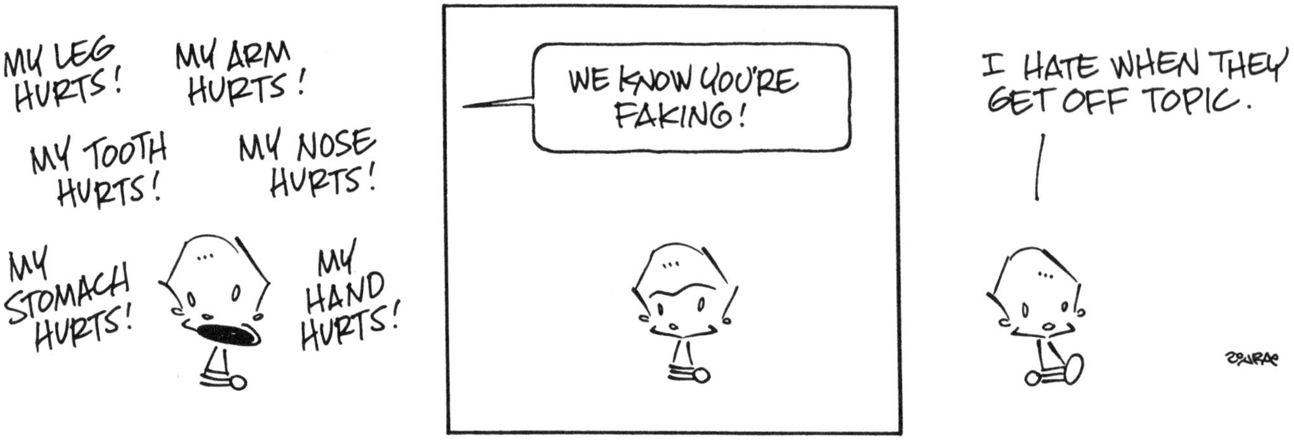
MY LEG HURTS!
MY ARM HURTS!
MY TOOTH HURTS!
MY NOSE HURTS!
MY STOMACH HURTS!
MY HAND HURTS!
WE KNOW YOU'RE FAKING!
I HATE WHEN THEY GET OFF TOPIC.

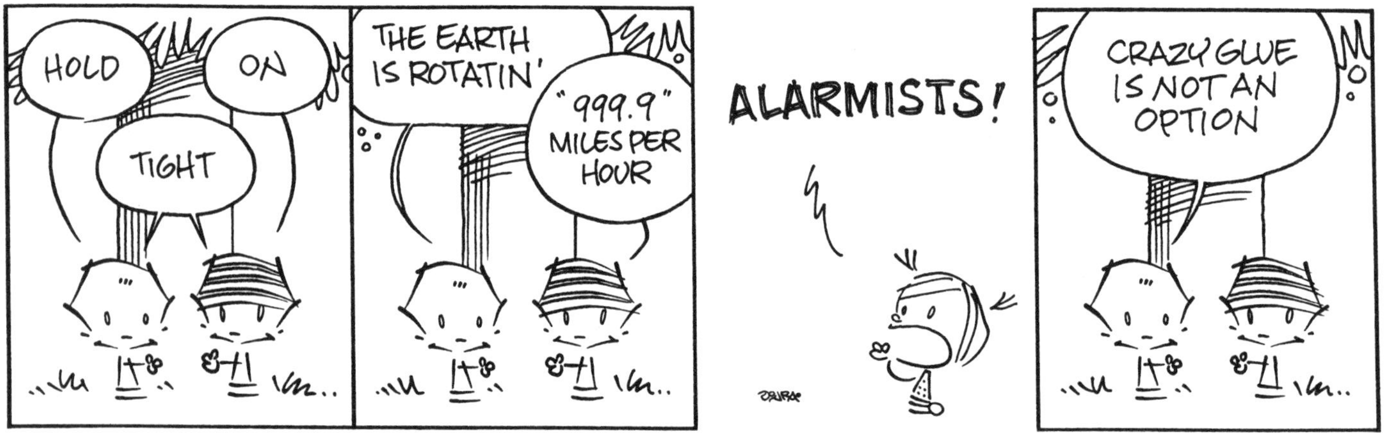
HOLD
ON
TIGHT
THE EARTH IS ROTATIN'
"999.9" MILES PER HOUR
ALARMISTS!
CRAZY GLUE IS NOT AN OPTION

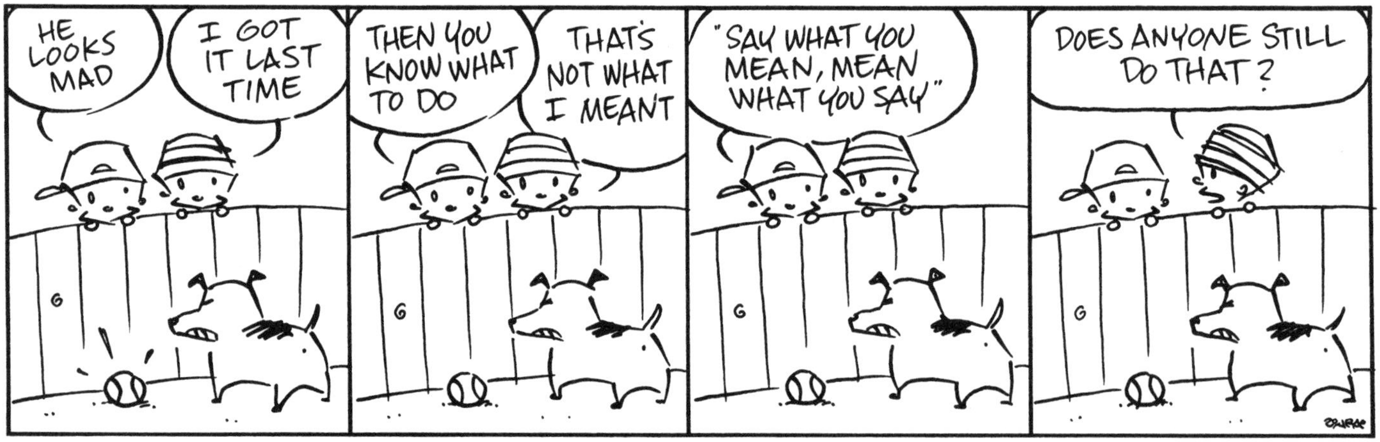
HE LOOKS MAD
I GOT IT LAST TIME
THEN YOU KNOW WHAT TO DO
THAT'S NOT WHAT I MEANT
"SAY WHAT YOU MEAN, MEAN WHAT YOU SAY"
DOES ANYONE STILL DO THAT?

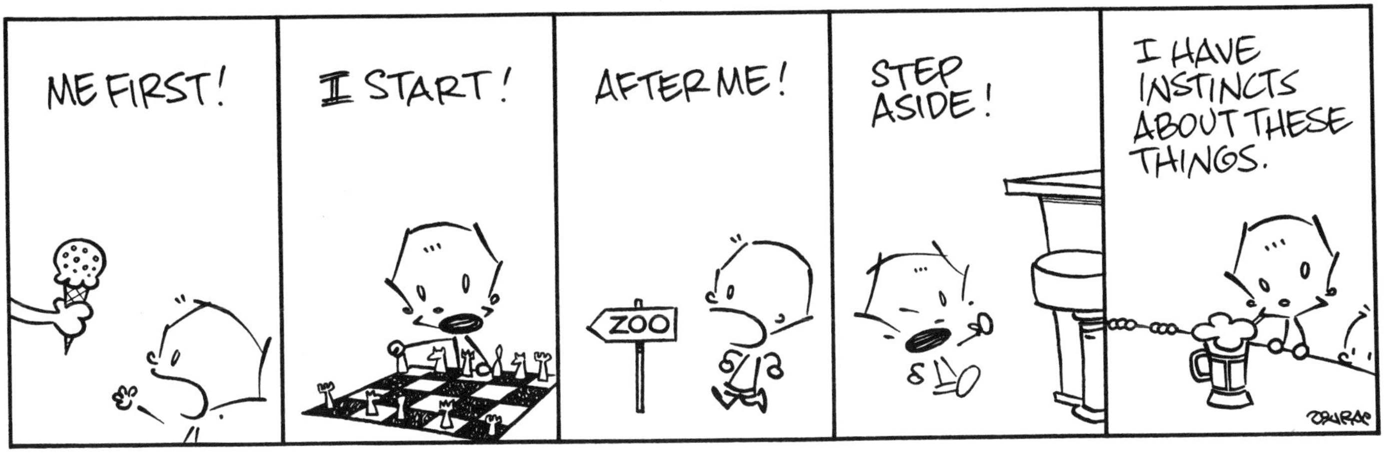
ME FIRST!
I START!
AFTER ME!
ZOO
STEP ASIDE!
I HAVE INSTINCTS ABOUT THESE THINGS.

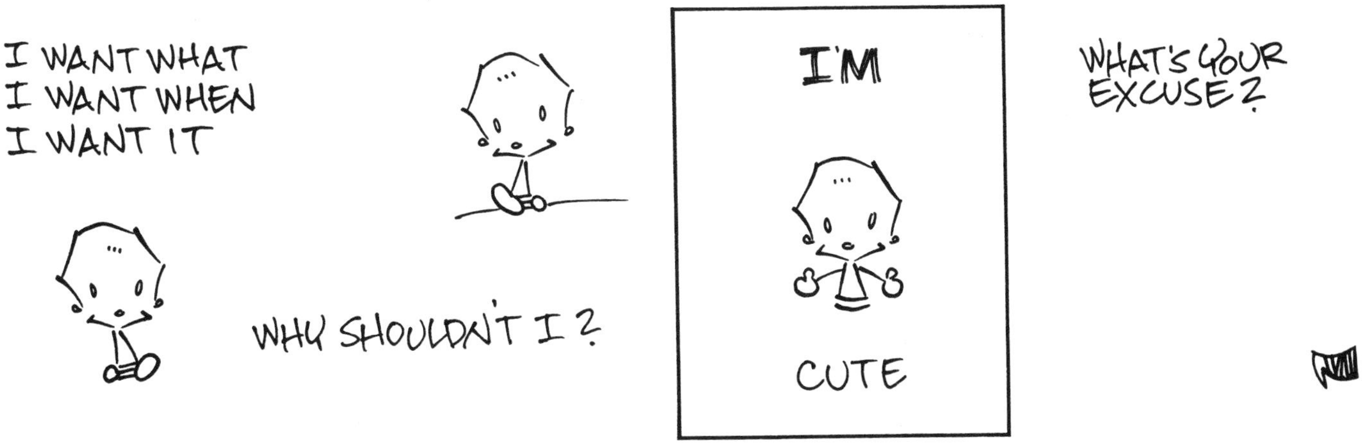
I WANT WHAT I WANT WHEN I WANT IT
WHY SHOULDN'T I?
I'M
CUTE
WHAT'S YOUR EXCUSE?

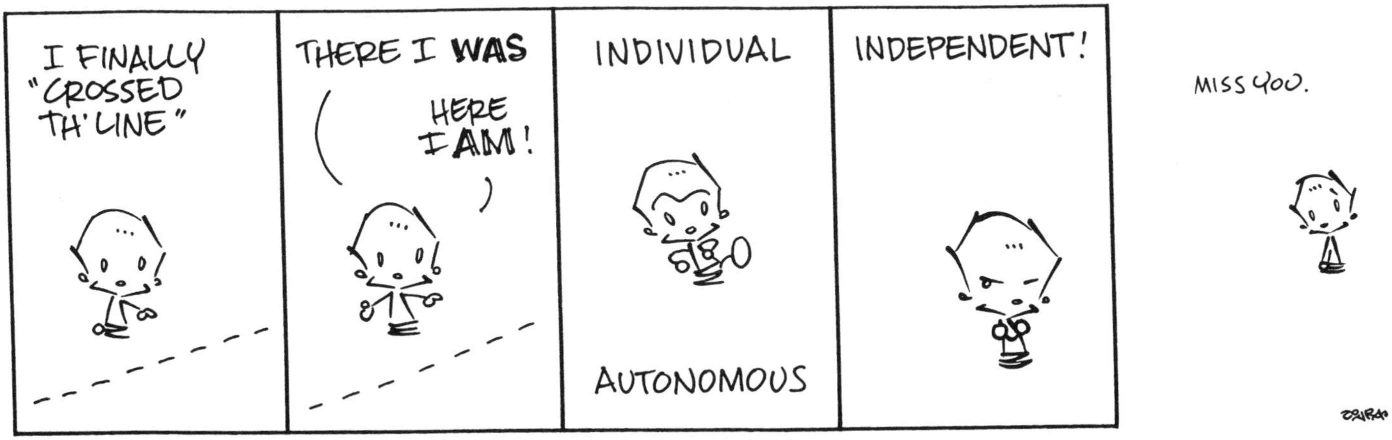
I FINALLY "CROSSED TH' LINE"
THERE I WAS
HERE I AM!
INDIVIDUAL
AUTONOMOUS
INDEPENDENT!
MISS YOU.

THE FACES OF JAMES!

I BLAME SOCIETY.

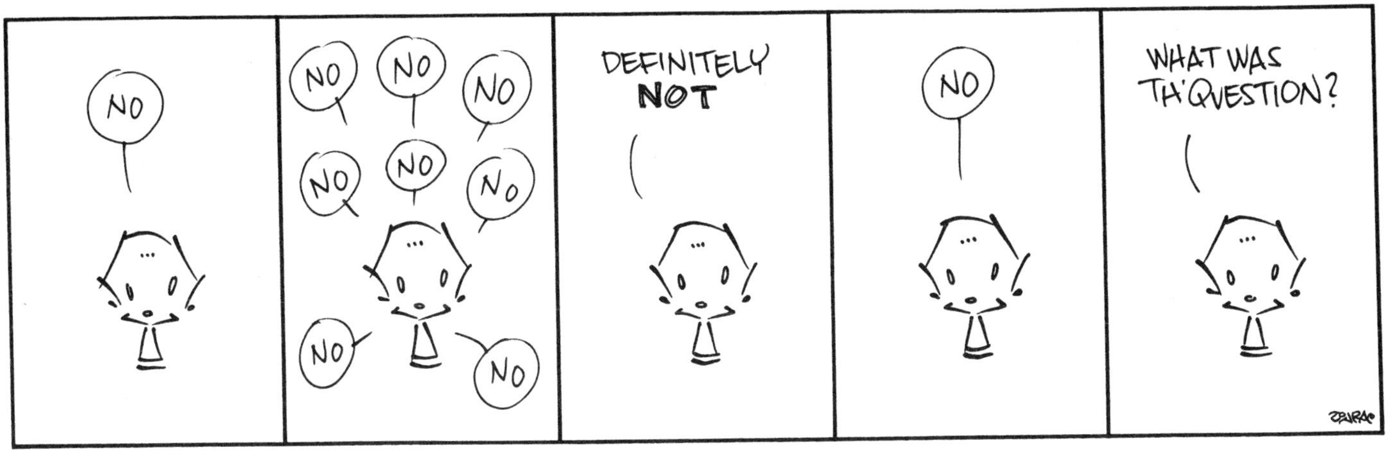
NO
NO NO NO NO NO NO NO NO
DEFINITELY **NOT**
NO
WHAT WAS TH' QUESTION?

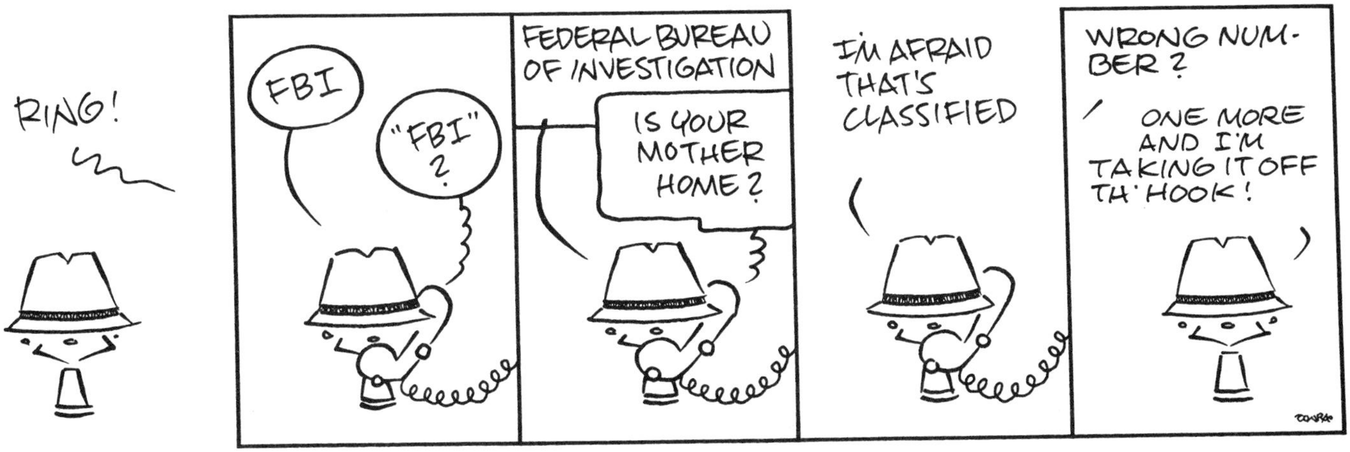
RING!
FBI
"FBI" ?
FEDERAL BUREAU OF INVESTIGATION
IS YOUR MOTHER HOME?
I'M AFRAID THAT'S CLASSIFIED
WRONG NUMBER?
ONE MORE AND I'M TAKING IT OFF TH' HOOK!

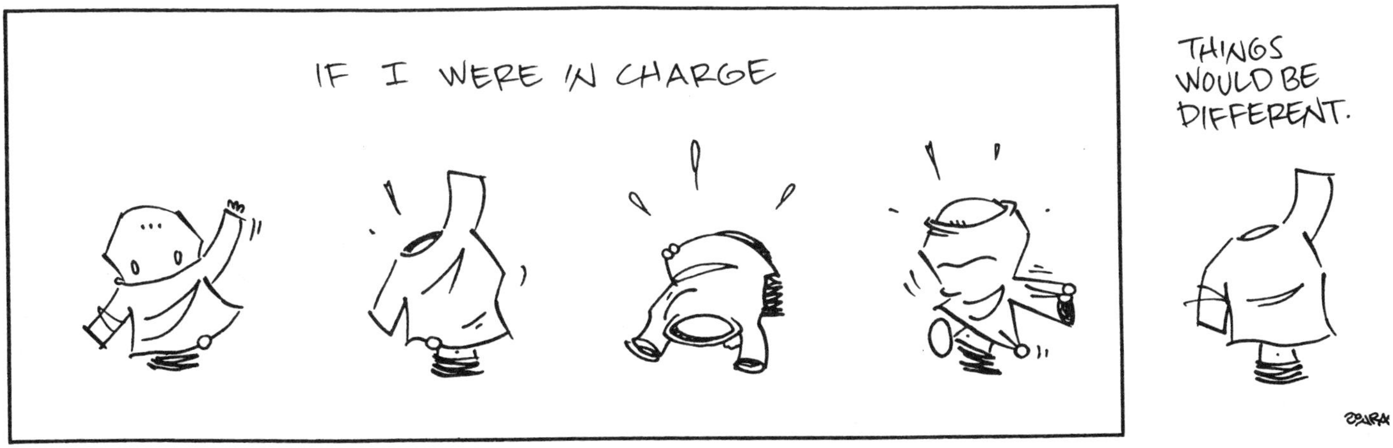
IF I WERE IN CHARGE
THINGS WOULD BE DIFFERENT.

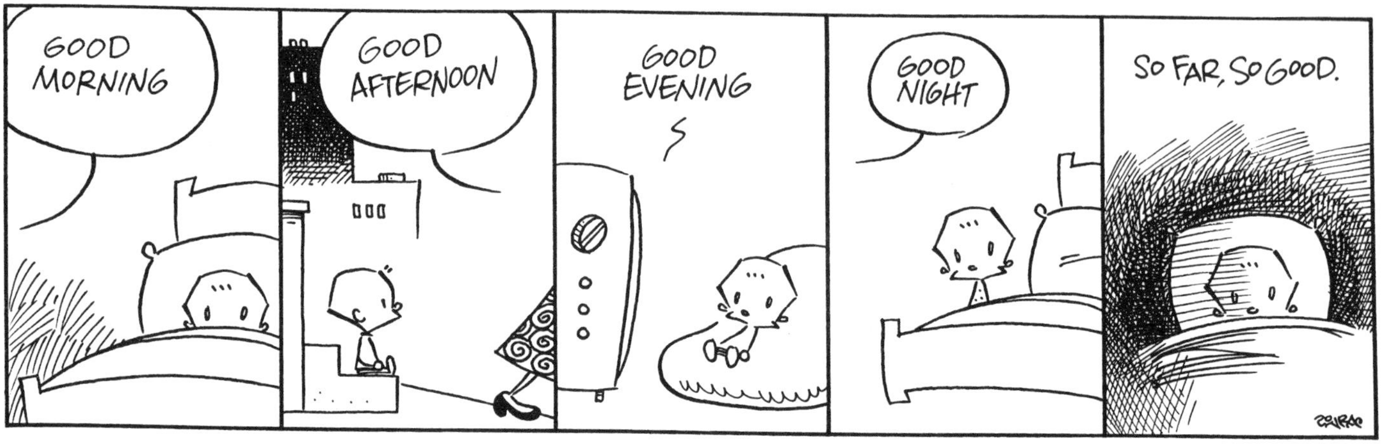
GOOD MORNING
GOOD AFTERNOON
GOOD EVENING
GOOD NIGHT
SO FAR, SO GOOD.

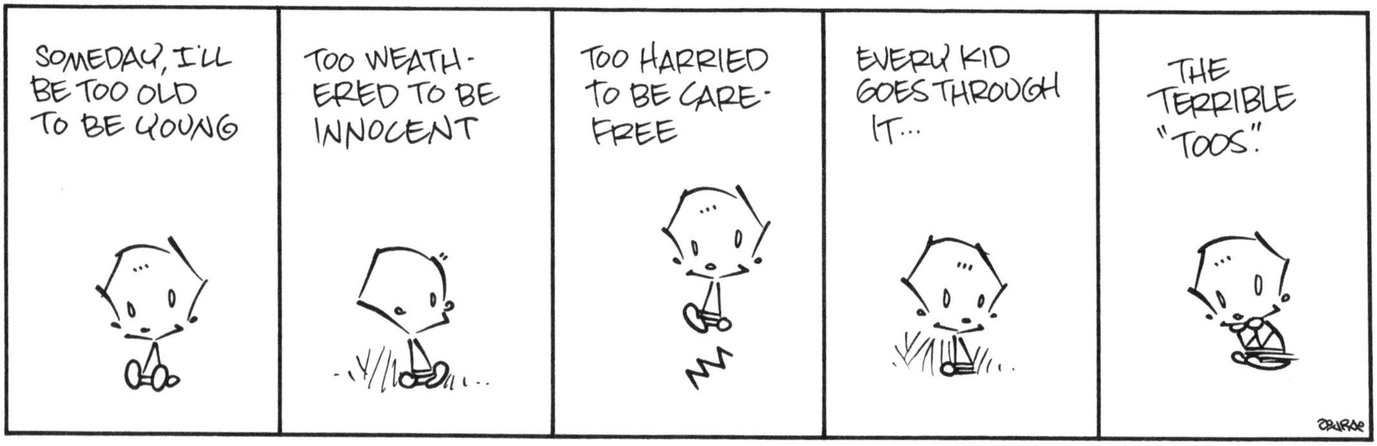
SOMEDAY, I'LL BE TOO OLD TO BE YOUNG
TOO WEATH-ERED TO BE INNOCENT
TOO HARRIED TO BE CARE-FREE
EVERY KID GOES THROUGH IT...
THE TERRIBLE "TOOS."

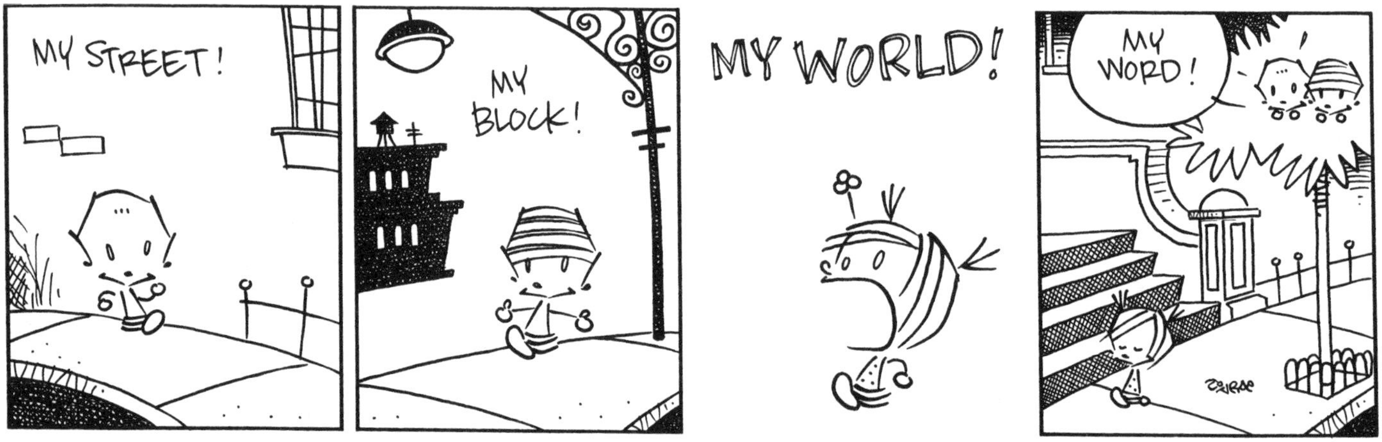
MY STREET!
MY BLOCK!
MY WORLD!
MY WORD!

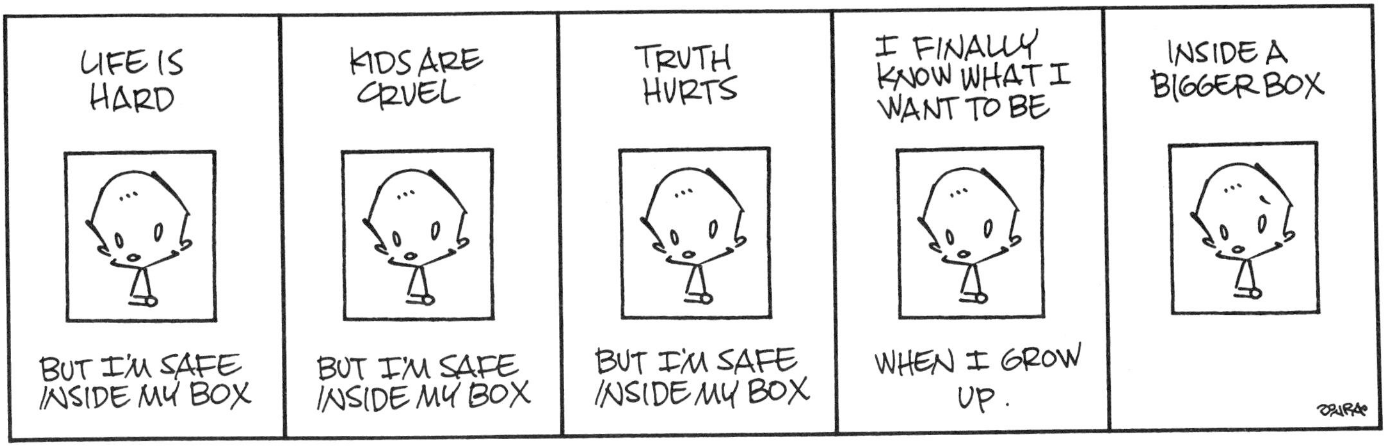
LIFE IS HARD
BUT I'M SAFE INSIDE MY BOX
KIDS ARE CRUEL
BUT I'M SAFE INSIDE MY BOX
TRUTH HURTS
BUT I'M SAFE INSIDE MY BOX
I FINALLY KNOW WHAT I WANT TO BE
WHEN I GROW UP.
INSIDE A BIGGER BOX

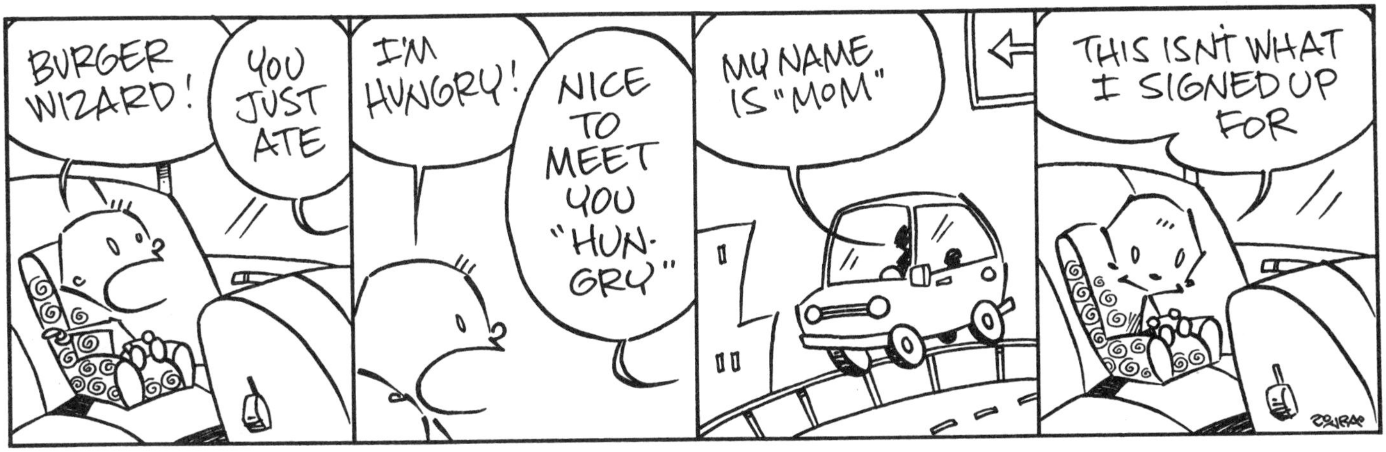
BURGER WIZARD!
YOU JUST ATE
I'M HUNGRY!
NICE TO MEET YOU "HUN-GRY"
MY NAME IS "MOM"
THIS ISN'T WHAT I SIGNED UP FOR

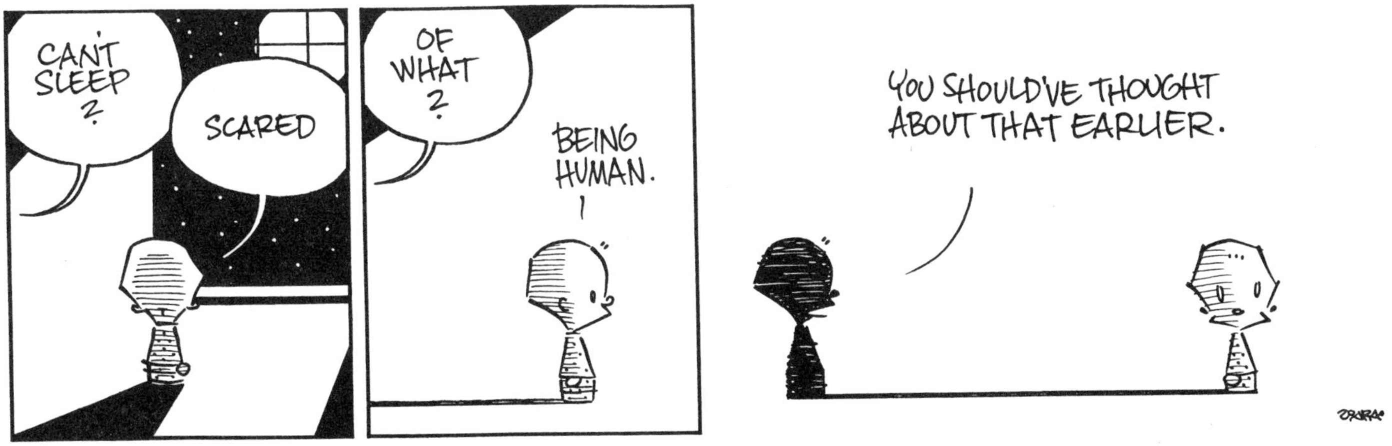
CAN'T SLEEP?
SCARED
OF WHAT?
BEING HUMAN.
YOU SHOULD'VE THOUGHT ABOUT THAT EARLIER.

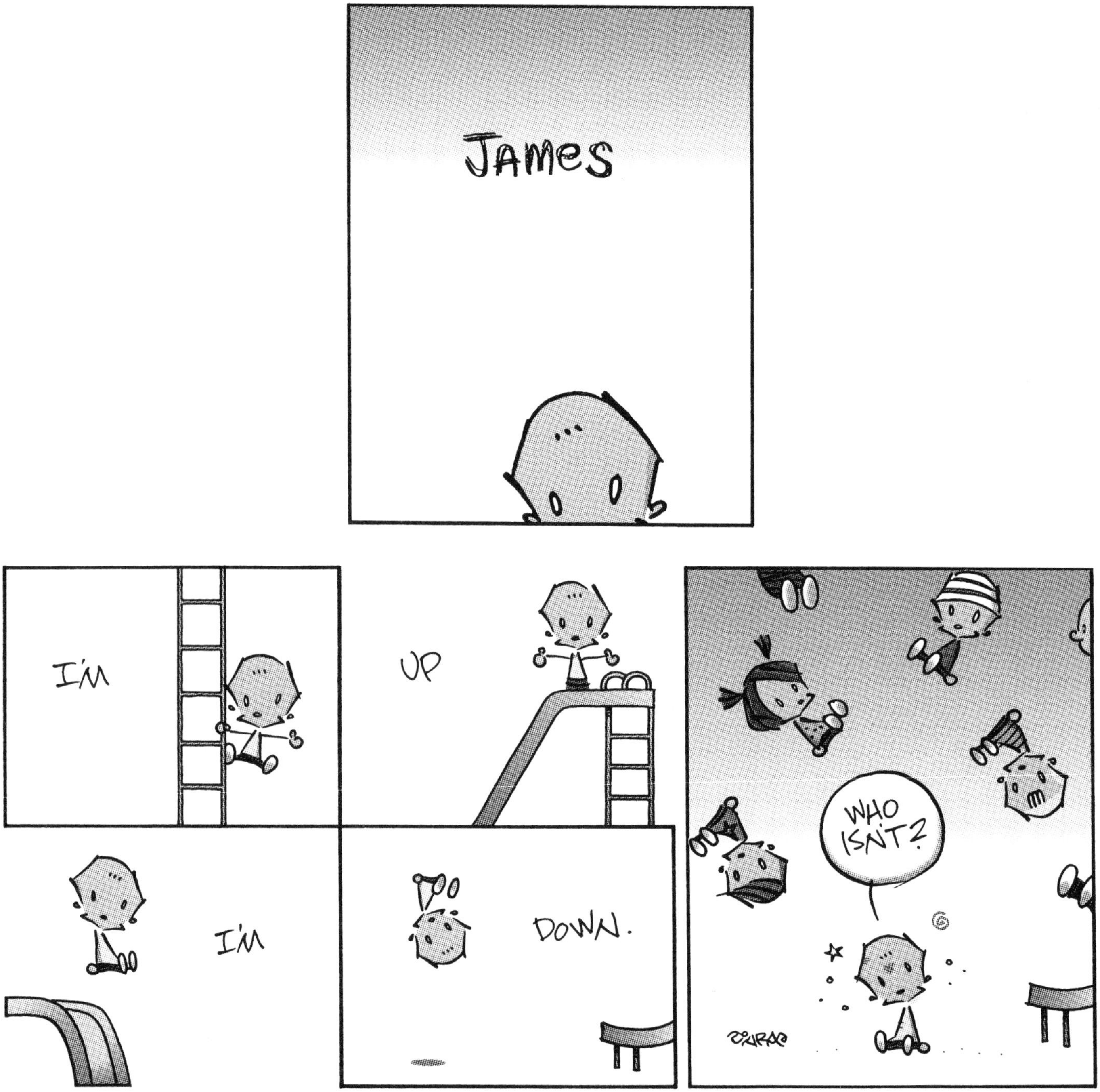
JAMES
I'M
UP
I'M
DOWN.
WHO ISN'T?

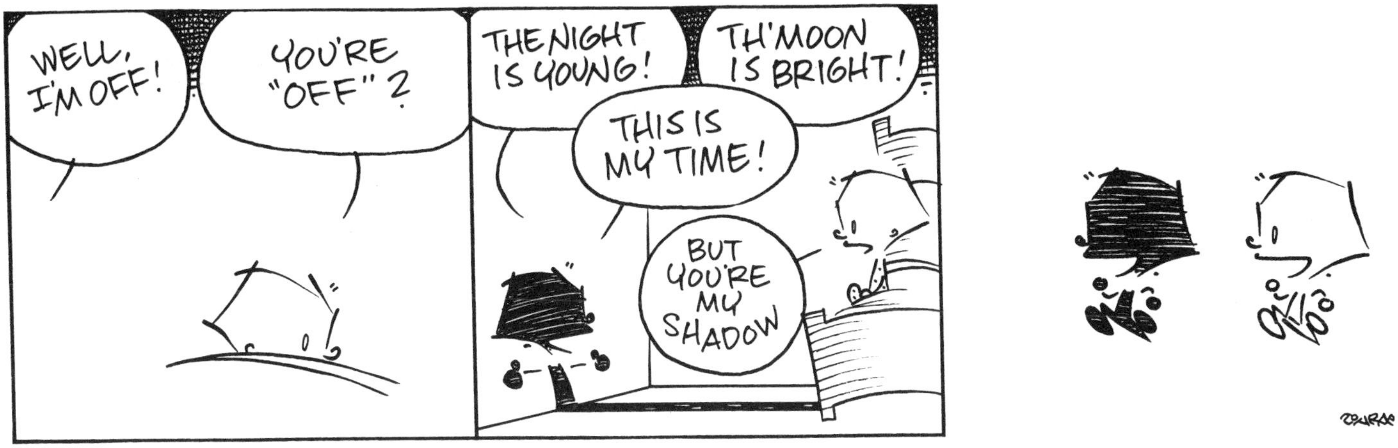
WELL, I'M OFF!
YOU'RE "OFF"?
THE NIGHT IS YOUNG!
TH' MOON IS BRIGHT!
THIS IS MY TIME!
BUT YOU'RE MY SHADOW

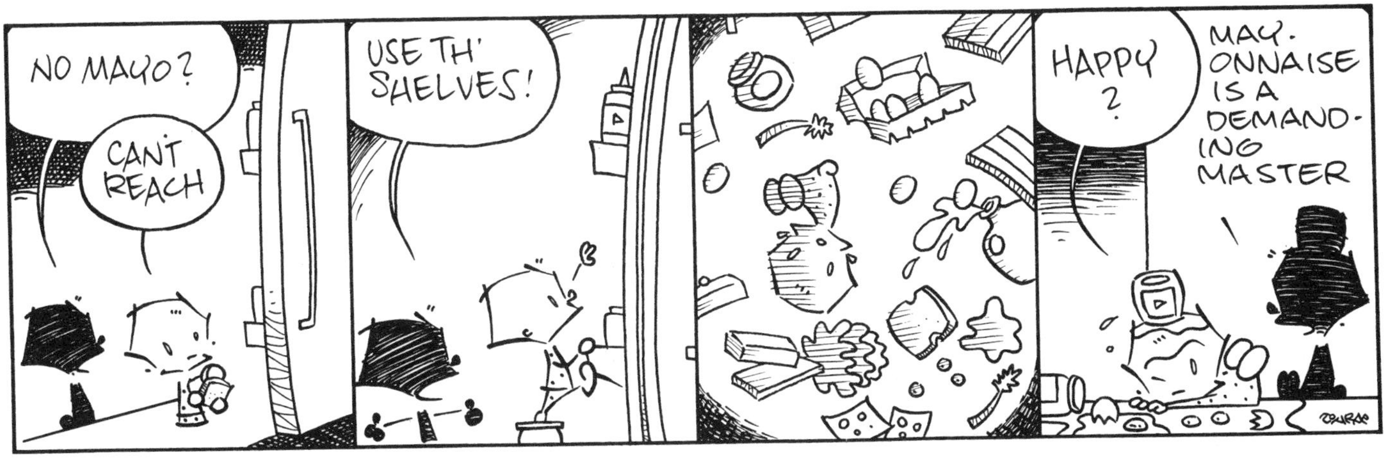
NO MAYO?
CAN'T REACH
USE TH' SHELVES!
HAPPY?
MAY-ONNAISE IS A DEMAND-ING MASTER

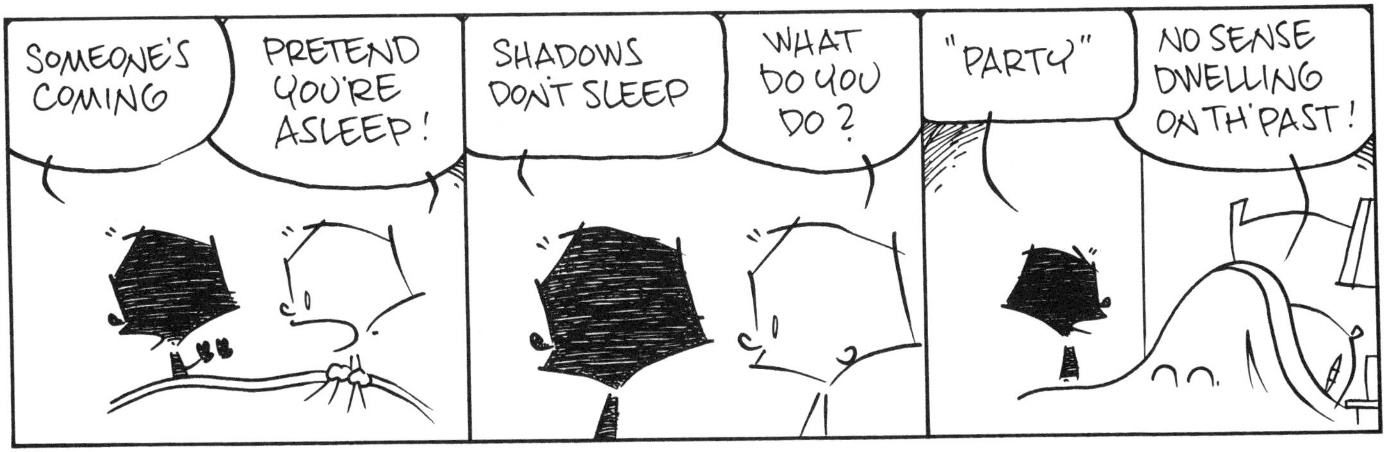
SOMEONE'S COMING
PRETEND YOU'RE ASLEEP!
SHADOWS DON'T SLEEP
WHAT DO YOU DO?
"PARTY"
NO SENSE DWELLING ON TH' PAST!

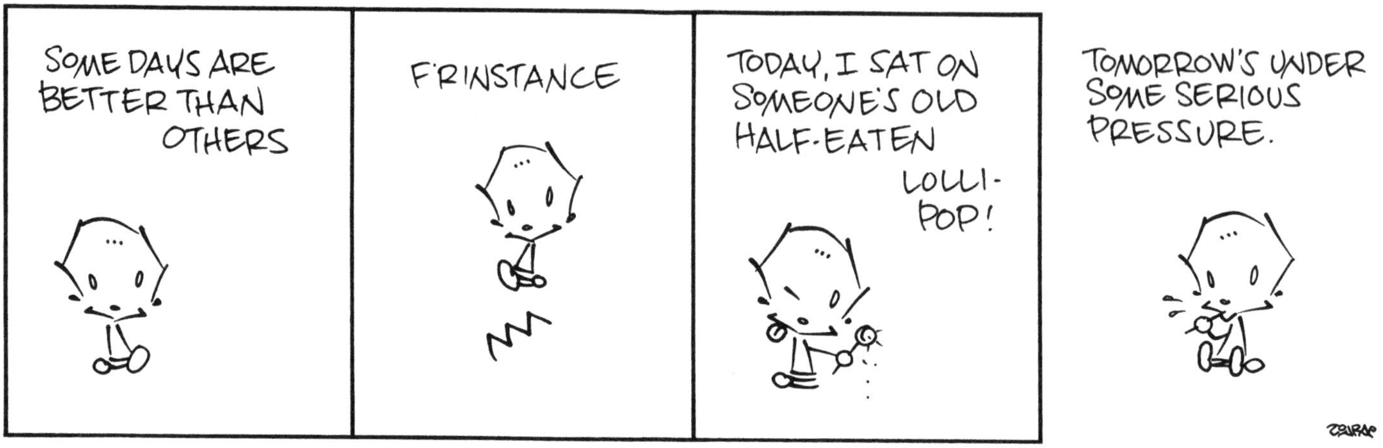
SOME DAYS ARE BETTER THAN OTHERS
F'RINSTANCE
TODAY, I SAT ON SOMEONE'S OLD HALF-EATEN
LOLLI-POP!
TOMORROW'S UNDER SOME SERIOUS PRESSURE.

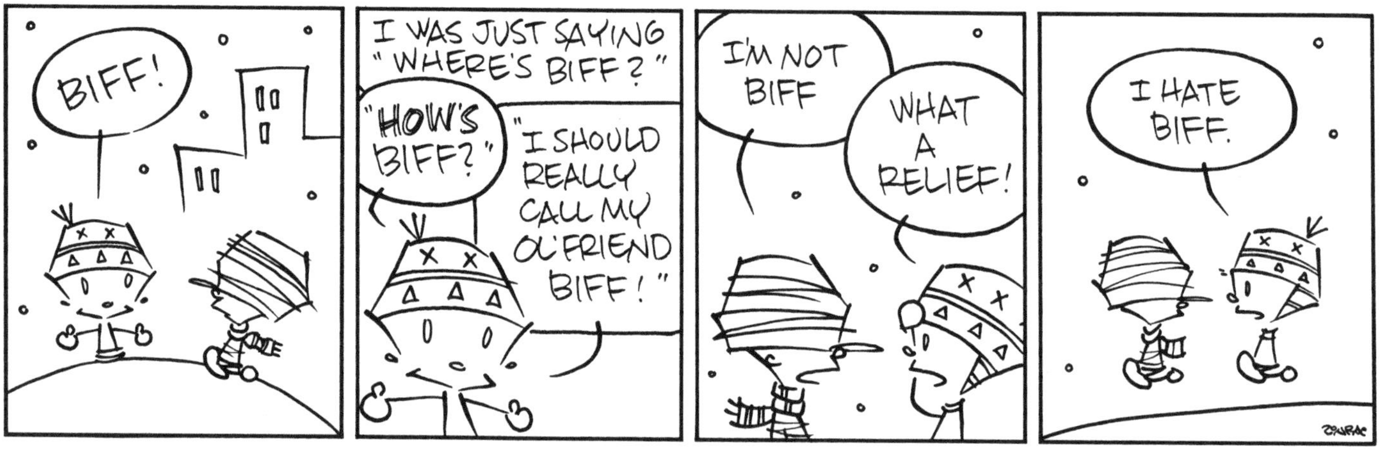
BIFF!
I WAS JUST SAYING "WHERE'S BIFF?"
"HOW'S BIFF?"
"I SHOULD REALLY CALL MY OL' FRIEND BIFF!"
I'M NOT BIFF
WHAT A RELIEF!
I HATE BIFF.

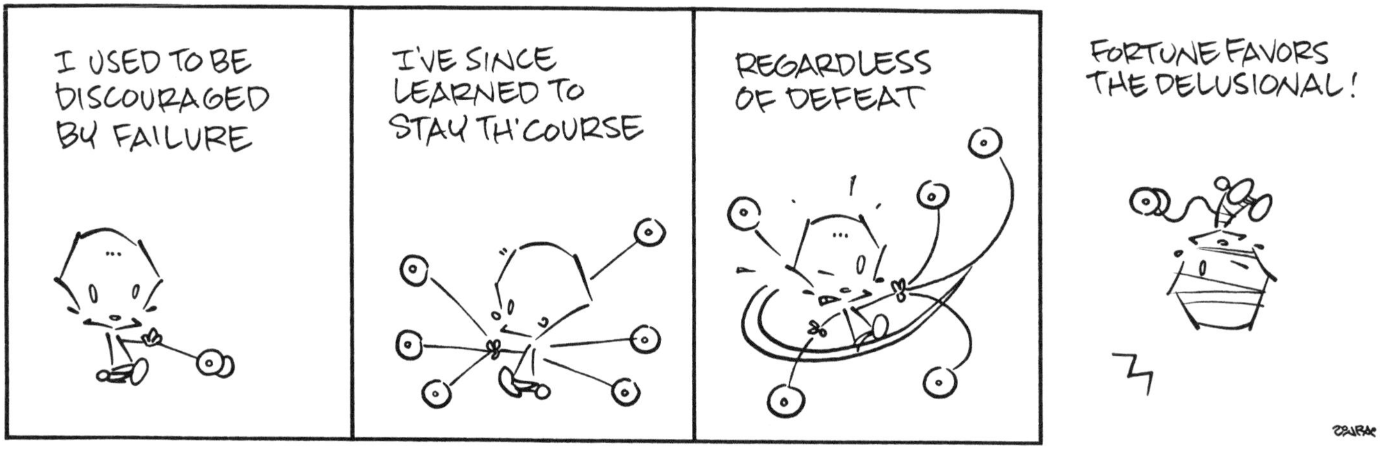
I USED TO BE DISCOURAGED BY FAILURE
I'VE SINCE LEARNED TO STAY TH' COURSE
REGARDLESS OF DEFEAT
FORTUNE FAVORS THE DELUSIONAL!

J
A
m
e
s

"IRRESPONSIBLE"
?

BECAUSE I DIDN'T CLEAN MY ROOM ?

BECAUSE I **LOST** MY SCHOOL BOOKS ?

BECAUSE I DIDN'T CLEAR TH' TABLE ??

MY LACK OF INTEREST IS OFTEN MISTAKEN FOR IRRESPONSIBILITY.

27

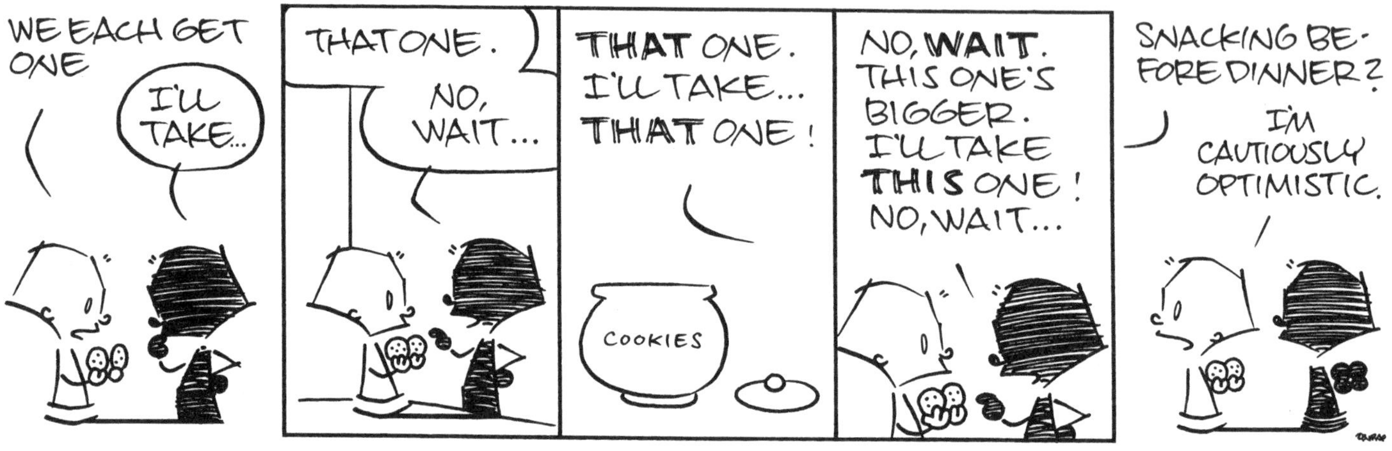
WE EACH GET ONE
I'LL TAKE...
THAT ONE.
NO, WAIT...
THAT ONE. I'LL TAKE... THAT ONE!
COOKIES
NO, WAIT. THIS ONE'S BIGGER. I'LL TAKE THIS ONE! NO, WAIT...
SNACKING BEFORE DINNER?
I'M CAUTIOUSLY OPTIMISTIC.

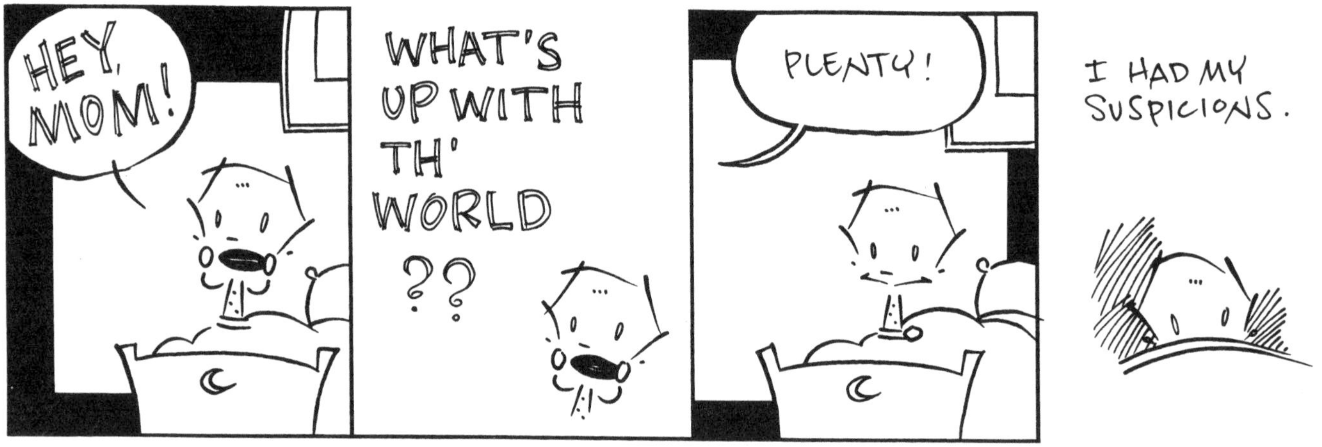
HEY, MOM!
WHAT'S UP WITH TH' WORLD ??
PLENTY!
I HAD MY SUSPICIONS.

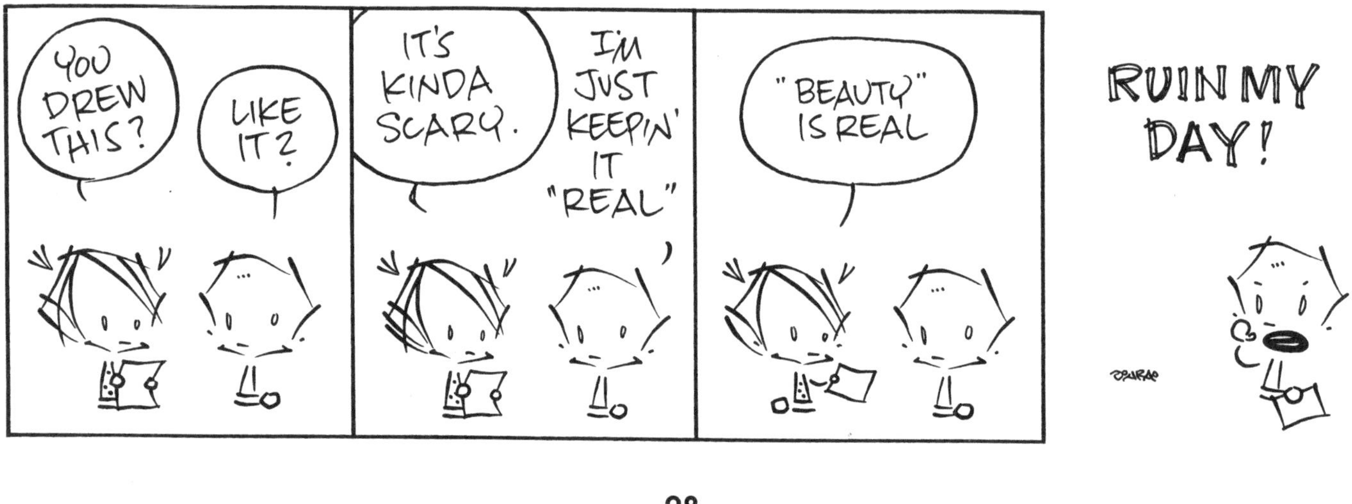
YOU DREW THIS?
LIKE IT?
IT'S KINDA SCARY.
I'M JUST KEEPIN' IT "REAL"
"BEAUTY" IS REAL
RUIN MY DAY!

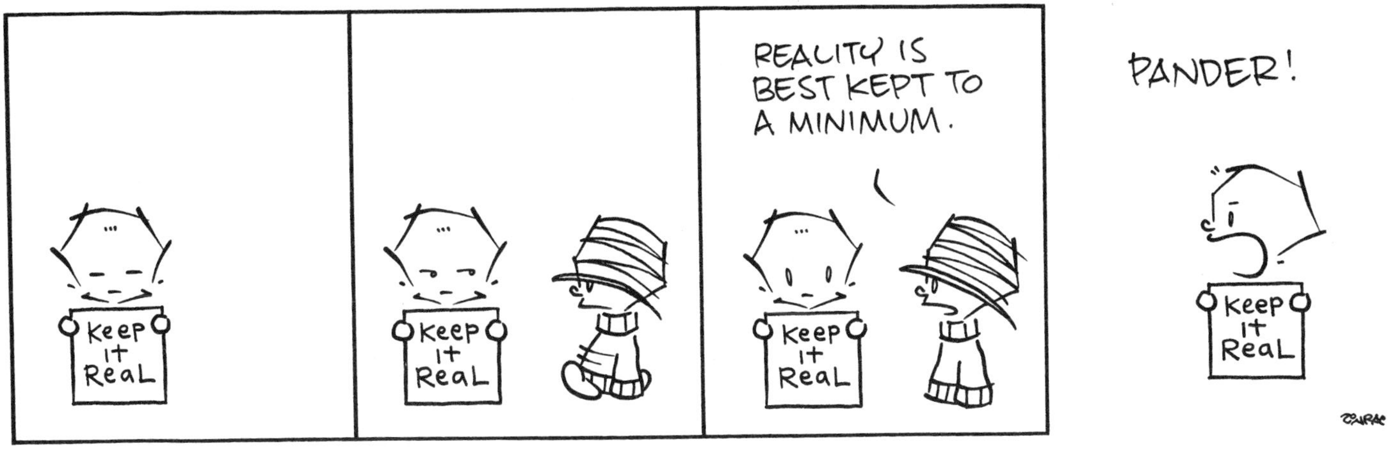
Keep it Real
Keep it Real
REALITY IS BEST KEPT TO A MINIMUM.
Keep it Real
PANDER!
Keep it Real

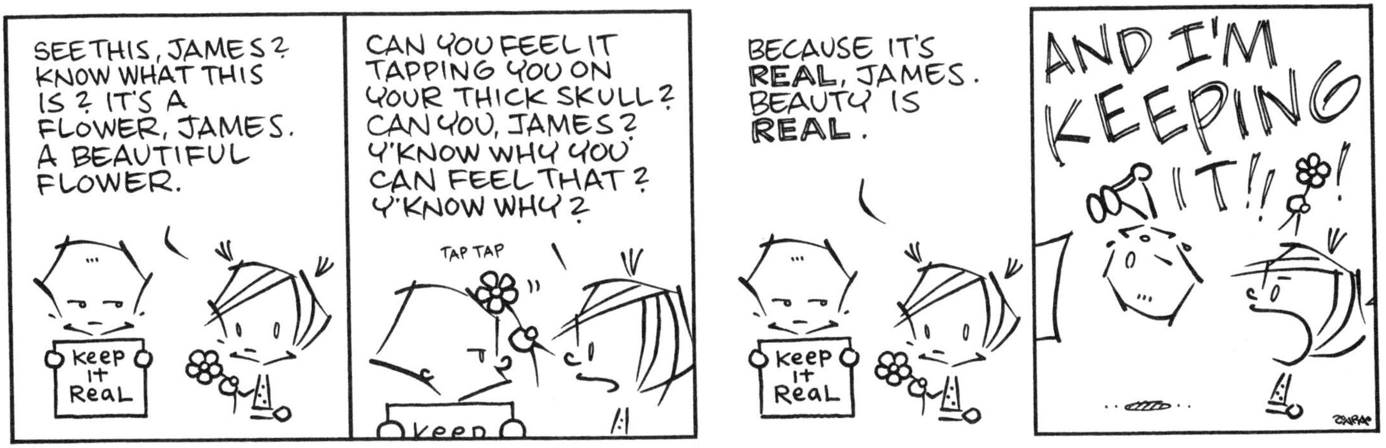
SEE THIS, JAMES? KNOW WHAT THIS IS? IT'S A FLOWER, JAMES. A BEAUTIFUL FLOWER.
Keep it Real
CAN YOU FEEL IT TAPPING YOU ON YOUR THICK SKULL? CAN YOU, JAMES? Y'KNOW WHY YOU CAN FEEL THAT? Y'KNOW WHY?
TAP TAP
BECAUSE IT'S **REAL**, JAMES. BEAUTY IS **REAL**.
Keep it Real
AND I'M KEEPING IT!!!

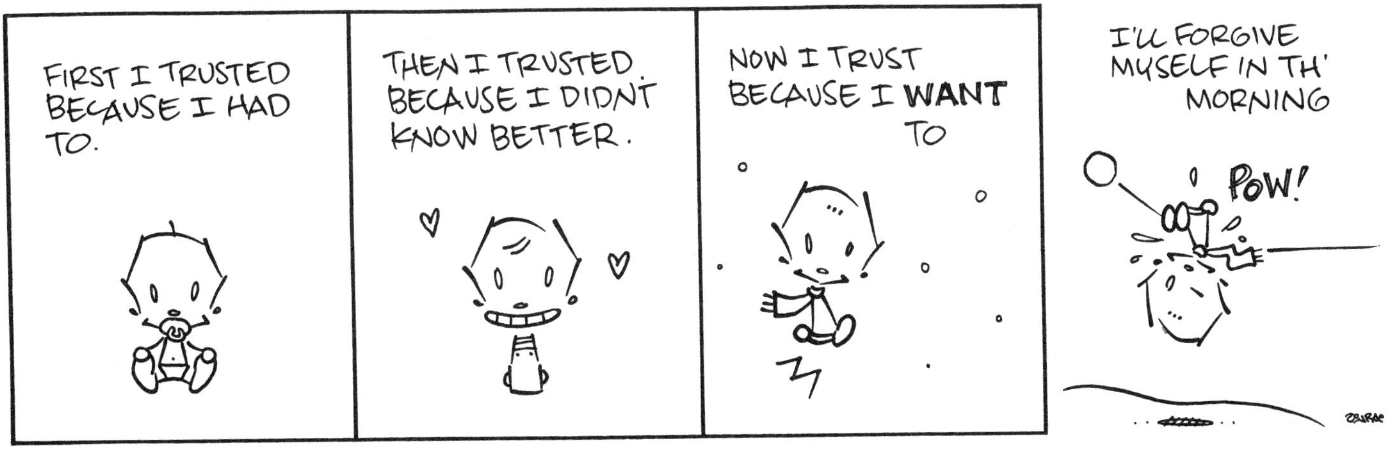
FIRST I TRUSTED BECAUSE I HAD TO.
THEN I TRUSTED BECAUSE I DIDN'T KNOW BETTER.
NOW I TRUST BECAUSE I **WANT** TO
I'LL FORGIVE MYSELF IN TH' MORNING
POW!

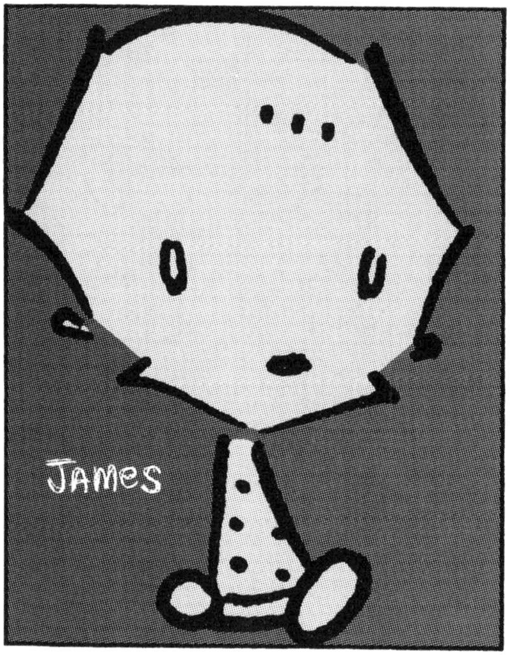
JAMES

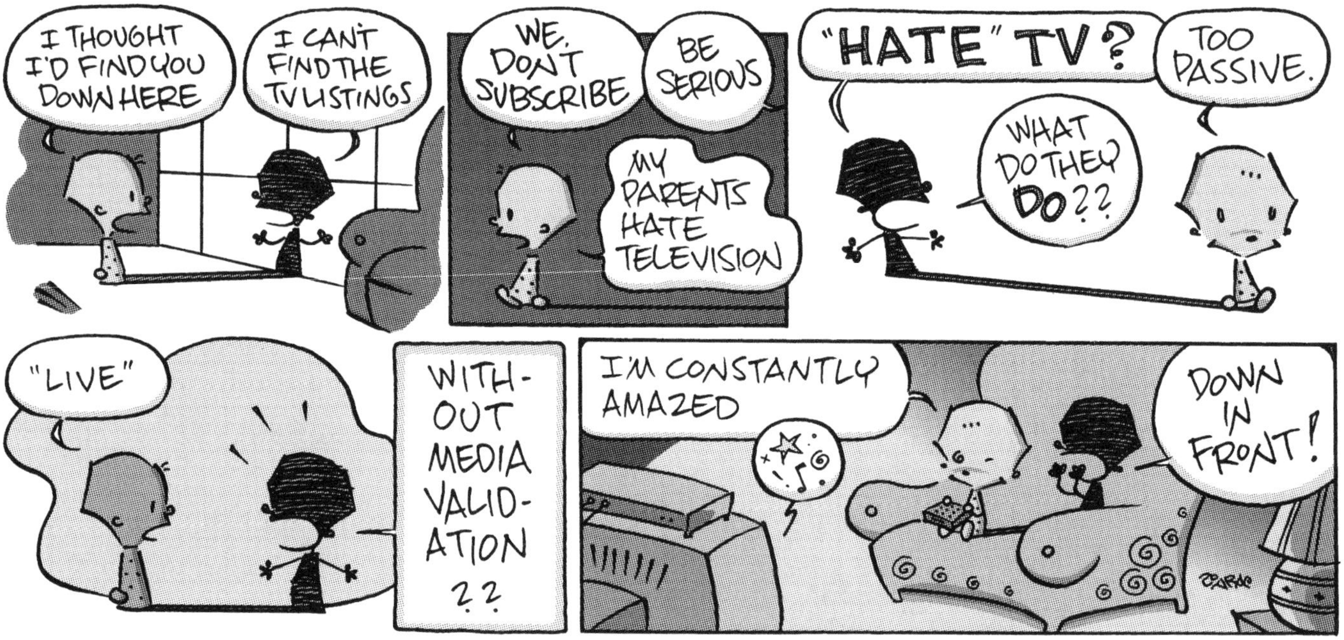
I THOUGHT I'D FIND YOU DOWN HERE
I CAN'T FIND THE TV LISTINGS
WE DON'T SUBSCRIBE
BE SERIOUS
MY PARENTS HATE TELEVISION
"HATE" TV?
WHAT DO THEY DO??
TOO PASSIVE.
"LIVE"
WITH-OUT MEDIA VALID-ATION ??
I'M CONSTANTLY AMAZED
DOWN IN FRONT!

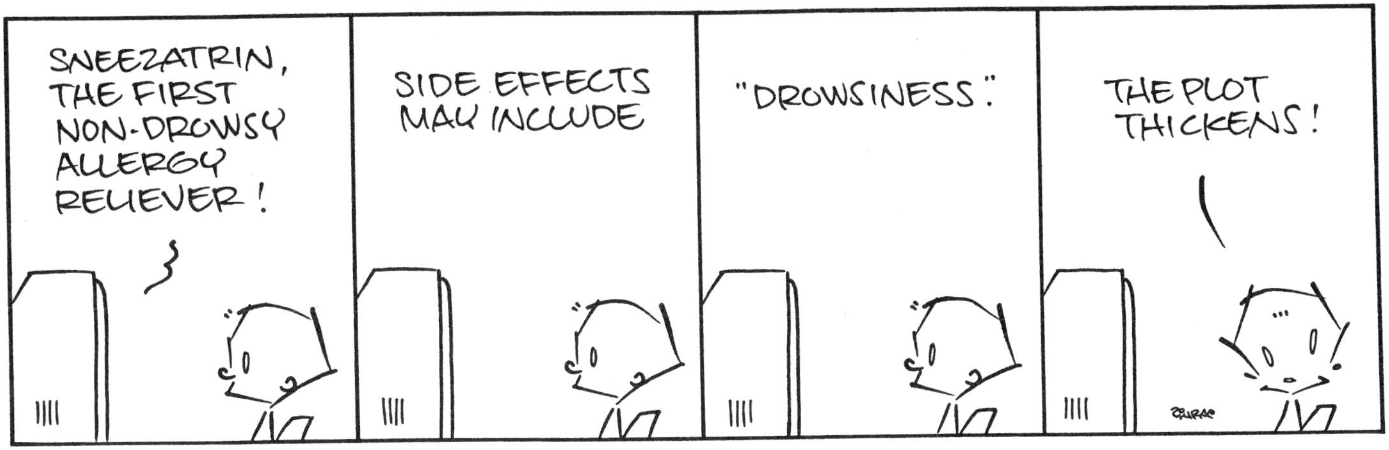
SNEEZATRIN, THE FIRST NON-DROWSY ALLERGY RELIEVER!
SIDE EFFECTS MAY INCLUDE
"DROWSINESS."
THE PLOT THICKENS!

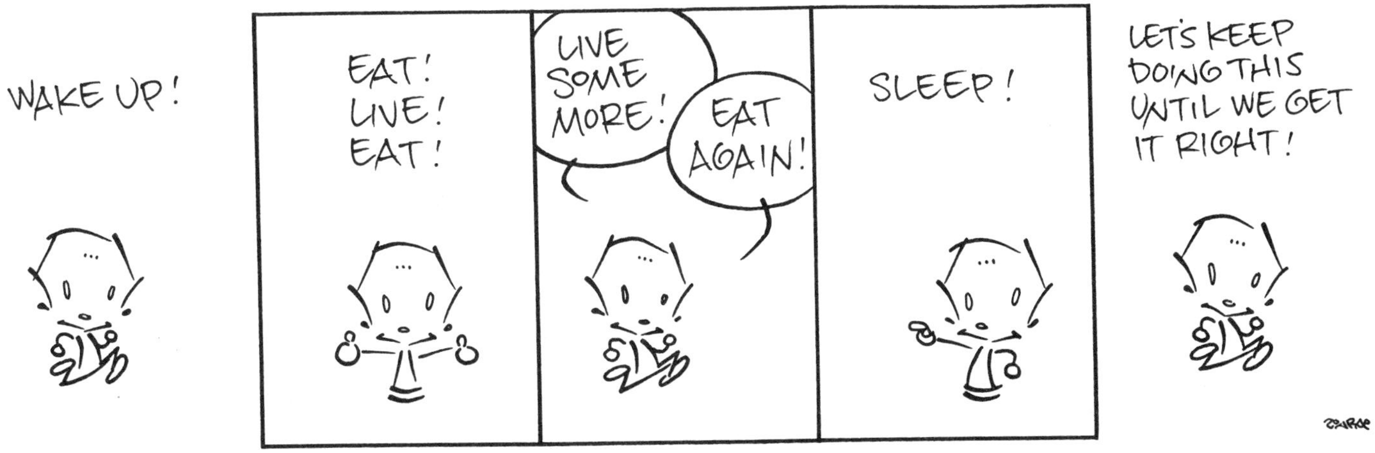
WAKE UP!
EAT! LIVE! EAT!
LIVE SOME MORE!
EAT AGAIN!
SLEEP!
LET'S KEEP DOING THIS UNTIL WE GET IT RIGHT!

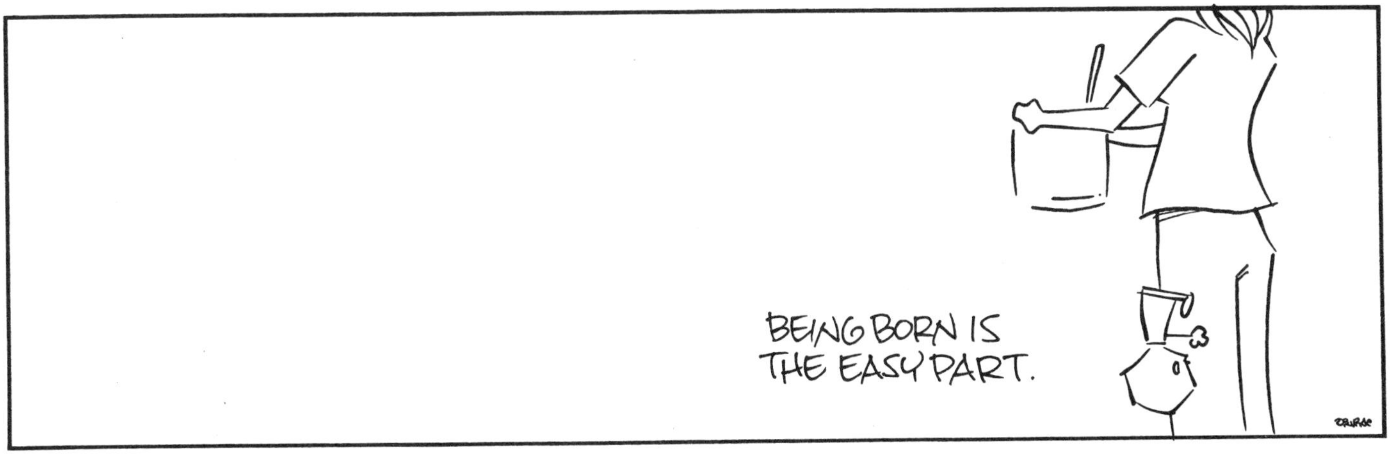
BEING BORN IS THE EASY PART.

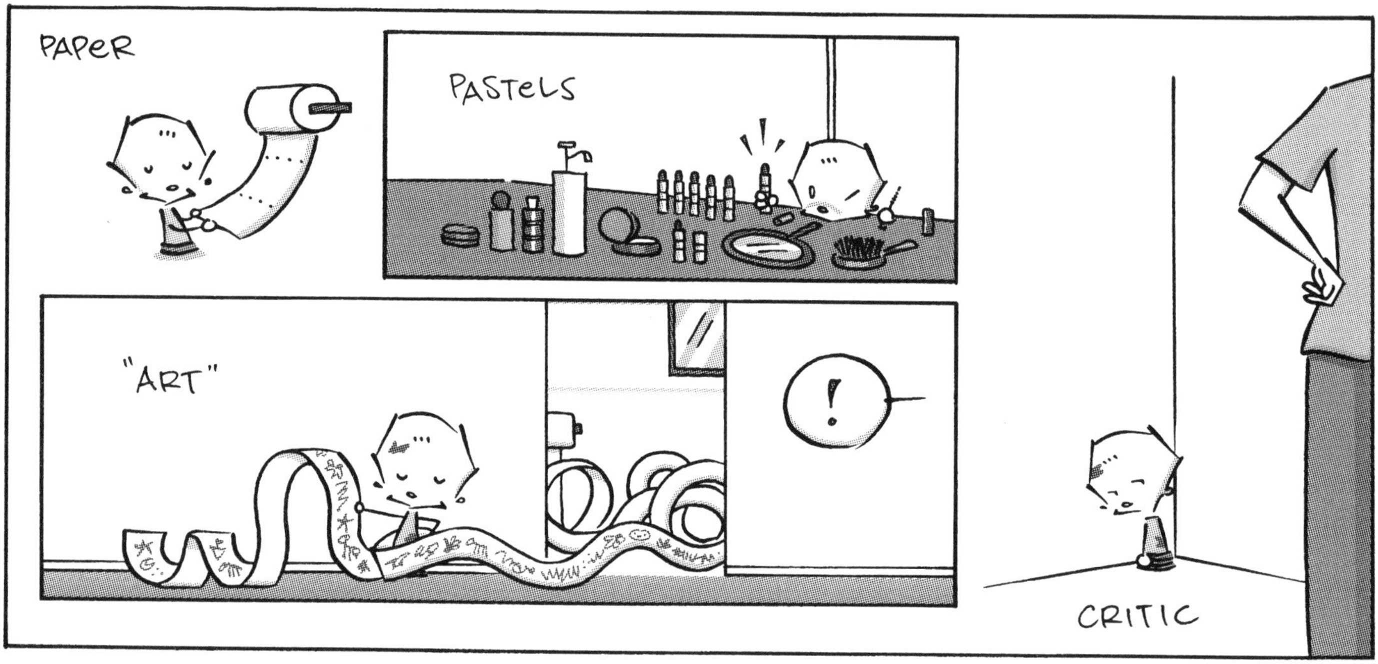
PAPER
PASTELS
"ART"
!
CRITIC

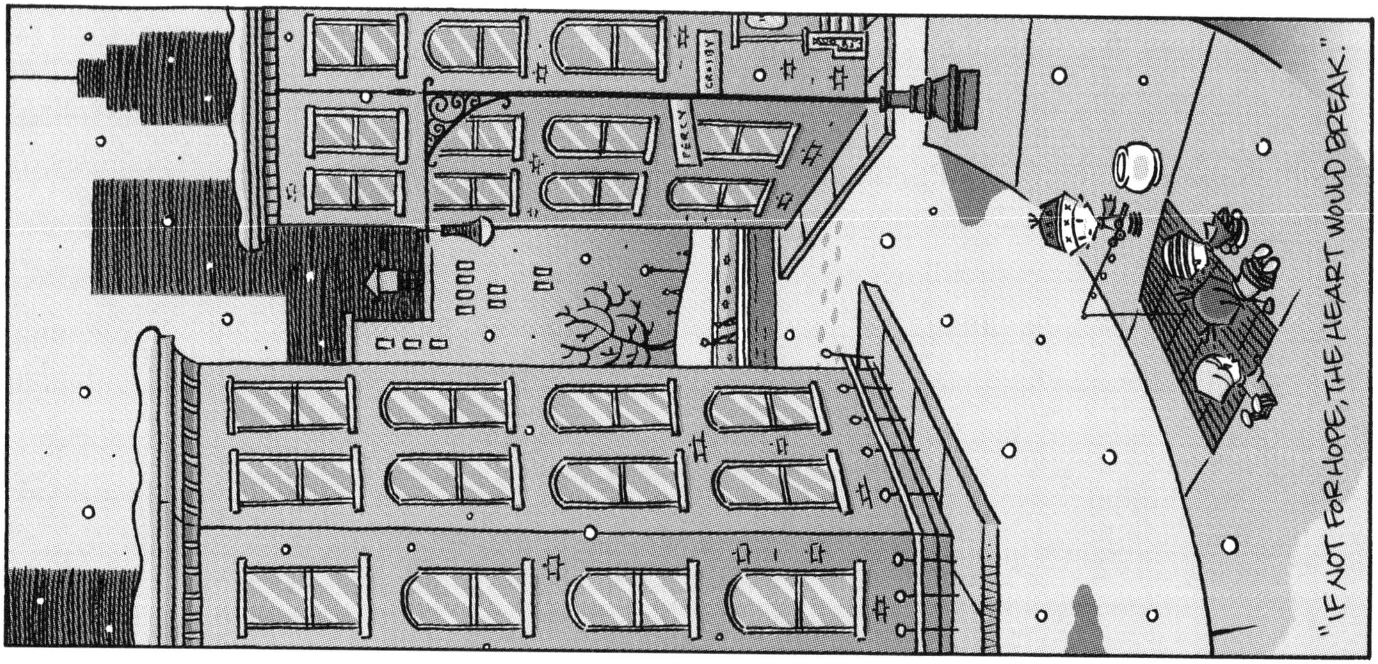
"IF NOT FOR HOPE, THE HEART WOULD BREAK."

James

DO YOU THINK PEOPLE ARE SMART?

SOMETIMES

LIKE WHEN?

LIKE WHEN THEY AGREE WITH ME

DOES THAT HAPPEN OFTEN?

NOT SO YOU'D NOTICE

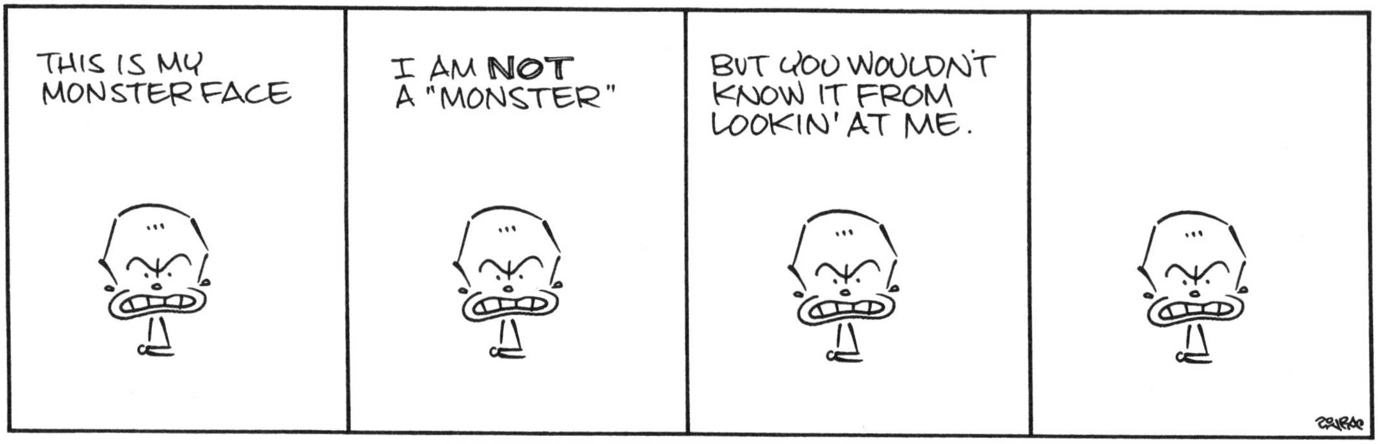
THIS IS MY MONSTER FACE
I AM **NOT** A "MONSTER"
BUT YOU WOULDN'T KNOW IT FROM LOOKIN' AT ME.

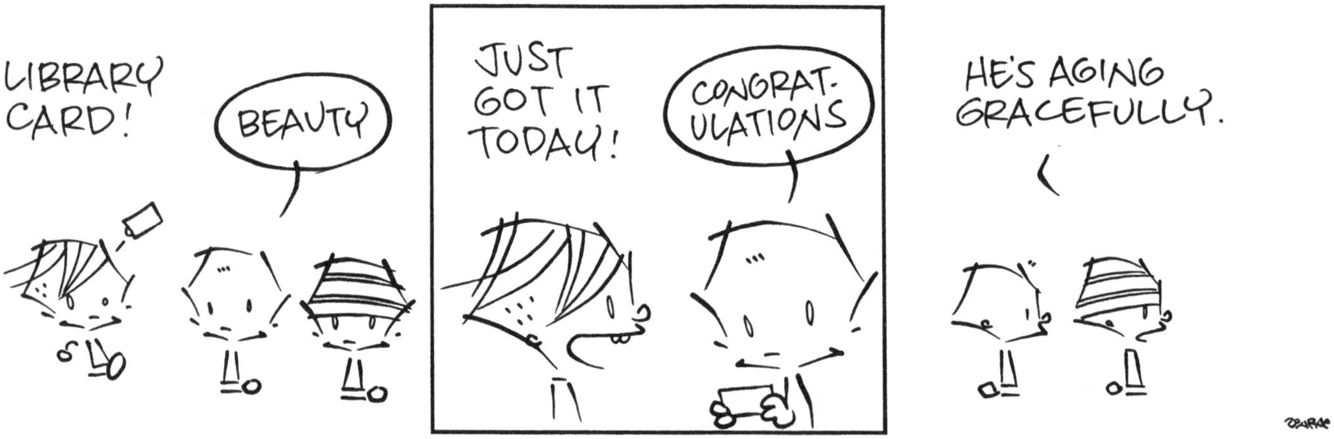
LIBRARY CARD!
BEAUTY
JUST GOT IT TODAY!
CONGRAT-ULATIONS
HE'S AGING GRACEFULLY.

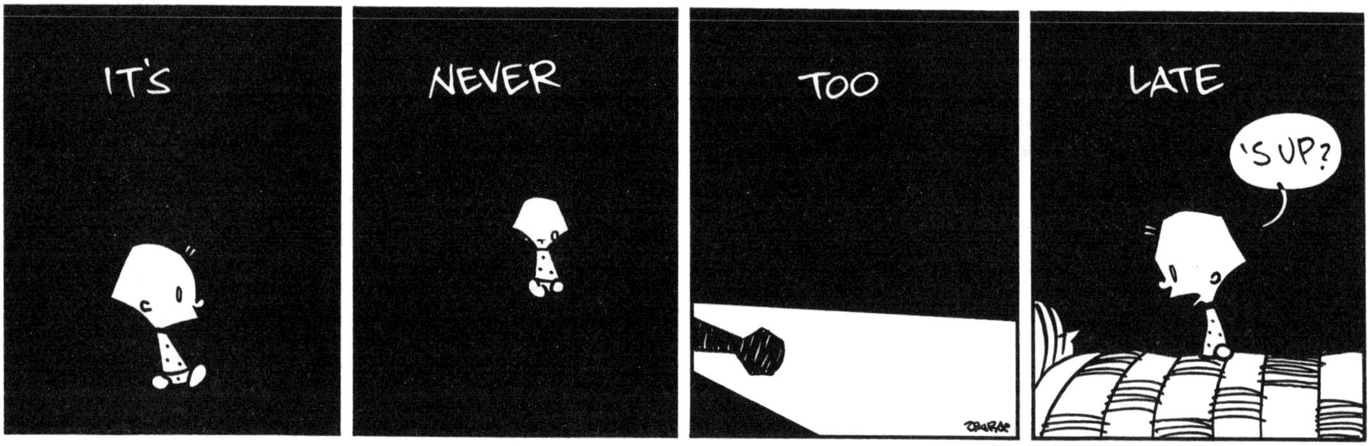
IT'S
NEVER
TOO
LATE
'S UP?

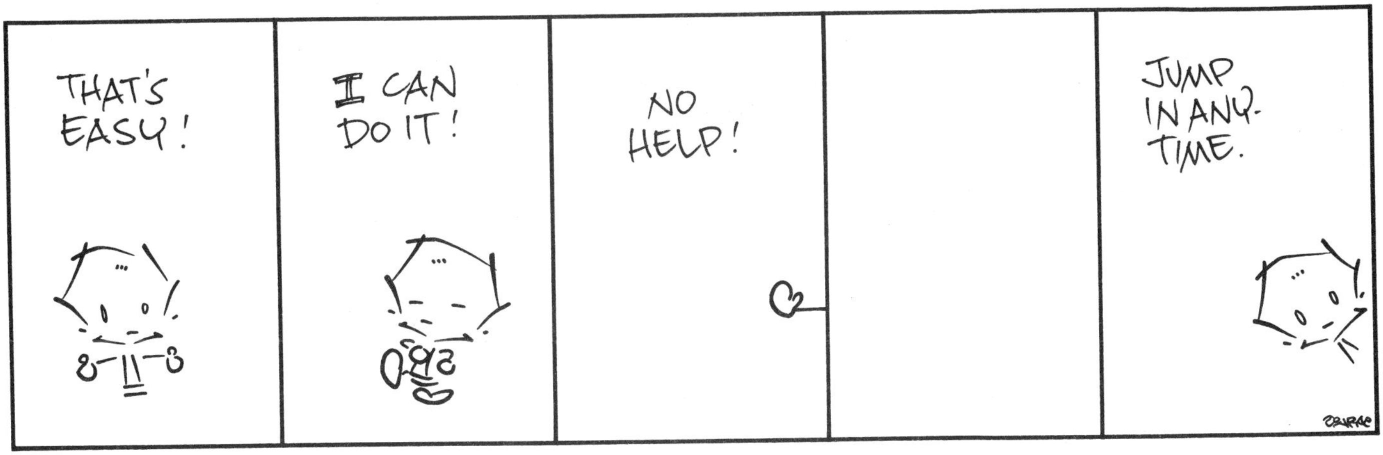
THAT'S EASY!
I CAN DO IT!
NO HELP!
JUMP IN ANY TIME.

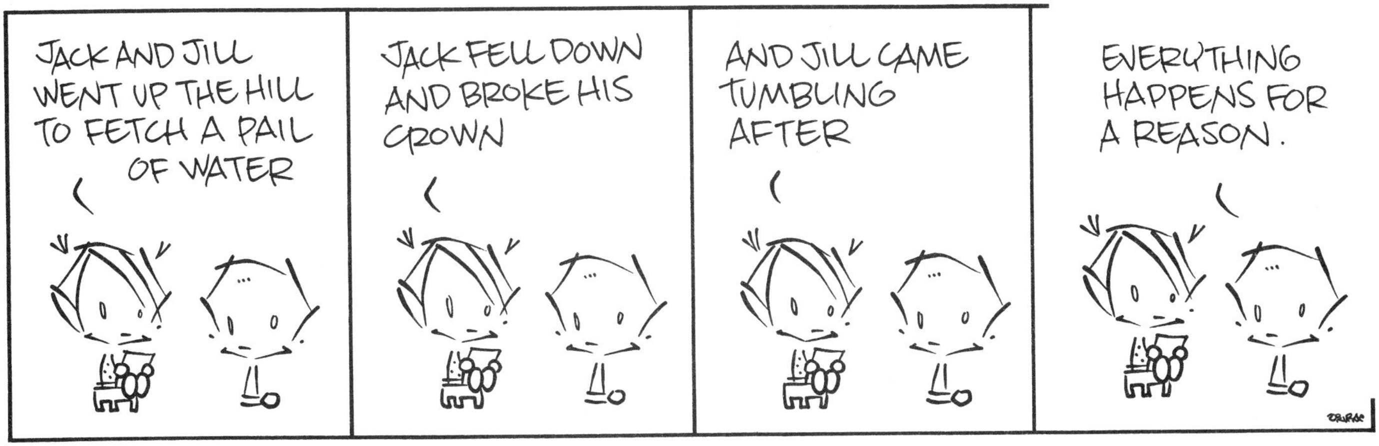
JACK AND JILL WENT UP THE HILL TO FETCH A PAIL OF WATER
JACK FELL DOWN AND BROKE HIS CROWN
AND JILL CAME TUMBLING AFTER
EVERYTHING HAPPENS FOR A REASON.

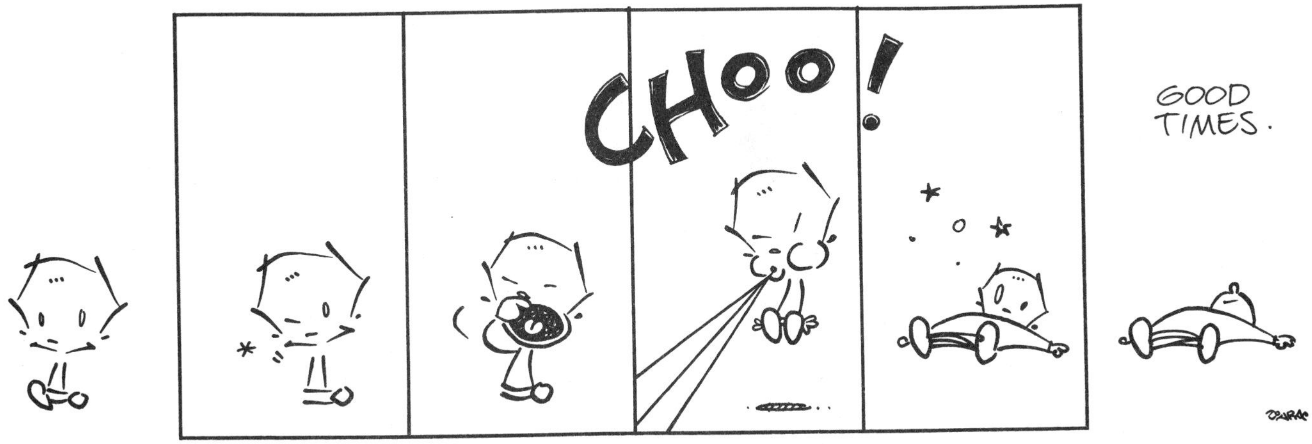
CHOO!
GOOD TIMES.

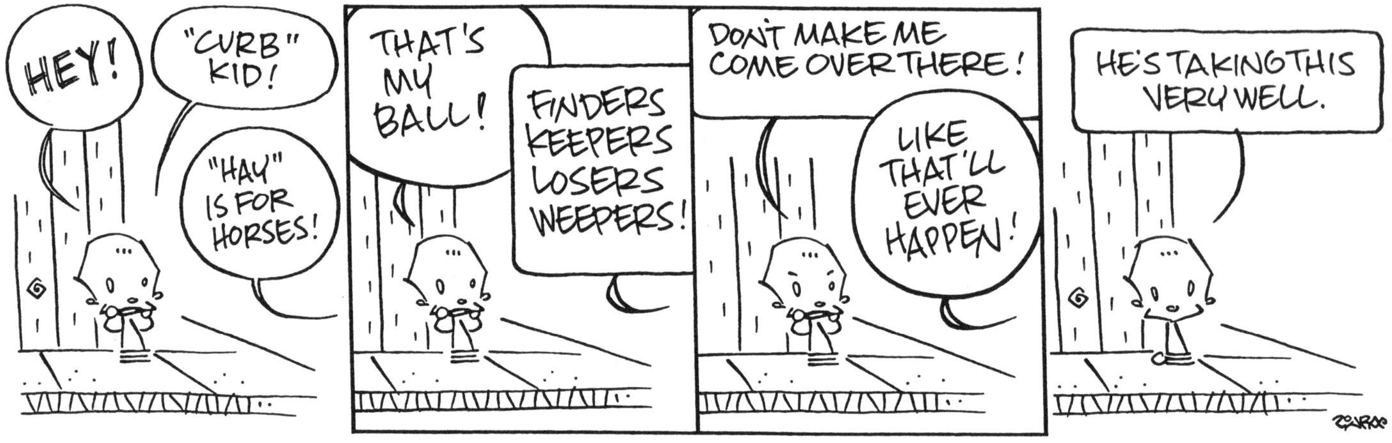
HEY!
"CURB" KID!
"HAY" IS FOR HORSES!
THAT'S MY BALL!
FINDERS KEEPERS LOSERS WEEPERS!
DON'T MAKE ME COME OVER THERE!
LIKE THAT'LL EVER HAPPEN!
HE'S TAKING THIS VERY WELL.

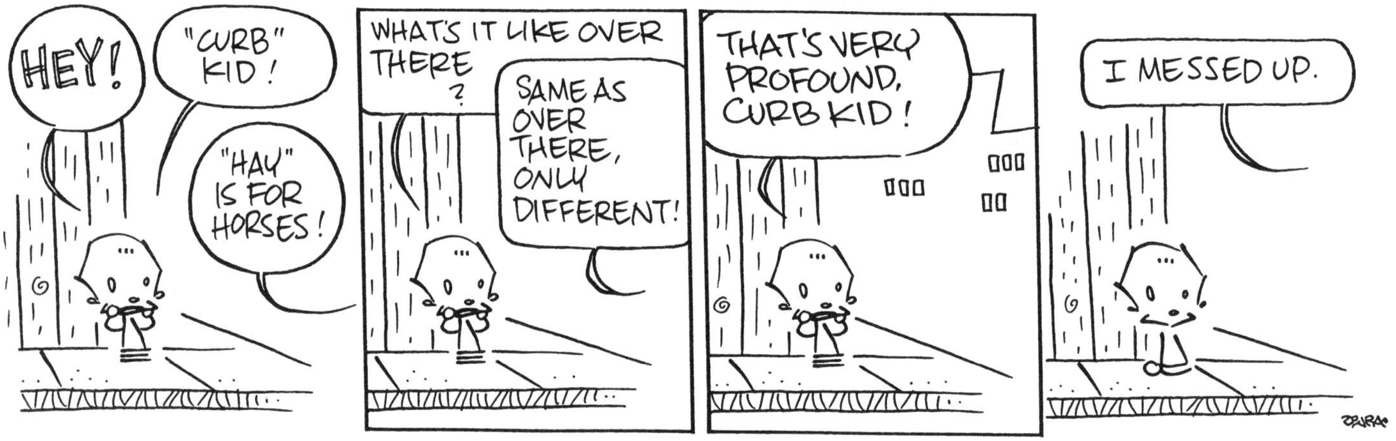
HEY!
"CURB" KID!
"HAY" IS FOR HORSES!
WHAT'S IT LIKE OVER THERE?
SAME AS OVER THERE, ONLY DIFFERENT!
THAT'S VERY PROFOUND, CURB KID!
I MESSED UP.

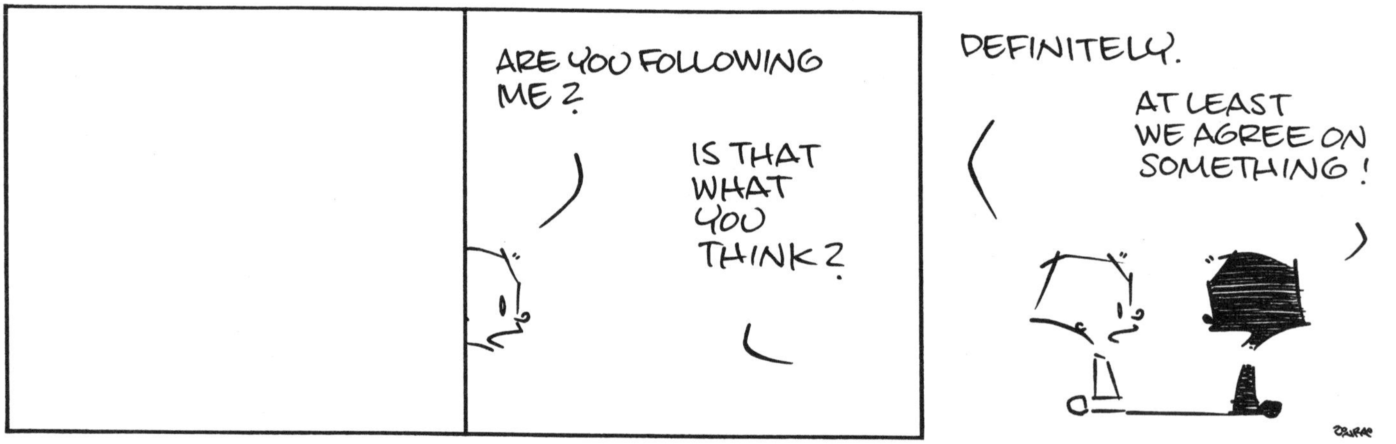
ARE YOU FOLLOWING ME?
IS THAT WHAT YOU THINK?
DEFINITELY.
AT LEAST WE AGREE ON SOMETHING!

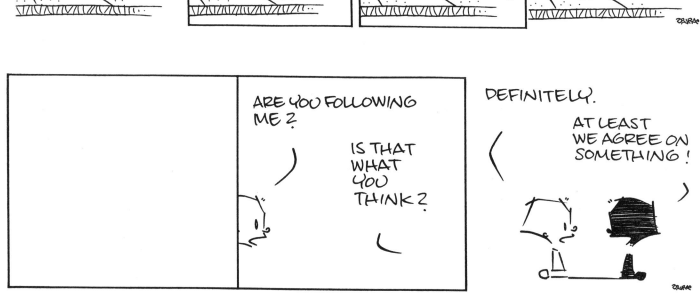

JAMES

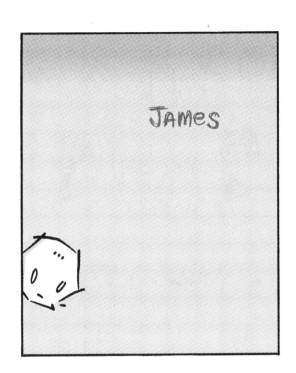

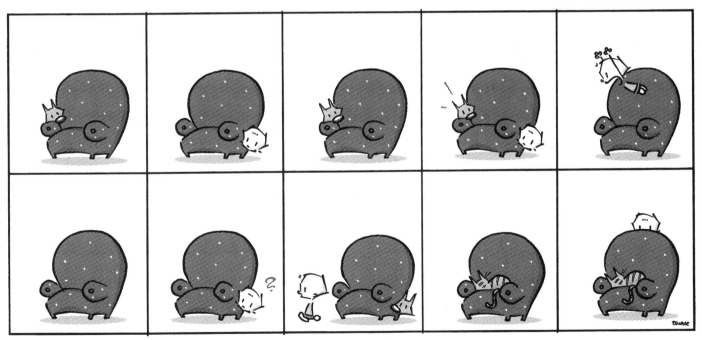

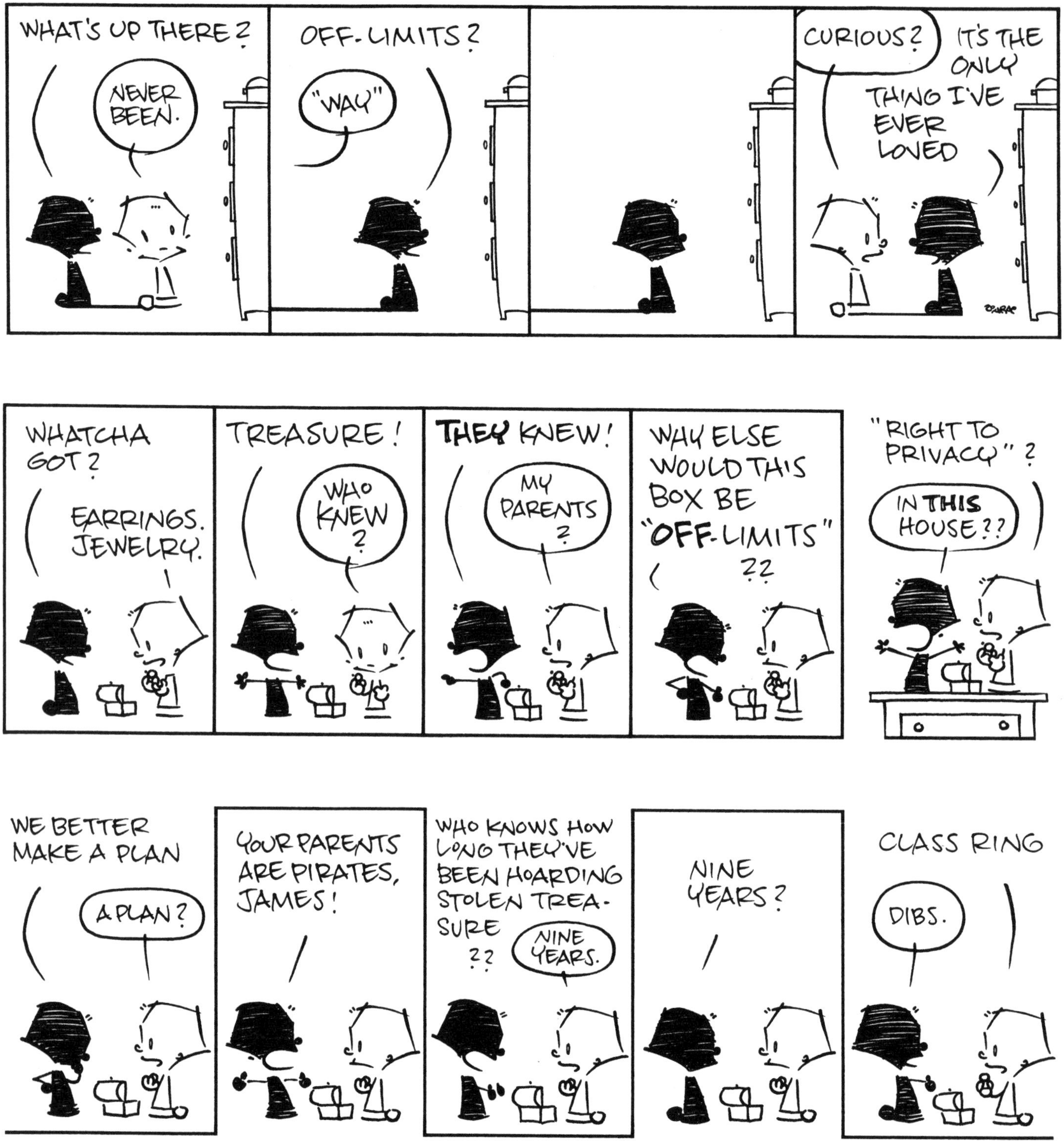
WHAT'S UP THERE?
NEVER BEEN.
OFF-LIMITS?
"WAY"
CURIOUS?
IT'S THE ONLY THING I'VE EVER LOVED
WHATCHA GOT?
EARRINGS. JEWELRY.
TREASURE!
WHO KNEW?
THEY KNEW!
MY PARENTS?
WHY ELSE WOULD THIS BOX BE "OFF-LIMITS"??
"RIGHT TO PRIVACY"?
IN THIS HOUSE??
WE BETTER MAKE A PLAN
A PLAN?
YOUR PARENTS ARE PIRATES, JAMES!
WHO KNOWS HOW LONG THEY'VE BEEN HOARDING STOLEN TREASURE??
NINE YEARS.
NINE YEARS?
CLASS RING
DIBS.

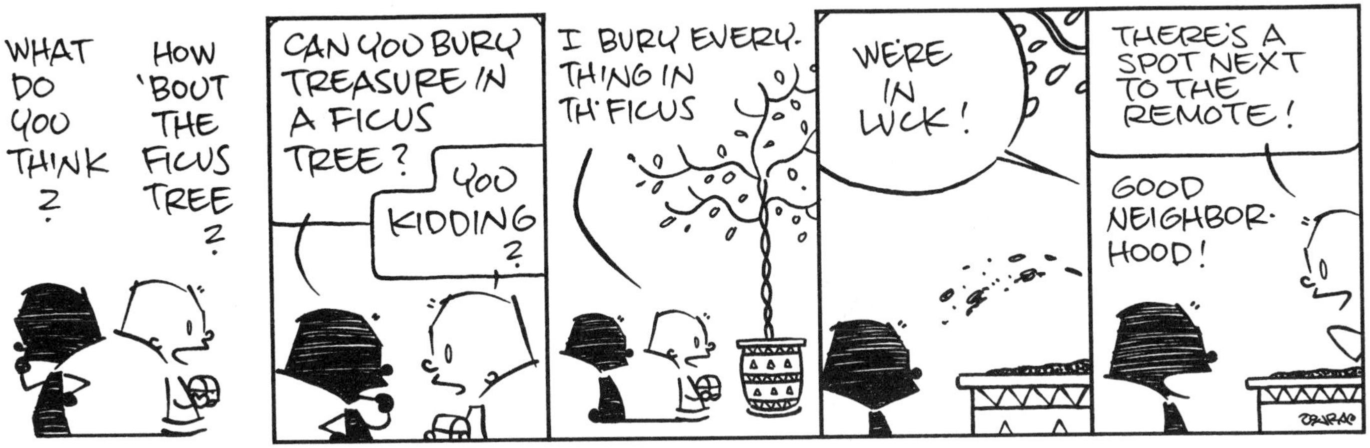
WHAT DO YOU THINK ?
HOW 'BOUT THE FICUS TREE ?
CAN YOU BURY TREASURE IN A FICUS TREE ?
YOU KIDDING ?
I BURY EVERY-THING IN TH' FICUS
WE'RE IN LUCK !
THERE'S A SPOT NEXT TO THE REMOTE !
GOOD NEIGHBOR-HOOD !

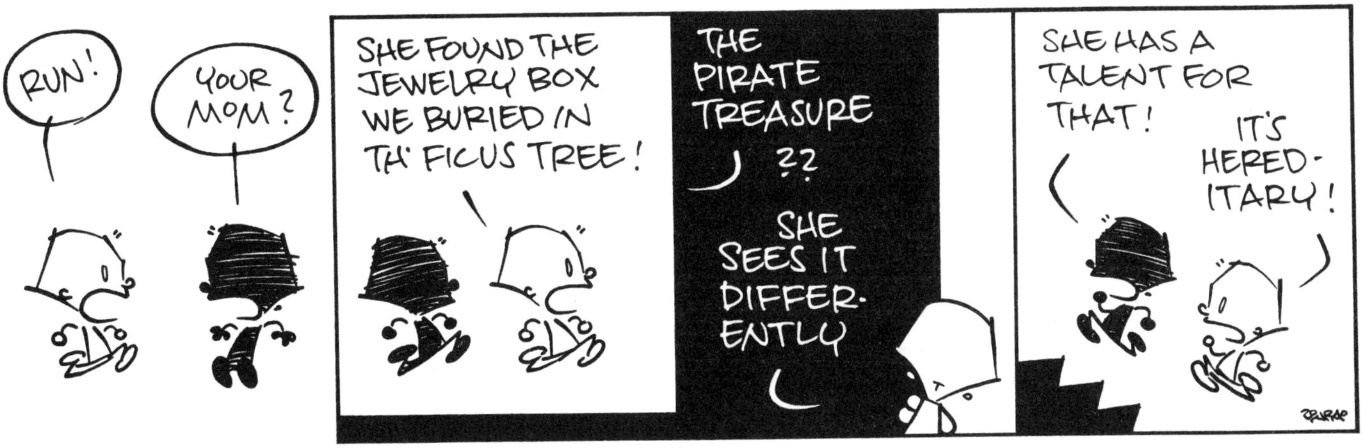
RUN !
YOUR MOM ?
SHE FOUND THE JEWELRY BOX WE BURIED IN TH' FICUS TREE !
THE PIRATE TREASURE ??
SHE SEES IT DIFFER-ENTLY
SHE HAS A TALENT FOR THAT !
IT'S HERED-ITARY !

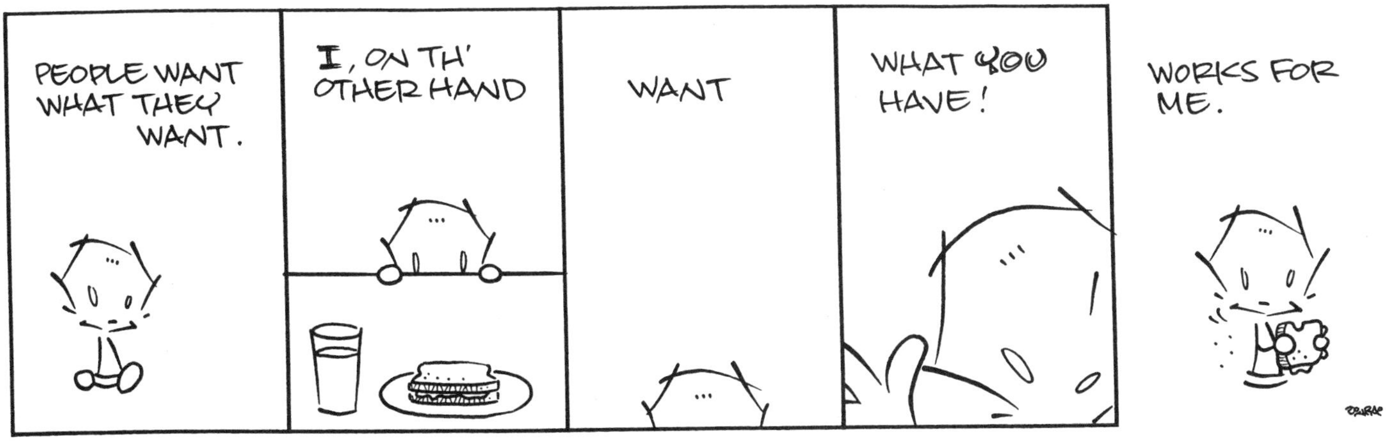
PEOPLE WANT WHAT THEY WANT.
I, ON TH' OTHER HAND
WANT
WHAT YOU HAVE !
WORKS FOR ME.

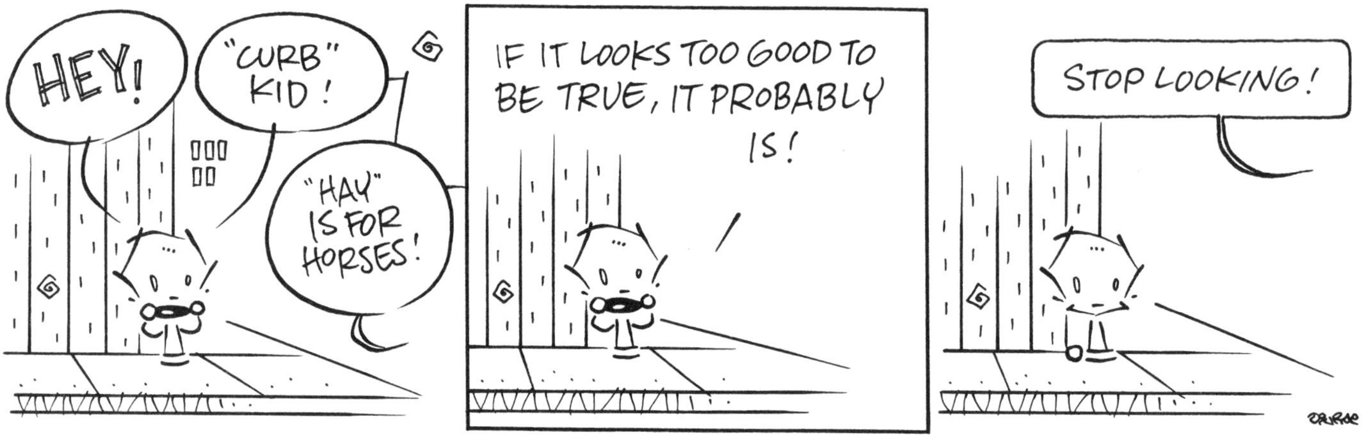
HEY!
"CURB" KID!
"HAY" IS FOR HORSES!
IF IT LOOKS TOO GOOD TO BE TRUE, IT PROBABLY IS!
STOP LOOKING!

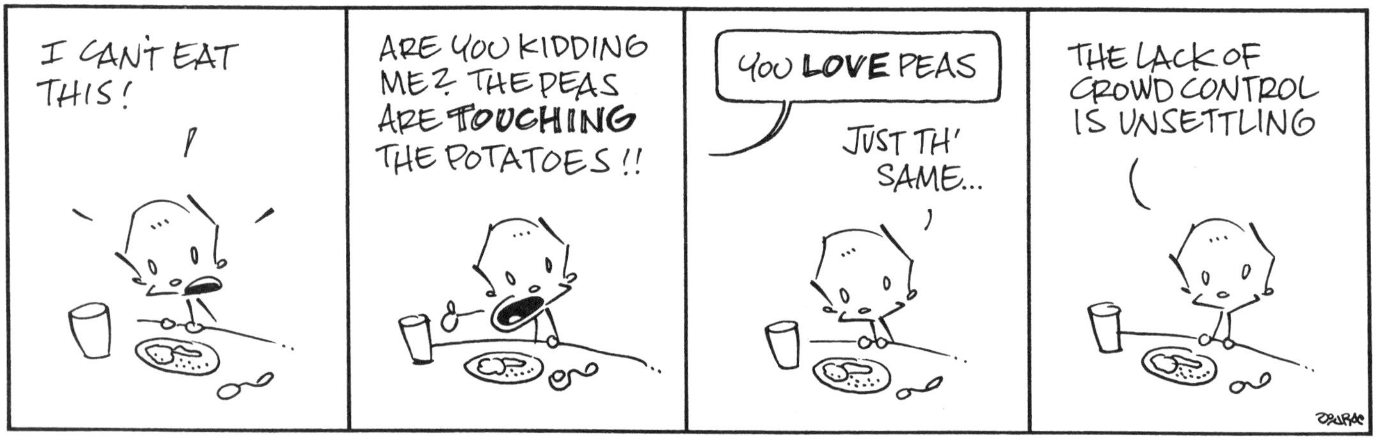
I CAN'T EAT THIS!
ARE YOU KIDDING ME? THE PEAS ARE TOUCHING THE POTATOES!!
YOU LOVE PEAS
JUST TH' SAME...
THE LACK OF CROWD CONTROL IS UNSETTLING

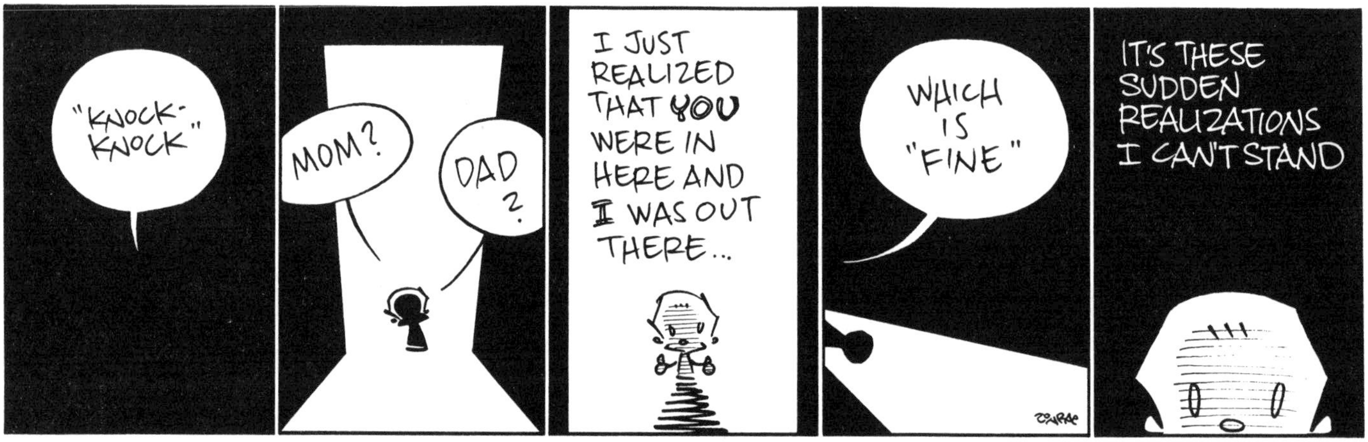
"KNOCK-KNOCK"
MOM?
DAD?
I JUST REALIZED THAT YOU WERE IN HERE AND I WAS OUT THERE...
WHICH IS "FINE"
IT'S THESE SUDDEN REALIZATIONS I CAN'T STAND

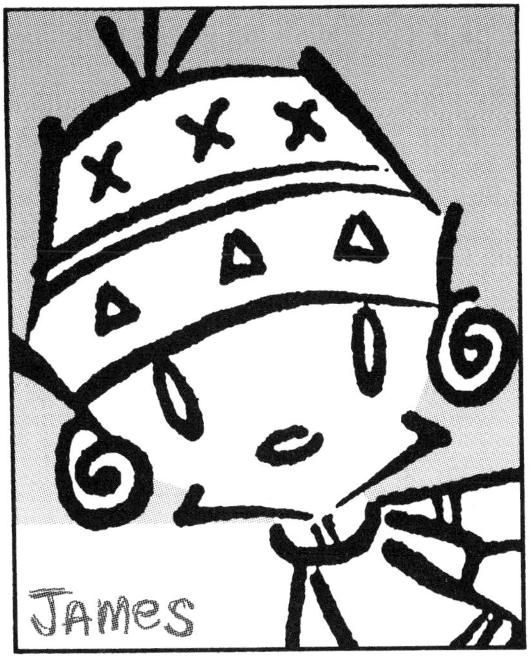
JAMES

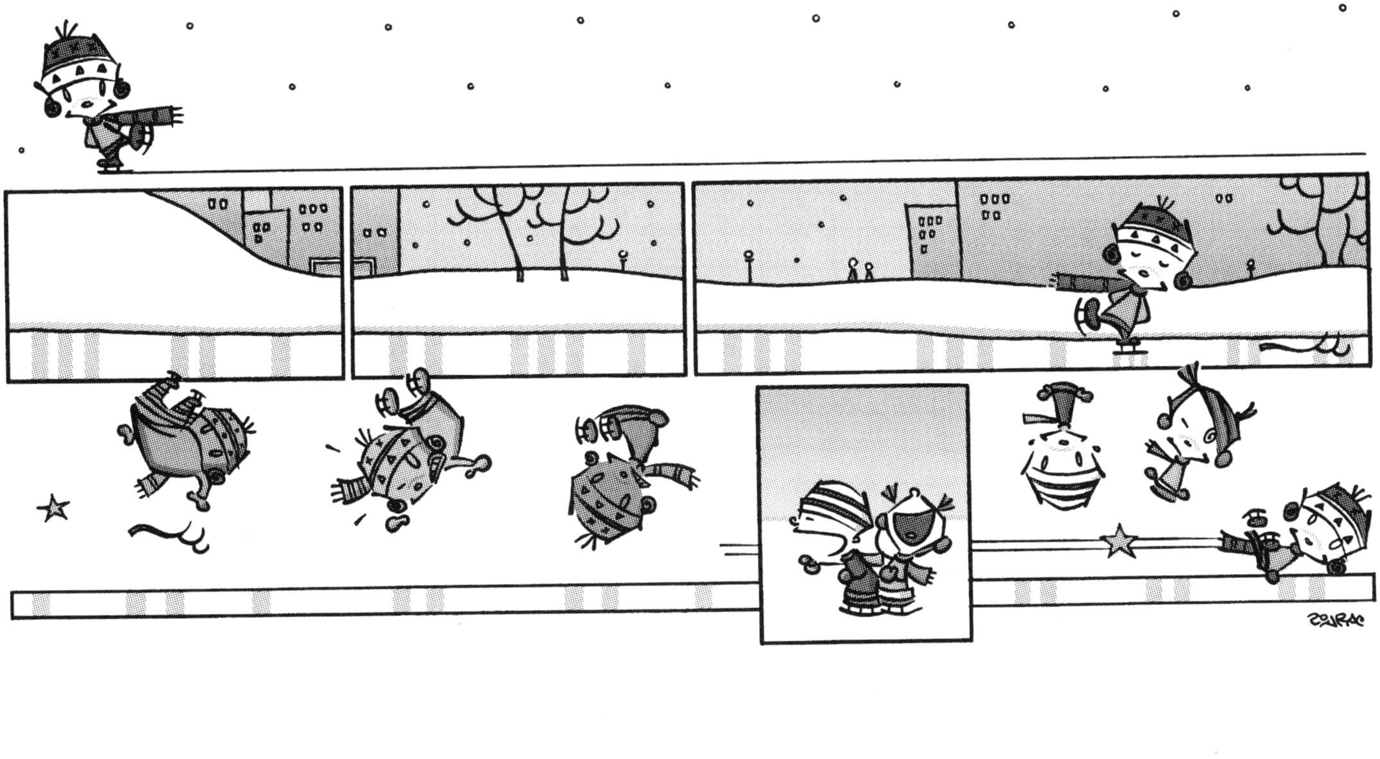

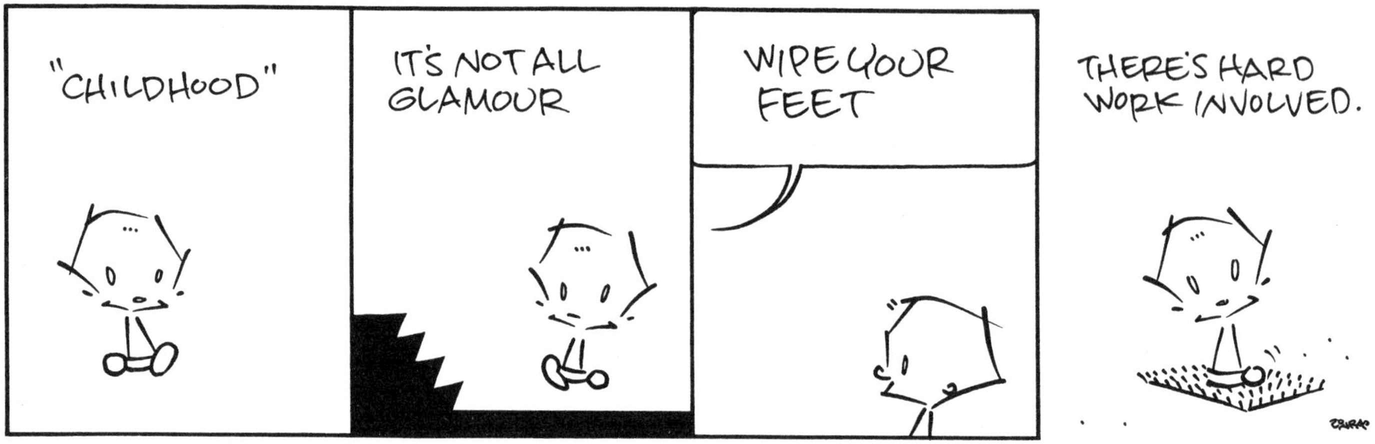
"CHILDHOOD"
IT'S NOT ALL GLAMOUR
WIPE YOUR FEET
THERE'S HARD WORK INVOLVED.

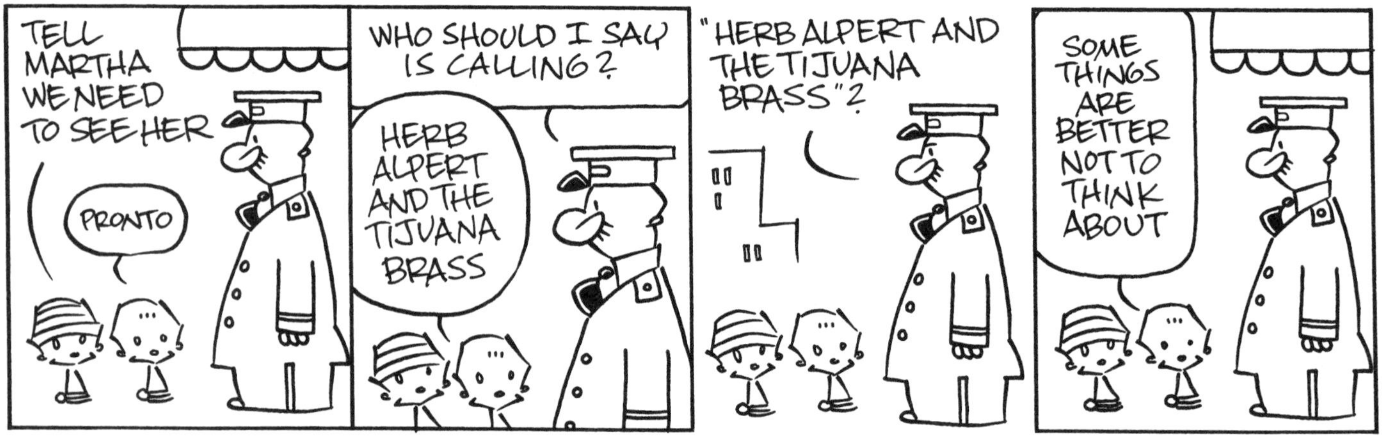
TELL MARTHA WE NEED TO SEE HER
PRONTO
WHO SHOULD I SAY IS CALLING?
HERB ALPERT AND THE TIJUANA BRASS
"HERB ALPERT AND THE TIJUANA BRASS"?
SOME THINGS ARE BETTER NOT TO THINK ABOUT

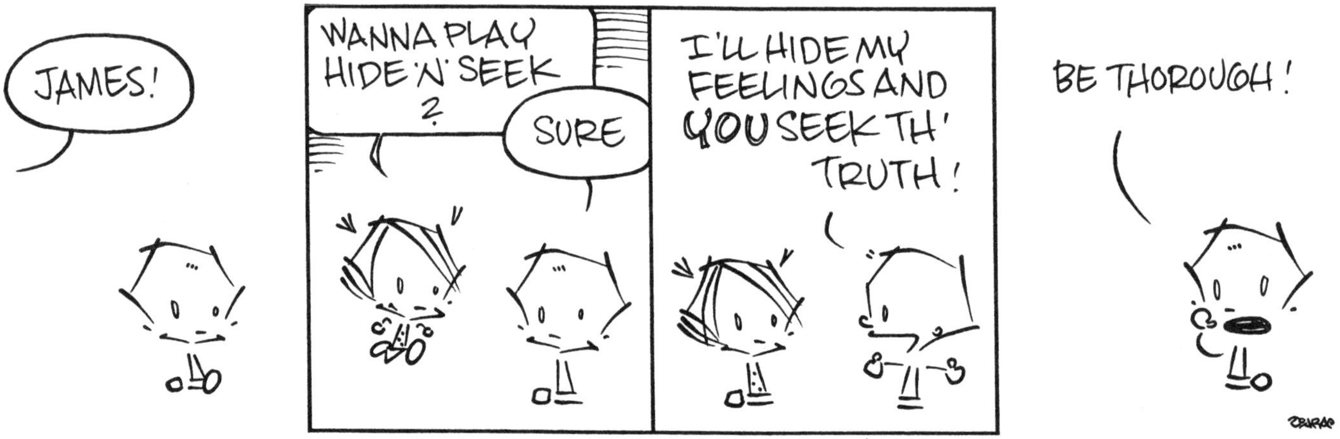
JAMES!
WANNA PLAY HIDE 'N' SEEK ?
SURE
I'LL HIDE MY FEELINGS AND YOU SEEK TH' TRUTH!
BE THOROUGH!

JAMES

1:00	1:15	1:30	1:45
WATER!	BLANKET!	RHINO!	COLD!

1:50

I DON'T KNOW WHAT THEY SEE IN ME.

I'M A "GOOD" BOY

MOM SAID SO

AND **I** BELIEVE HER!

I'M WAY TOO TRUSTING.

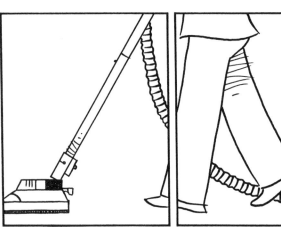

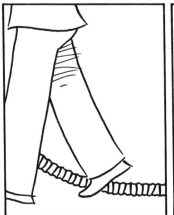

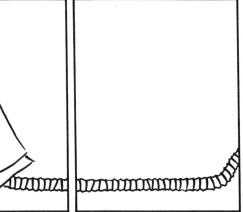

CHIPS

THEY WANT ME TO BE "HAPPY"

BUT THEY **WON'T** LET ME SWING ON TH' CURTAINS!

THEY WANT ME TO BE "HAPPY"

BUT THEY **WON'T** LET ME PUT A WAFFLE IN TH' VCR!

I'D SEND THEM TO A THERAPIST IF I THOUGHT IT WOULD HELP.

James

JAMES!
TH'SNOW STORM'S GOING TO MISS US
I KNEW YOU'D BE DIS-APPOINTED SO I BROUGHT YOU SOME CRUSHED ICE FROM OUR REFRIGERATOR
LET TH' HEALING BEGIN!

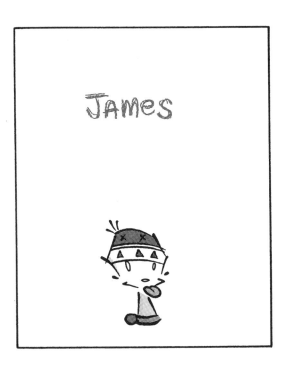

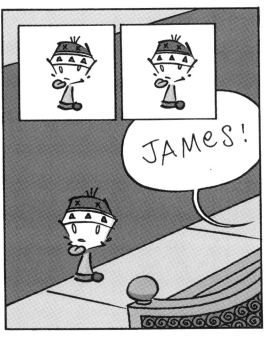

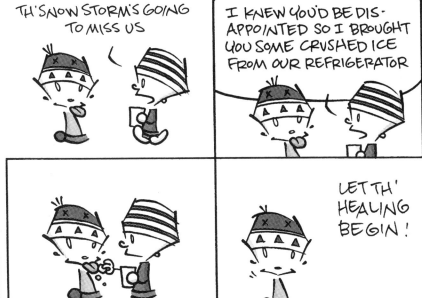

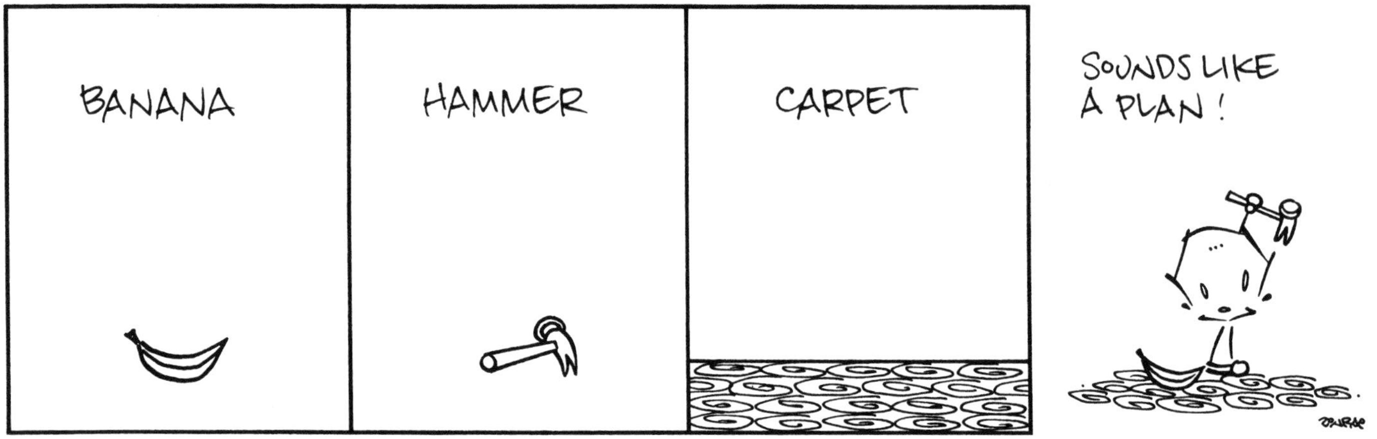
BANANA
HAMMER
CARPET
SOUNDS LIKE A PLAN!

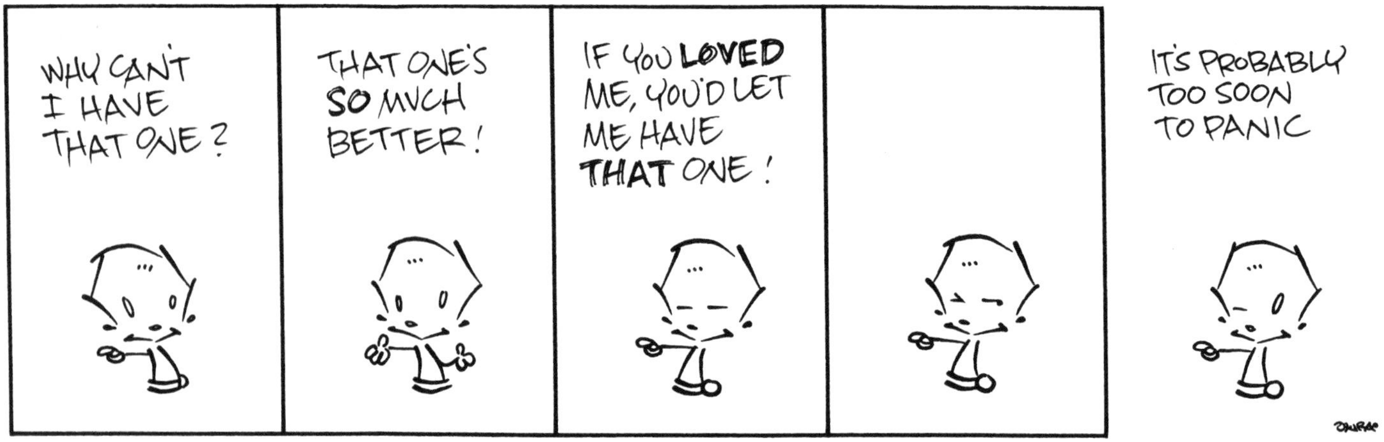
WHY CAN'T I HAVE THAT ONE?
THAT ONE'S SO MUCH BETTER!
IF YOU LOVED ME, YOU'D LET ME HAVE THAT ONE!
IT'S PROBABLY TOO SOON TO PANIC

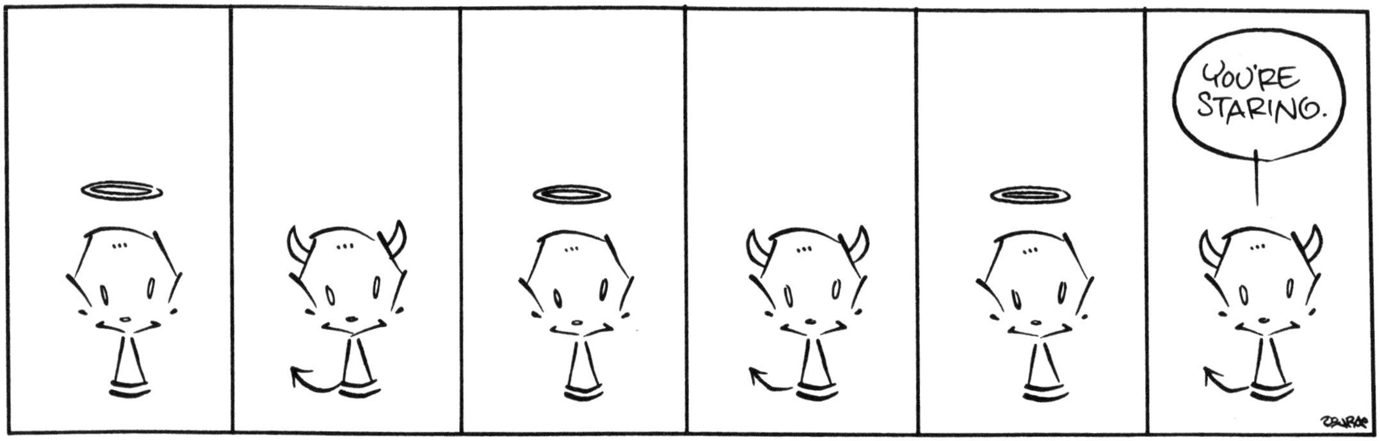
YOU'RE STARING.

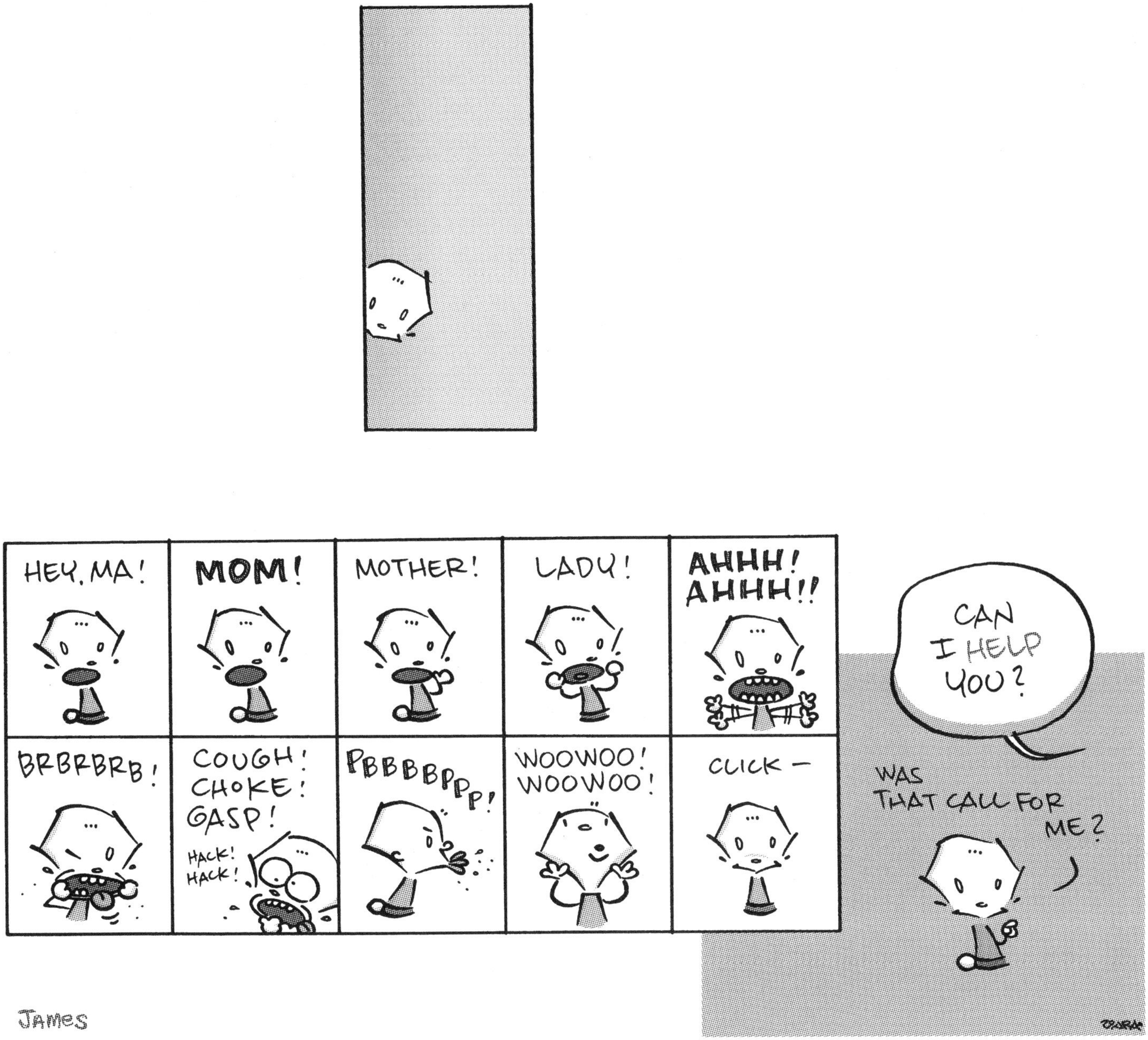
HEY, MA!
MOM!
MOTHER!
LADY!
AHHH! AHHH!!
BRBRBRBRB!
COUGH! CHOKE! GASP!
HACK! HACK!
PBBBBBPPPP!
WOOWOO! WOOWOO!
CLICK –
CAN I HELP YOU?
WAS THAT CALL FOR ME?
JAMES

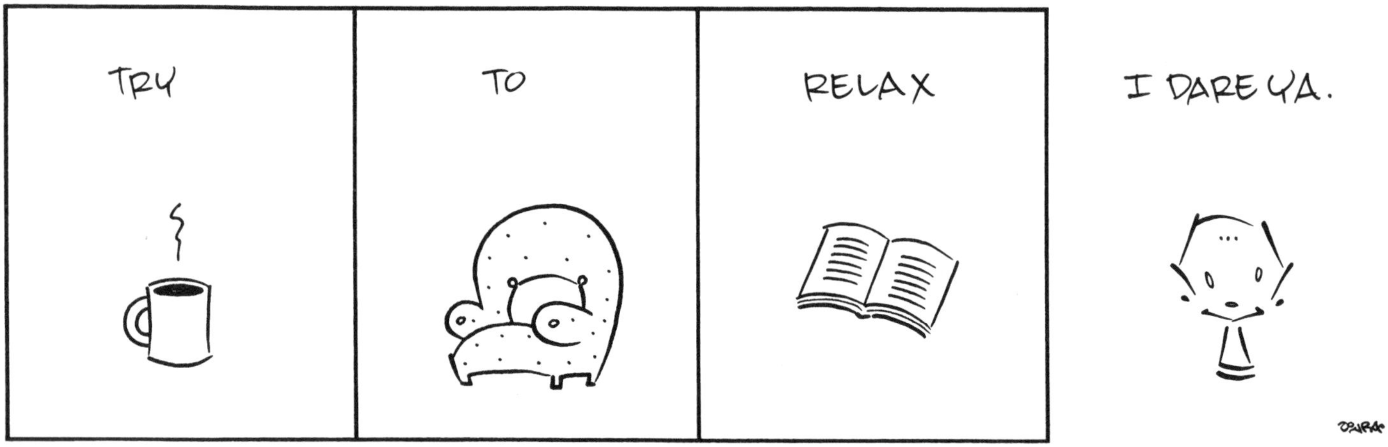
TRY
TO
RELAX
I DARE YA.

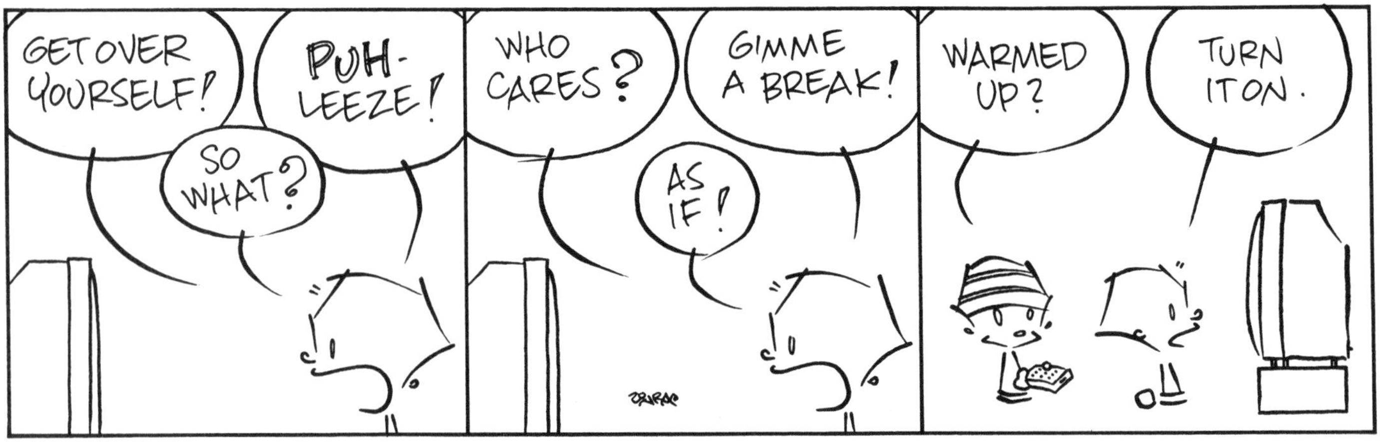
GET OVER YOURSELF!
SO WHAT?
PUH-LEEZE!
WHO CARES?
AS IF!
GIMME A BREAK!
WARMED UP?
TURN IT ON.

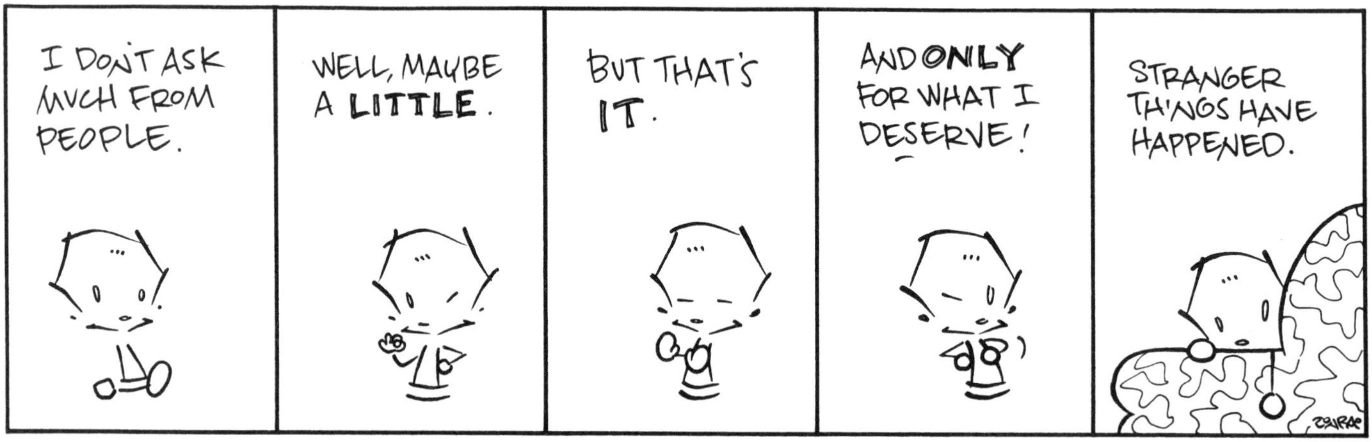
I DON'T ASK MUCH FROM PEOPLE.
WELL, MAYBE A **LITTLE**.
BUT THAT'S **IT**.
AND **ONLY** FOR WHAT I DESERVE!
STRANGER THINGS HAVE HAPPENED.

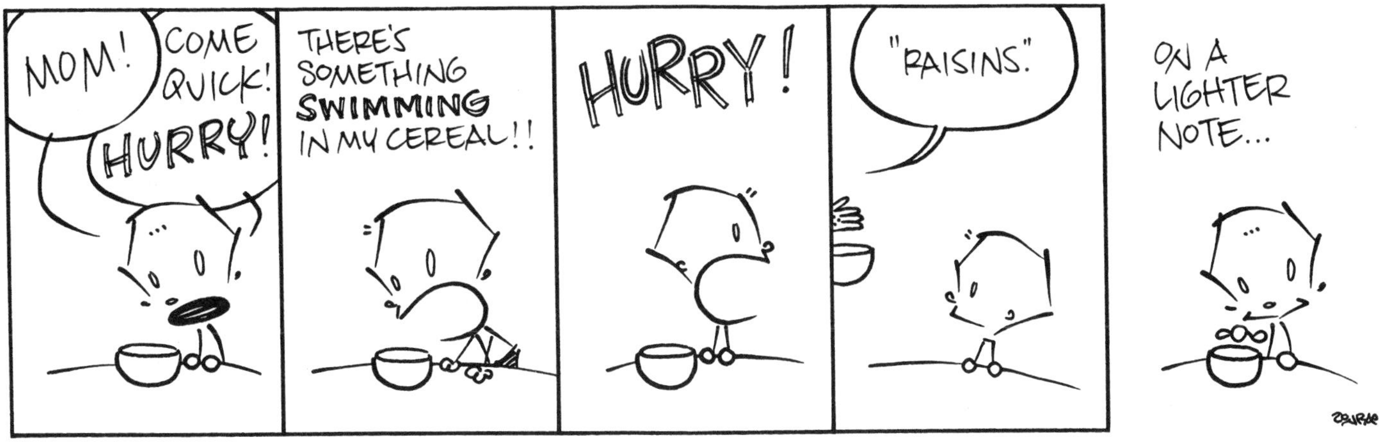
MOM!
COME QUICK!
HURRY!
THERE'S SOMETHING SWIMMING IN MY CEREAL!!
HURRY!
"RAISINS."
ON A LIGHTER NOTE...

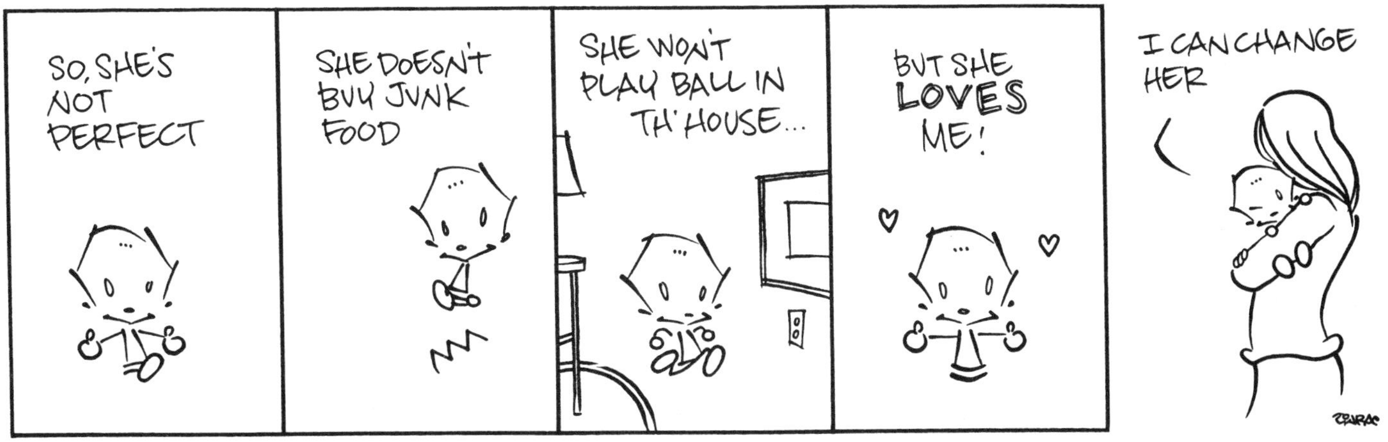
SO, SHE'S NOT PERFECT
SHE DOESN'T BUY JUNK FOOD
SHE WON'T PLAY BALL IN TH' HOUSE...
BUT SHE LOVES ME!
I CAN CHANGE HER

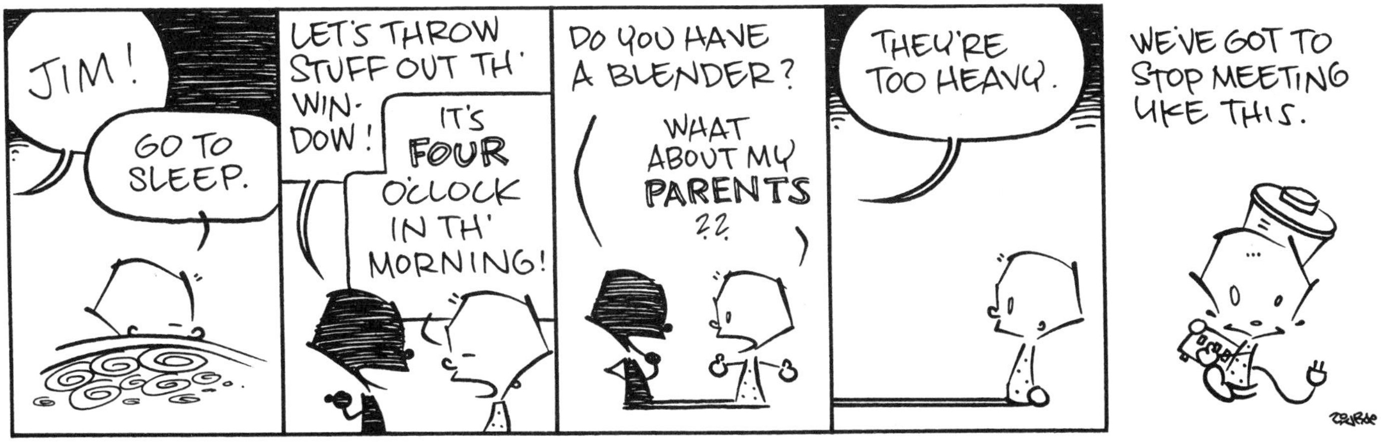
JIM!
GO TO SLEEP.
LET'S THROW STUFF OUT TH' WIN-DOW!
IT'S FOUR O'CLOCK IN TH' MORNING!
DO YOU HAVE A BLENDER?
WHAT ABOUT MY PARENTS??
THEY'RE TOO HEAVY.
WE'VE GOT TO STOP MEETING LIKE THIS.

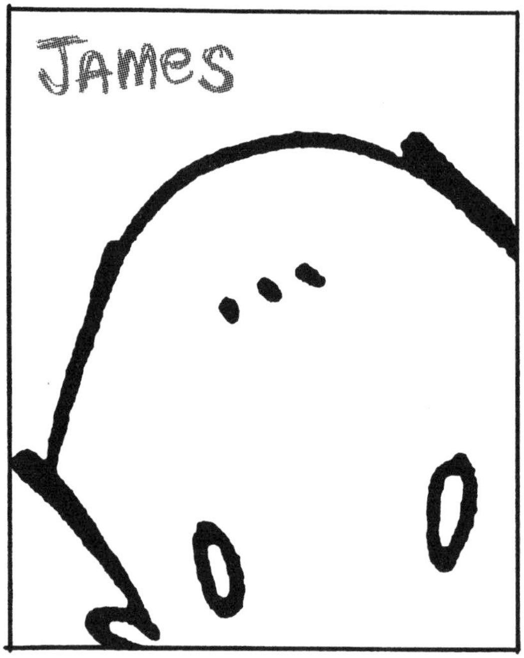
JAMES
...

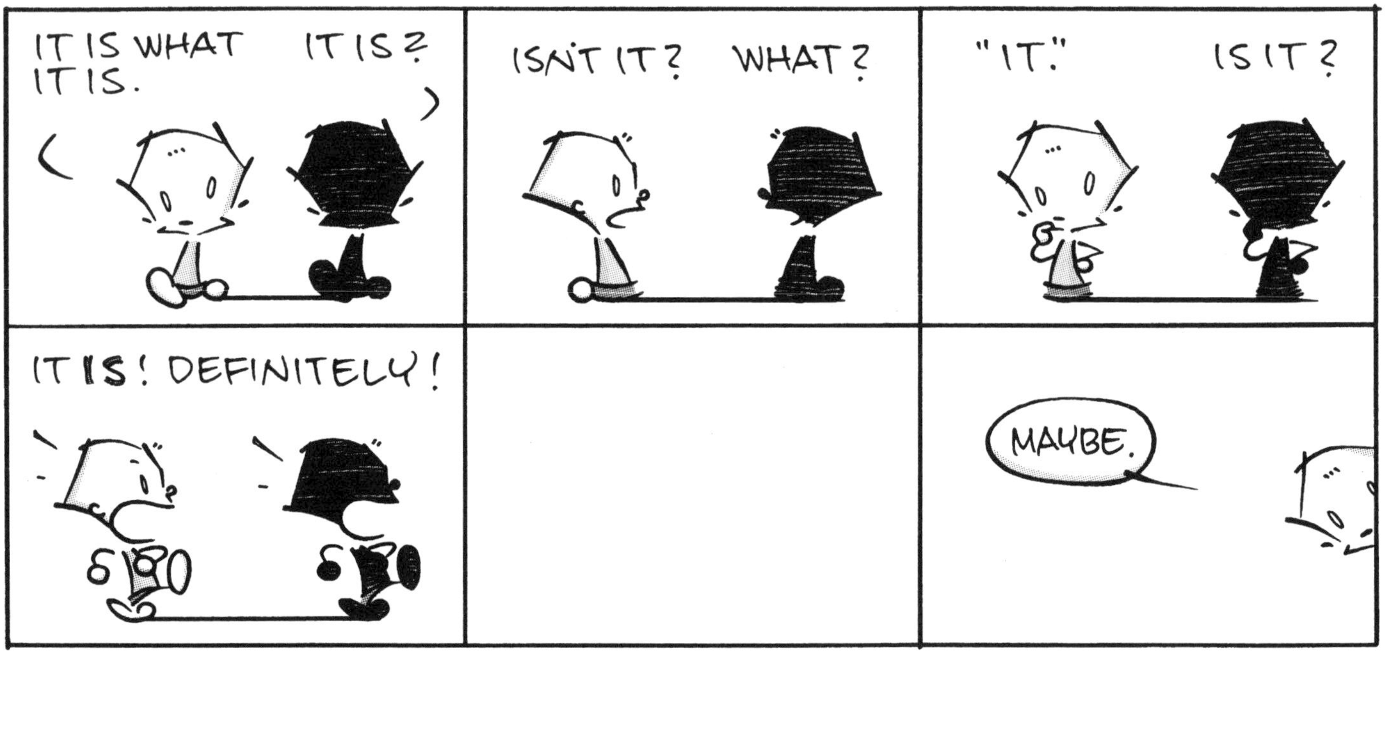
IT IS WHAT IT IS.
IT IS?
ISN'T IT?
WHAT?
"IT."
IS IT?
IT IS! DEFINITELY!
MAYBE.

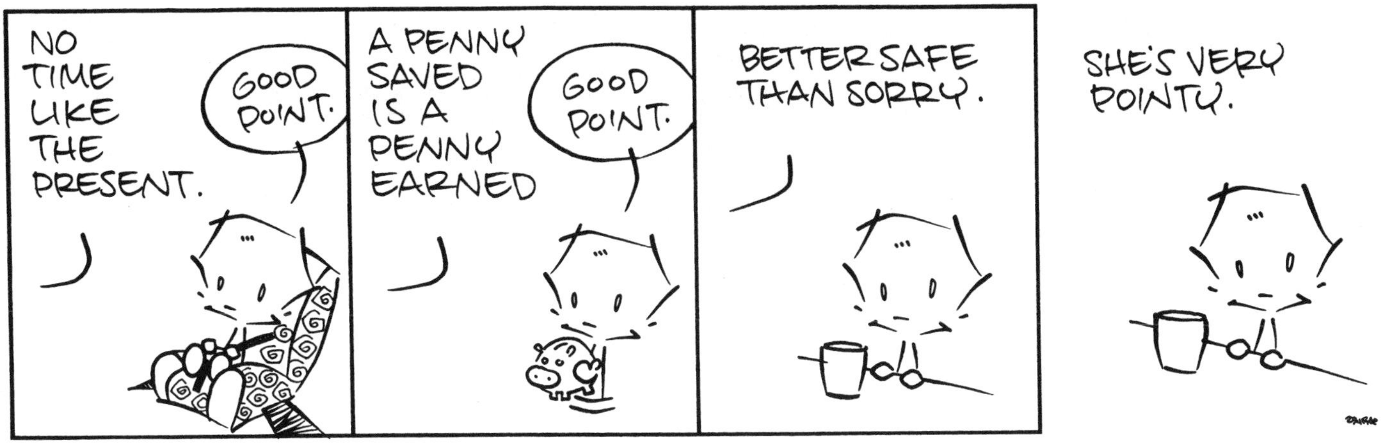
NO TIME LIKE THE PRESENT.
GOOD POINT.
A PENNY SAVED IS A PENNY EARNED
GOOD POINT.
BETTER SAFE THAN SORRY.
SHE'S VERY POINTY.

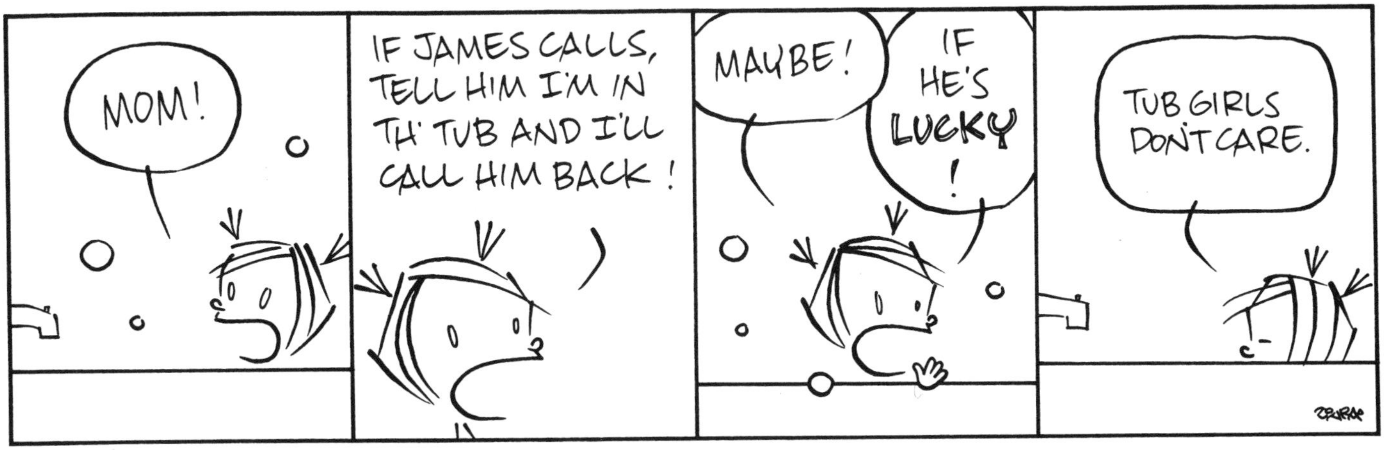
MOM!
IF JAMES CALLS, TELL HIM I'M IN TH' TUB AND I'LL CALL HIM BACK!
MAYBE!
IF HE'S **LUCKY**!
TUB GIRLS DON'T CARE.

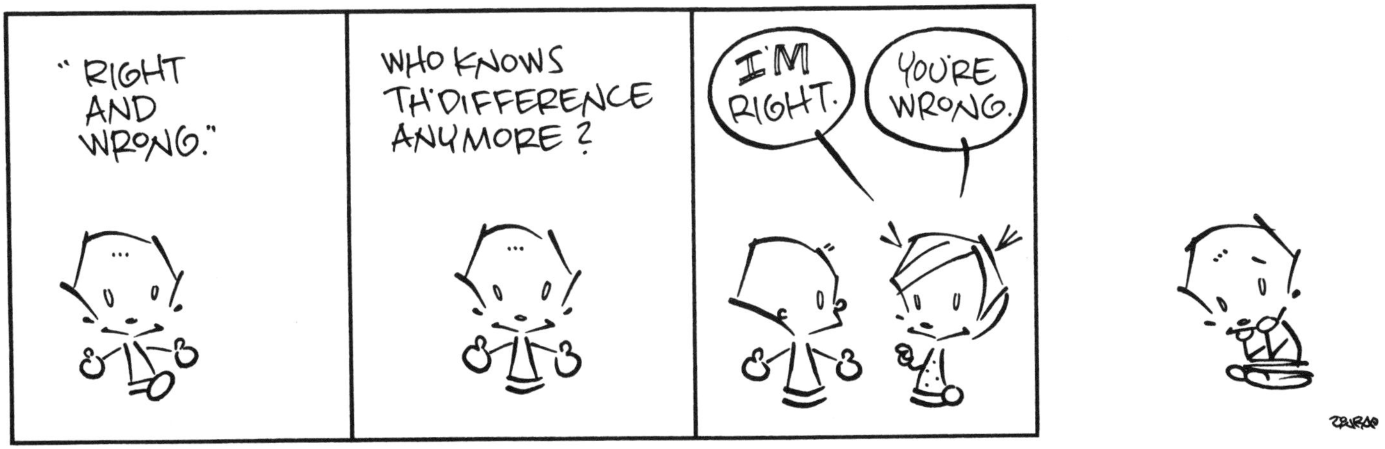
"RIGHT AND WRONG."
WHO KNOWS TH' DIFFERENCE ANYMORE?
I'M RIGHT.
YOU'RE WRONG.

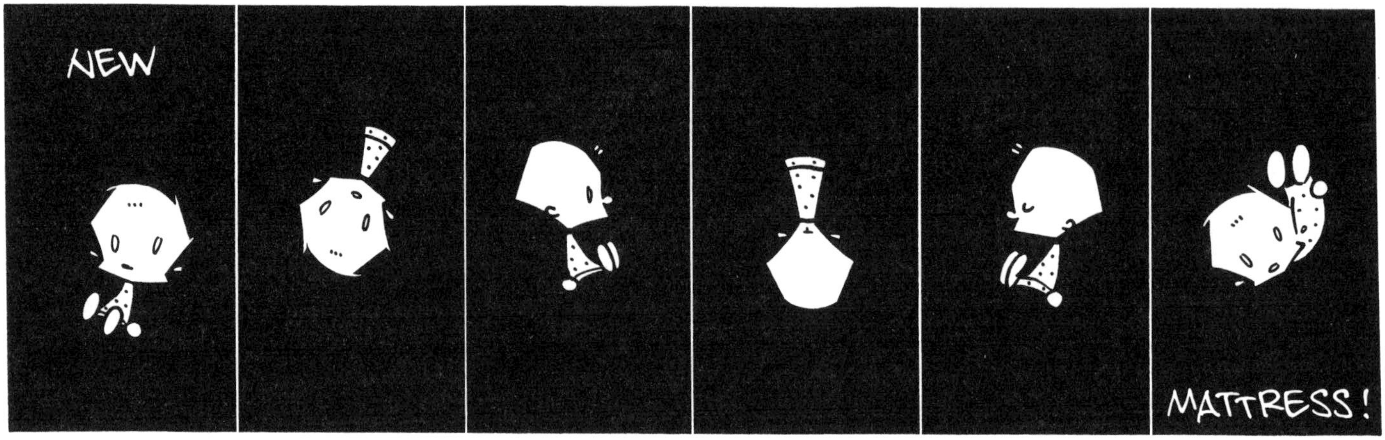
NEW
MATTRESS!

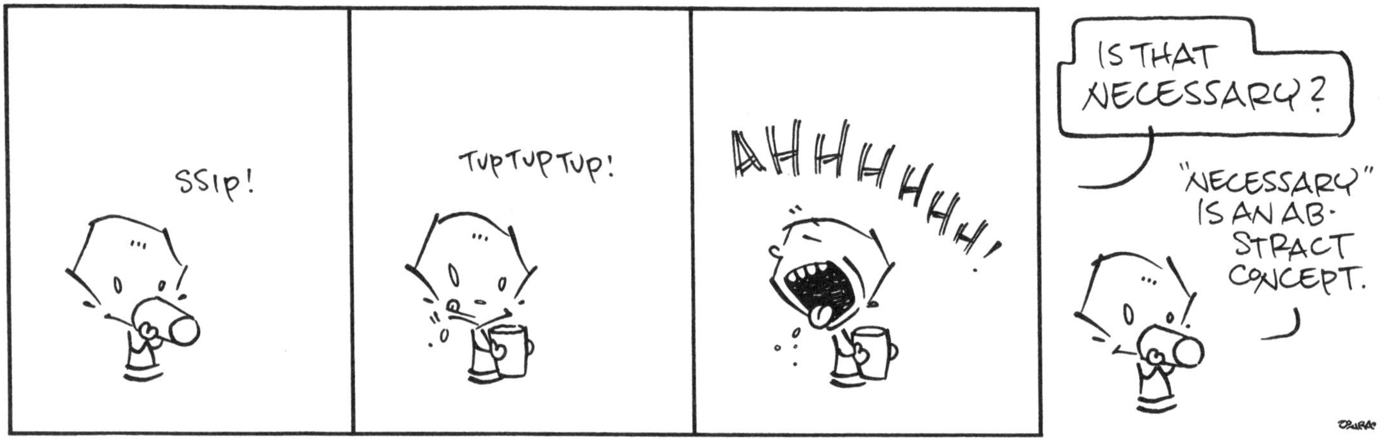
SSIP!
TUPTUPTUP!
AHHHHHHH!
IS THAT NECESSARY?
"NECESSARY" IS AN AB-STRACT CONCEPT.

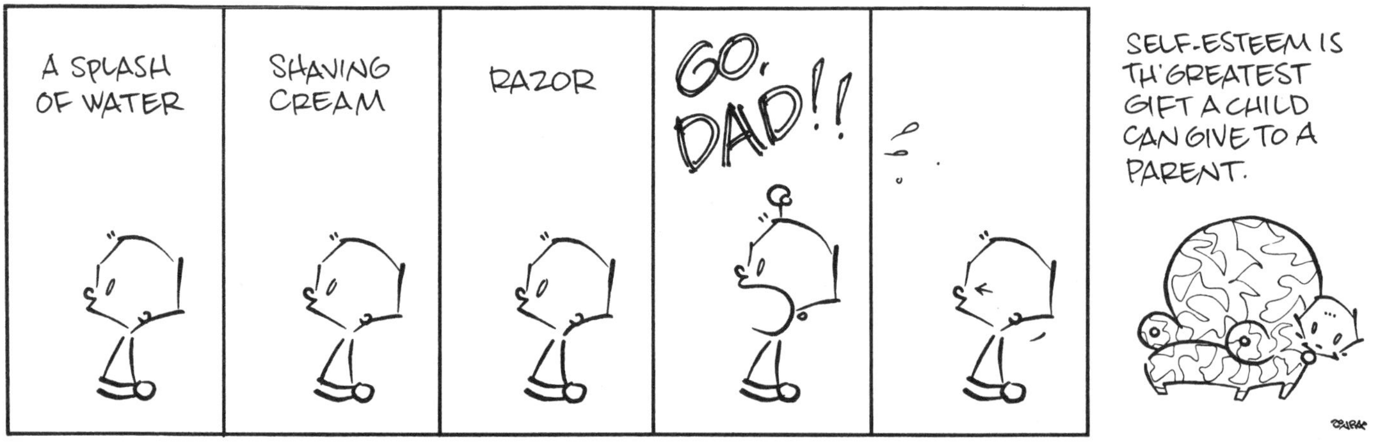
A SPLASH OF WATER
SHAVING CREAM
RAZOR
GO, DAD!!
SELF-ESTEEM IS TH' GREATEST GIFT A CHILD CAN GIVE TO A PARENT.

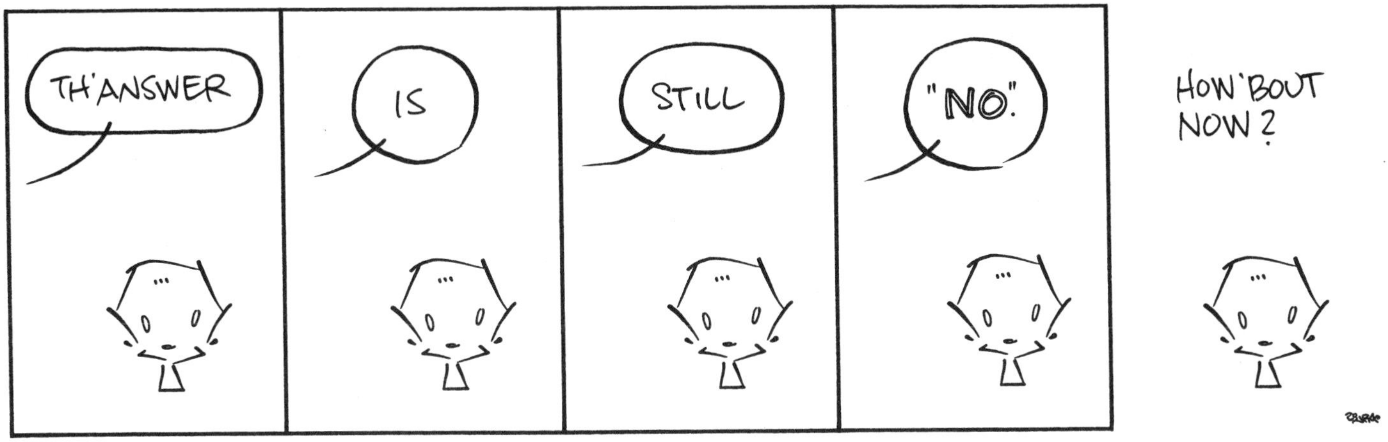
TH'ANSWER
IS
STILL
"NO."
HOW 'BOUT NOW?

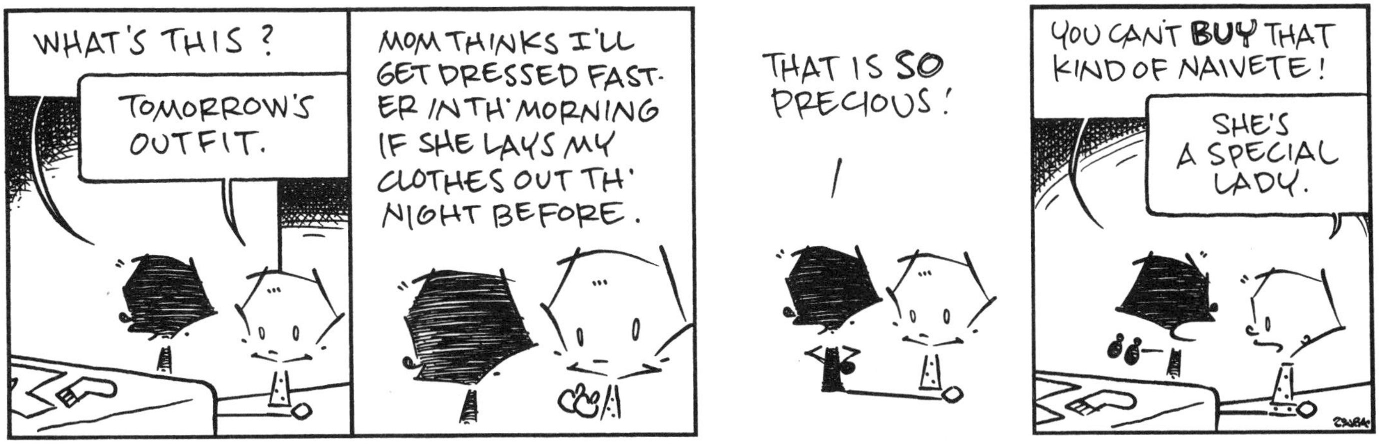
WHAT'S THIS?
TOMORROW'S OUTFIT.
MOM THINKS I'LL GET DRESSED FASTER IN TH' MORNING IF SHE LAYS MY CLOTHES OUT TH' NIGHT BEFORE.
THAT IS SO PRECIOUS!
YOU CAN'T BUY THAT KIND OF NAIVETE!
SHE'S A SPECIAL LADY.

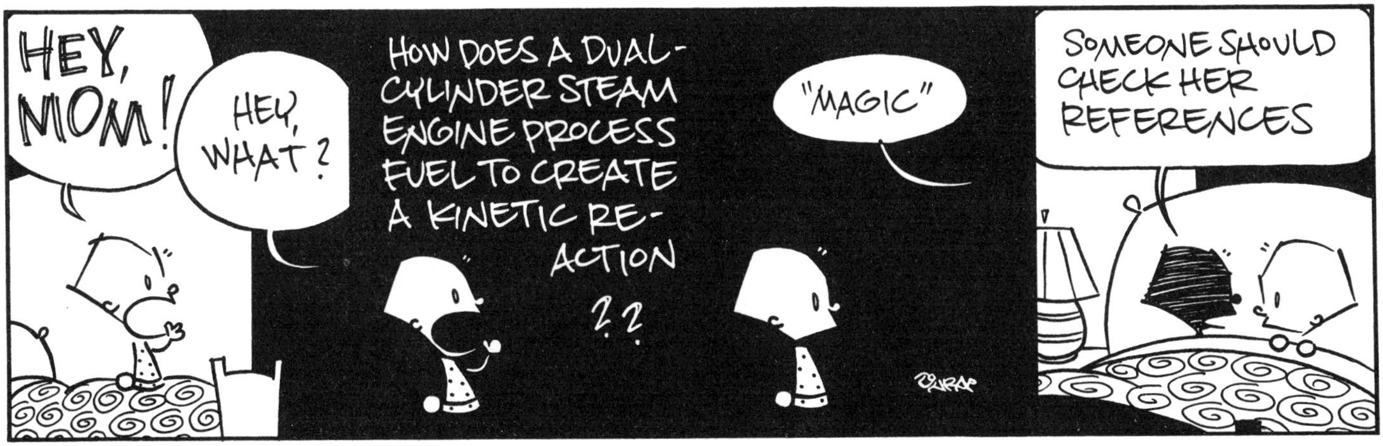
HEY, MOM!
HEY, WHAT?
HOW DOES A DUAL-CYLINDER STEAM ENGINE PROCESS FUEL TO CREATE A KINETIC RE-ACTION
??
"MAGIC"
SOMEONE SHOULD CHECK HER REFERENCES

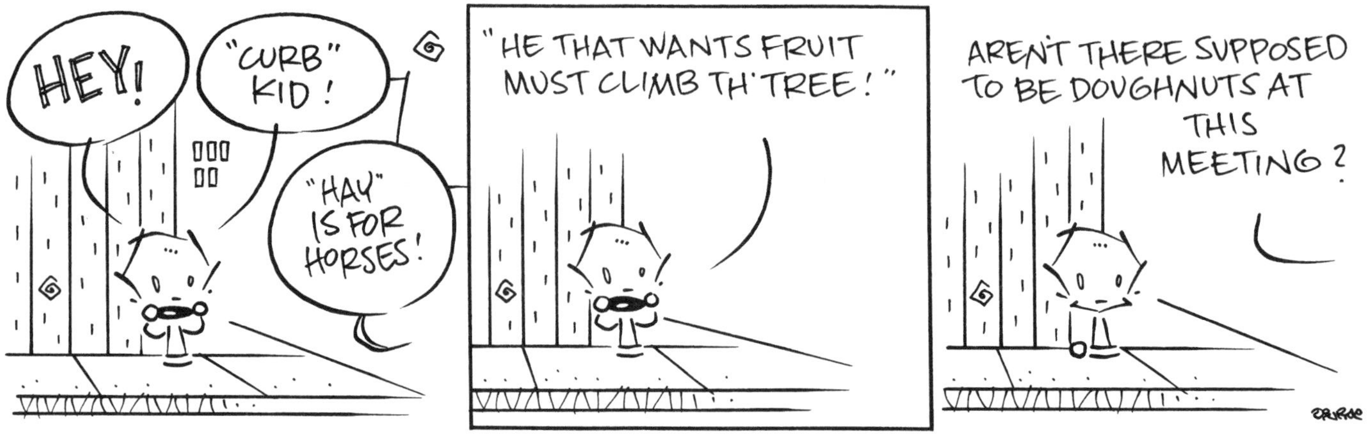
HEY!
"CURB" KID!
"HAY" IS FOR HORSES!
"HE THAT WANTS FRUIT MUST CLIMB TH' TREE!"
AREN'T THERE SUPPOSED TO BE DOUGHNUTS AT THIS MEETING?

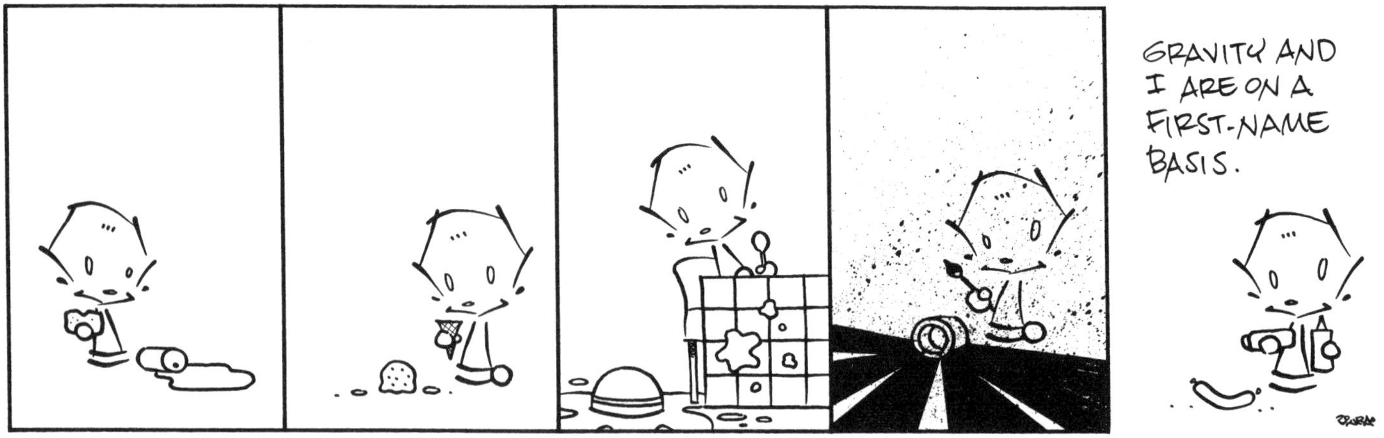
GRAVITY AND I ARE ON A FIRST-NAME BASIS.

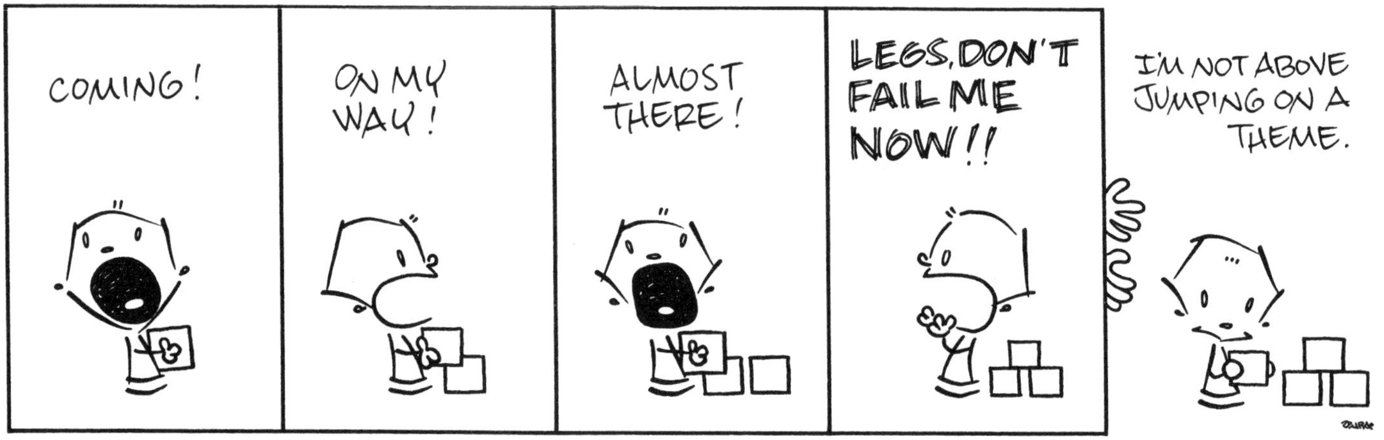
COMING!
ON MY WAY!
ALMOST THERE!
LEGS, DON'T FAIL ME NOW!!
I'M NOT ABOVE JUMPING ON A THEME.

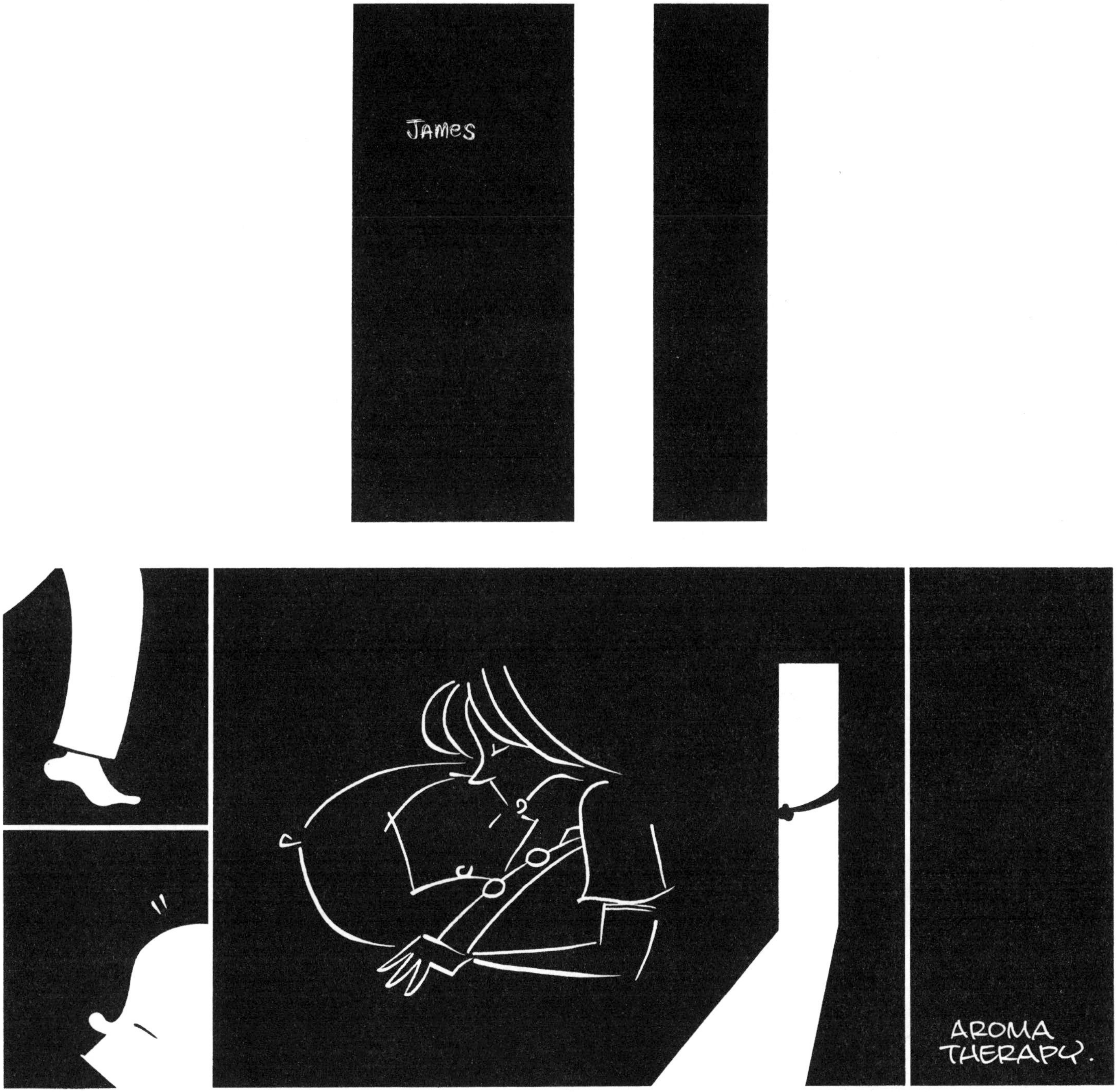
JAMES
AROMA THERAPY.

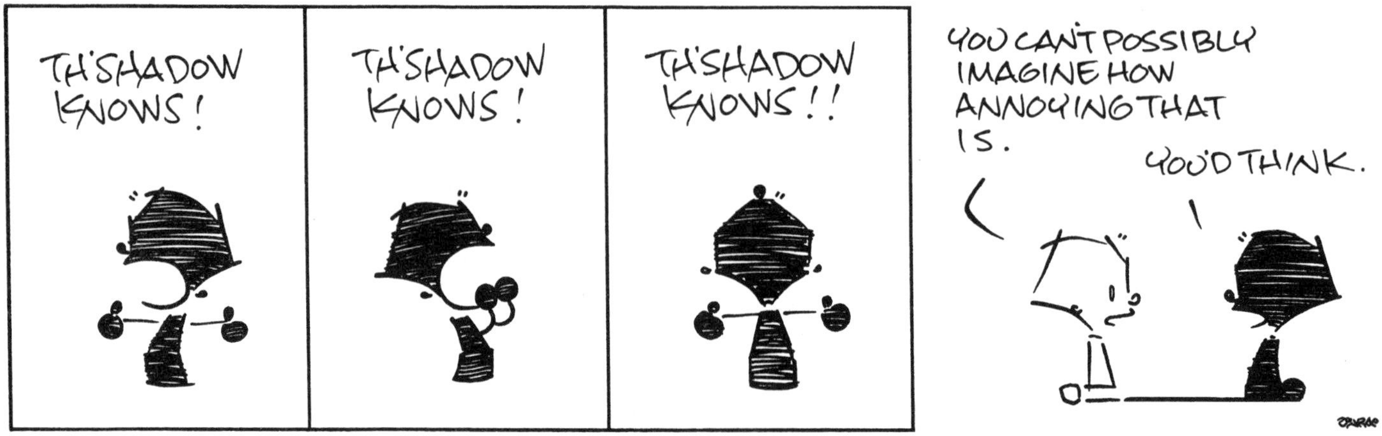
TH'SHADOW KNOWS!
TH'SHADOW KNOWS!
TH'SHADOW KNOWS!!
YOU CAN'T POSSIBLY IMAGINE HOW ANNOYING THAT IS.
YOU'D THINK.

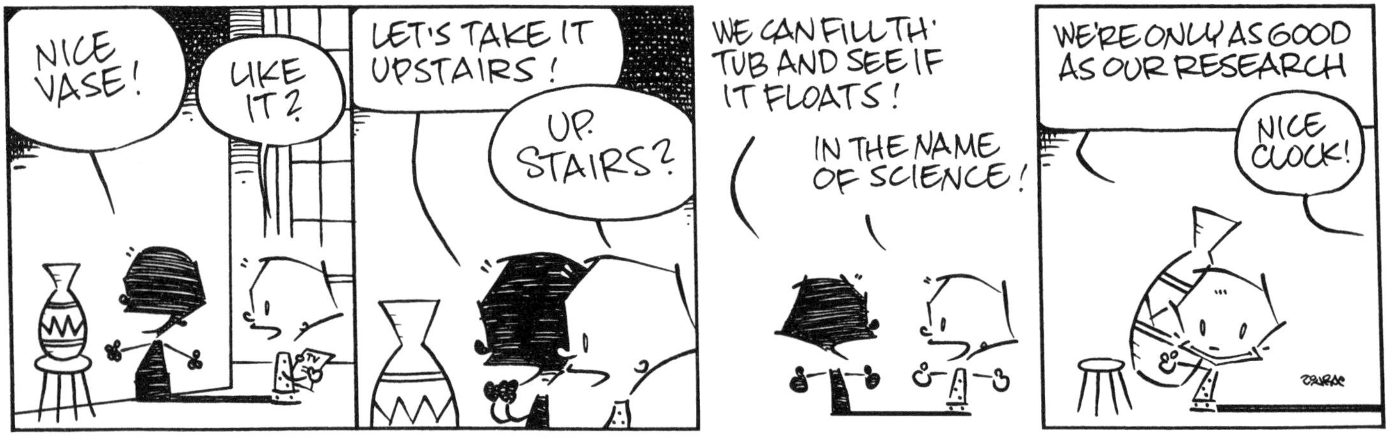
NICE VASE!
LIKE IT?
LET'S TAKE IT UPSTAIRS!
UP. STAIRS?
WE CAN FILL TH' TUB AND SEE IF IT FLOATS!
IN THE NAME OF SCIENCE!
WE'RE ONLY AS GOOD AS OUR RESEARCH
NICE CLOCK!

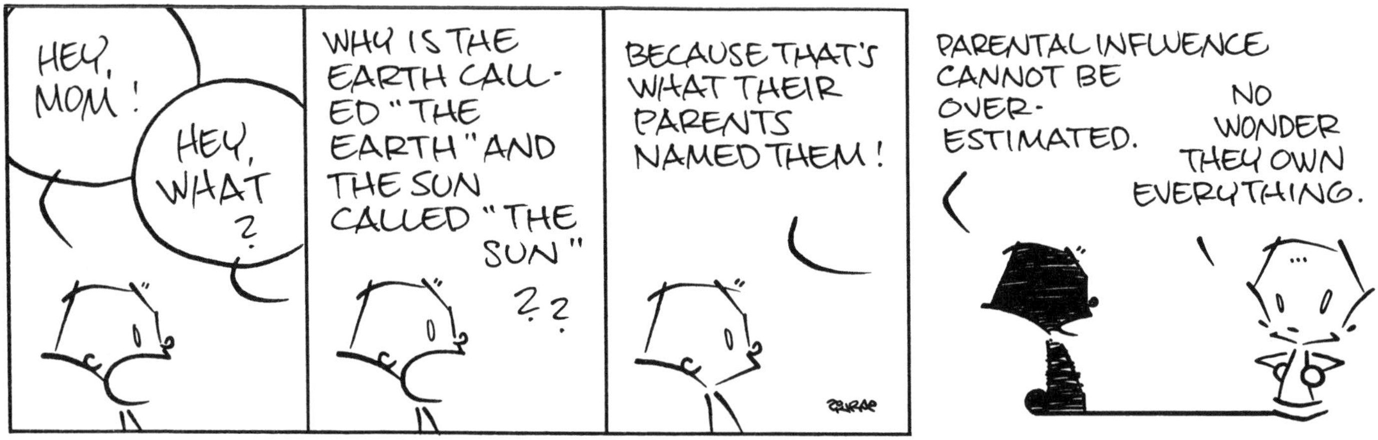
HEY, MOM!
HEY, WHAT?
WHY IS THE EARTH CALLED "THE EARTH" AND THE SUN CALLED "THE SUN"
??
BECAUSE THAT'S WHAT THEIR PARENTS NAMED THEM!
PARENTAL INFLUENCE CANNOT BE OVER-ESTIMATED.
NO WONDER THEY OWN EVERYTHING.

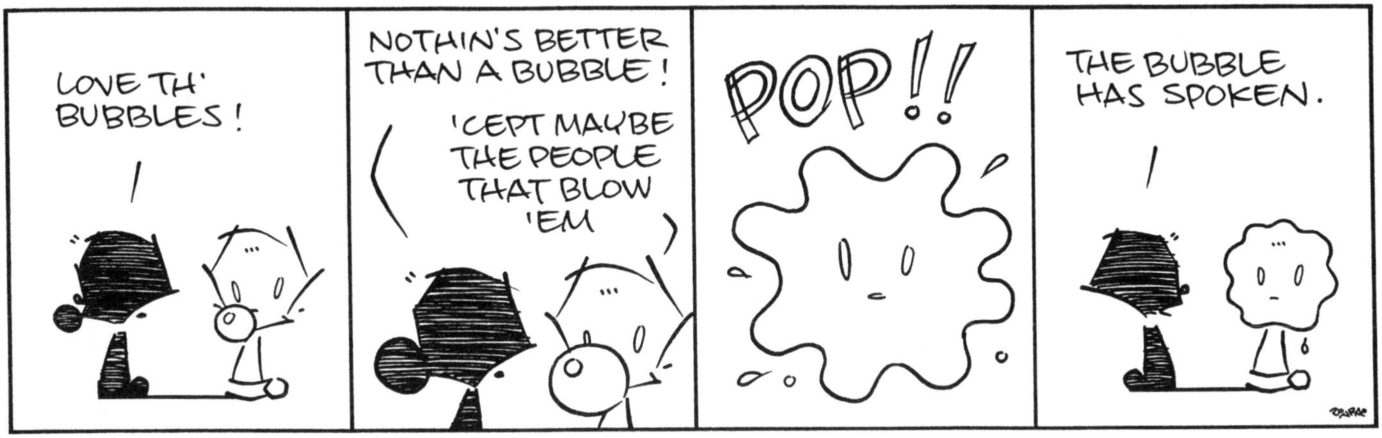
LOVE TH' BUBBLES!
NOTHIN'S BETTER THAN A BUBBLE!
'CEPT MAYBE THE PEOPLE THAT BLOW 'EM
POP!!
THE BUBBLE HAS SPOKEN.

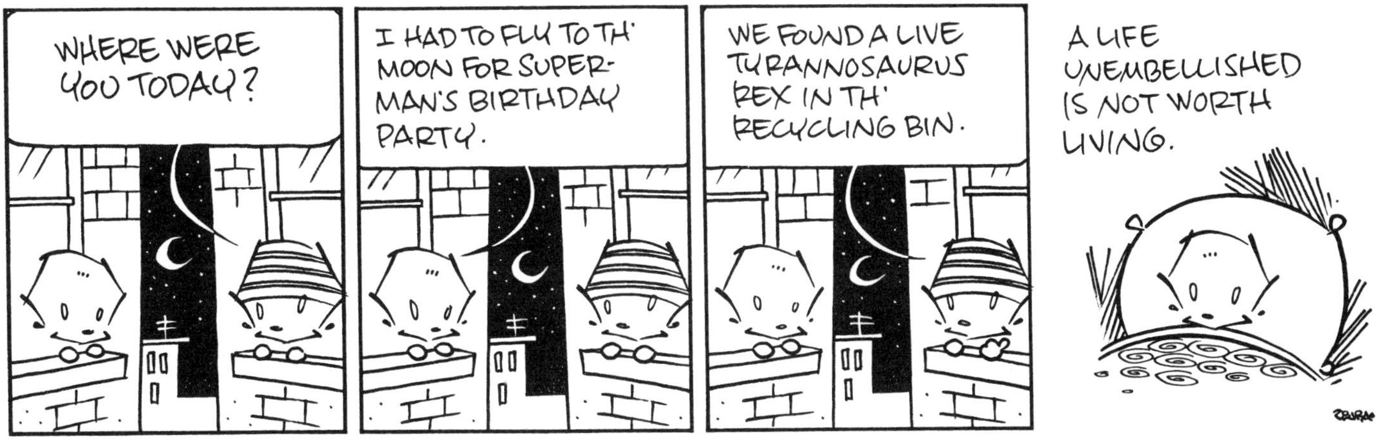
WHERE WERE YOU TODAY?
I HAD TO FLY TO TH' MOON FOR SUPER-MAN'S BIRTHDAY PARTY.
WE FOUND A LIVE TYRANNOSAURUS REX IN TH' RECYCLING BIN.
A LIFE UNEMBELLISHED IS NOT WORTH LIVING.

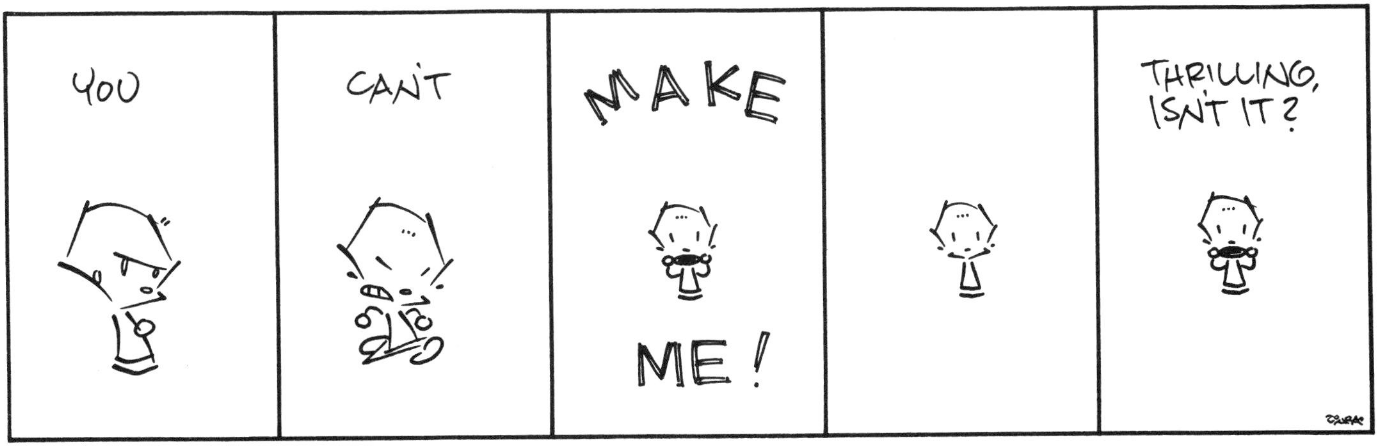
YOU
CAN'T
MAKE
ME!
THRILLING, ISN'T IT?

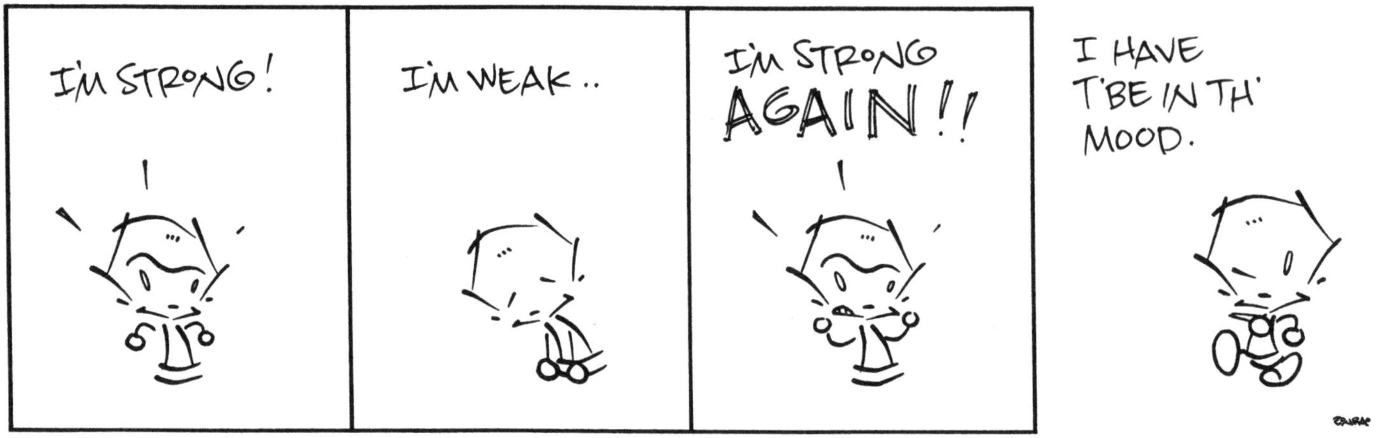
I'M STRONG!
I'M WEAK..
I'M STRONG AGAIN!!
I HAVE T'BE IN TH' MOOD.

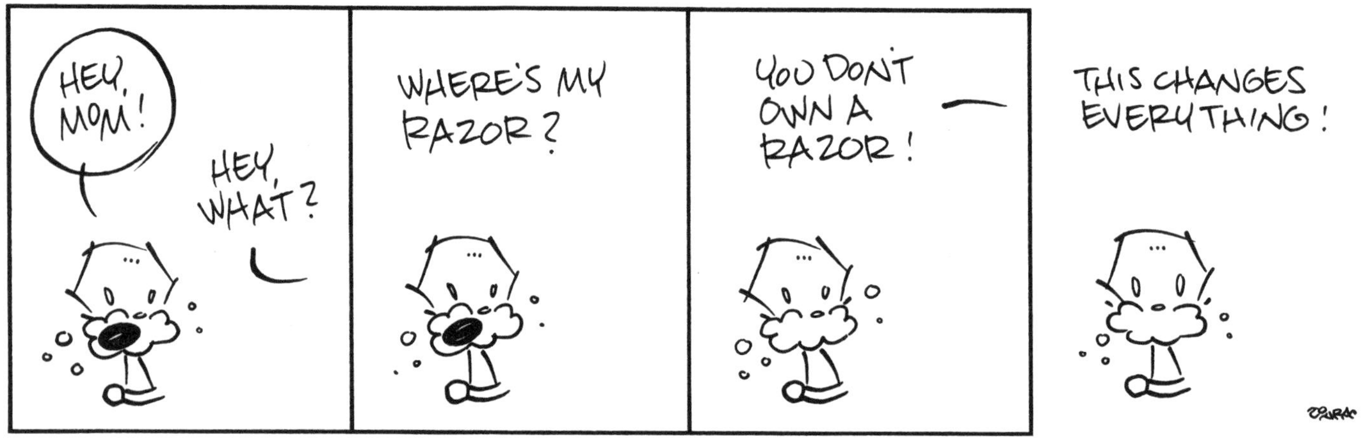
HEY, MOM!
HEY WHAT?
WHERE'S MY RAZOR?
YOU DON'T OWN A RAZOR!
THIS CHANGES EVERYTHING!

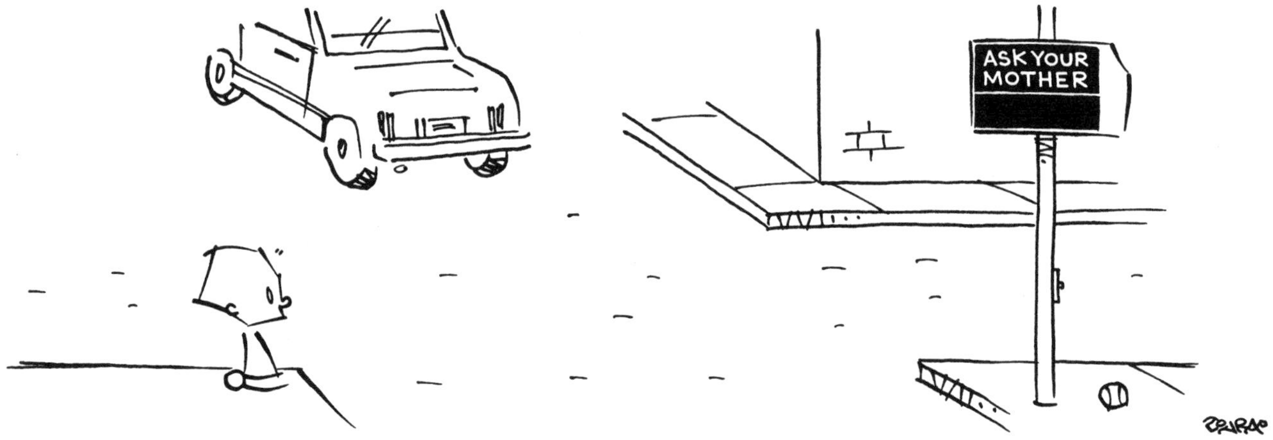
ASK YOUR MOTHER

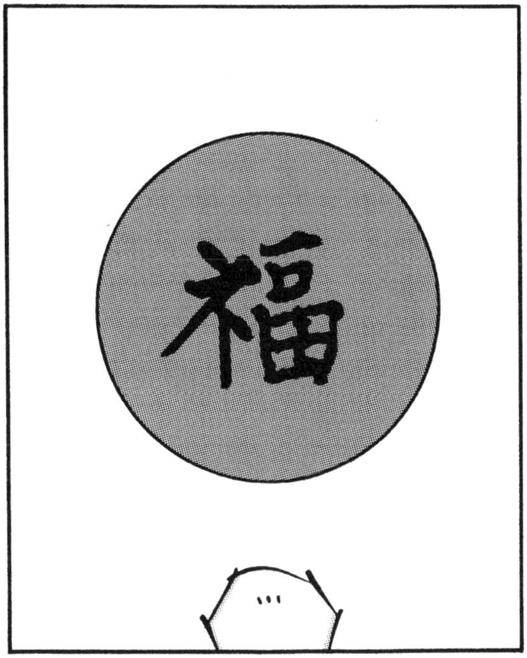
福

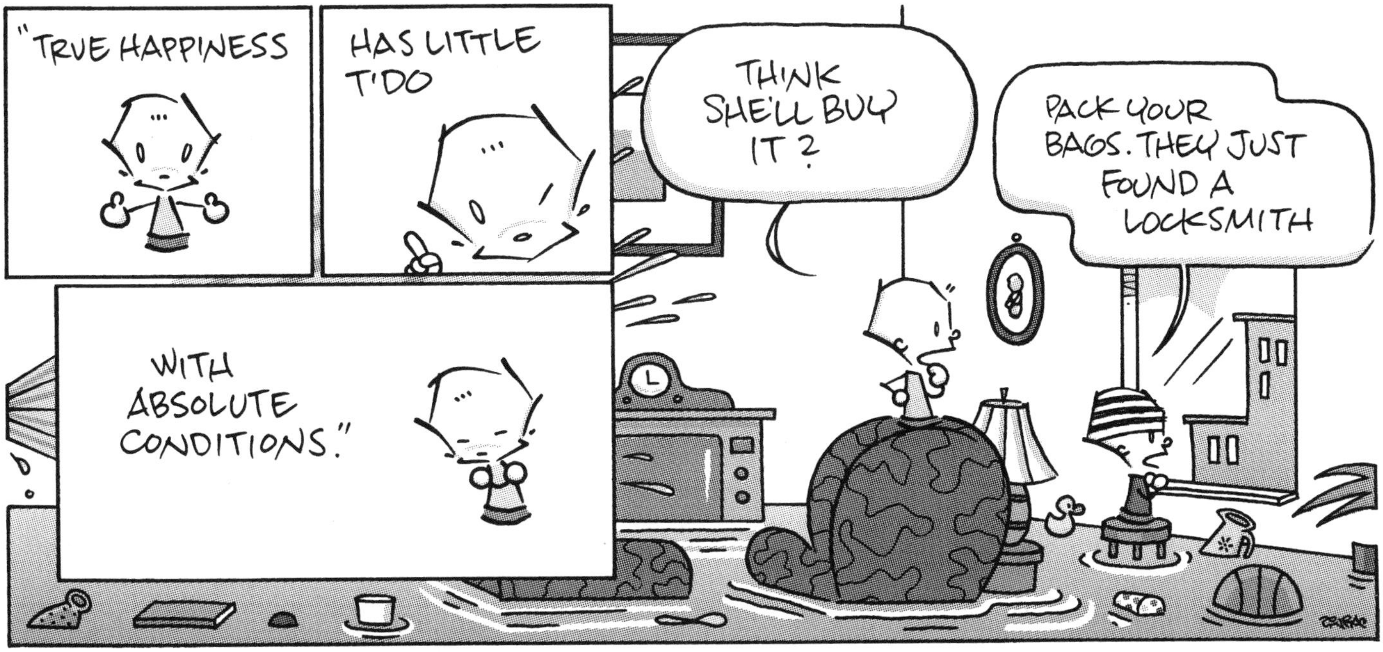
"TRUE HAPPINESS
HAS LITTLE T'DO
WITH ABSOLUTE CONDITIONS."
THINK SHE'LL BUY IT?
PACK YOUR BAGS. THEY JUST FOUND A LOCKSMITH

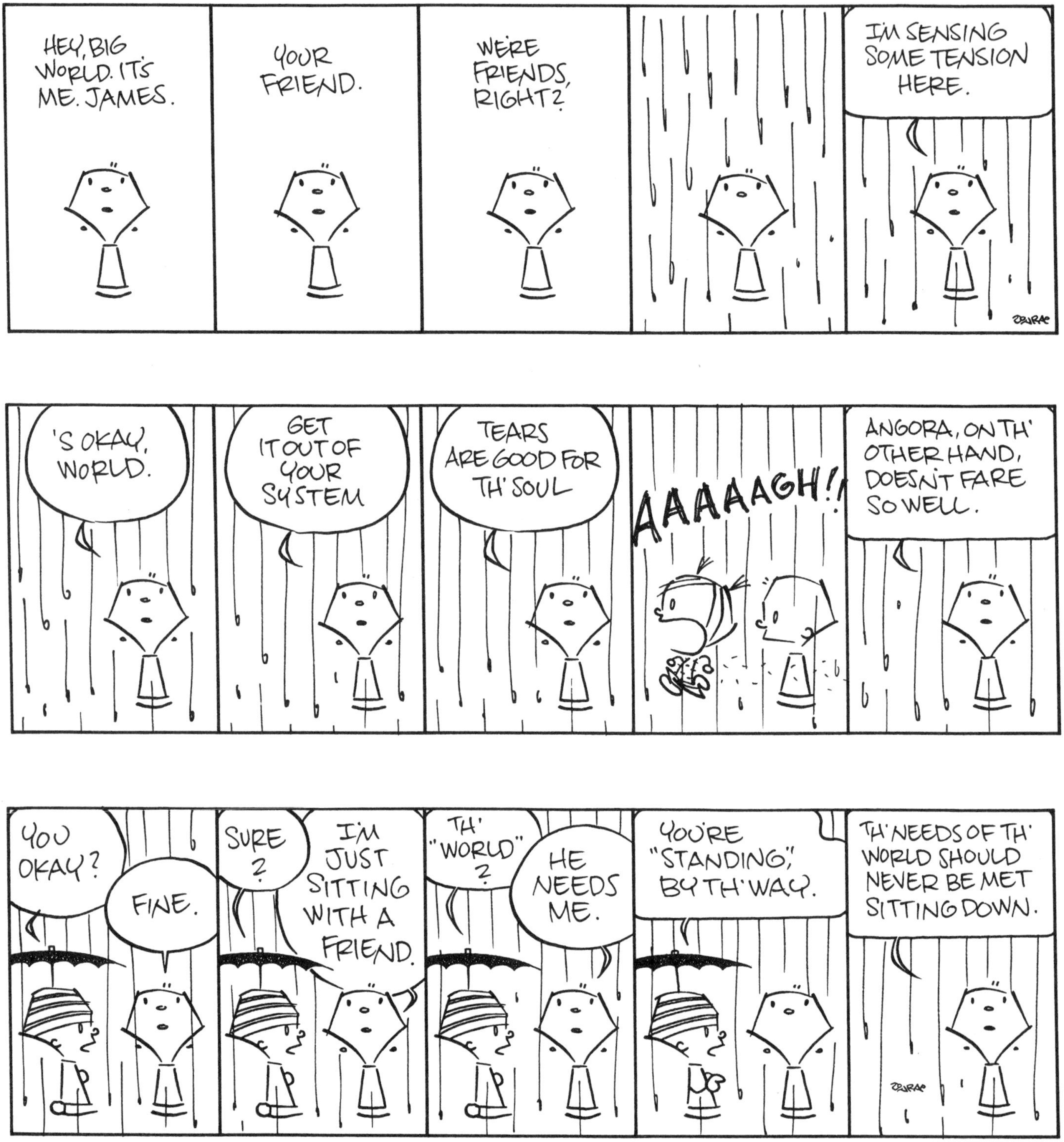
HEY, BIG WORLD. IT'S ME. JAMES.
YOUR FRIEND.
WE'RE FRIENDS, RIGHT?
I'M SENSING SOME TENSION HERE.
'S OKAY, WORLD.
GET IT OUT OF YOUR SYSTEM
TEARS ARE GOOD FOR TH' SOUL
AAAAAGH!!
ANGORA, ON TH' OTHER HAND, DOESN'T FARE SO WELL.
YOU OKAY?
FINE.
SURE?
I'M JUST SITTING WITH A FRIEND.
TH' "WORLD"?
HE NEEDS ME.
YOU'RE "STANDING," BY TH' WAY.
TH' NEEDS OF TH' WORLD SHOULD NEVER BE MET SITTING DOWN.

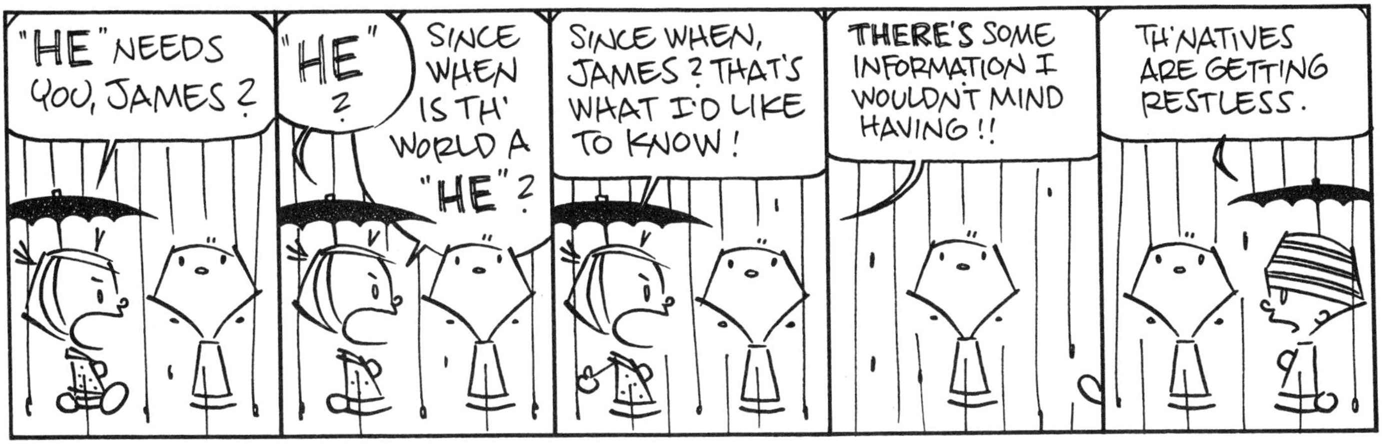
"HE" NEEDS YOU, JAMES?
"HE"?
SINCE WHEN IS TH' WORLD A "HE"?
SINCE WHEN, JAMES? THAT'S WHAT I'D LIKE TO KNOW!
THERE'S SOME INFORMATION I WOULDN'T MIND HAVING!!
TH' NATIVES ARE GETTING RESTLESS.

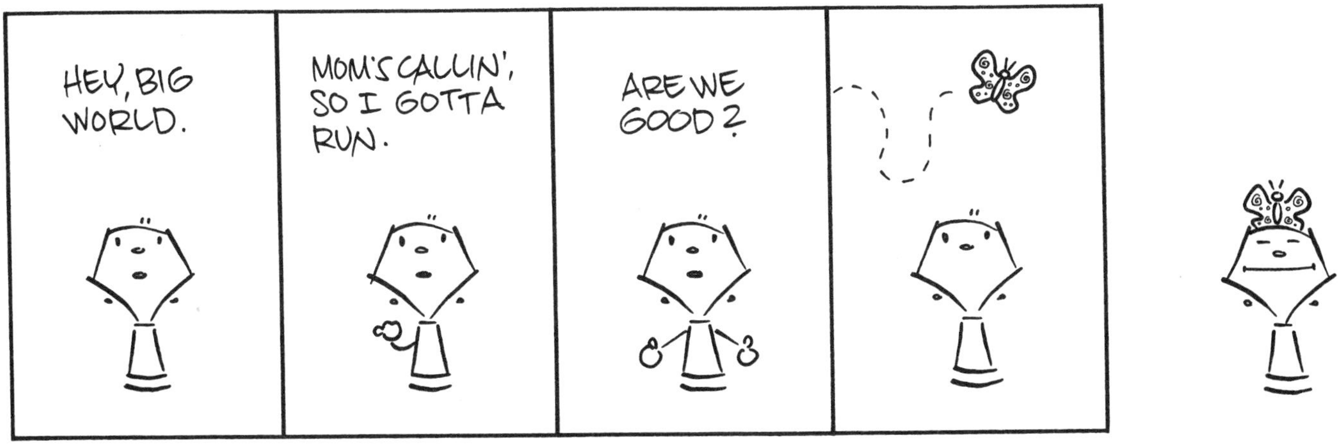
HEY, BIG WORLD.
MOM'S CALLIN', SO I GOTTA RUN.
ARE WE GOOD?

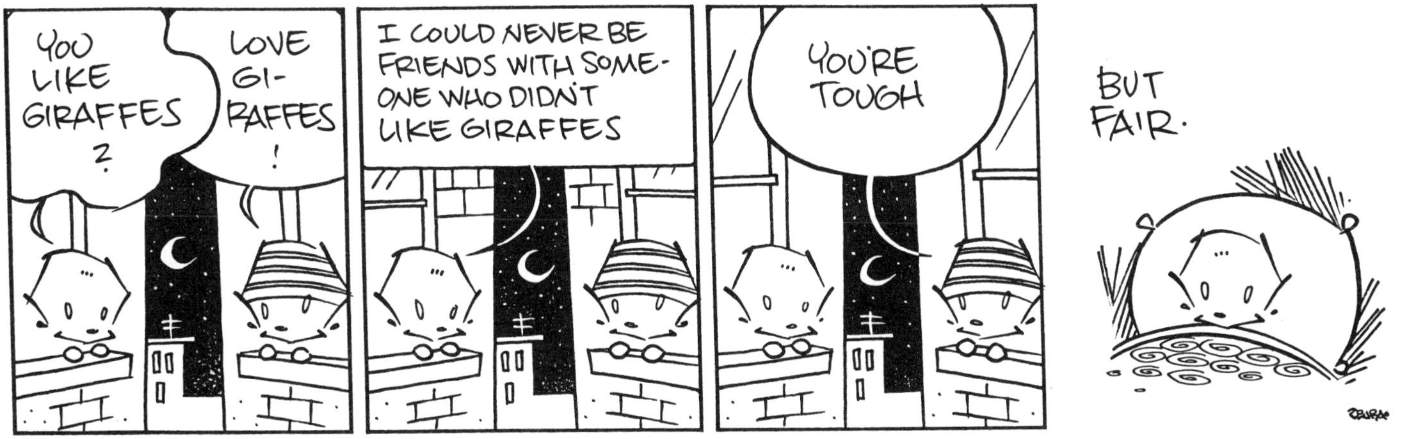
YOU LIKE GIRAFFES?
LOVE GI-RAFFES!
I COULD NEVER BE FRIENDS WITH SOME-ONE WHO DIDN'T LIKE GIRAFFES
YOU'RE TOUGH
BUT FAIR.

JAMES

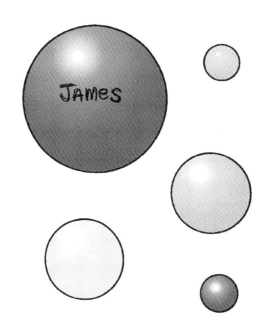

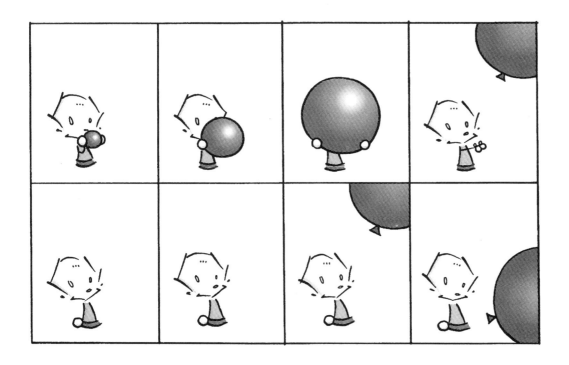

I KNOW TH' FEELING.

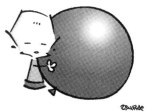

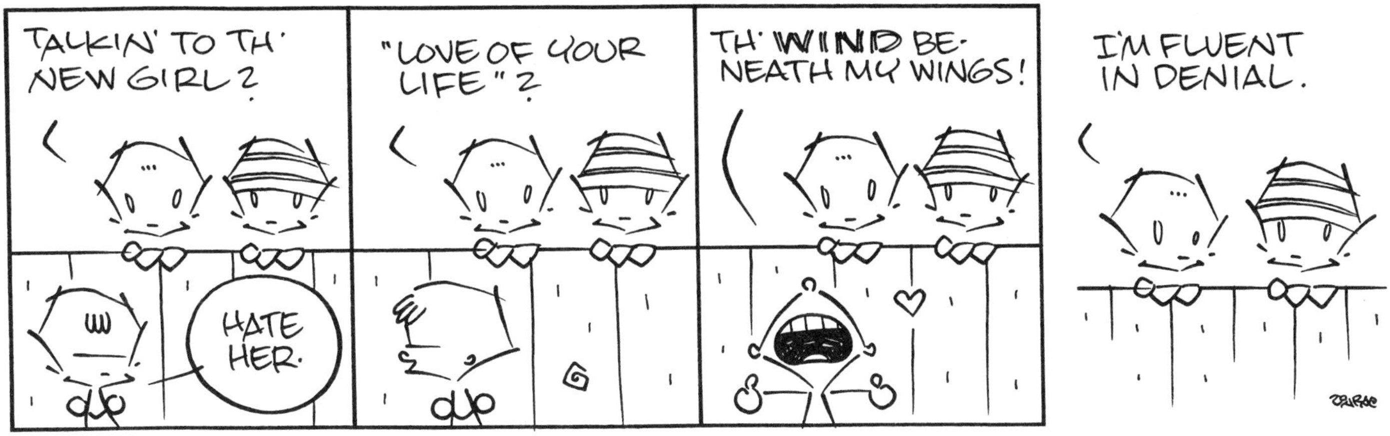
TALKIN' TO TH' NEW GIRL ?
HATE HER.
"LOVE OF YOUR LIFE" ?
TH' WIND BE-NEATH MY WINGS!
I'M FLUENT IN DENIAL.

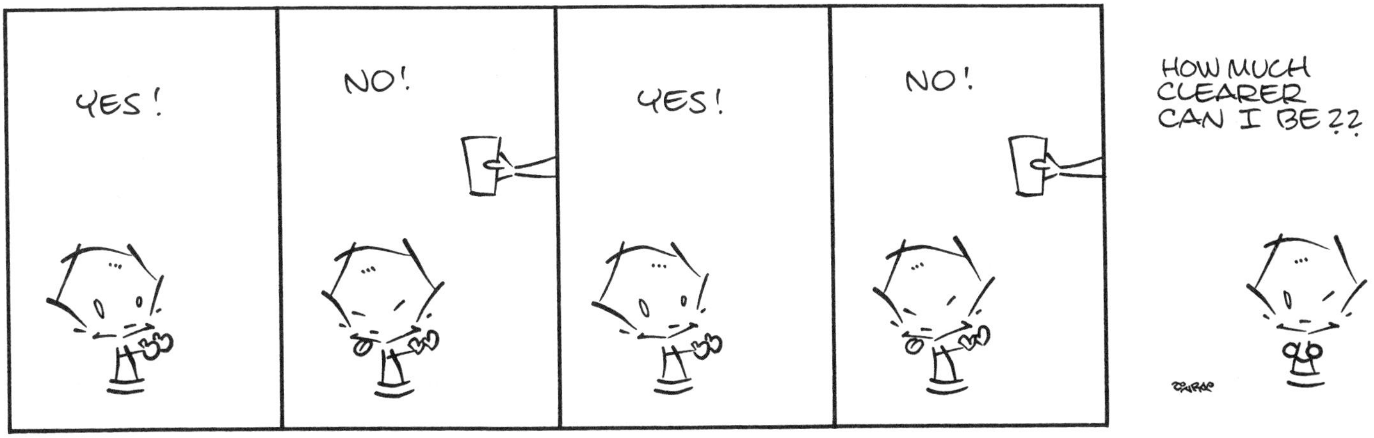
YES!
NO!
YES!
NO!
HOW MUCH CLEARER CAN I BE ??

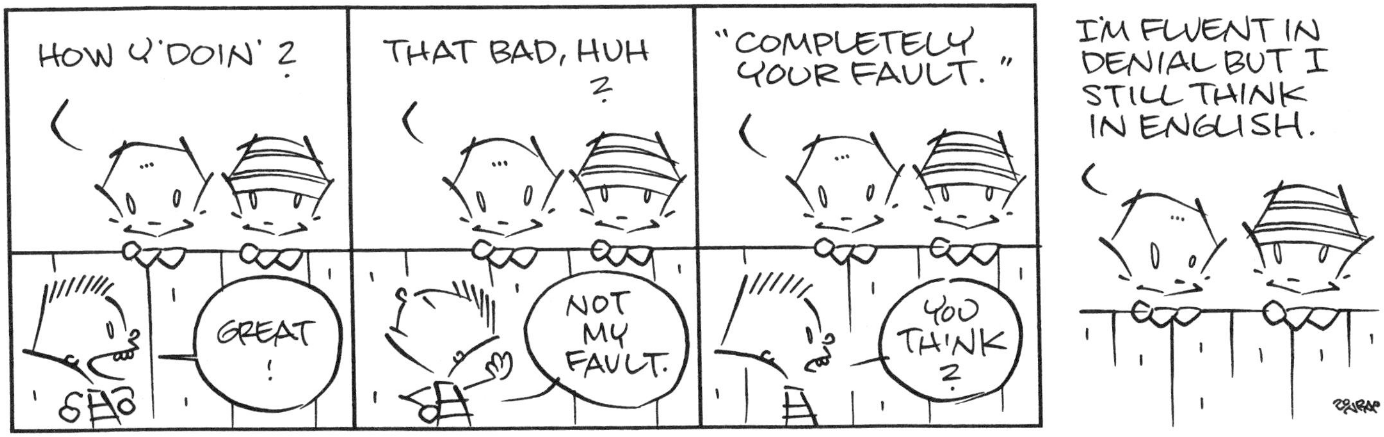
HOW Y'DOIN' ?
GREAT !
THAT BAD, HUH ?
NOT MY FAULT.
"COMPLETELY YOUR FAULT."
YOU THINK ?
I'M FLUENT IN DENIAL BUT I STILL THINK IN ENGLISH.

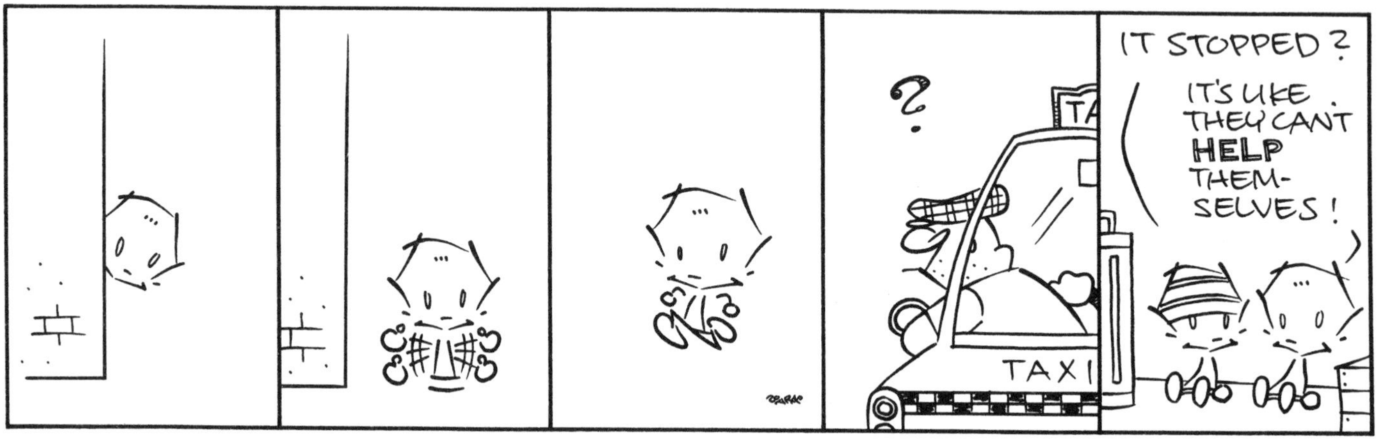
?
IT STOPPED?
IT'S LIKE THEY CAN'T **HELP** THEM-SELVES!
TAXI

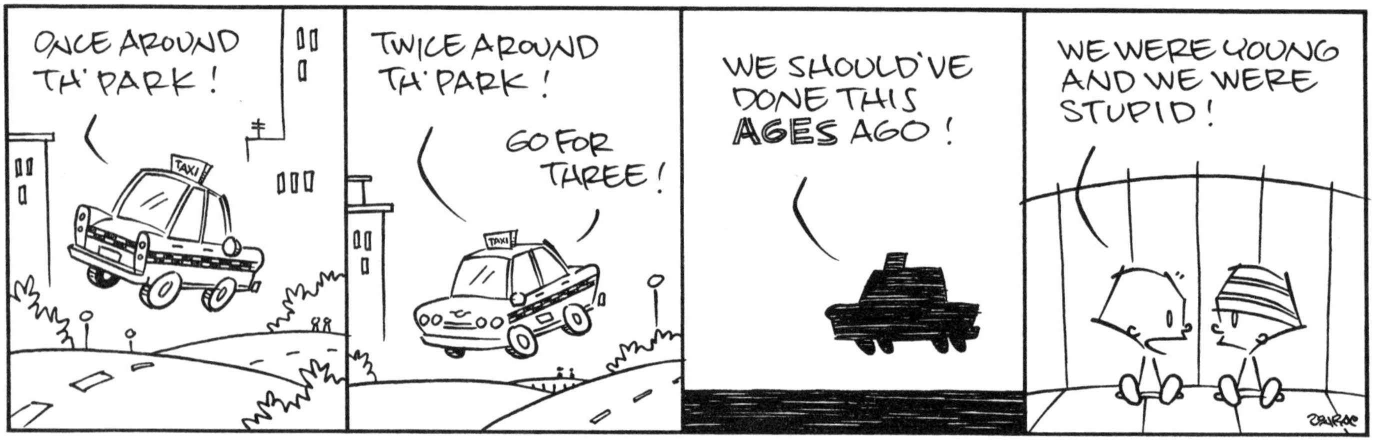
ONCE AROUND TH' PARK!
TAXI
TWICE AROUND TH' PARK!
GO FOR THREE!
WE SHOULD'VE DONE THIS **AGES** AGO!
WE WERE YOUNG AND WE WERE STUPID!

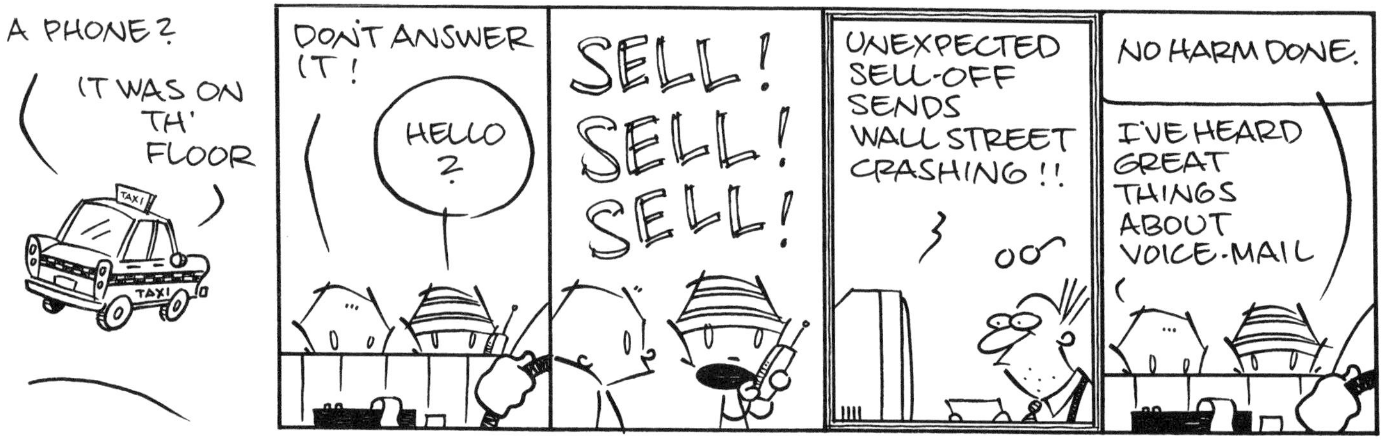
A PHONE?
IT WAS ON TH' FLOOR
TAXI
DON'T ANSWER IT!
HELLO?
SELL! SELL! SELL!
UNEXPECTED SELL-OFF SENDS WALL STREET CRASHING!!
NO HARM DONE.
I'VE HEARD GREAT THINGS ABOUT VOICE-MAIL

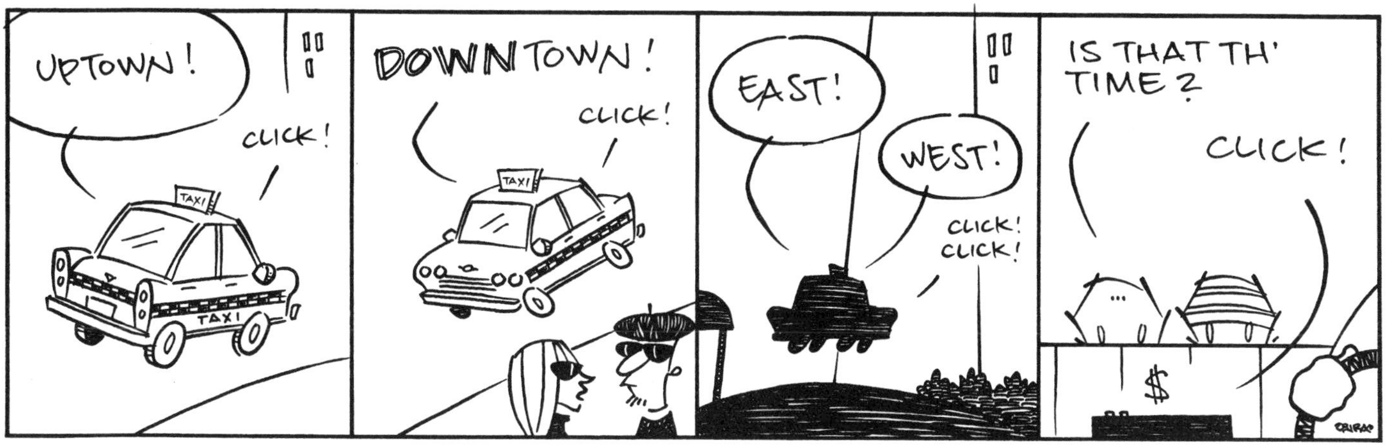
UPTOWN!
CLICK!
DOWNTOWN!
CLICK!
EAST!
WEST!
CLICK! CLICK!
IS THAT TH' TIME?
CLICK!

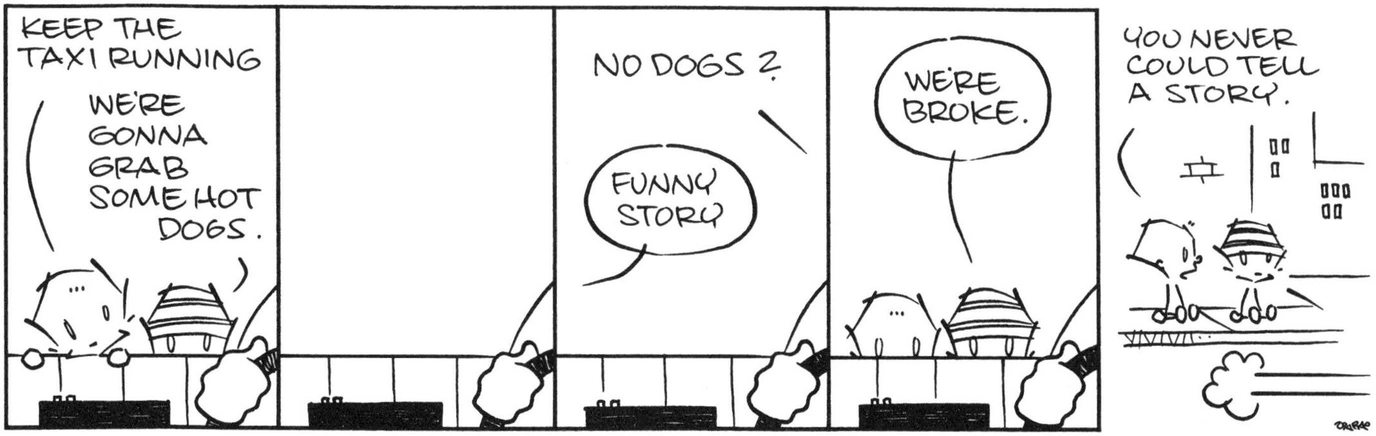
KEEP THE TAXI RUNNING
WE'RE GONNA GRAB SOME HOT DOGS.
NO DOGS?
FUNNY STORY
WE'RE BROKE.
YOU NEVER COULD TELL A STORY.

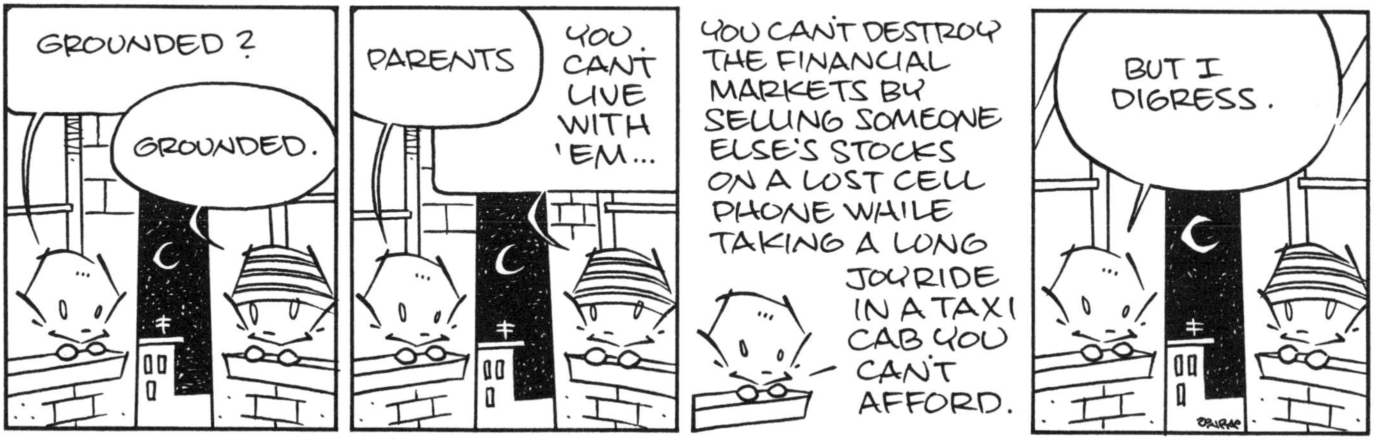
GROUNDED?
GROUNDED.
PARENTS
YOU CAN'T LIVE WITH 'EM...
YOU CAN'T DESTROY THE FINANCIAL MARKETS BY SELLING SOMEONE ELSE'S STOCKS ON A LOST CELL PHONE WHILE TAKING A LONG JOYRIDE IN A TAXI CAB YOU CAN'T AFFORD.
BUT I DIGRESS.

JAMES

 IF I WERE AS BRAVE AS I WANT TO BE

I'D LET **EVERY**ONE KNOW EXACTLY WHAT I THOUGHT OF 'EM !

BIG PEOPLE ! LITTLE PEOPLE ! WEAK PEOPLE ! **STRONG** PEOPLE !

NOONE WOULD BE FREE FROM MY HONEST ASSESS· MENT !

INCLUDING YOUR· SELF ?

I'M JUST NOT THAT BRAVE.

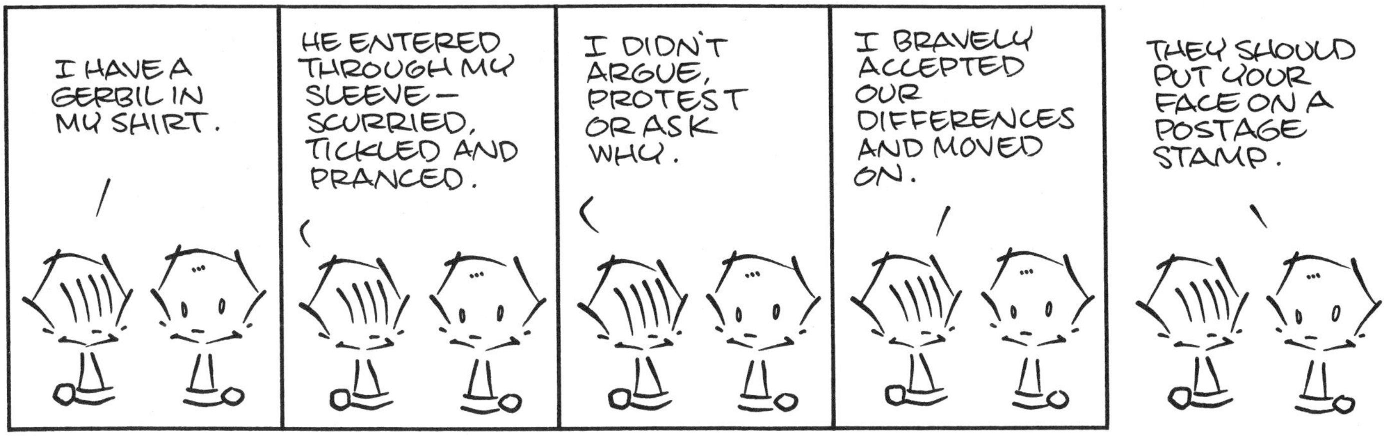
I HAVE A GERBIL IN MY SHIRT.
HE ENTERED THROUGH MY SLEEVE— SCURRIED, TICKLED AND PRANCED.
I DIDN'T ARGUE, PROTEST OR ASK WHY.
I BRAVELY ACCEPTED OUR DIFFERENCES AND MOVED ON.
THEY SHOULD PUT YOUR FACE ON A POSTAGE STAMP.

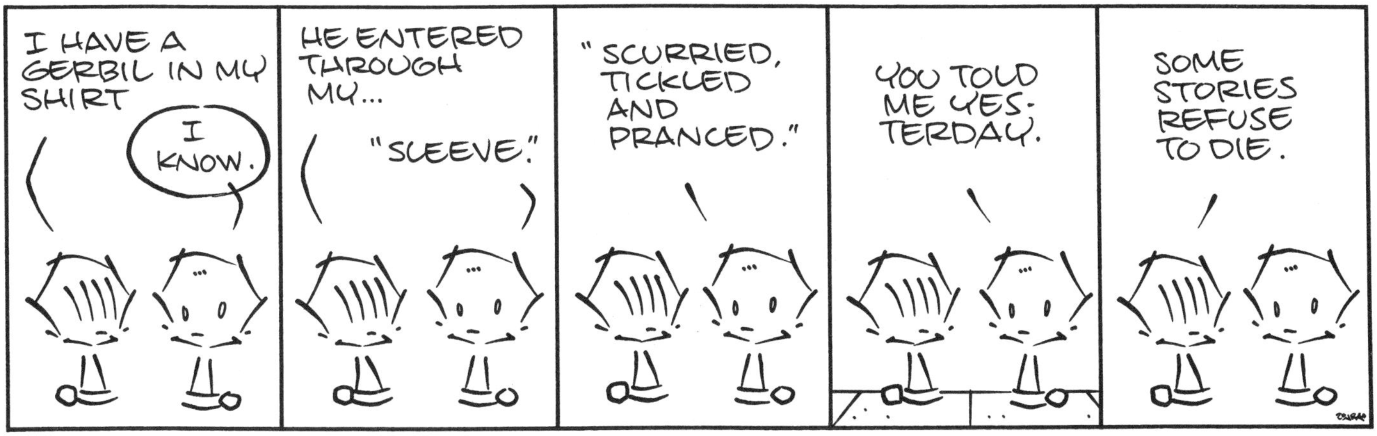
I HAVE A GERBIL IN MY SHIRT
I KNOW.
HE ENTERED THROUGH MY...
"SLEEVE."
"SCURRIED, TICKLED AND PRANCED."
YOU TOLD ME YES-TERDAY.
SOME STORIES REFUSE TO DIE.

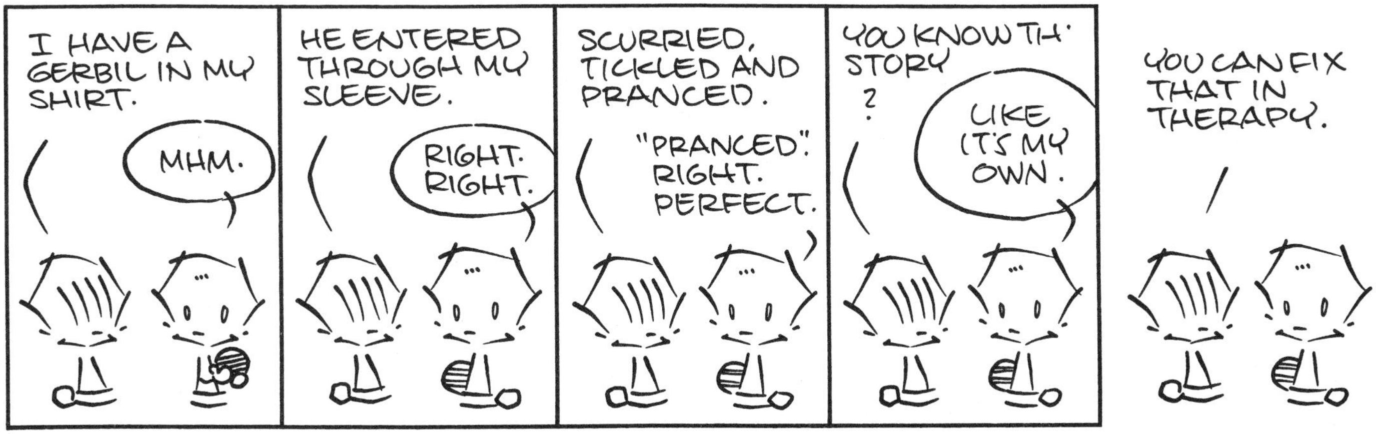
I HAVE A GERBIL IN MY SHIRT.
MHM.
HE ENTERED THROUGH MY SLEEVE.
RIGHT. RIGHT.
SCURRIED, TICKLED AND PRANCED.
"PRANCED." RIGHT. PERFECT.
YOU KNOW TH' STORY?
LIKE IT'S MY OWN.
YOU CAN FIX THAT IN THERAPY.

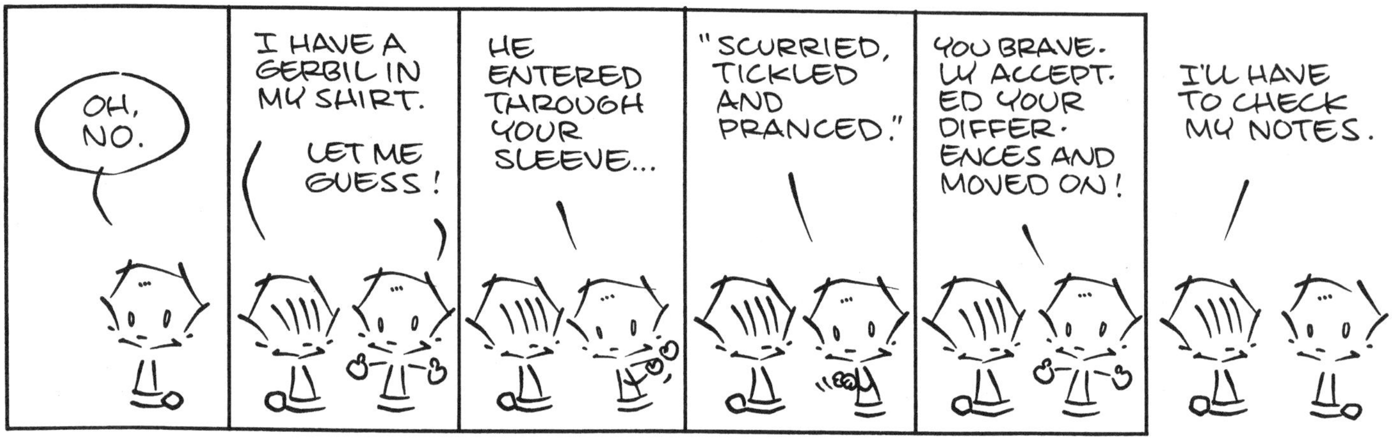
OH, NO.
I HAVE A GERBIL IN MY SHIRT.
LET ME GUESS!
HE ENTERED THROUGH YOUR SLEEVE...
"SCURRIED, TICKLED AND PRANCED."
YOU BRAVELY ACCEPTED YOUR DIFFERENCES AND MOVED ON!
I'LL HAVE TO CHECK MY NOTES.

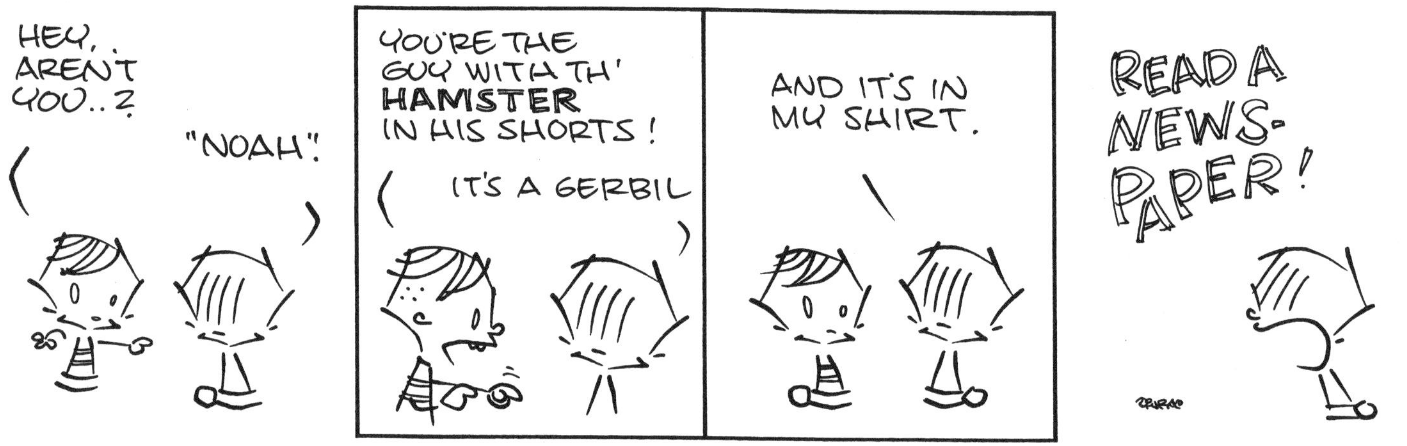
HEY, ARENT YOU..?
"NOAH"!
YOU'RE THE GUY WITH TH' HAMSTER IN HIS SHORTS!
IT'S A GERBIL
AND IT'S IN MY SHIRT.
READ A NEWSPAPER!

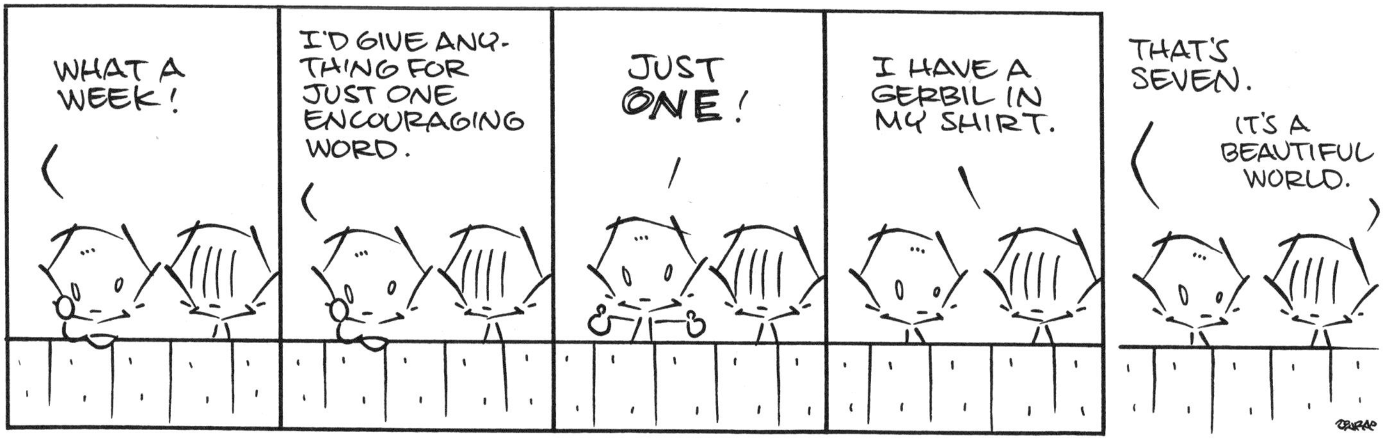
WHAT A WEEK!
I'D GIVE ANYTHING FOR JUST ONE ENCOURAGING WORD.
JUST ONE!
I HAVE A GERBIL IN MY SHIRT.
THAT'S SEVEN.
IT'S A BEAUTIFUL WORLD.

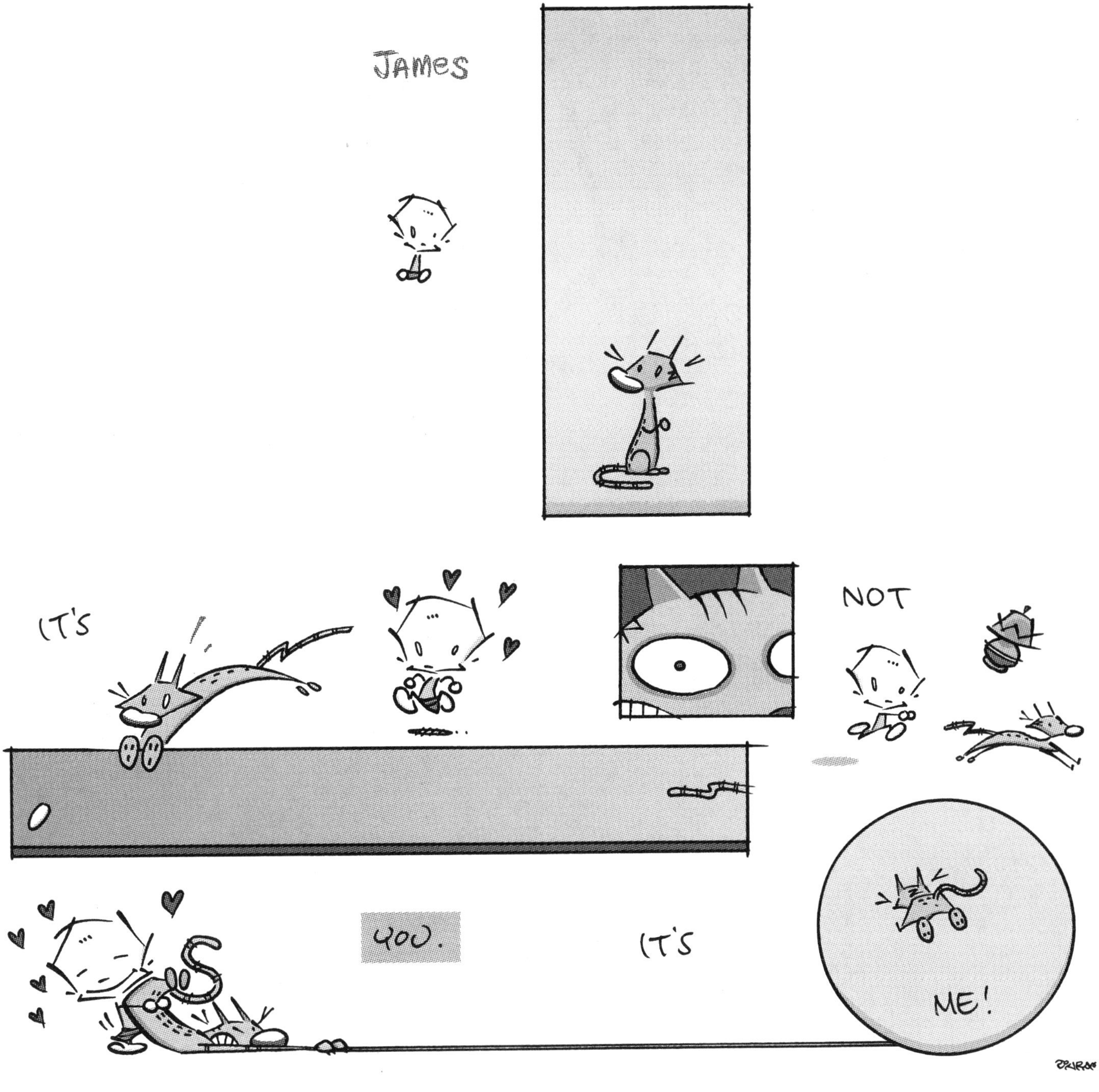
JAMES
IT'S
NOT
YOU.
IT'S
ME!

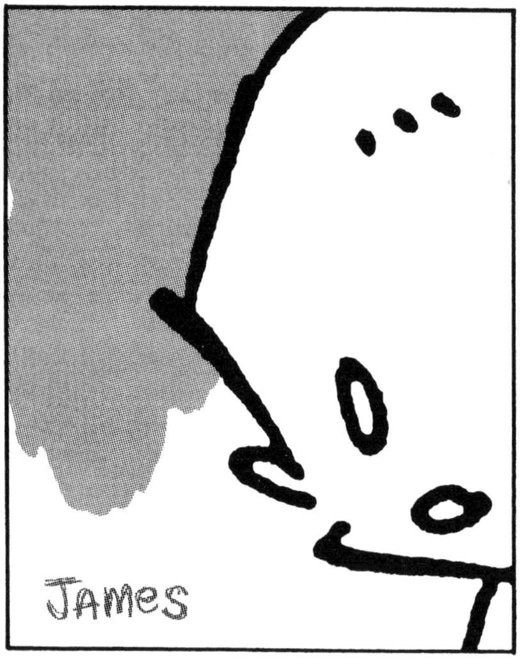
JAMES

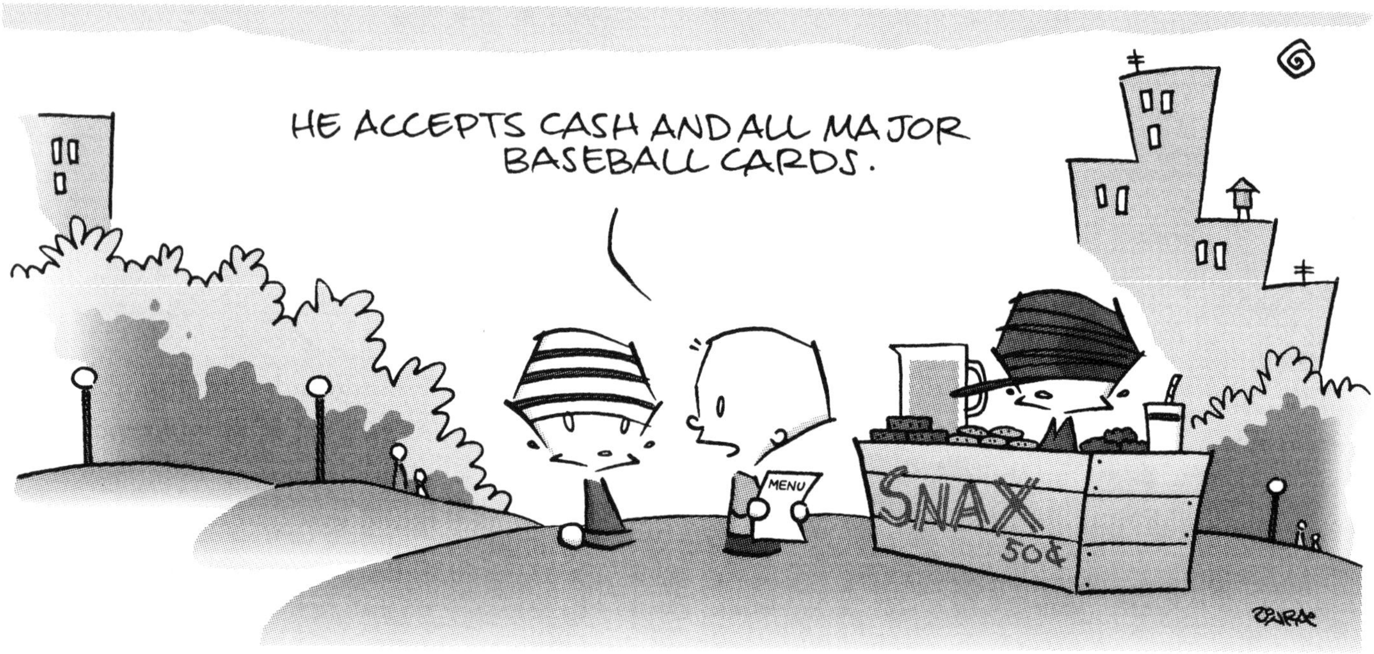
HE ACCEPTS CASH AND ALL MAJOR BASEBALL CARDS.
MENU
SNAX
50¢

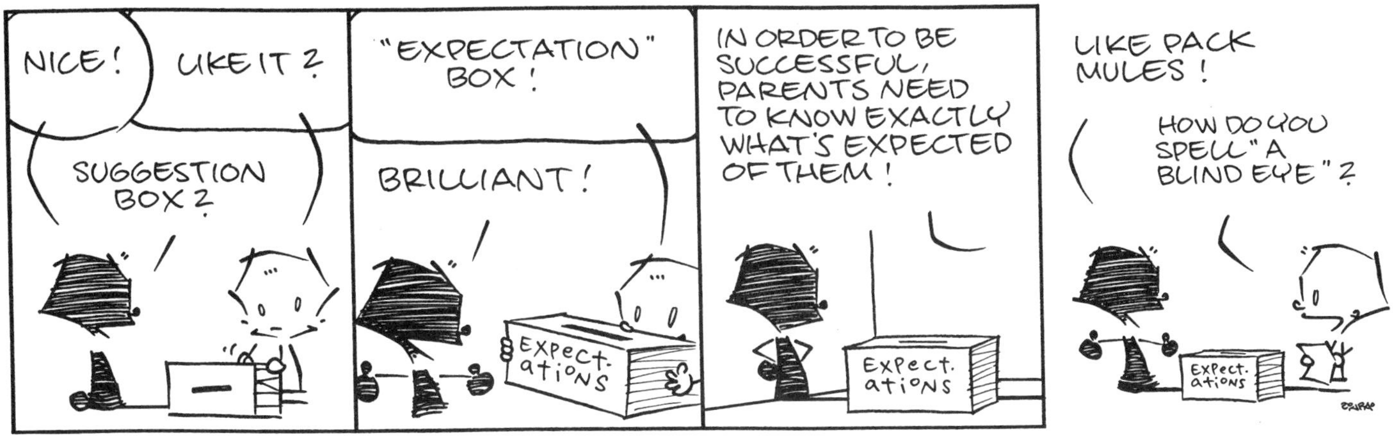
NICE!
SUGGESTION BOX?
LIKE IT?
"EXPECTATION" BOX!
BRILLIANT!
Expect-ations
IN ORDER TO BE SUCCESSFUL, PARENTS NEED TO KNOW EXACTLY WHAT'S EXPECTED OF THEM!
LIKE PACK MULES!
HOW DO YOU SPELL "A BLIND EYE"?

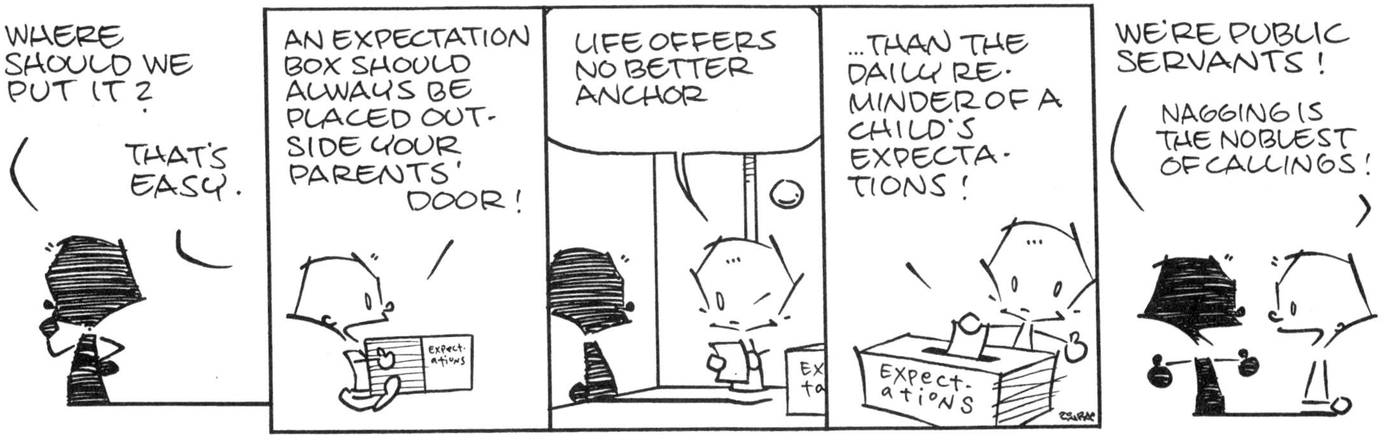
WHERE SHOULD WE PUT IT?
THAT'S EASY.
AN EXPECTATION BOX SHOULD ALWAYS BE PLACED OUTSIDE YOUR PARENTS' DOOR!
LIFE OFFERS NO BETTER ANCHOR
...THAN THE DAILY REMINDER OF A CHILD'S EXPECTATIONS!
Expect-ations
WE'RE PUBLIC SERVANTS!
NAGGING IS THE NOBLEST OF CALLINGS!

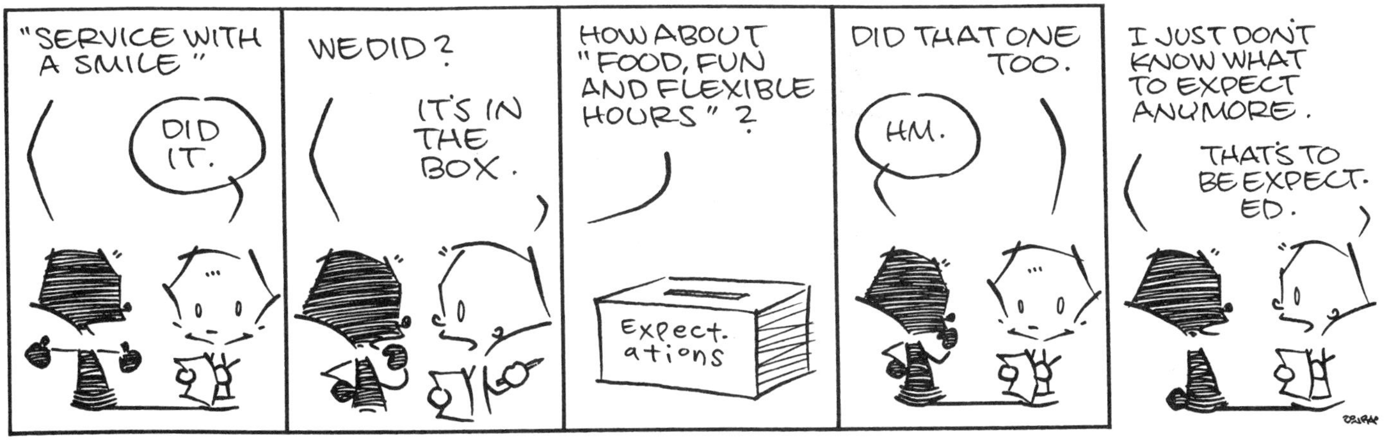
"SERVICE WITH A SMILE"
DID IT.
WE DID?
IT'S IN THE BOX.
HOW ABOUT "FOOD, FUN AND FLEXIBLE HOURS"?
Expect-ations
DID THAT ONE TOO.
HM.
I JUST DON'T KNOW WHAT TO EXPECT ANYMORE.
THAT'S TO BE EXPECTED.

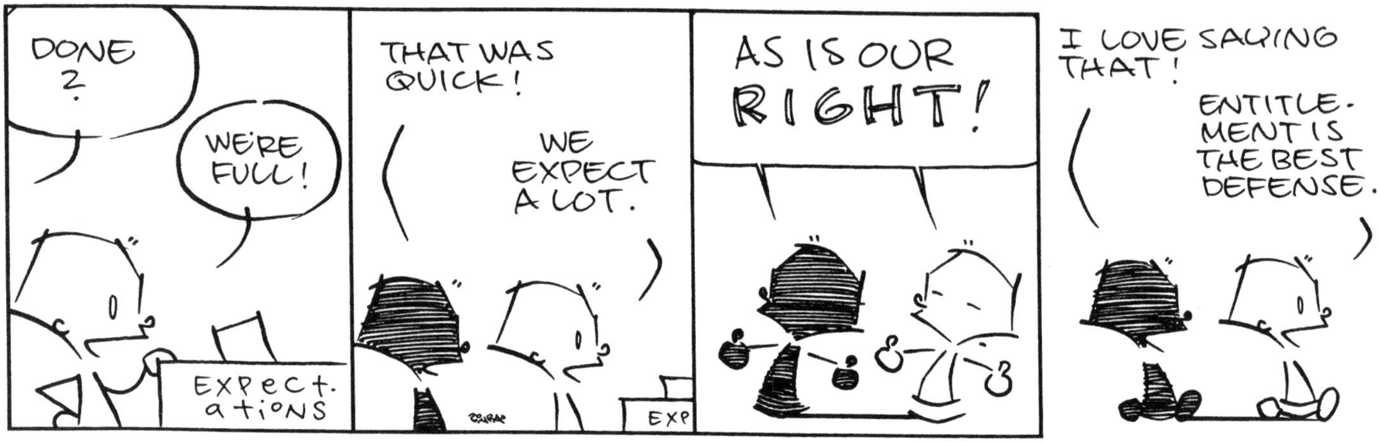
DONE?
WE'RE FULL!
EXPECTATIONS
THAT WAS QUICK!
WE EXPECT A LOT.
EXP
AS IS OUR RIGHT!
I LOVE SAYING THAT!
ENTITLEMENT IS THE BEST DEFENSE.

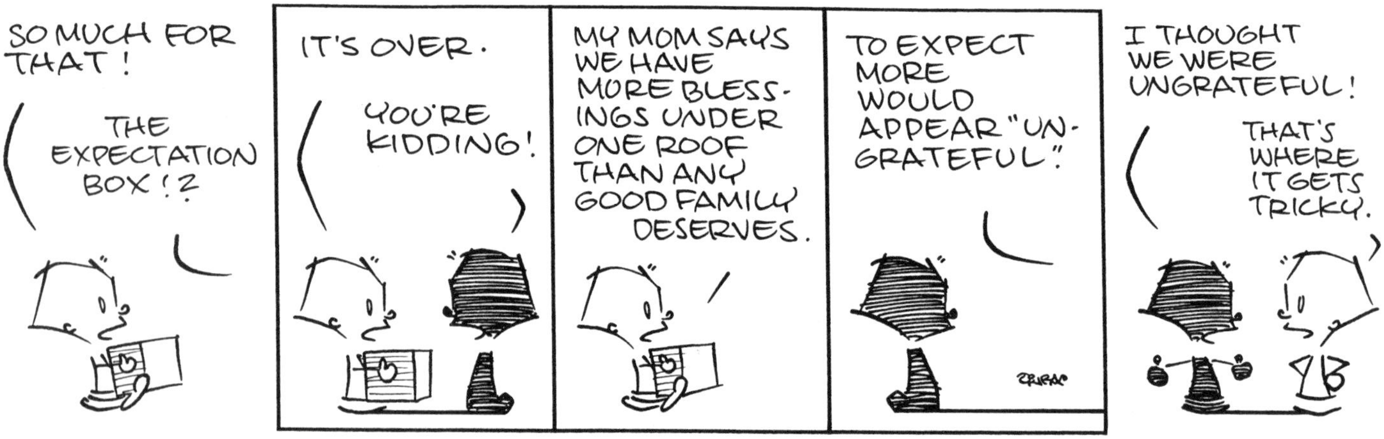
SO MUCH FOR THAT!
THE EXPECTATION BOX!?
IT'S OVER.
YOU'RE KIDDING!
MY MOM SAYS WE HAVE MORE BLESSINGS UNDER ONE ROOF THAN ANY GOOD FAMILY DESERVES.
TO EXPECT MORE WOULD APPEAR "UNGRATEFUL".
I THOUGHT WE WERE UNGRATEFUL!
THAT'S WHERE IT GETS TRICKY.

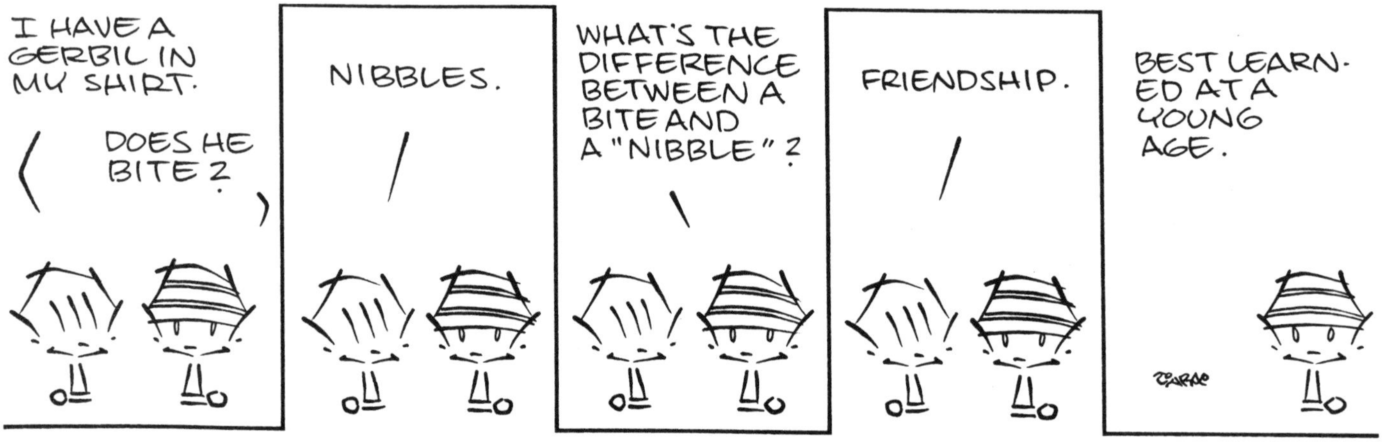
I HAVE A GERBIL IN MY SHIRT.
DOES HE BITE?
NIBBLES.
WHAT'S THE DIFFERENCE BETWEEN A BITE AND A "NIBBLE"?
FRIENDSHIP.
BEST LEARNED AT A YOUNG AGE.

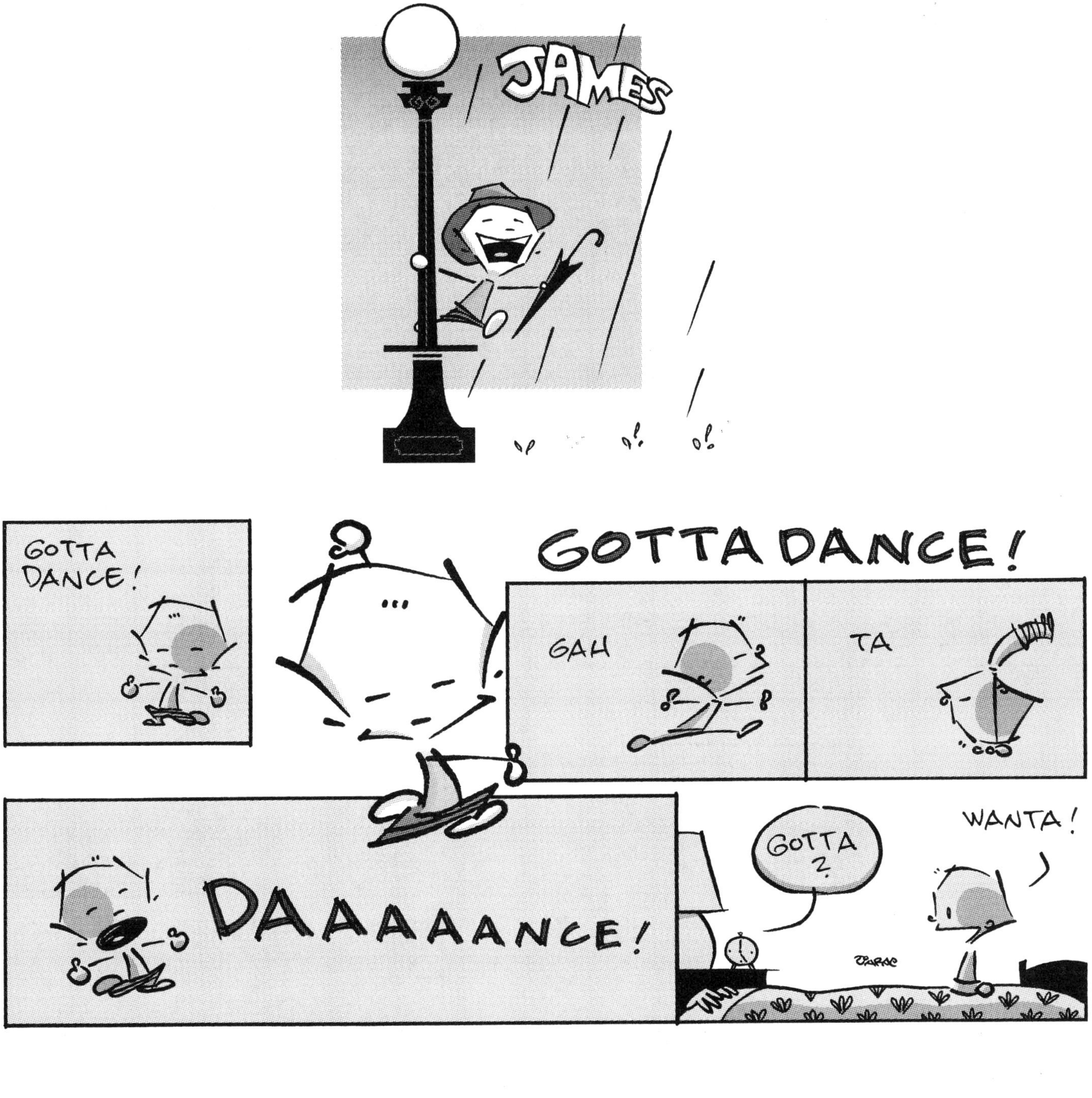
JAMES
GOTTA DANCE!
GOTTA DANCE!
GAH
TA
DAAAAANCE!
GOTTA ?
WANTA!

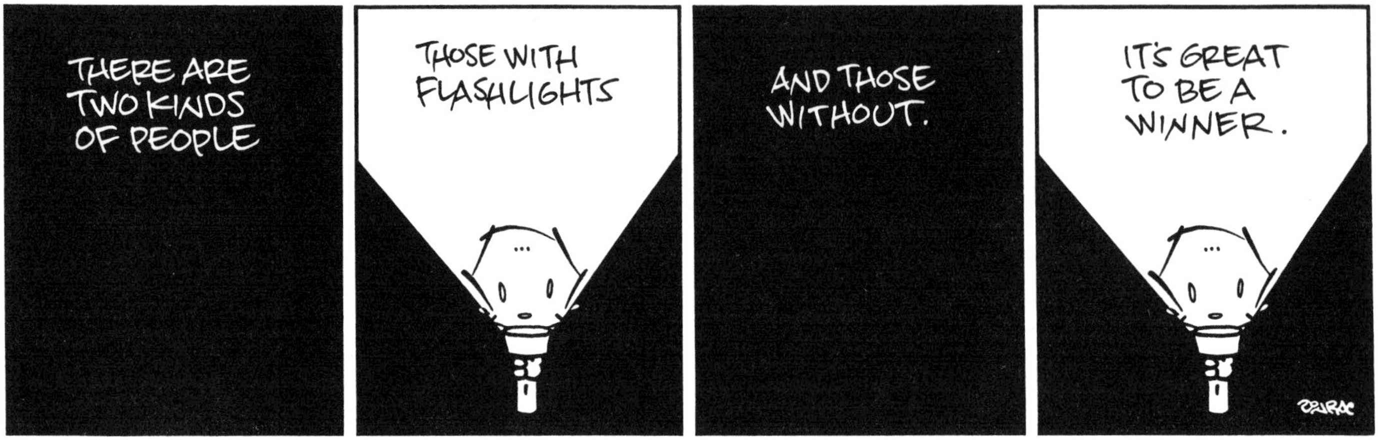
THERE ARE TWO KINDS OF PEOPLE
THOSE WITH FLASHLIGHTS
AND THOSE WITHOUT.
IT'S GREAT TO BE A WINNER.

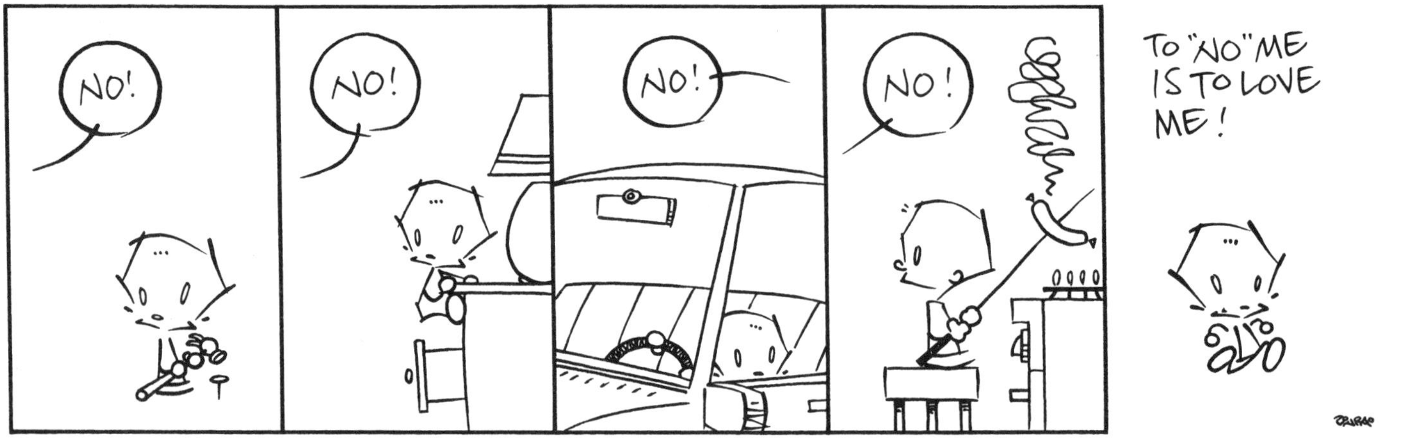
NO!
NO!
NO!
NO!
TO "NO" ME IS TO LOVE ME!

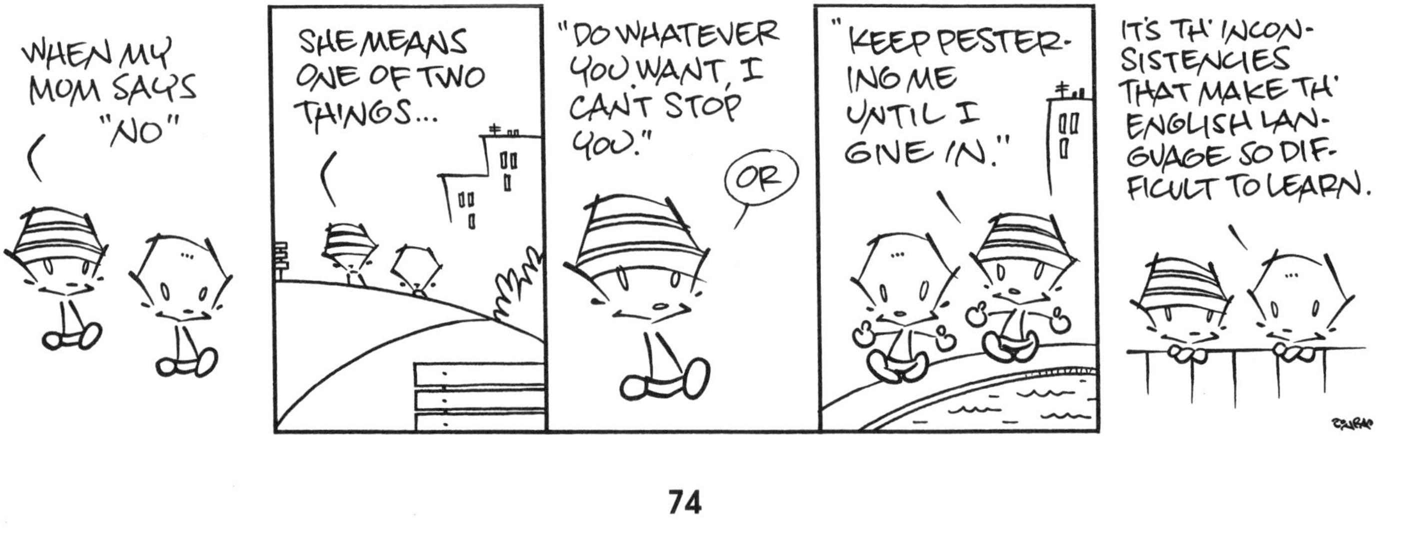
WHEN MY MOM SAYS "NO"
SHE MEANS ONE OF TWO THINGS...
"DO WHATEVER YOU WANT, I CAN'T STOP YOU."
OR
"KEEP PESTERING ME UNTIL I GIVE IN."
IT'S TH' INCONSISTENCIES THAT MAKE TH' ENGLISH LANGUAGE SO DIFFICULT TO LEARN.

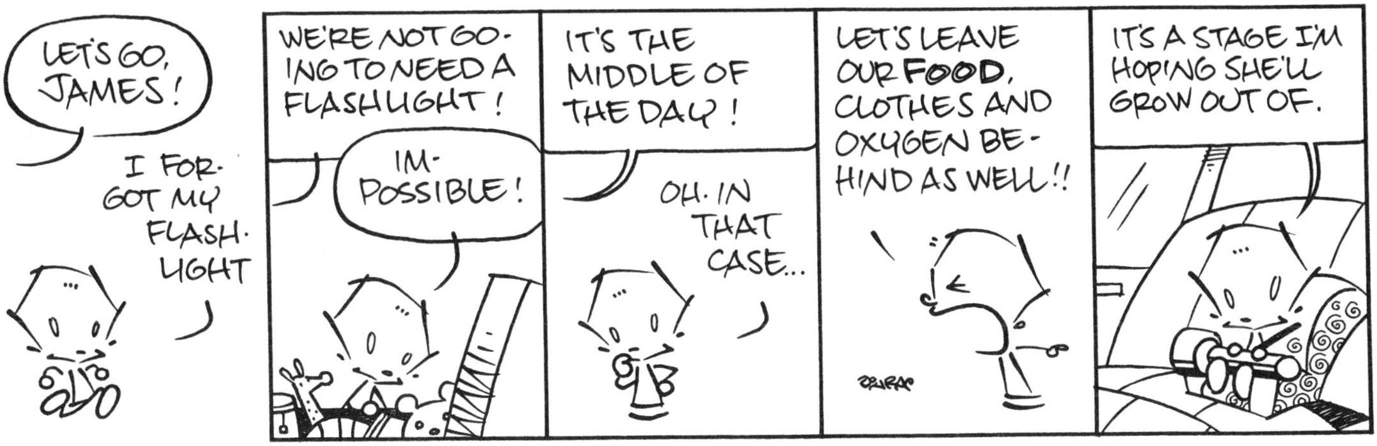
LET'S GO, JAMES!
I FORGOT MY FLASHLIGHT
WE'RE NOT GOING TO NEED A FLASHLIGHT!
IMPOSSIBLE!
IT'S THE MIDDLE OF THE DAY!
OH. IN THAT CASE...
LET'S LEAVE OUR FOOD, CLOTHES AND OXYGEN BEHIND AS WELL!!
IT'S A STAGE I'M HOPING SHE'LL GROW OUT OF.

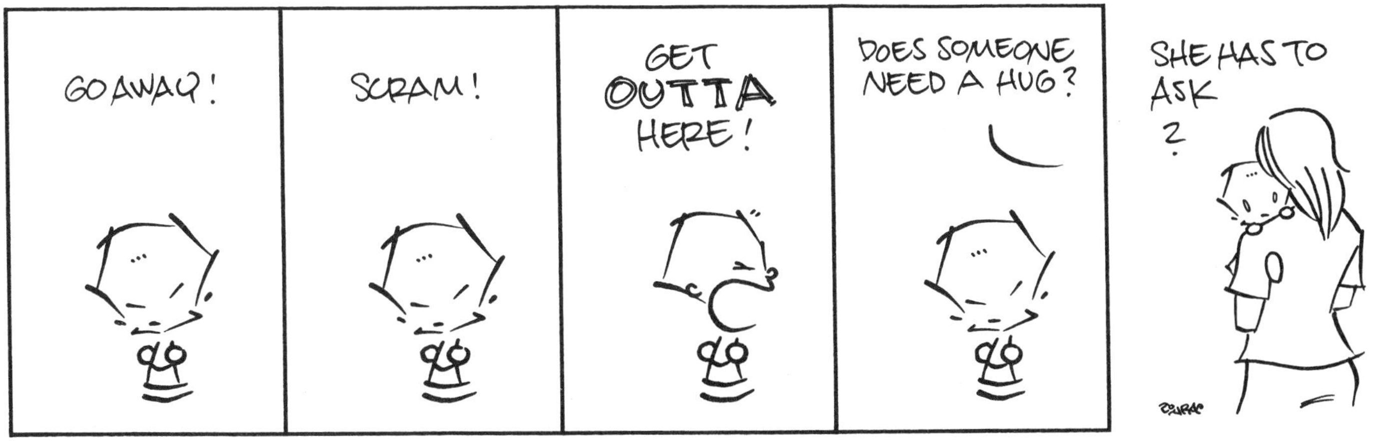
GO AWAY!
SCRAM!
GET OUTTA HERE!
DOES SOMEONE NEED A HUG?
SHE HAS TO ASK?

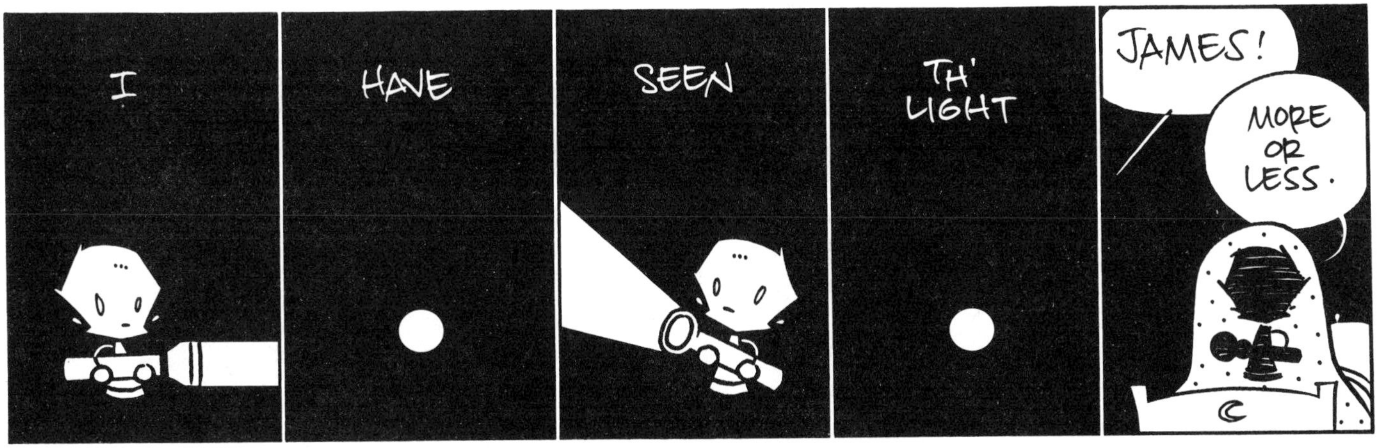
I
HAVE
SEEN
TH' LIGHT
JAMES!
MORE OR LESS.

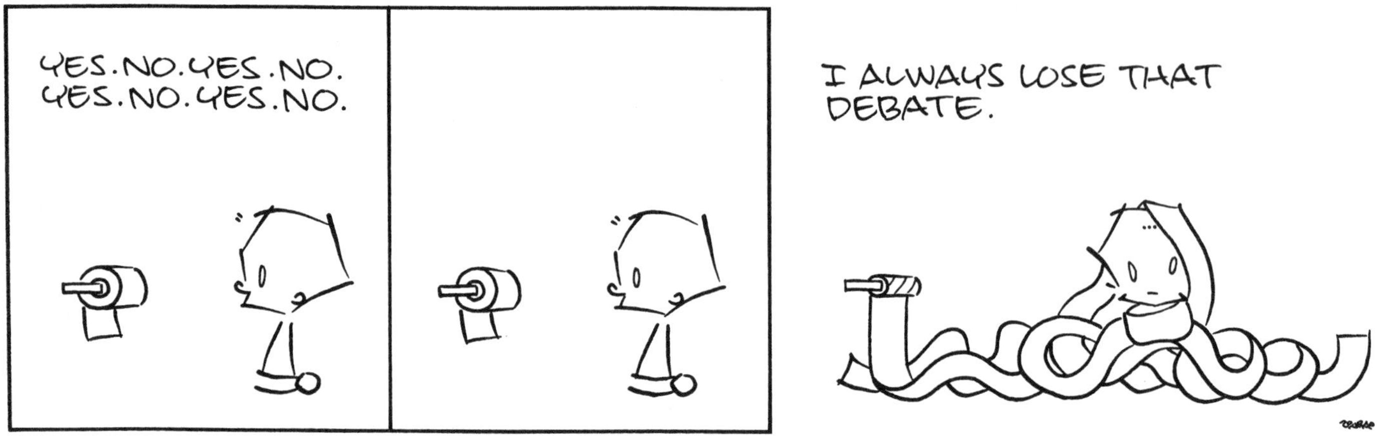

YES.NO.YES.NO.
YES.NO.YES.NO.
I ALWAYS LOSE THAT DEBATE.

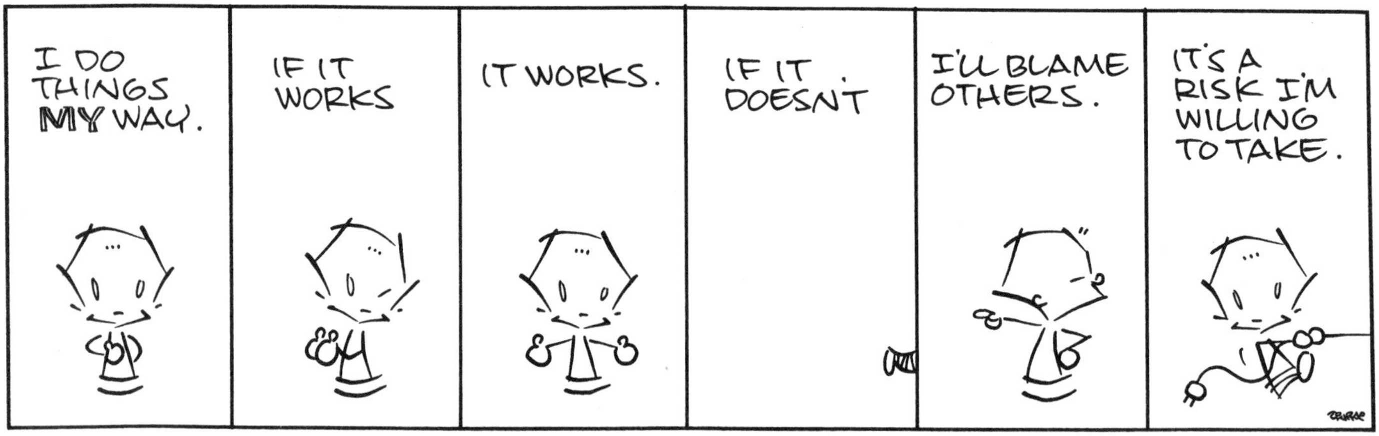

I DO THINGS MY WAY.
IF IT WORKS
IT WORKS.
IF IT DOESN'T
I'LL BLAME OTHERS.
IT'S A RISK I'M WILLING TO TAKE.

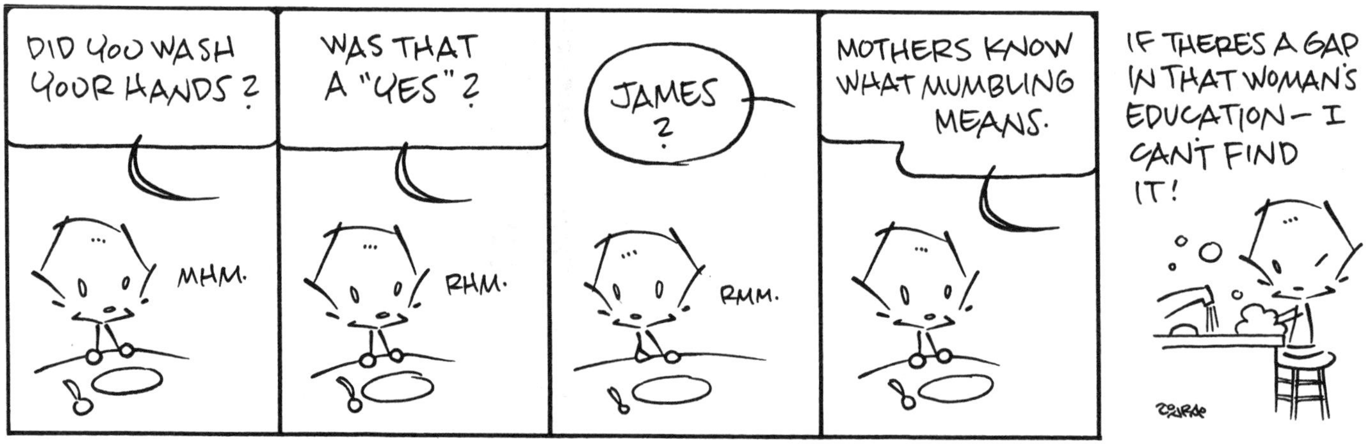

DID YOU WASH YOUR HANDS?
MHM.
WAS THAT A "YES"?
RHM.
JAMES?
RMM.
MOTHERS KNOW WHAT MUMBLING MEANS.
IF THERE'S A GAP IN THAT WOMAN'S EDUCATION – I CAN'T FIND IT!

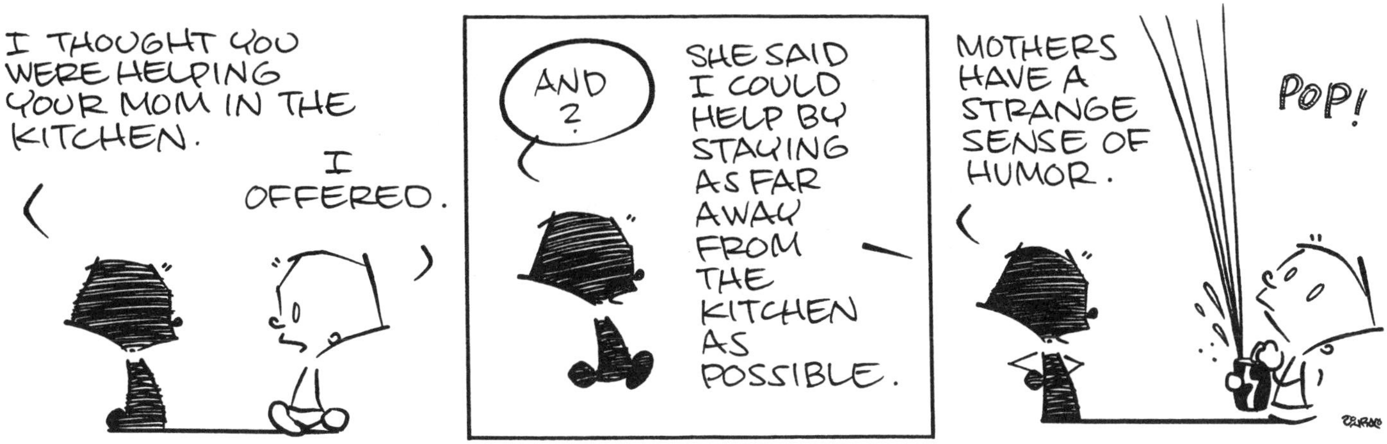
I THOUGHT YOU WERE HELPING YOUR MOM IN THE KITCHEN.
I OFFERED.
AND ?
SHE SAID I COULD HELP BY STAYING AS FAR AWAY FROM THE KITCHEN AS POSSIBLE.
MOTHERS HAVE A STRANGE SENSE OF HUMOR.
POP!

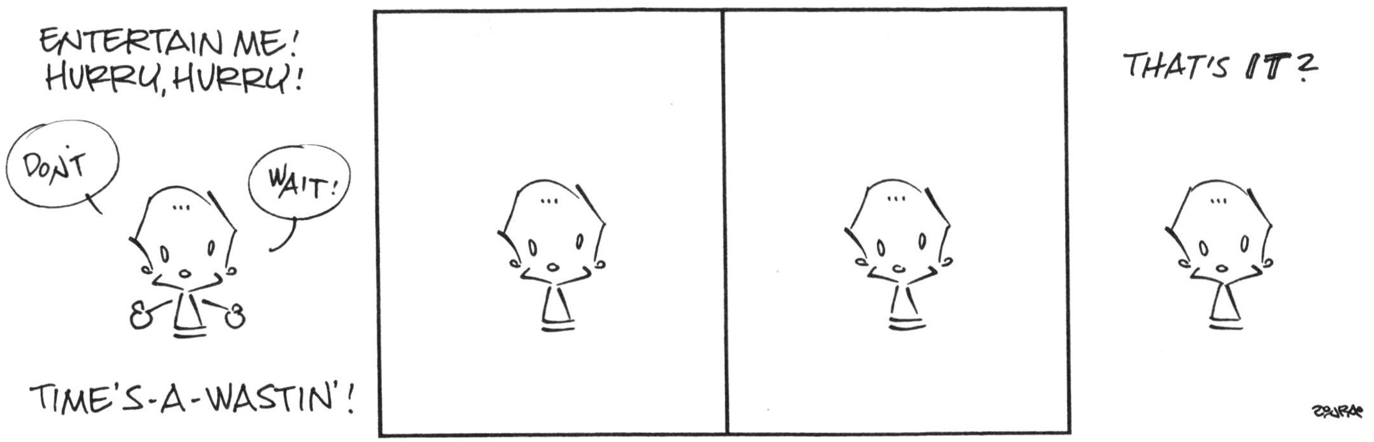
ENTERTAIN ME! HURRY, HURRY!
DON'T
WAIT!
TIME'S-A-WASTIN'!
THAT'S IT?

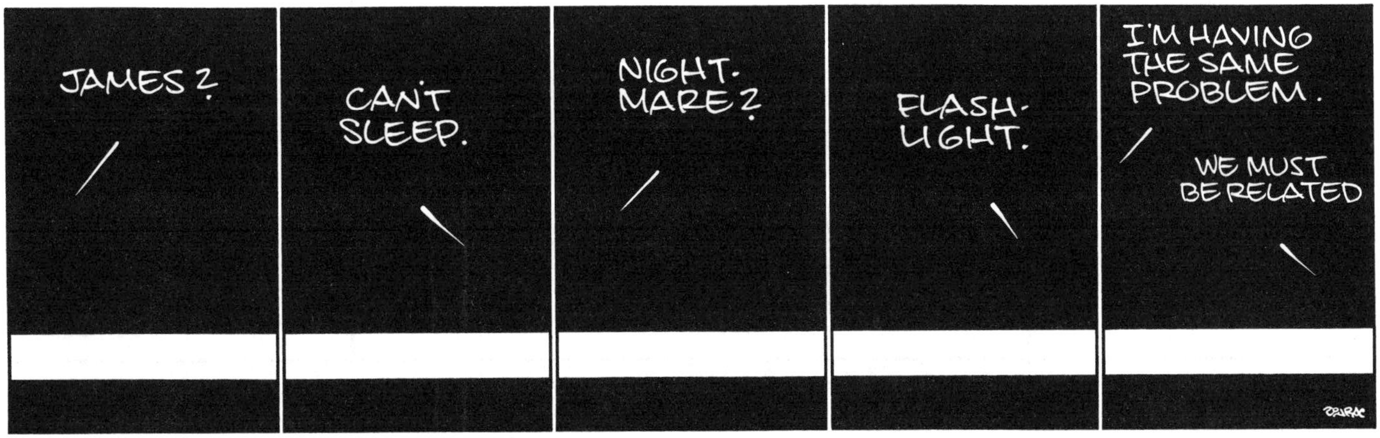
JAMES?
CAN'T SLEEP.
NIGHT-MARE?
FLASH-LIGHT.
I'M HAVING THE SAME PROBLEM.
WE MUST BE RELATED

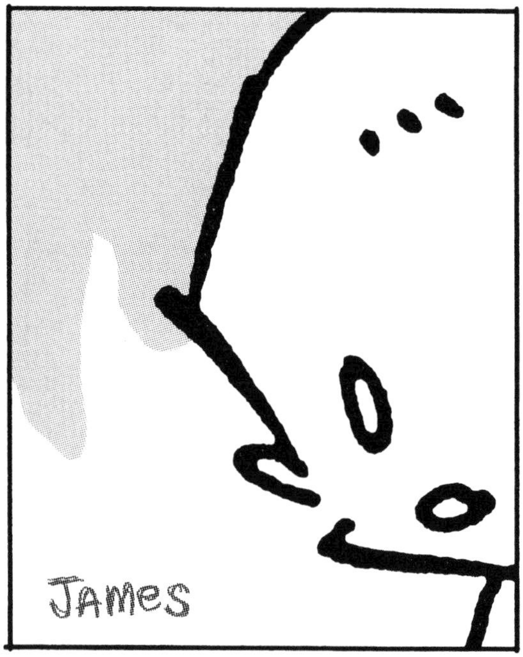
JAMES

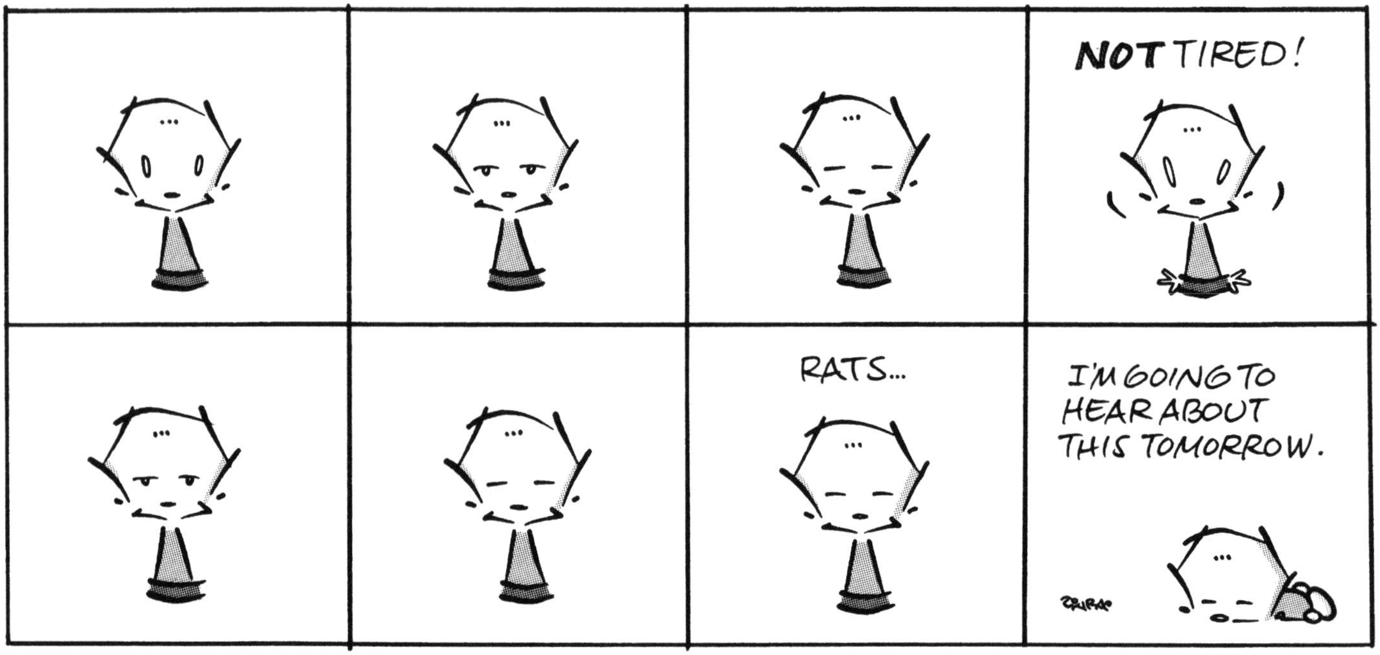
NOT TIRED!
RATS...
I'M GOING TO HEAR ABOUT THIS TOMORROW.

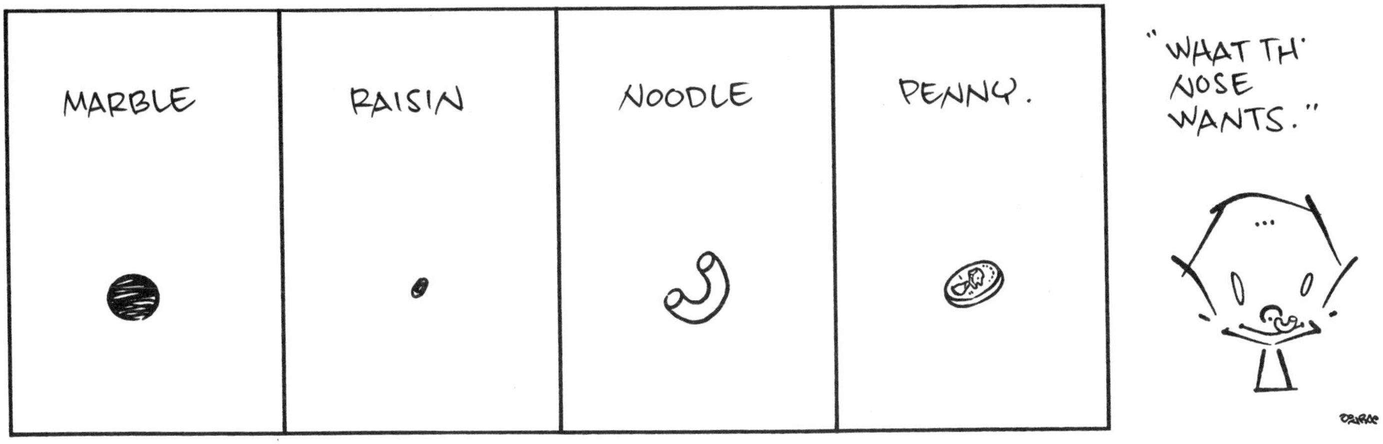
MARBLE
RAISIN
NOODLE
PENNY.
"WHAT TH' NOSE WANTS."

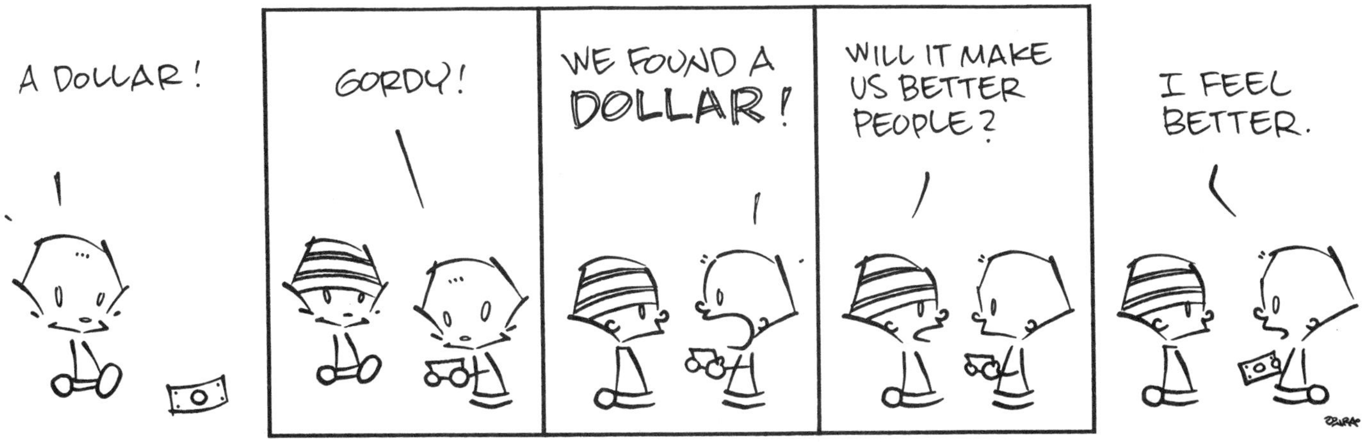
A DOLLAR!
GORDY!
WE FOUND A DOLLAR!
WILL IT MAKE US BETTER PEOPLE?
I FEEL BETTER.

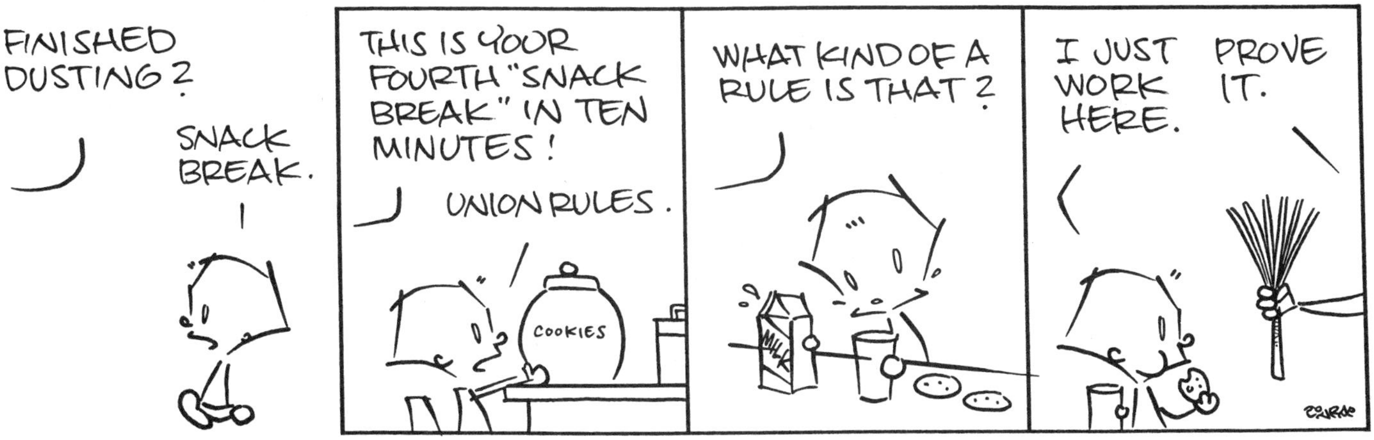
FINISHED DUSTING?
SNACK BREAK.
THIS IS YOUR FOURTH "SNACK BREAK" IN TEN MINUTES!
UNION RULES.
COOKIES
WHAT KIND OF A RULE IS THAT?
I JUST WORK HERE.
PROVE IT.

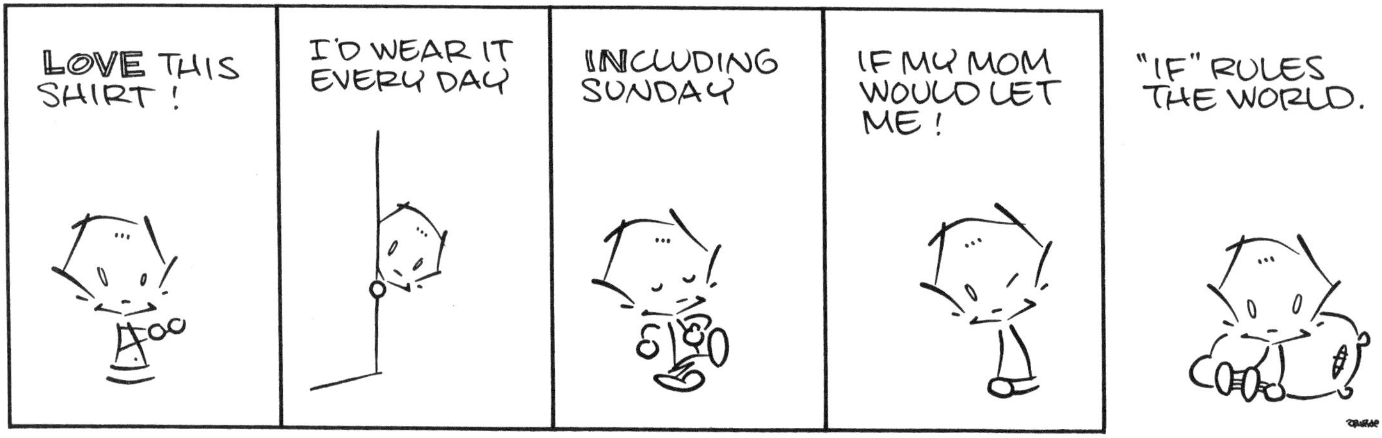
LOVE THIS SHIRT!
I'D WEAR IT EVERY DAY
INCLUDING SUNDAY
IF MY MOM WOULD LET ME!
"IF" RULES THE WORLD.

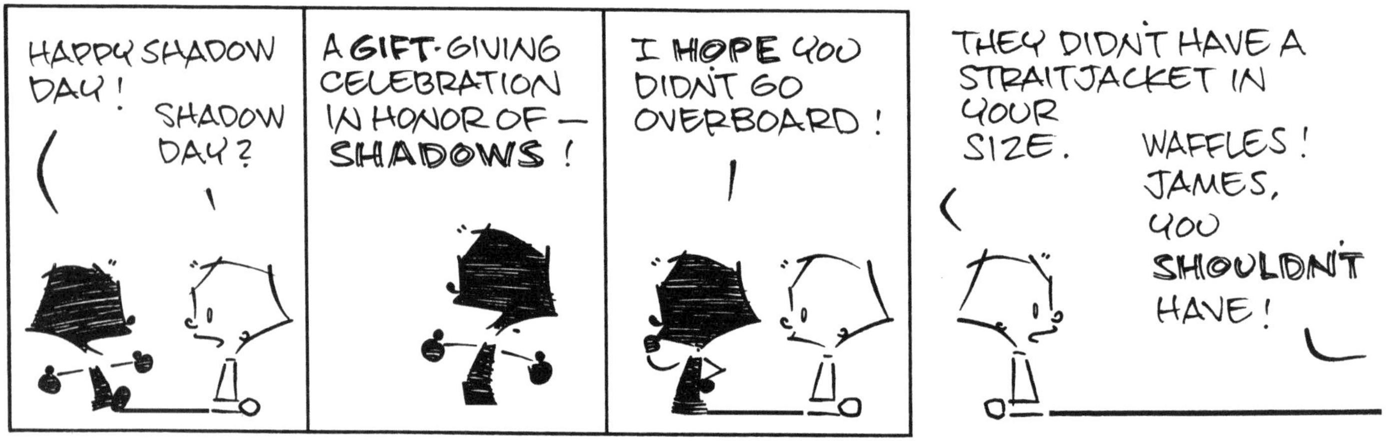
HAPPY SHADOW DAY!
SHADOW DAY?
A GIFT-GIVING CELEBRATION IN HONOR OF— SHADOWS!
I HOPE YOU DIDN'T GO OVERBOARD!
THEY DIDN'T HAVE A STRAITJACKET IN YOUR SIZE.
WAFFLES! JAMES, YOU SHOULDN'T HAVE!

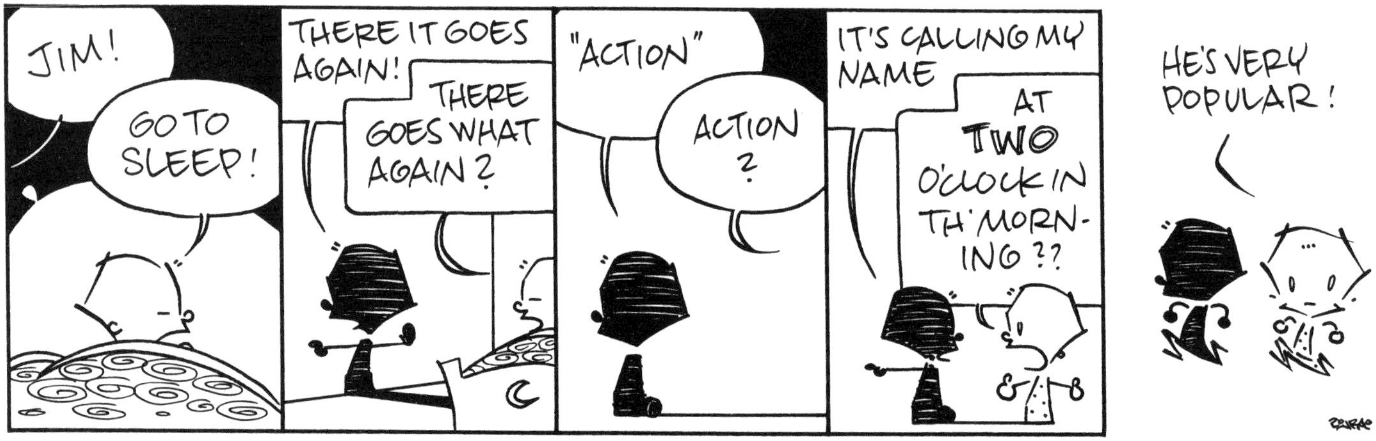
JIM!
GO TO SLEEP!
THERE IT GOES AGAIN!
THERE GOES WHAT AGAIN?
"ACTION"
ACTION?
IT'S CALLING MY NAME
AT TWO O'CLOCK IN TH' MORNING??
HE'S VERY POPULAR!

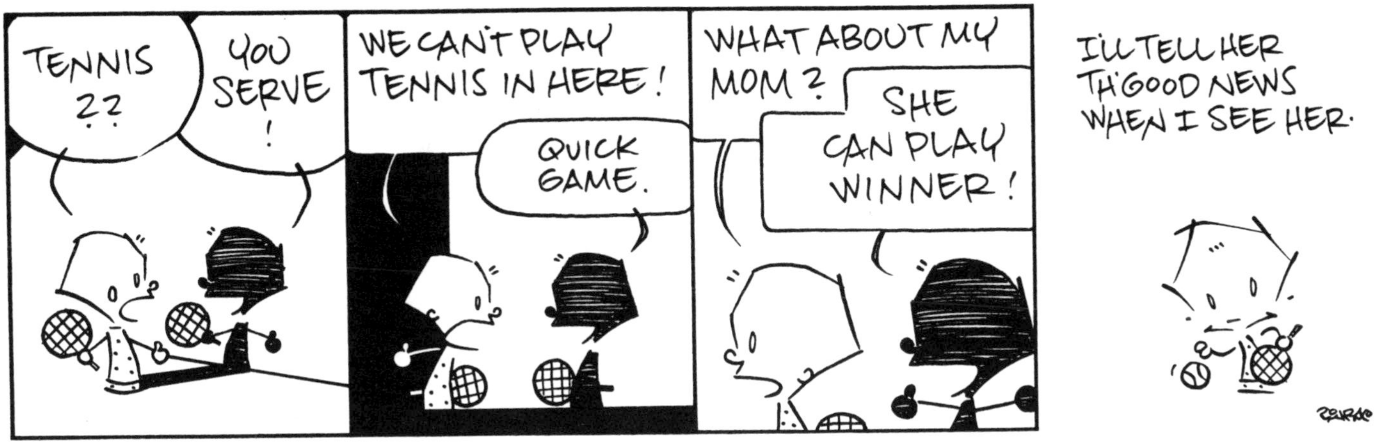
TENNIS ??
YOU SERVE!
WE CAN'T PLAY TENNIS IN HERE!
QUICK GAME.
WHAT ABOUT MY MOM?
SHE CAN PLAY WINNER!
I'LL TELL HER TH' GOOD NEWS WHEN I SEE HER.

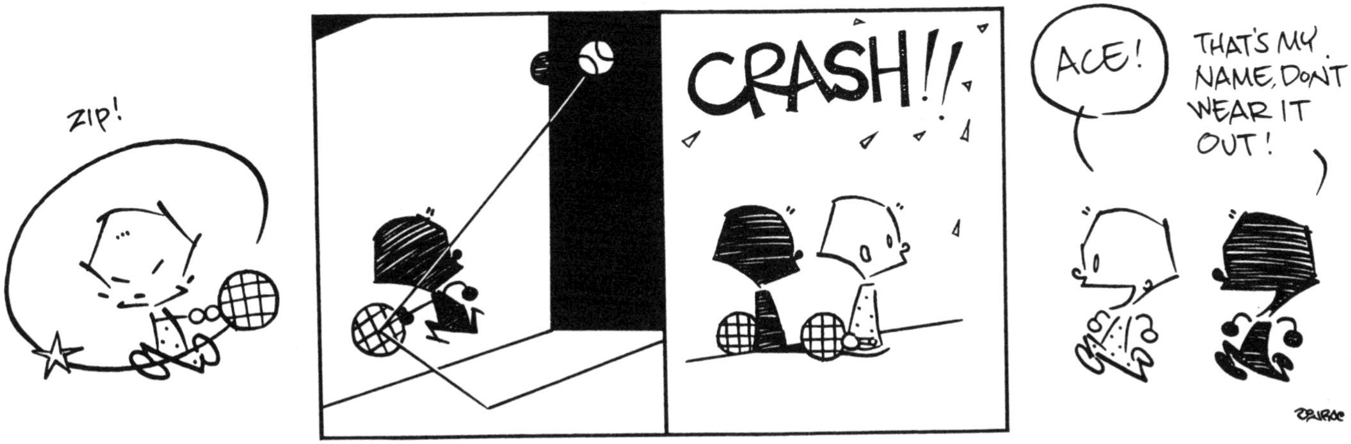
ZIP!
CRASH!!!
ACE!
THAT'S MY NAME, DON'T WEAR IT OUT!

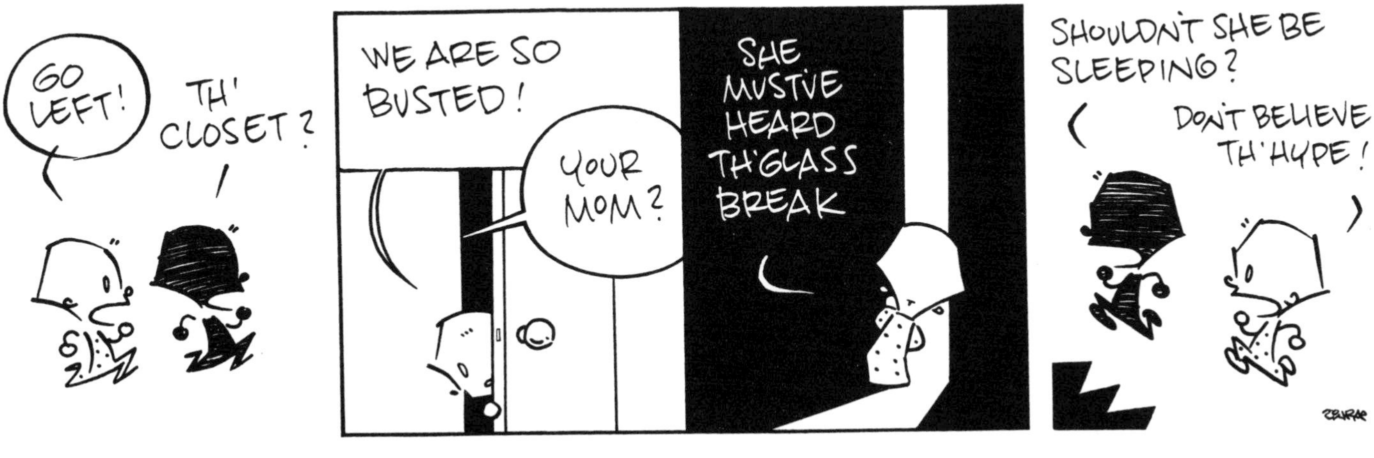
GO LEFT!
TH' CLOSET?
WE ARE SO BUSTED!
YOUR MOM?
SHE MUST'VE HEARD TH' GLASS BREAK
SHOULDN'T SHE BE SLEEPING?
DON'T BELIEVE TH' HYPE!

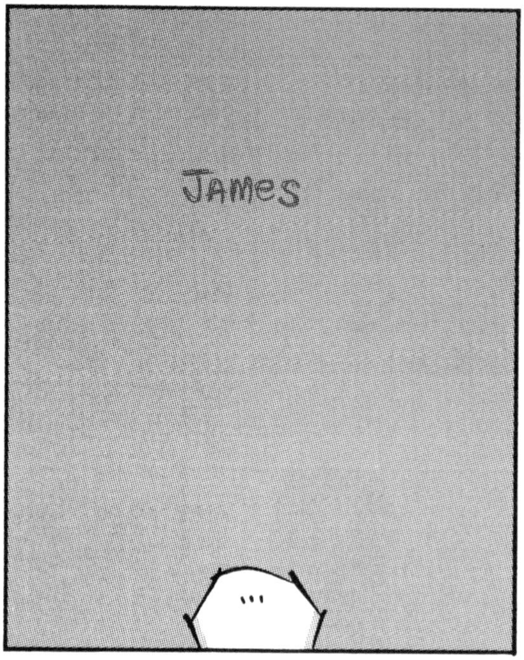
James

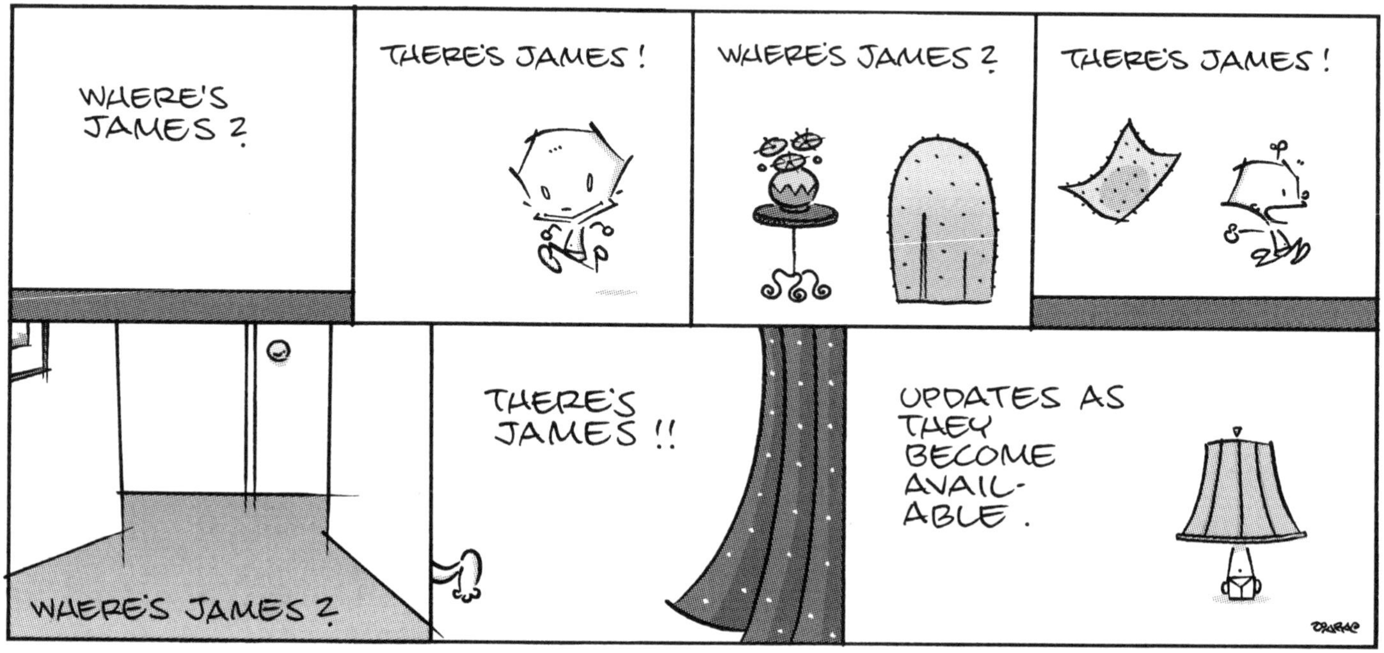
WHERE'S JAMES?
THERE'S JAMES!
WHERE'S JAMES?
THERE'S JAMES!
WHERE'S JAMES?
THERE'S JAMES!!
UPDATES AS THEY BECOME AVAIL-ABLE.

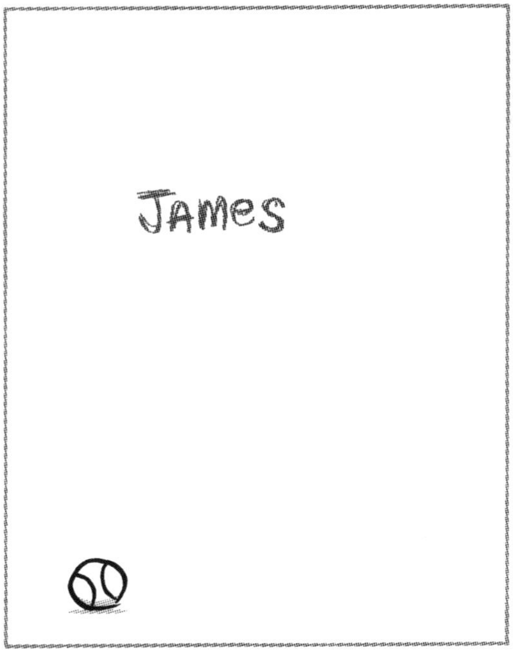
James

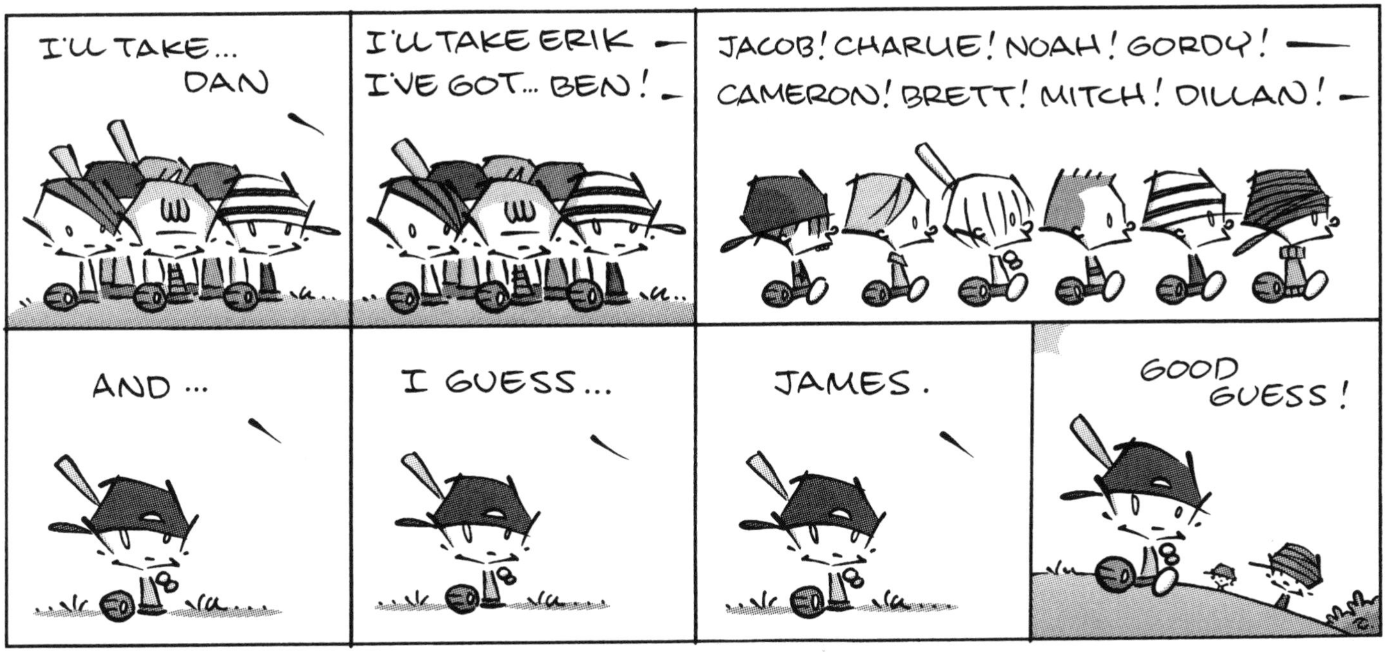
I'LL TAKE... DAN
I'LL TAKE ERIK —
I'VE GOT... BEN! —
JACOB! CHARLIE! NOAH! GORDY! —
CAMERON! BRETT! MITCH! DILLAN! —
AND ...
I GUESS...
JAMES.
GOOD GUESS!

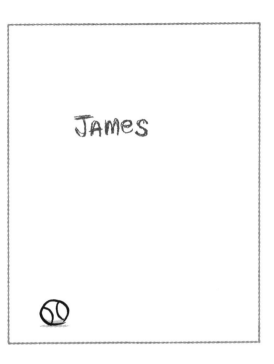

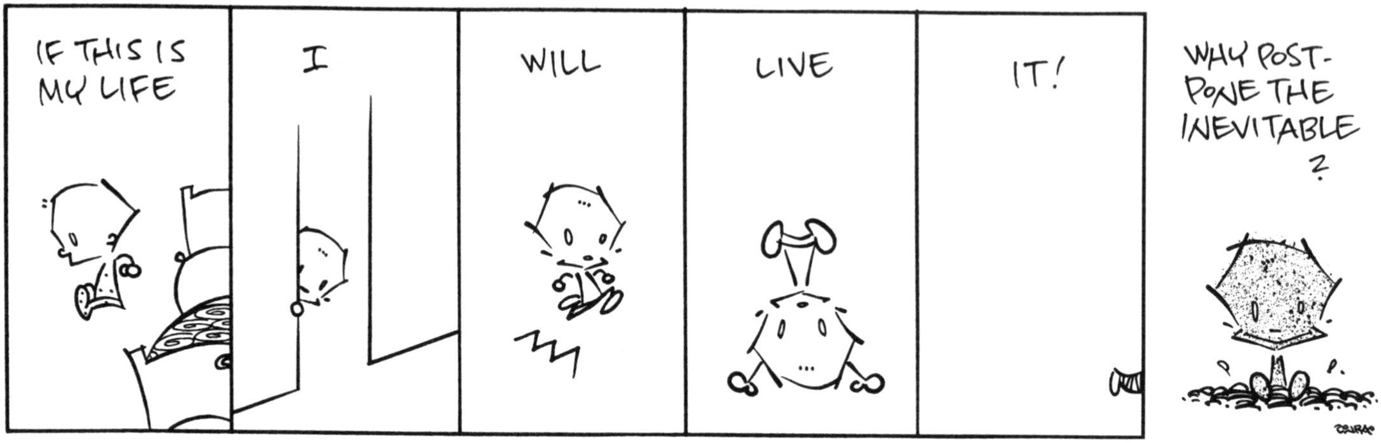
IF THIS IS MY LIFE
I
WILL
LIVE
IT!
WHY POST-PONE THE INEVITABLE?

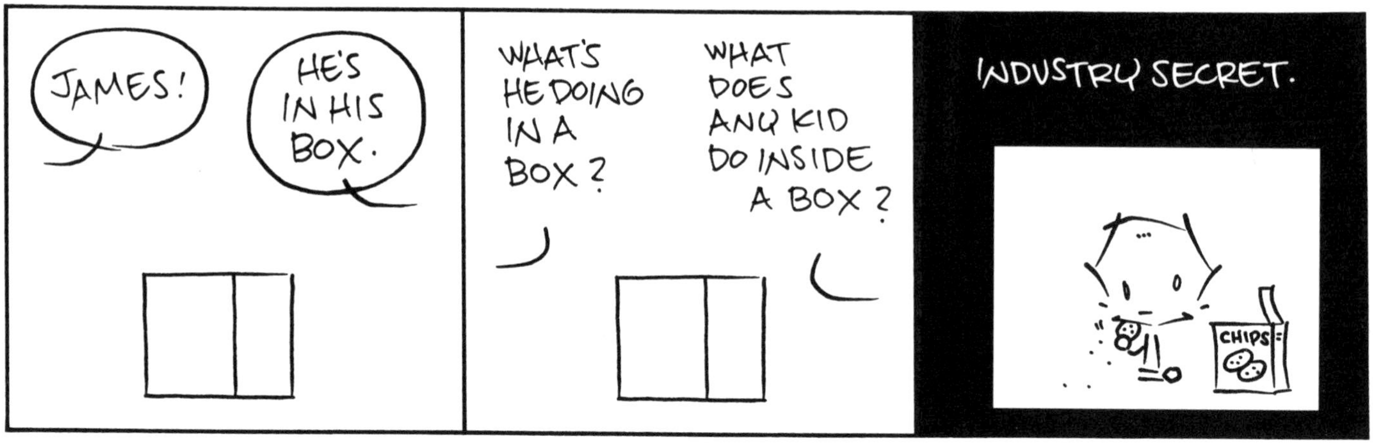
JAMES!
HE'S IN HIS BOX.
WHAT'S HE DOING IN A BOX?
WHAT DOES ANY KID DO INSIDE A BOX?
INDUSTRY SECRET.
CHIPS

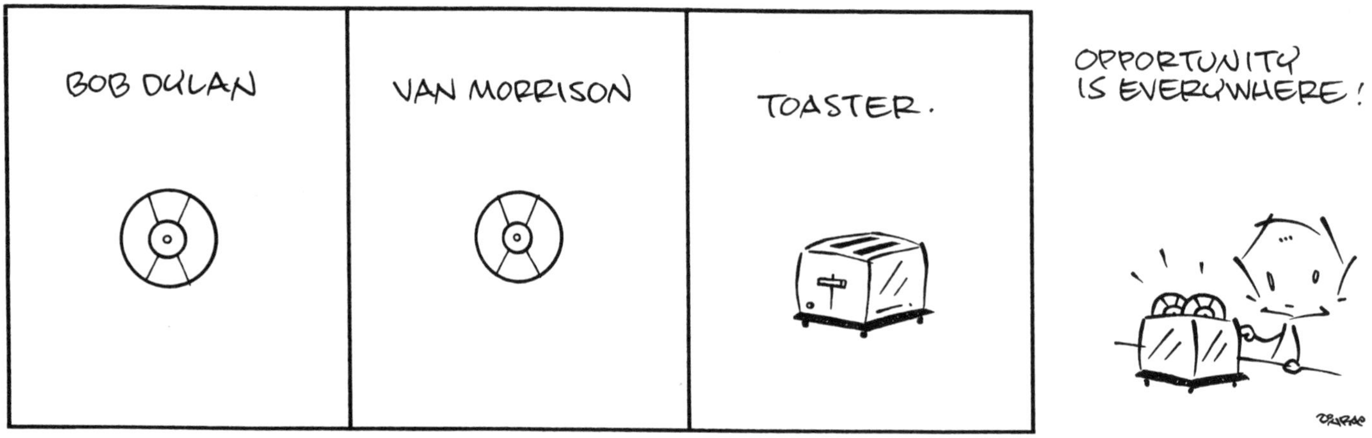
BOB DYLAN
VAN MORRISON
TOASTER.
OPPORTUNITY IS EVERYWHERE!

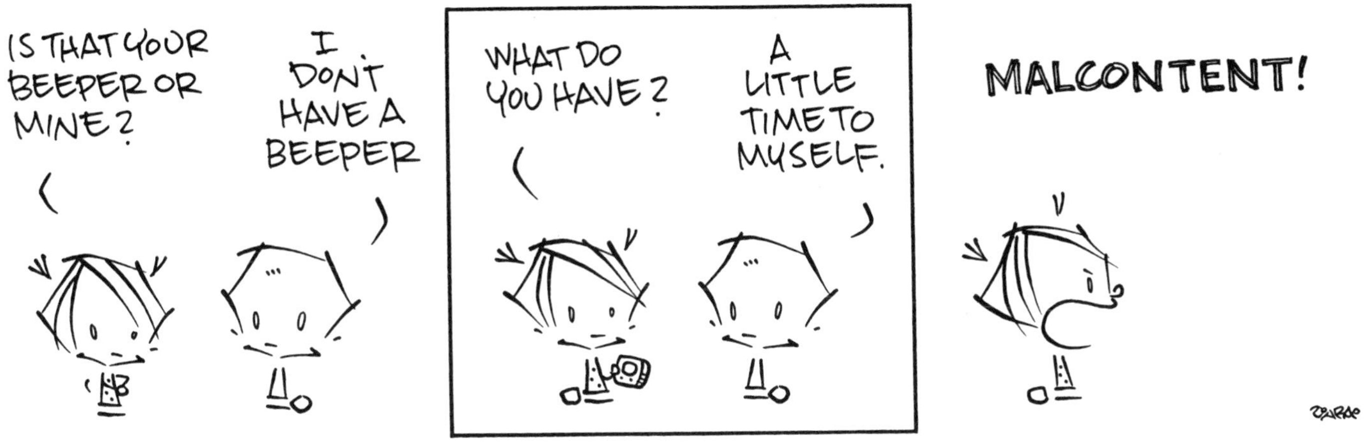
IS THAT YOUR BEEPER OR MINE?
I DON'T HAVE A BEEPER
WHAT DO YOU HAVE?
A LITTLE TIME TO MYSELF.
MALCONTENT!

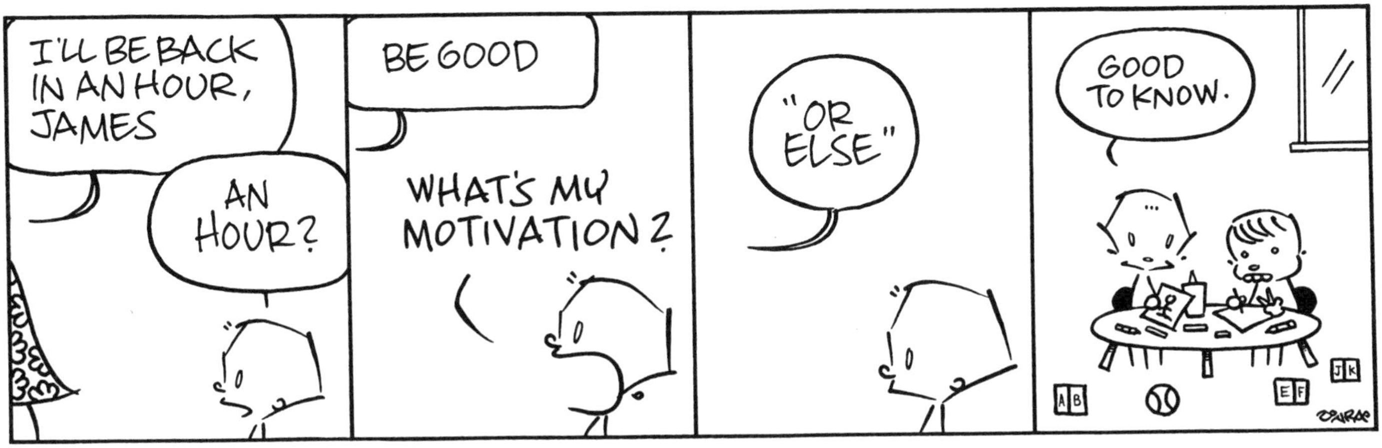
I'LL BE BACK IN AN HOUR, JAMES
AN HOUR?
BE GOOD
WHAT'S MY MOTIVATION?
"OR ELSE"
GOOD TO KNOW.
AB
JK
EF

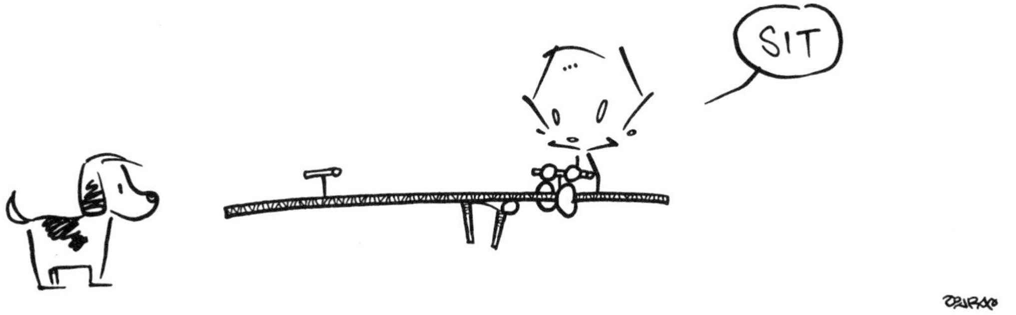
SIT

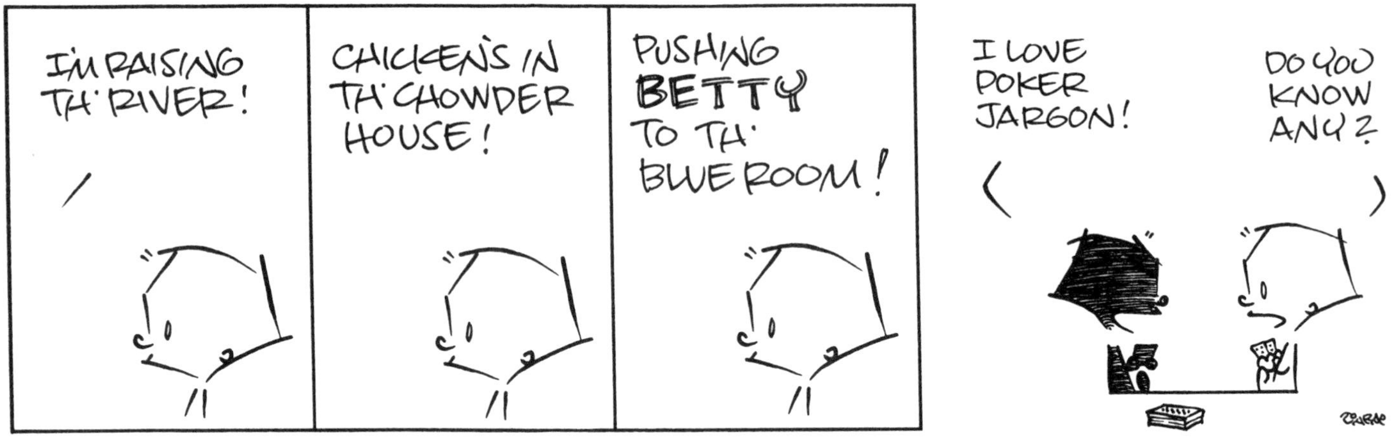
I'M RAISING TH' RIVER!
CHICKEN'S IN TH' CHOWDER HOUSE!
PUSHING BETTY TO TH' BLUE ROOM!
I LOVE POKER JARGON!
DO YOU KNOW ANY?

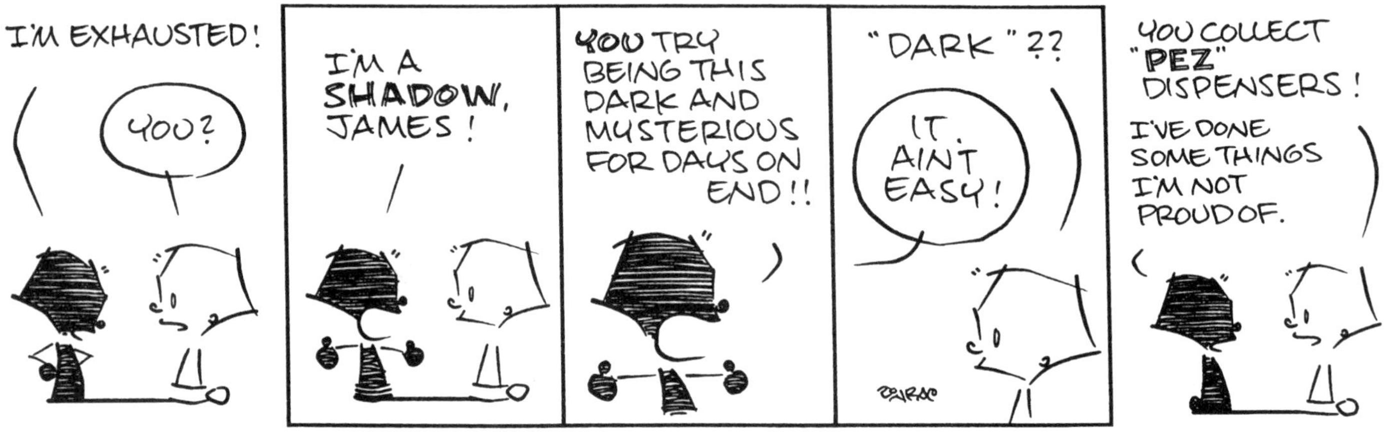
I'M EXHAUSTED!
YOU?
I'M A SHADOW, JAMES!
YOU TRY BEING THIS DARK AND MYSTERIOUS FOR DAYS ON END!!
"DARK"??
IT AIN'T EASY!
YOU COLLECT "PEZ" DISPENSERS!
I'VE DONE SOME THINGS I'M NOT PROUD OF.

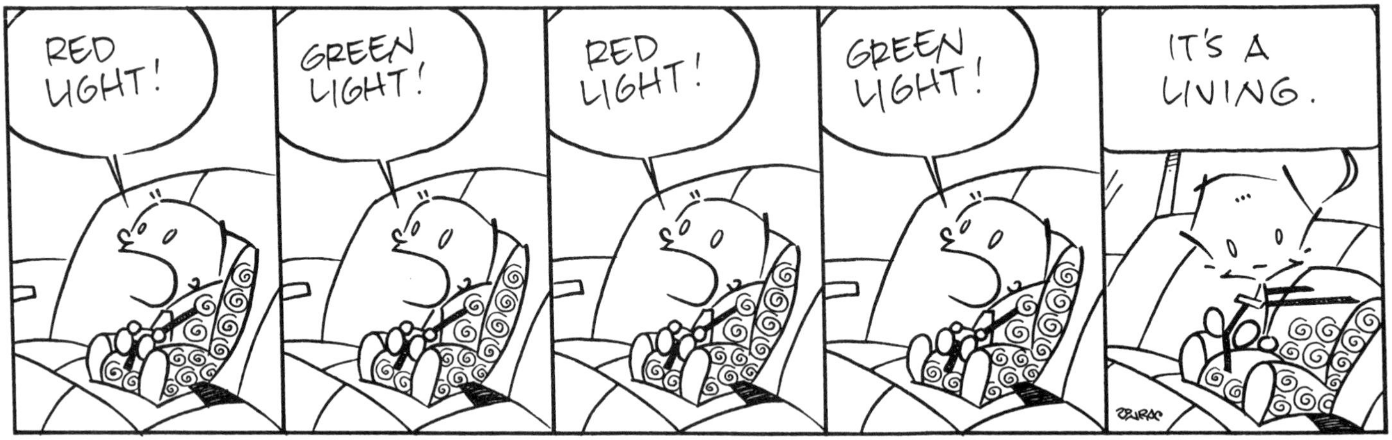
RED LIGHT!
GREEN LIGHT!
RED LIGHT!
GREEN LIGHT!
IT'S A LIVING.

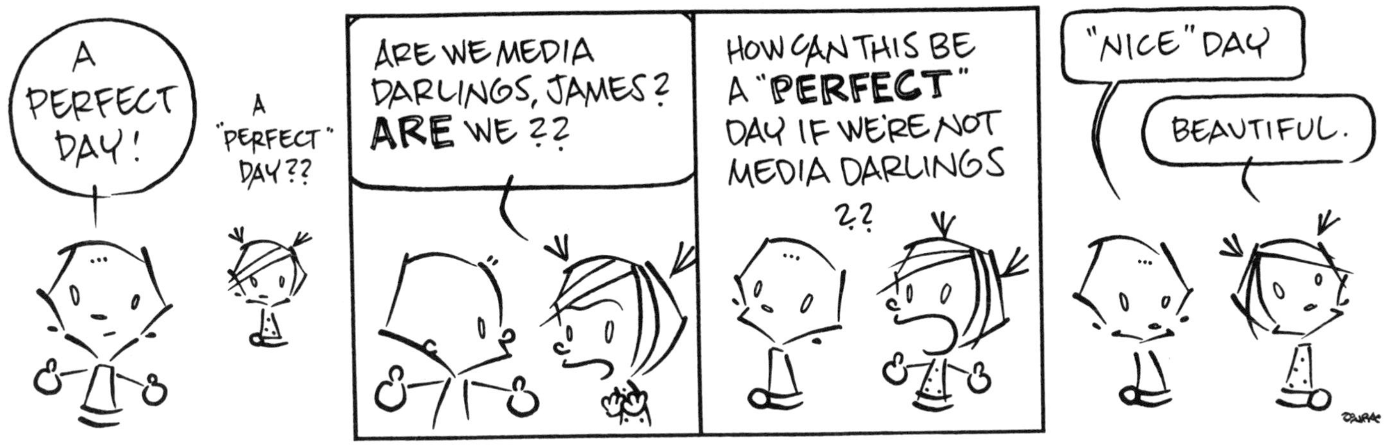
A PERFECT DAY!
A "PERFECT" DAY??
ARE WE MEDIA DARLINGS, JAMES? **ARE** WE??
HOW CAN THIS BE A "**PERFECT**" DAY IF WE'RE NOT MEDIA DARLINGS
??
"NICE" DAY
BEAUTIFUL.

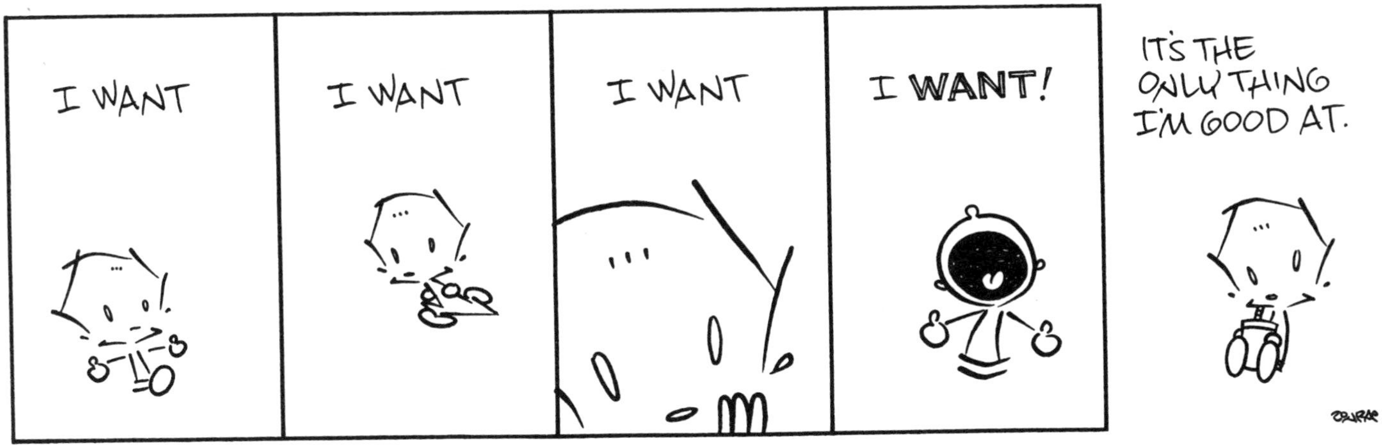
I WANT
I WANT
I WANT
I **WANT**!
IT'S THE ONLY THING I'M GOOD AT.

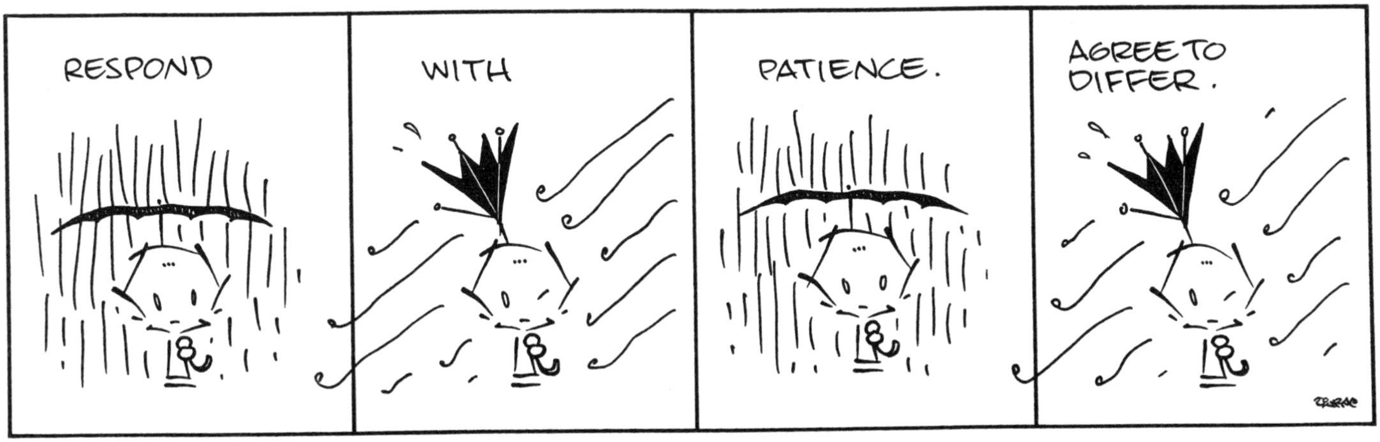
RESPOND
WITH
PATIENCE.
AGREE TO DIFFER.

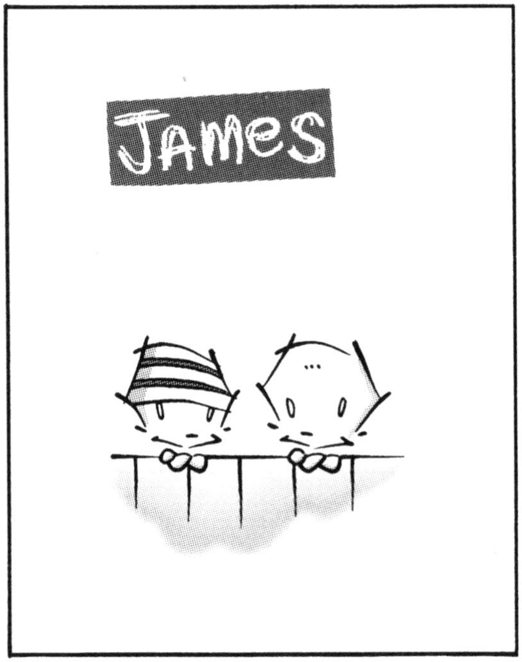
James
...

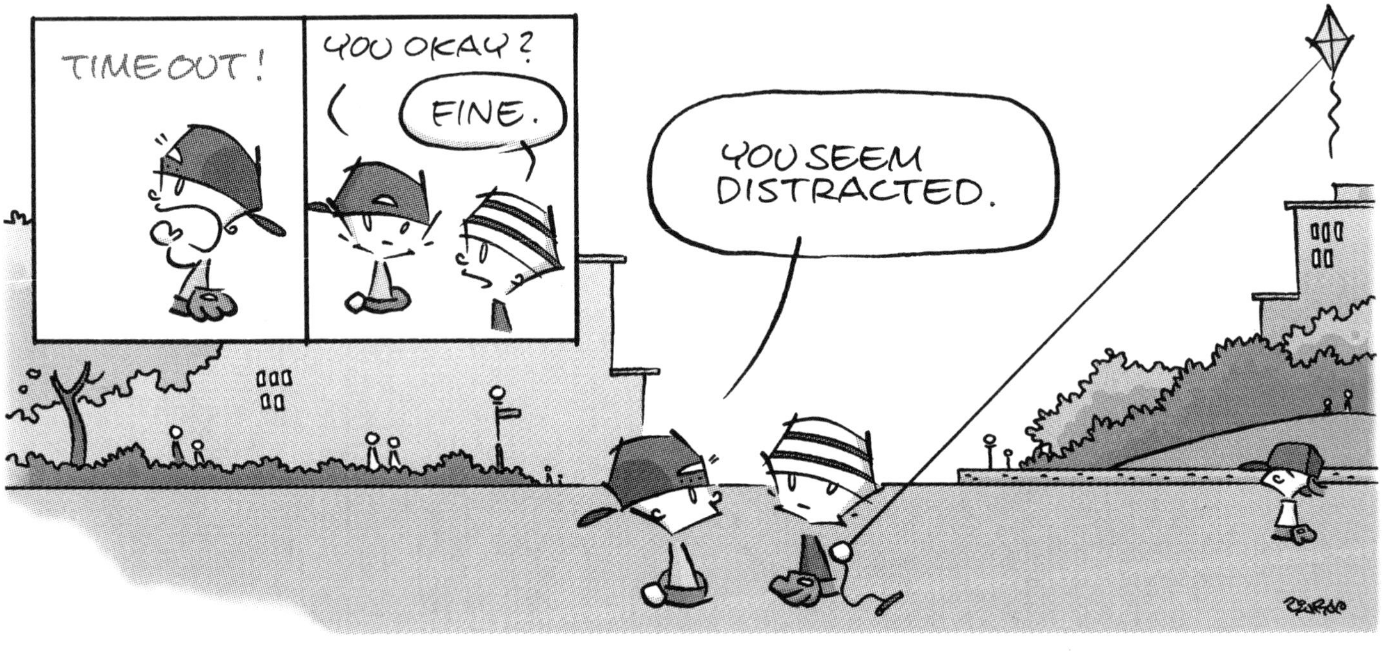
TIME OUT!
YOU OKAY?
FINE.
YOU SEEM DISTRACTED.

James

I WANTED TO BE AN ASTRO- NAUT

UNTIL THEY TOLD ME I COULDN'T BE AN ASTRO- NAUT.

I WANTED TO BE AN ARTIST

UNTIL THEY TOLD ME I COULDN'T BE AN ARTIST.

I WANTED TO BE AN ACTOR, ATHLETE AND MUSICIAN

UNTIL THEY TOLD ME I COULDN'T.

IT'S AMAZING WHAT YOU CAN'T ACCOM- PLISH

ONCE THEY PUT THEIR MIND TO IT.

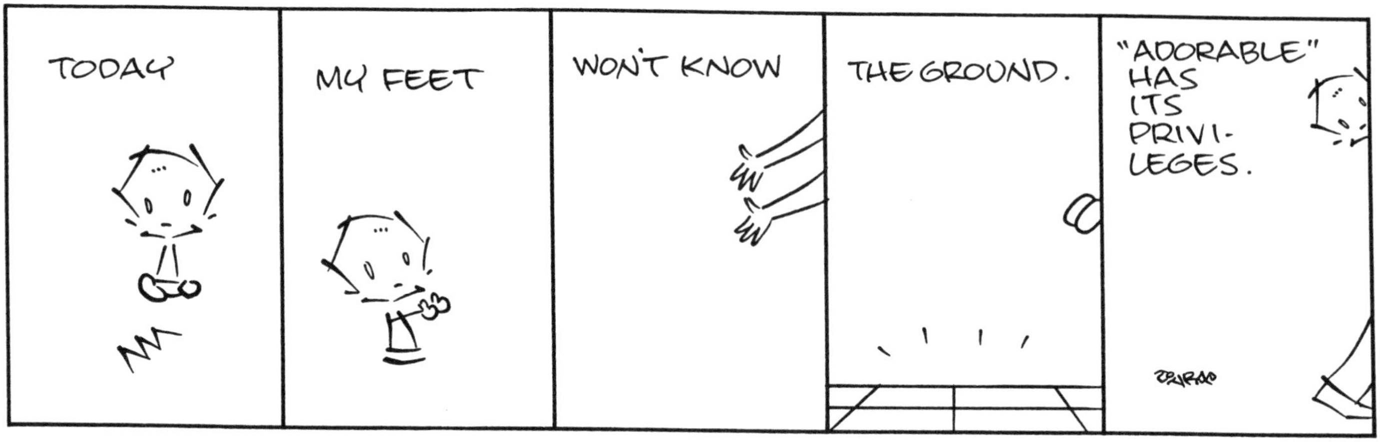
TODAY
MY FEET
WON'T KNOW
THE GROUND.
"ADORABLE" HAS ITS PRIVI-LEGES.

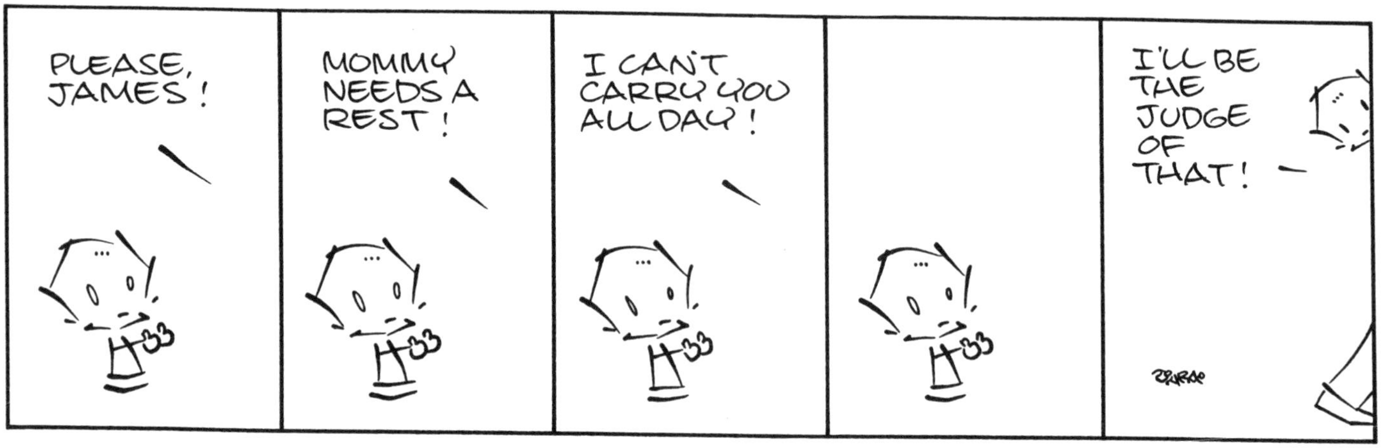
PLEASE, JAMES!
MOMMY NEEDS A REST!
I CAN'T CARRY YOU ALL DAY!
I'LL BE THE JUDGE OF THAT!

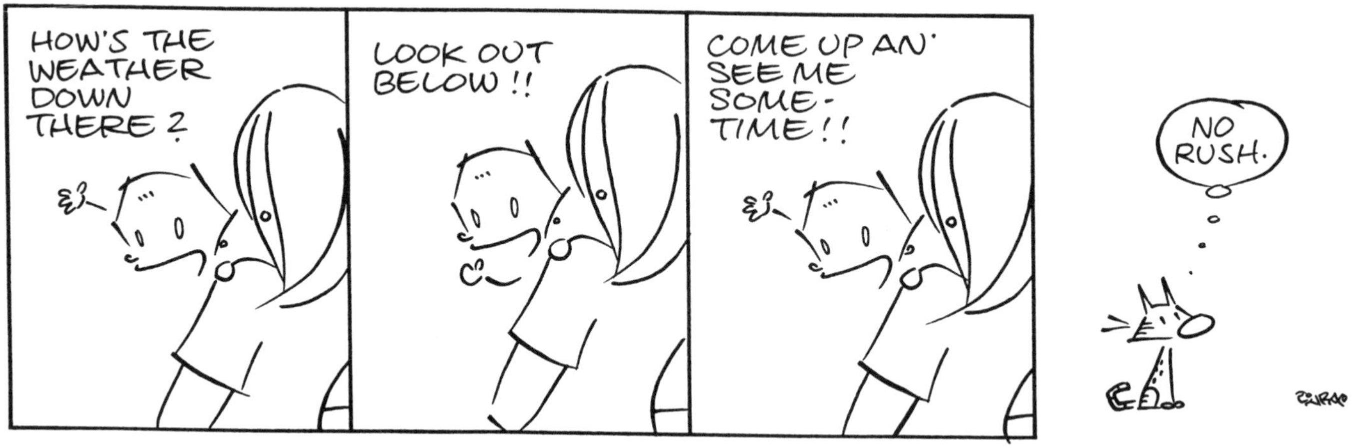
HOW'S THE WEATHER DOWN THERE?
LOOK OUT BELOW!!
COME UP AN' SEE ME SOME-TIME!!
NO RUSH.

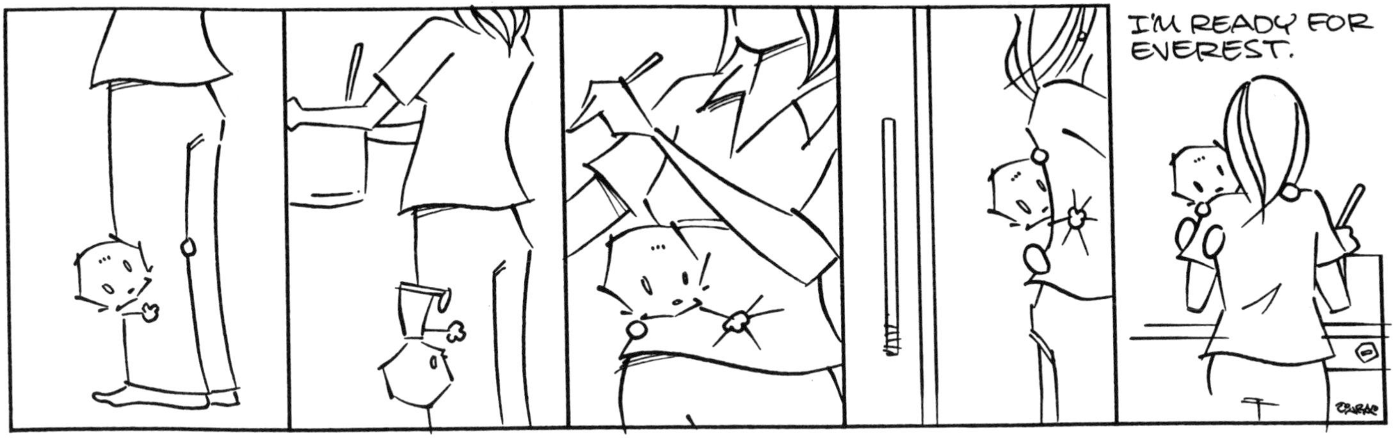
I'M READY FOR EVEREST.

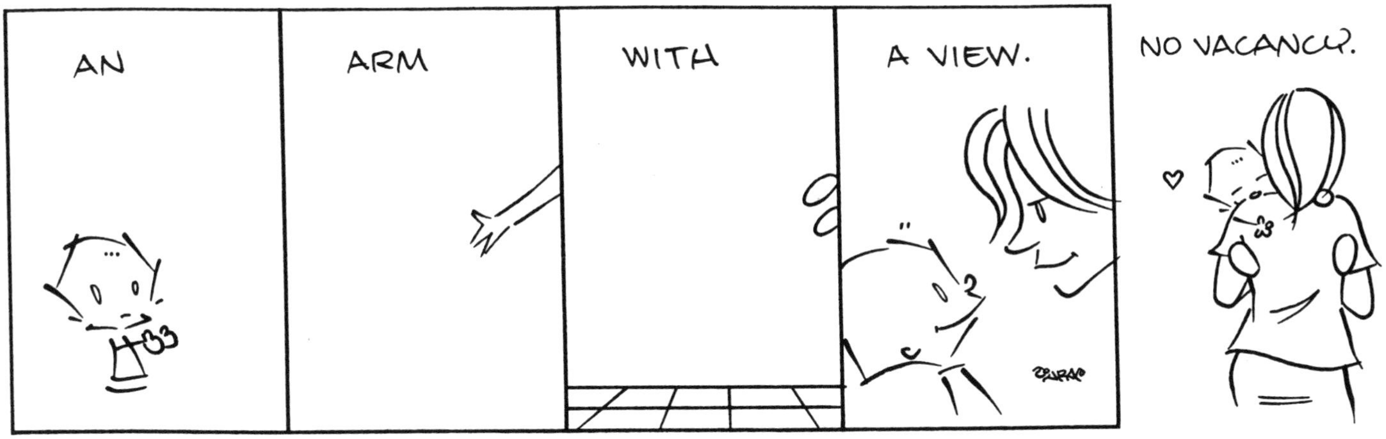
AN
ARM
WITH
A VIEW.
NO VACANCY.

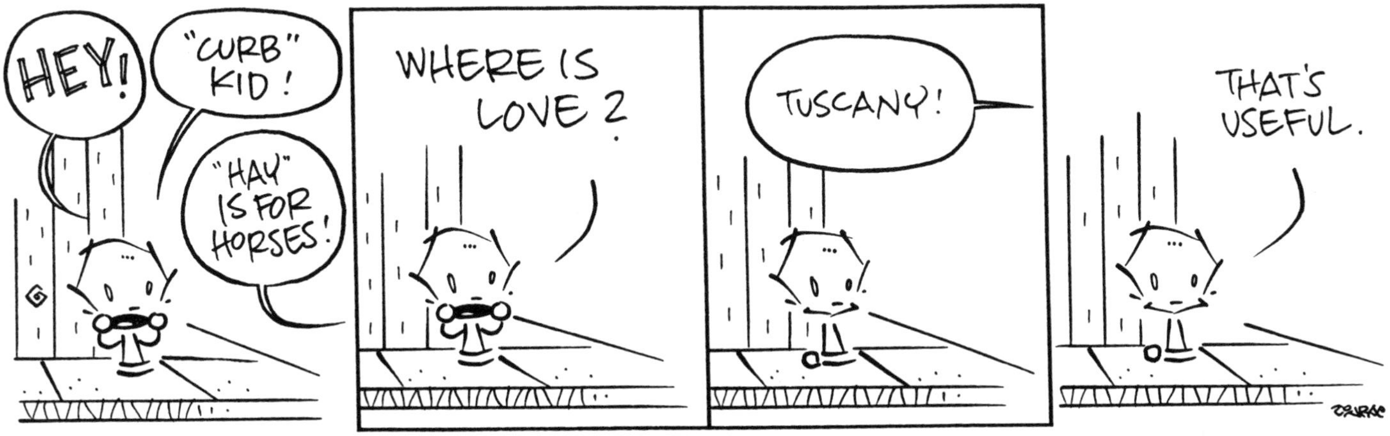
HEY!
"CURB" KID!
"HAY" IS FOR HORSES!
WHERE IS LOVE?
TUSCANY!
THAT'S USEFUL.

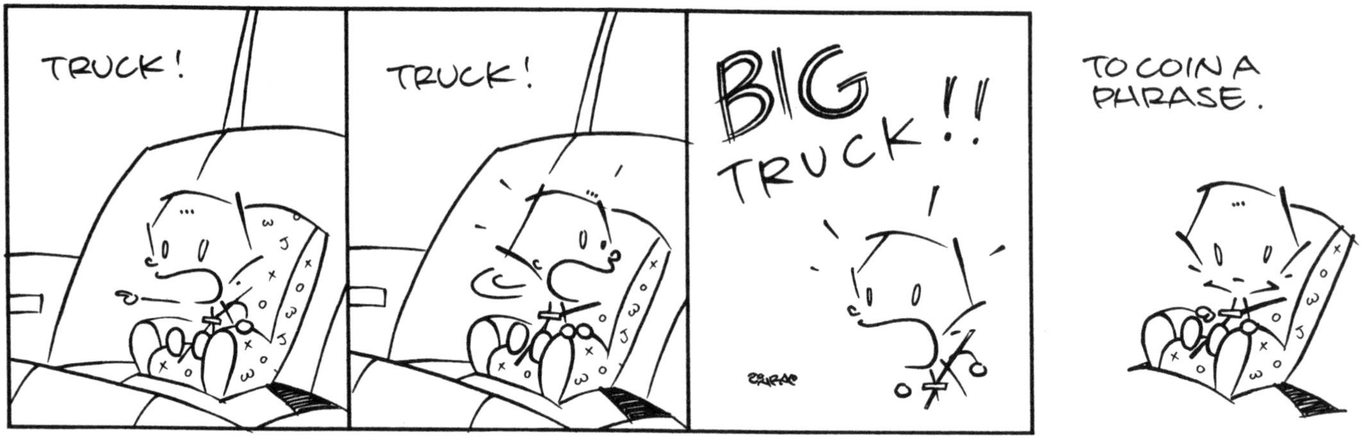
TRUCK!
TRUCK!
BIG TRUCK!!
TO COIN A PHRASE.

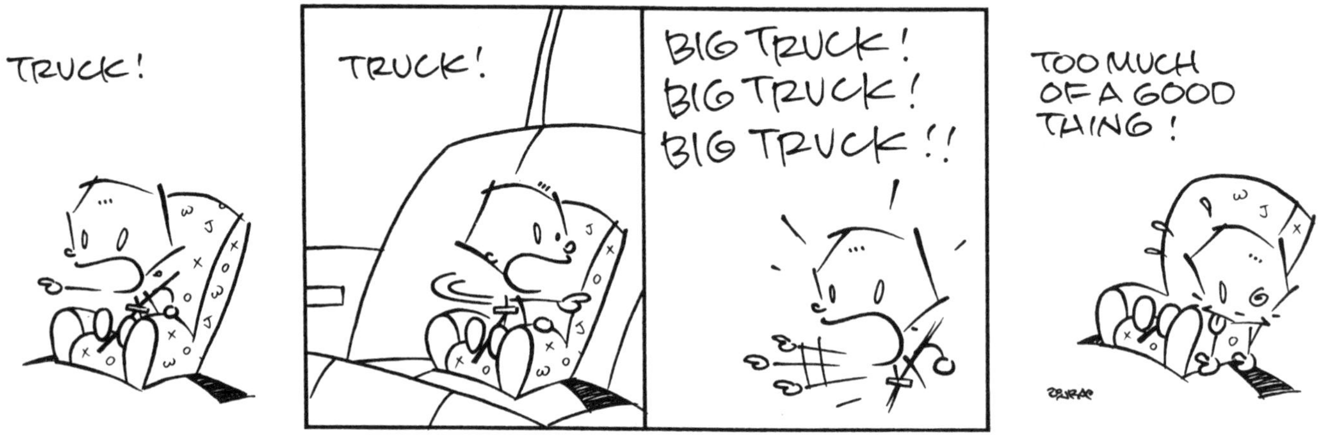
TRUCK!
TRUCK!
BIG TRUCK! BIG TRUCK! BIG TRUCK!!
TOO MUCH OF A GOOD THING!

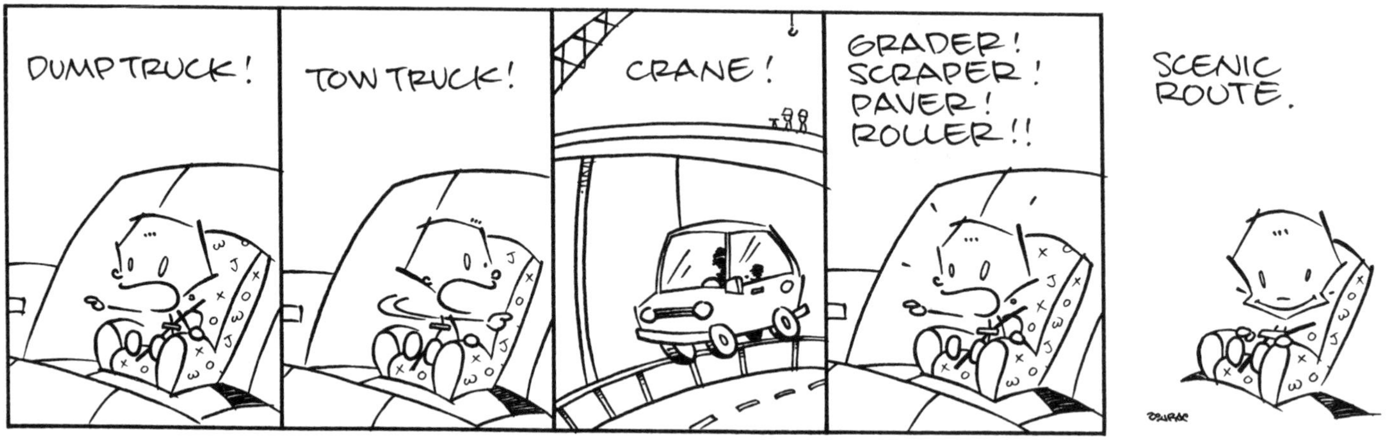
DUMP TRUCK!
TOW TRUCK!
CRANE!
GRADER! SCRAPER! PAVER! ROLLER!!
SCENIC ROUTE.

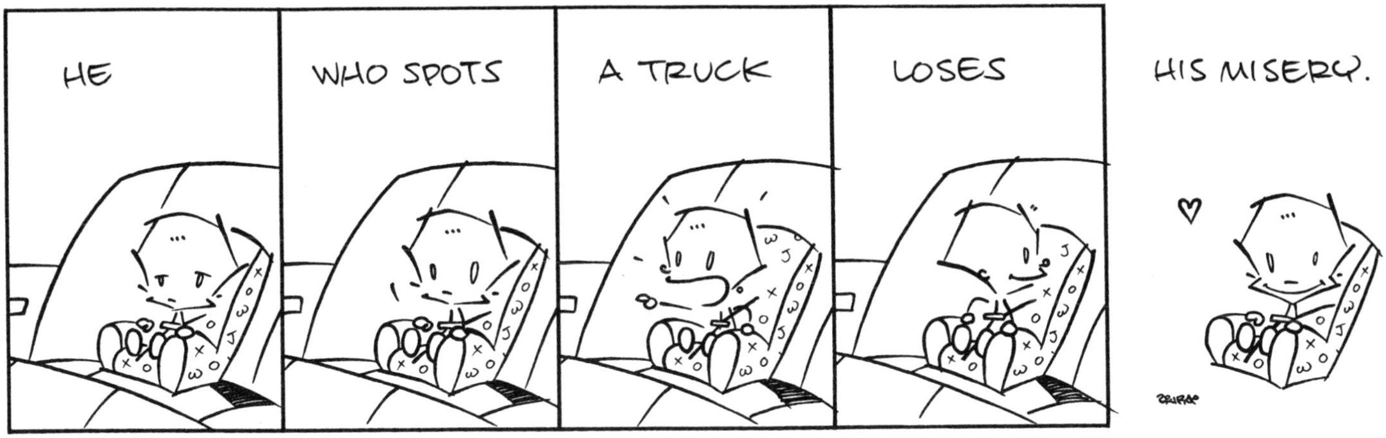
HE
WHO SPOTS
A TRUCK
LOSES
HIS MISERY.

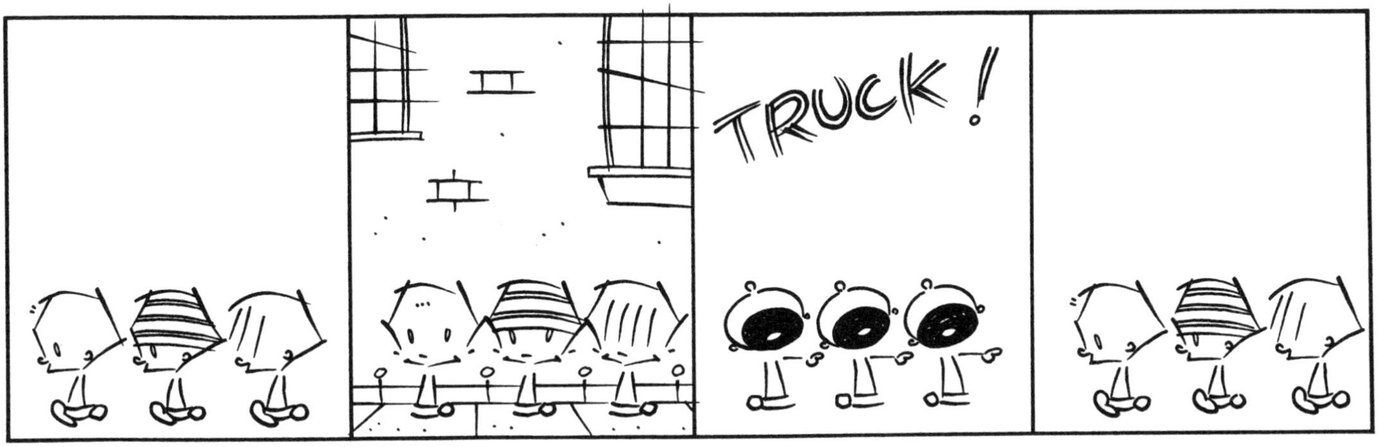
TRUCK!

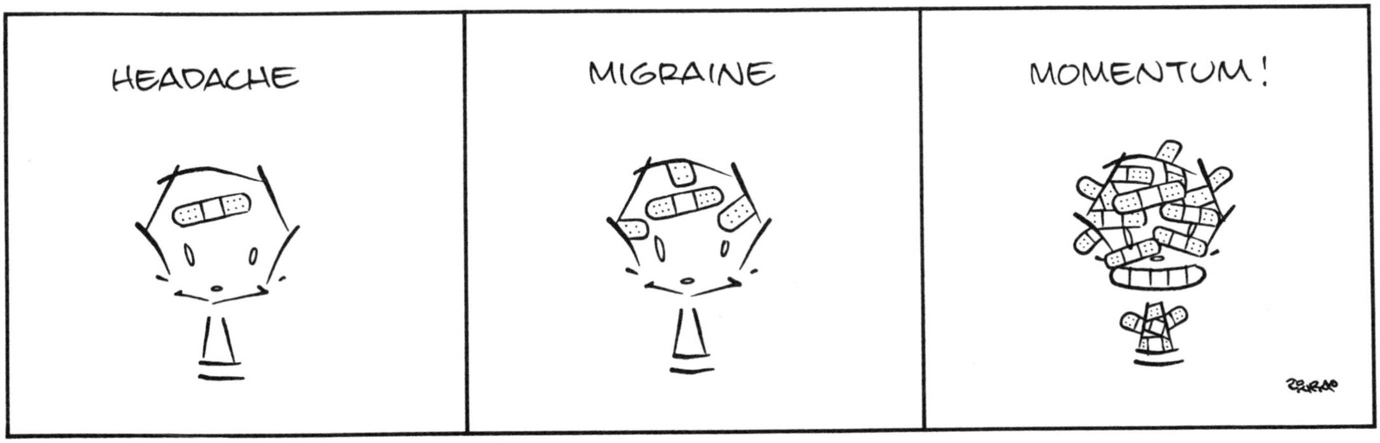
HEADACHE
MIGRAINE
MOMENTUM!

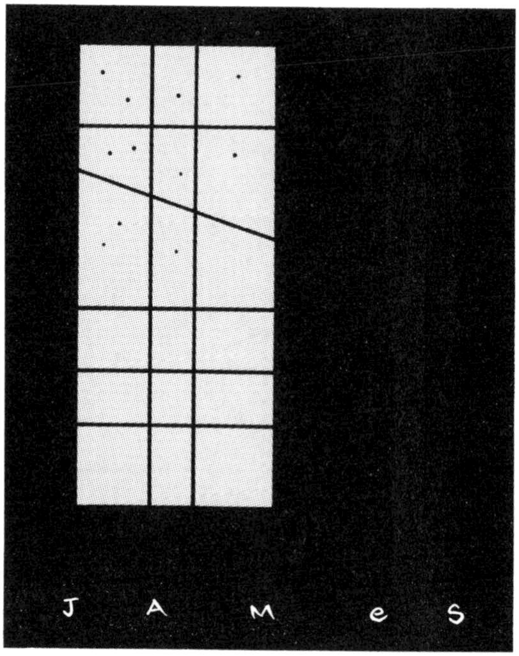
J A M e S

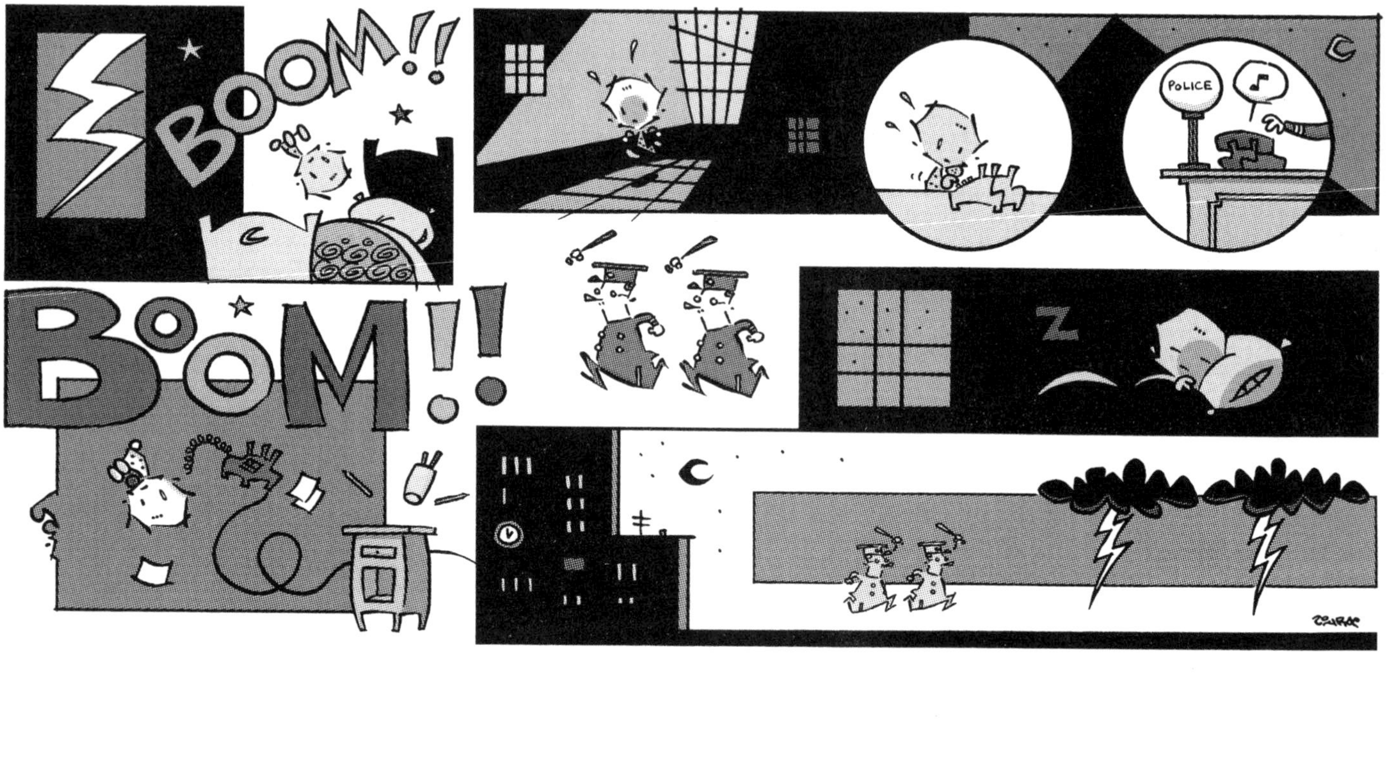
BOOM!!
POLICE
Z
BOOM!!

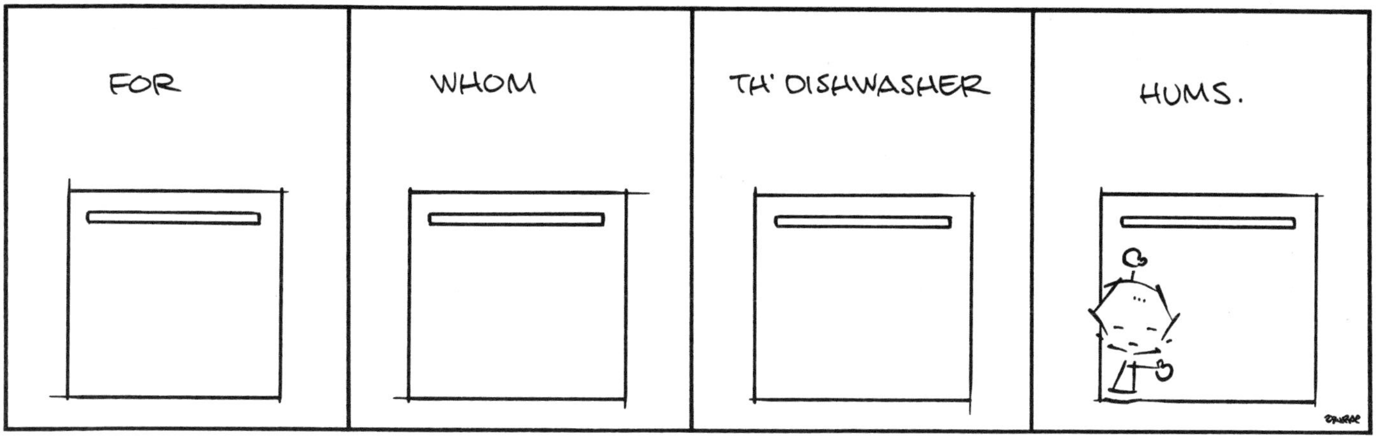
FOR
WHOM
TH' DISHWASHER
HUMS.

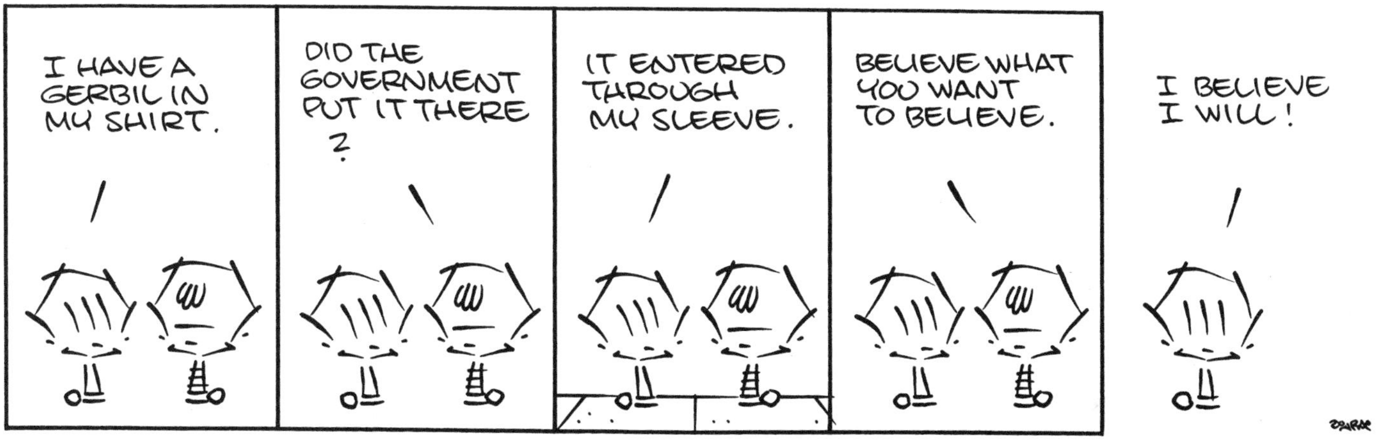
I HAVE A GERBIL IN MY SHIRT.
DID THE GOVERNMENT PUT IT THERE?
IT ENTERED THROUGH MY SLEEVE.
BELIEVE WHAT YOU WANT TO BELIEVE.
I BELIEVE I WILL!

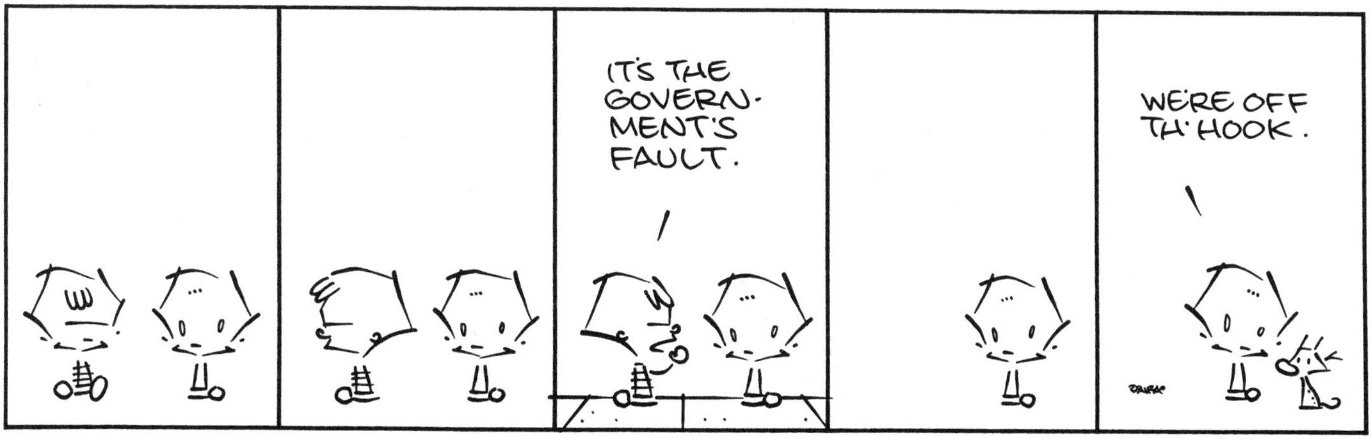
IT'S THE GOVERN-MENT'S FAULT.
WE'RE OFF TH' HOOK.

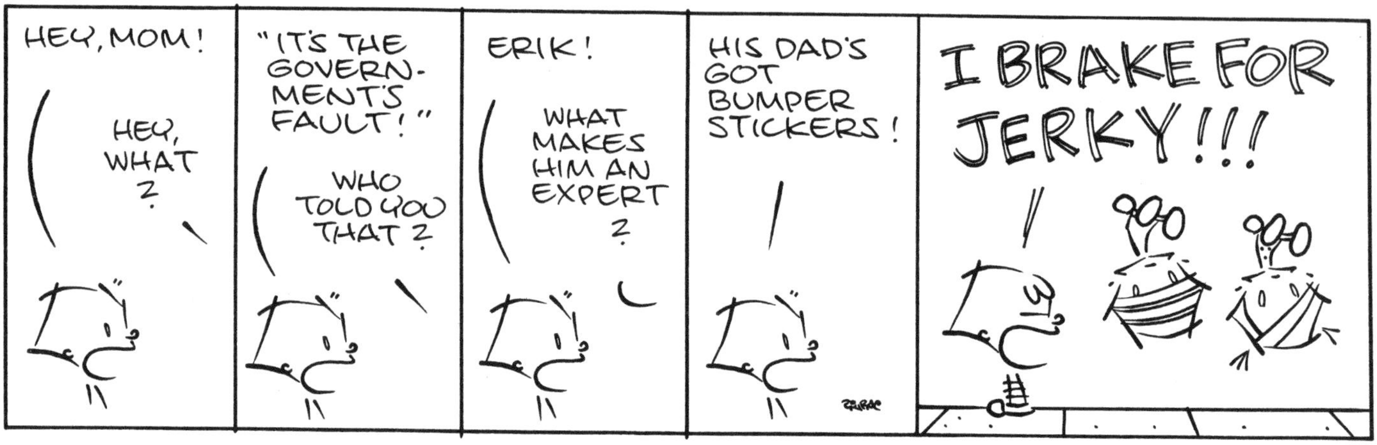
HEY, MOM!
HEY, WHAT?
"IT'S THE GOVERNMENT'S FAULT!"
WHO TOLD YOU THAT?
ERIK!
WHAT MAKES HIM AN EXPERT?
HIS DAD'S GOT BUMPER STICKERS!
I BRAKE FOR JERKY!!!

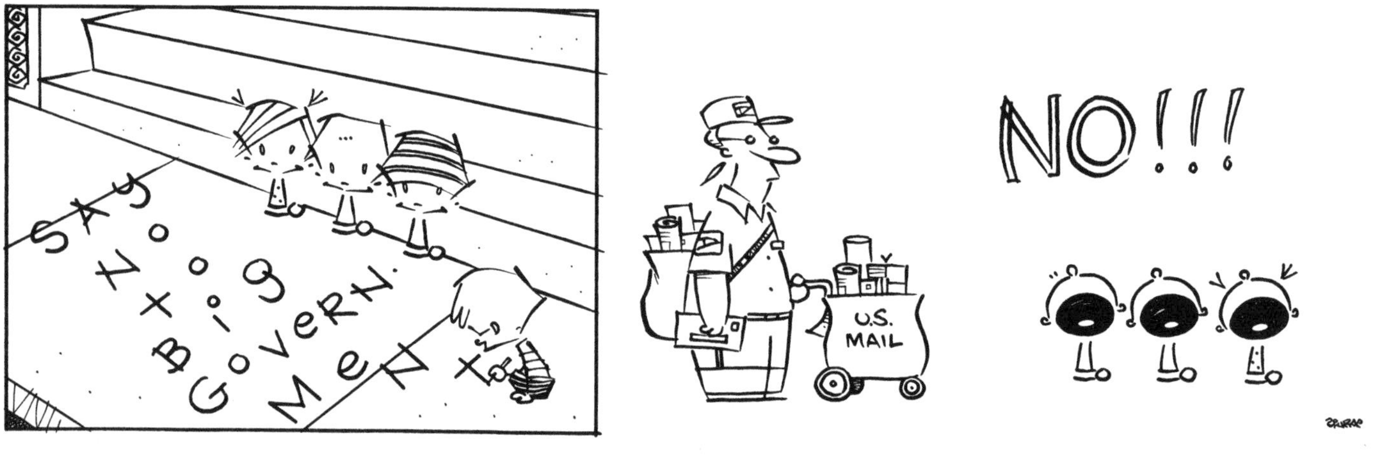
SAY NO TO BIG GOVERNMENT
U.S. MAIL
NO!!!

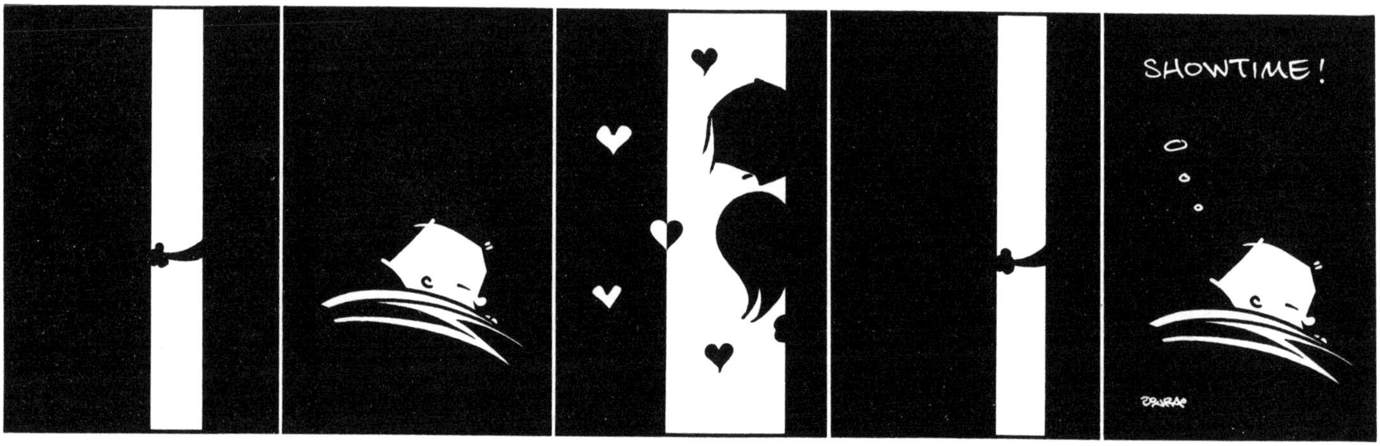
SHOWTIME!

James

PLEASE, JAMES!
MOMMY CAN'T HOLD YOU
AND COOK
AT THE SAME TIME!
LEARN.
EDUCATION IS EVERY-THING.

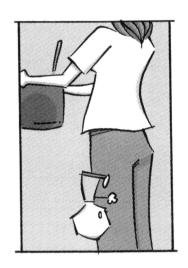

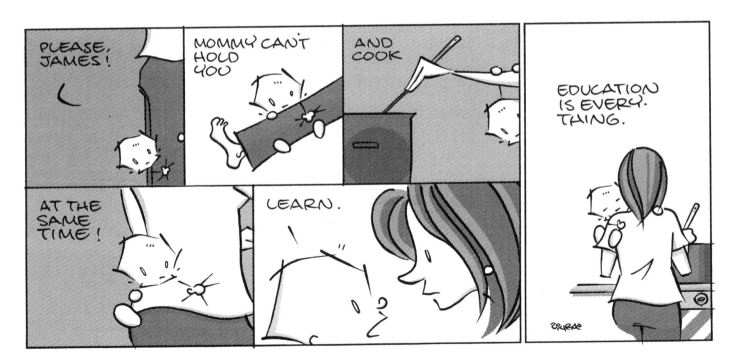

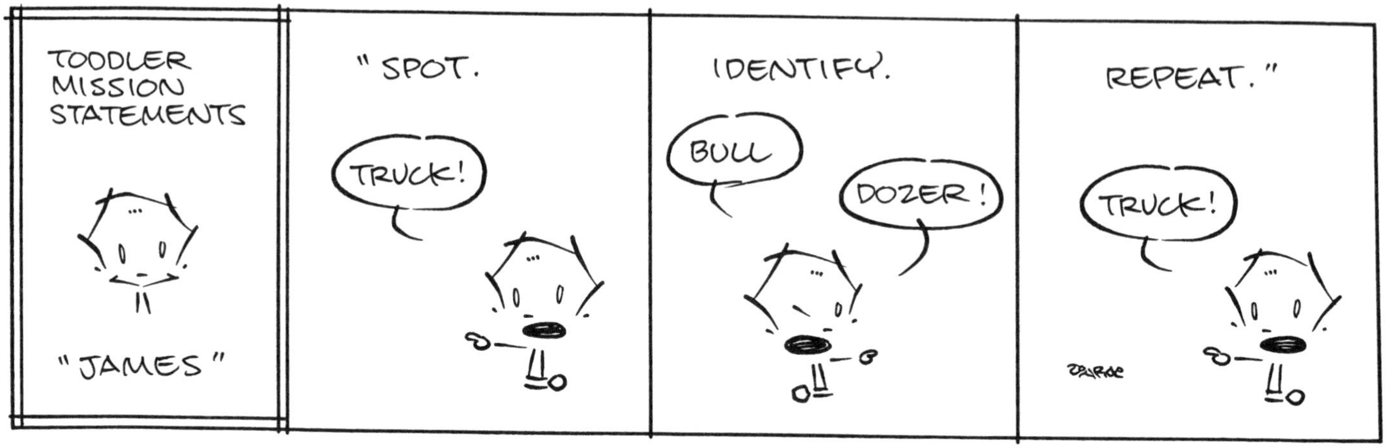
TODDLER MISSION STATEMENTS
"JAMES"
"SPOT.
TRUCK!
IDENTIFY.
BULL
DOZER!
REPEAT."
TRUCK!

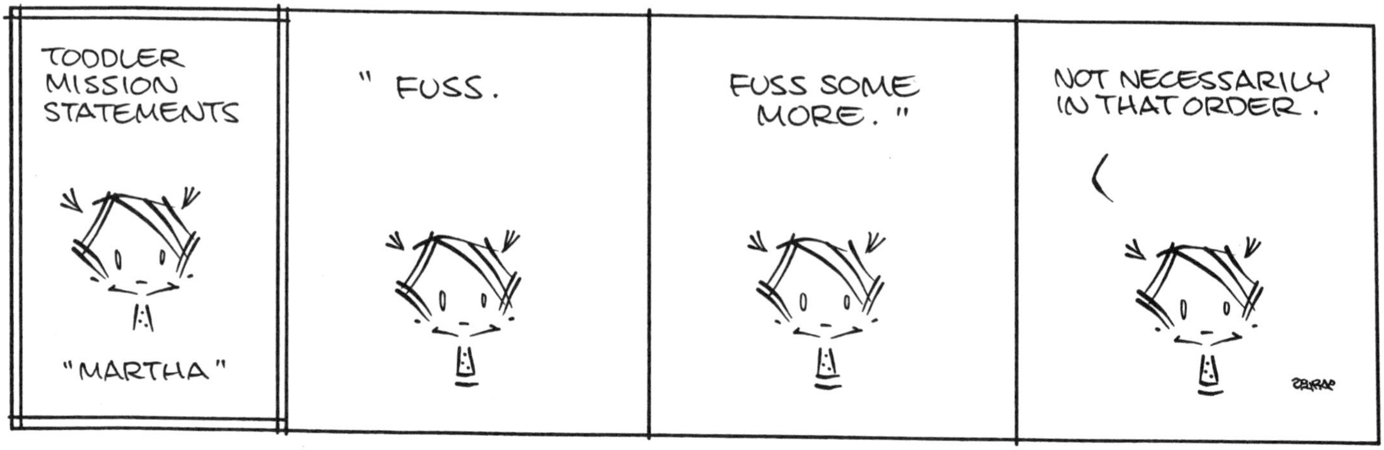
TODDLER MISSION STATEMENTS
"MARTHA"
" FUSS.
FUSS SOME MORE."
NOT NECESSARILY IN THAT ORDER.

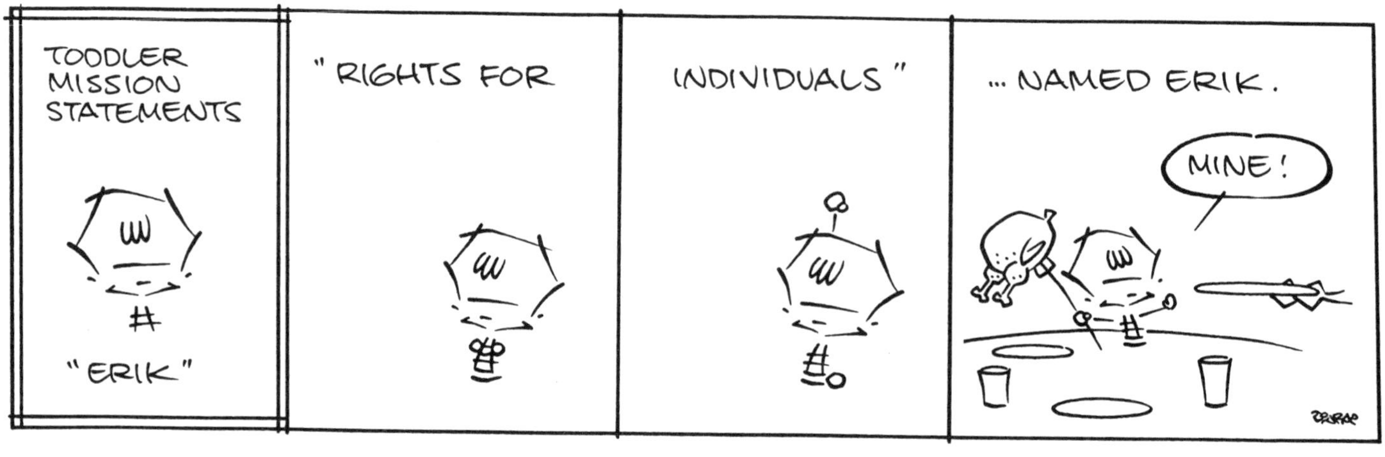
TODDLER MISSION STATEMENTS
"ERIK"
"RIGHTS FOR
INDIVIDUALS"
...NAMED ERIK.
MINE!

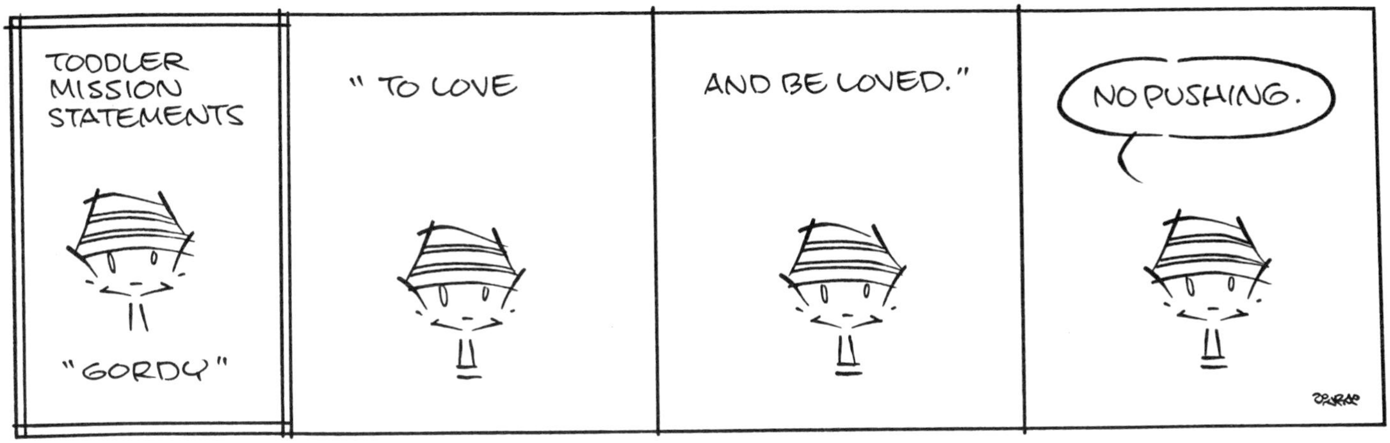
TODDLER MISSION STATEMENTS
"GORDY"
" TO LOVE
AND BE LOVED."
NO PUSHING.

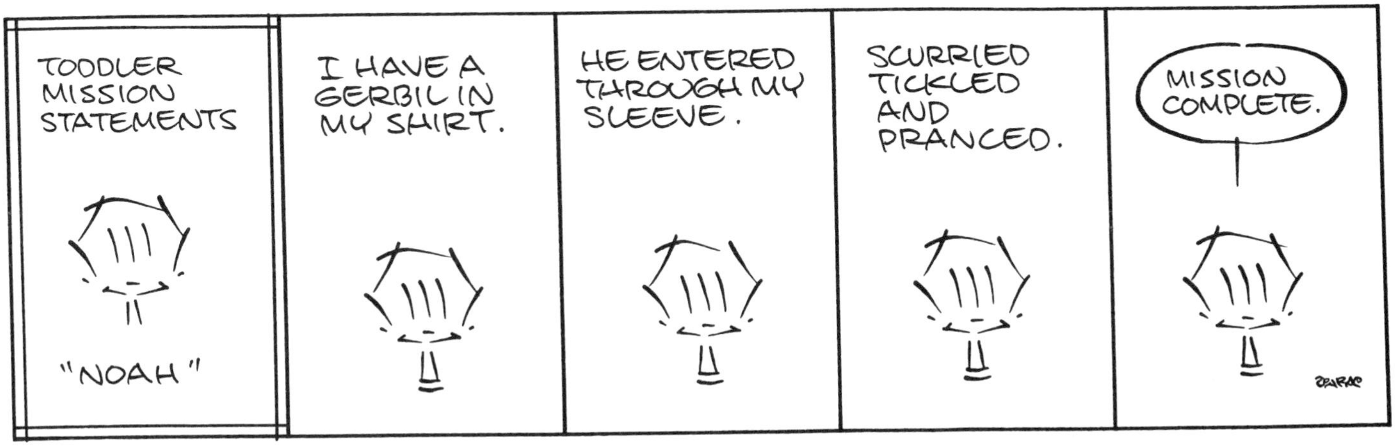
TODDLER MISSION STATEMENTS
"NOAH"
I HAVE A GERBIL IN MY SHIRT.
HE ENTERED THROUGH MY SLEEVE.
SCURRIED TICKLED AND PRANCED.
MISSION COMPLETE.

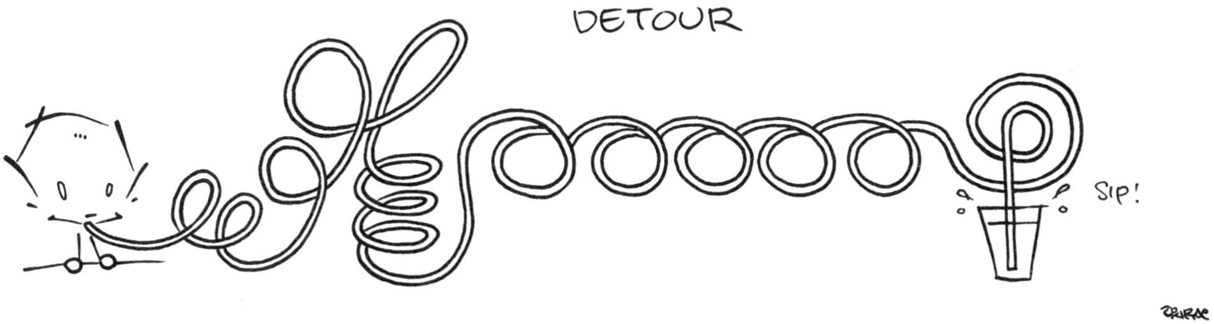
DETOUR
SIP!

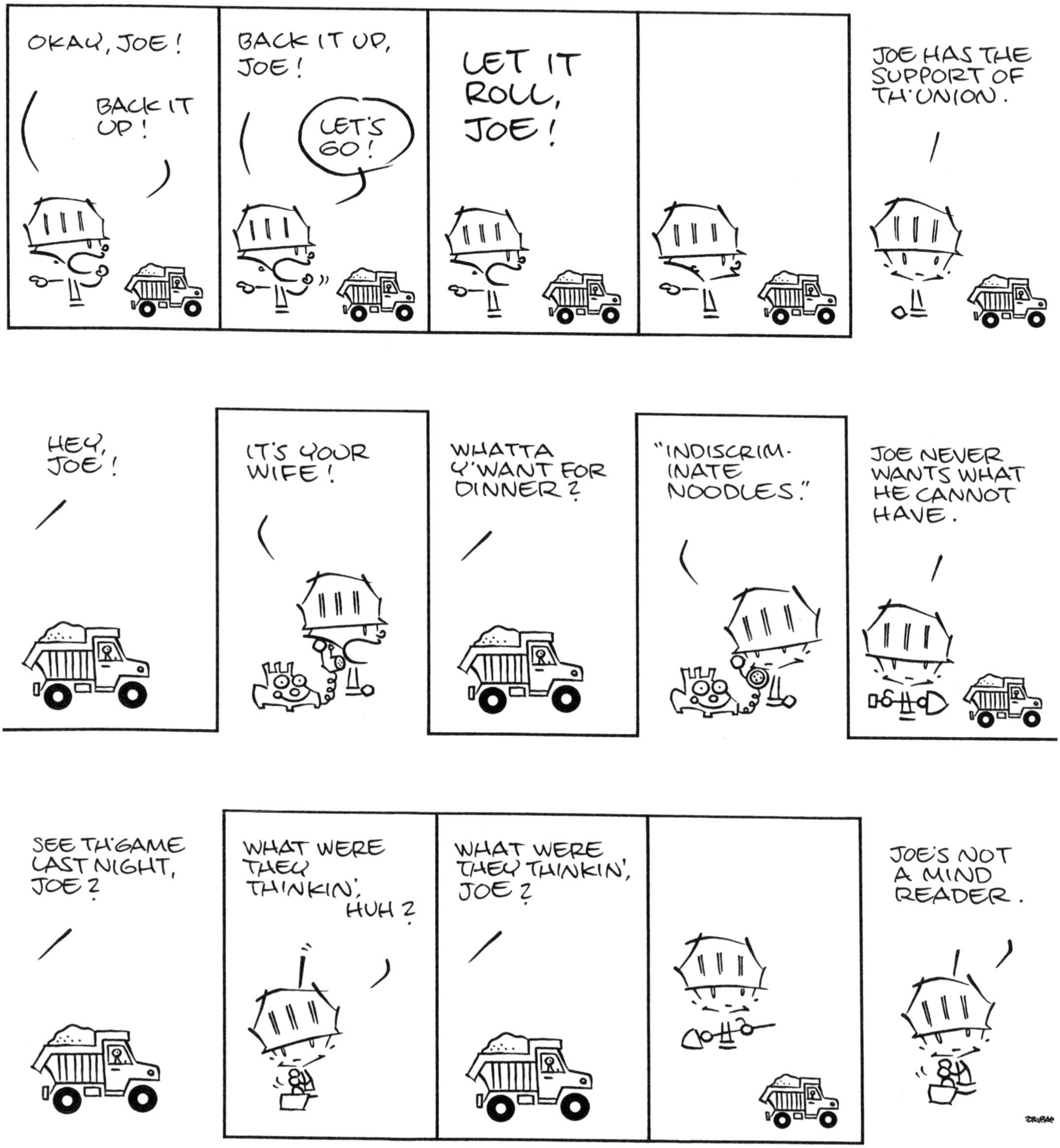
OKAY, JOE!
BACK IT UP!
BACK IT UP, JOE!
LET'S GO!
LET IT ROLL, JOE!
JOE HAS THE SUPPORT OF TH'UNION.
HEY, JOE!
IT'S YOUR WIFE!
WHATTA Y'WANT FOR DINNER?
"INDISCRIMINATE NOODLES."
JOE NEVER WANTS WHAT HE CANNOT HAVE.
SEE TH'GAME LAST NIGHT, JOE?
WHAT WERE THEY THINKIN',
HUH?
WHAT WERE THEY THINKIN', JOE?
JOE'S NOT A MIND READER.

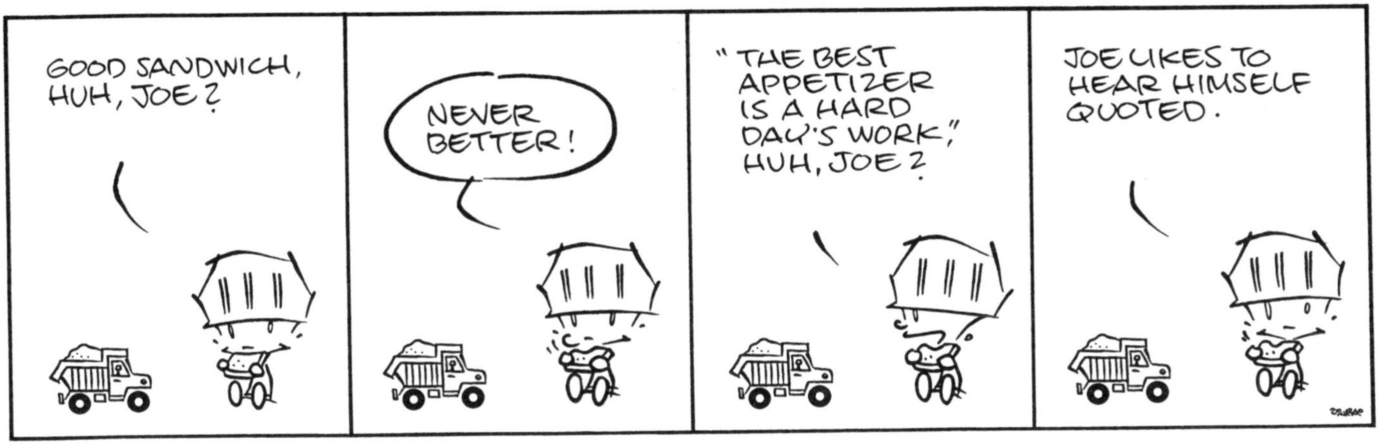
GOOD SANDWICH, HUH, JOE?
NEVER BETTER!
"THE BEST APPETIZER IS A HARD DAY'S WORK," HUH, JOE?
JOE LIKES TO HEAR HIMSELF QUOTED.

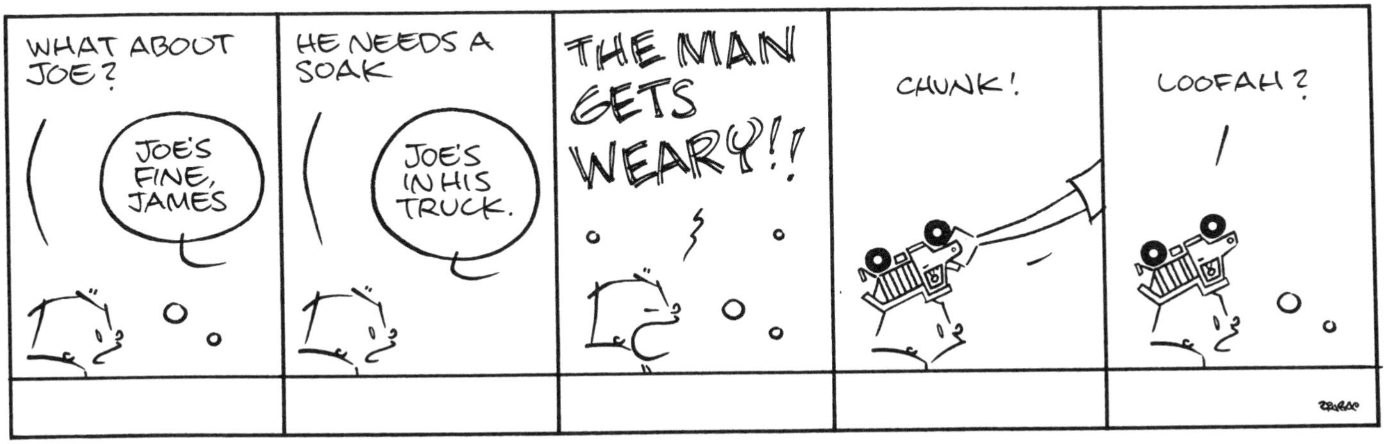
WHAT ABOUT JOE?
JOE'S FINE, JAMES
HE NEEDS A SOAK
JOE'S IN HIS TRUCK.
THE MAN GETS WEARY!!
CHUNK!
LOOFAH?

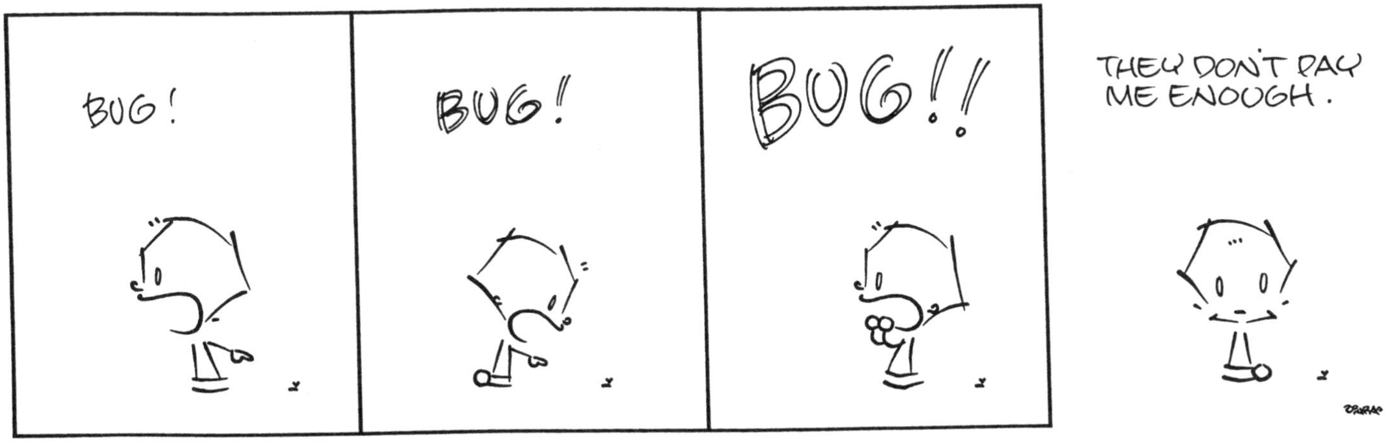
BUG!
BUG!
BUG!!
THEY DON'T PAY ME ENOUGH.

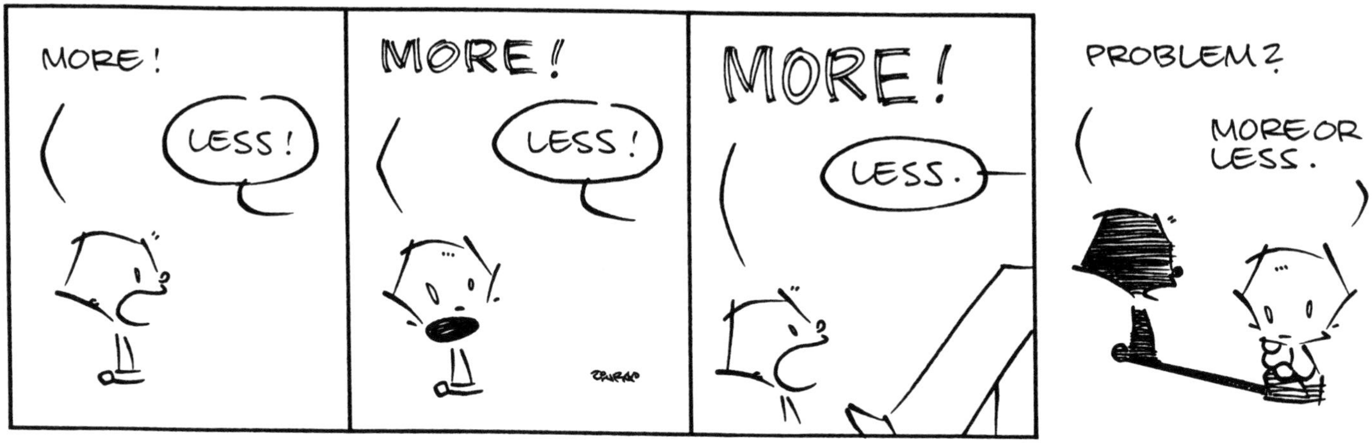
MORE!
LESS!
MORE!
LESS!
MORE!
LESS.
PROBLEM?
MORE OR LESS.

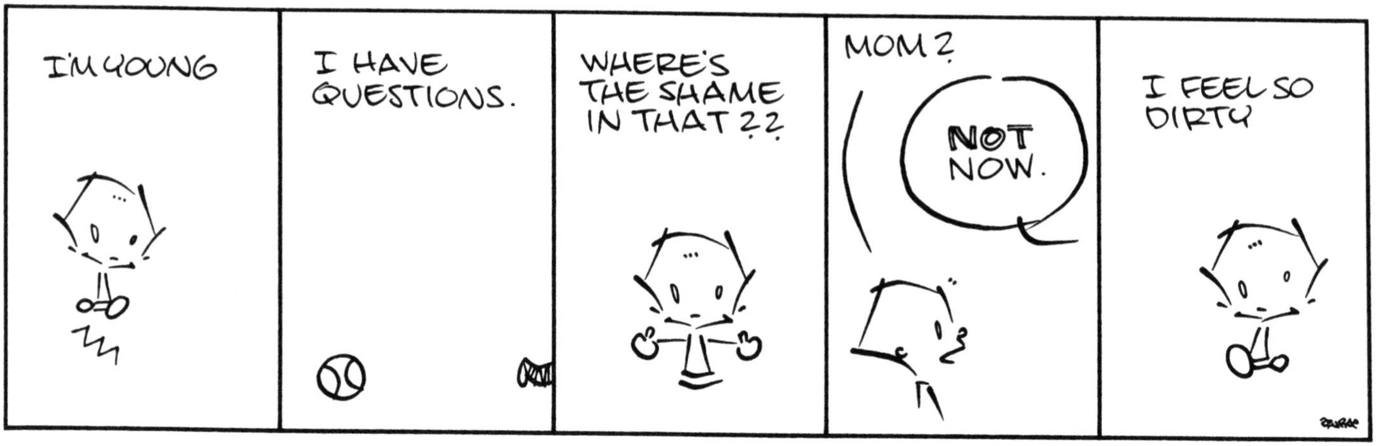
I'M YOUNG
I HAVE QUESTIONS.
WHERE'S THE SHAME IN THAT??
MOM?
NOT NOW.
I FEEL SO DIRTY

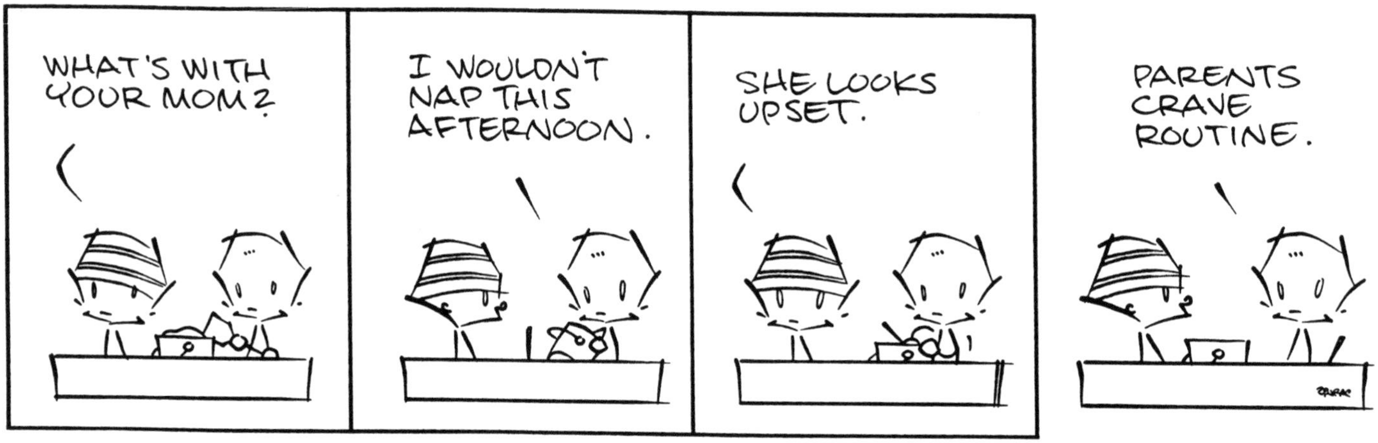
WHAT'S WITH YOUR MOM?
I WOULDN'T NAP THIS AFTERNOON.
SHE LOOKS UPSET.
PARENTS CRAVE ROUTINE.

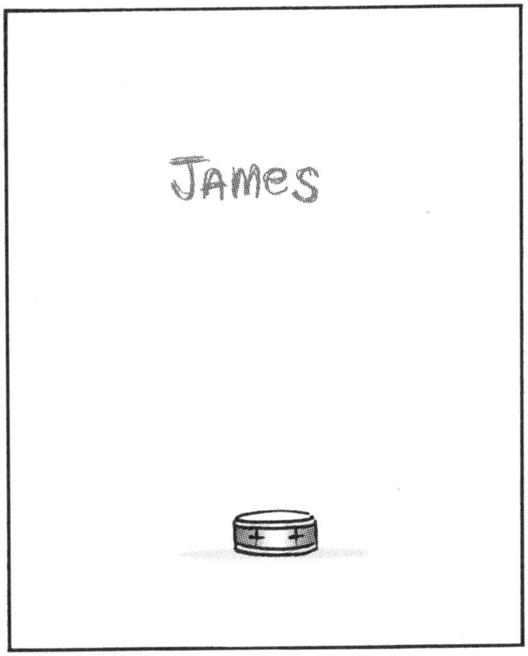
JAMES

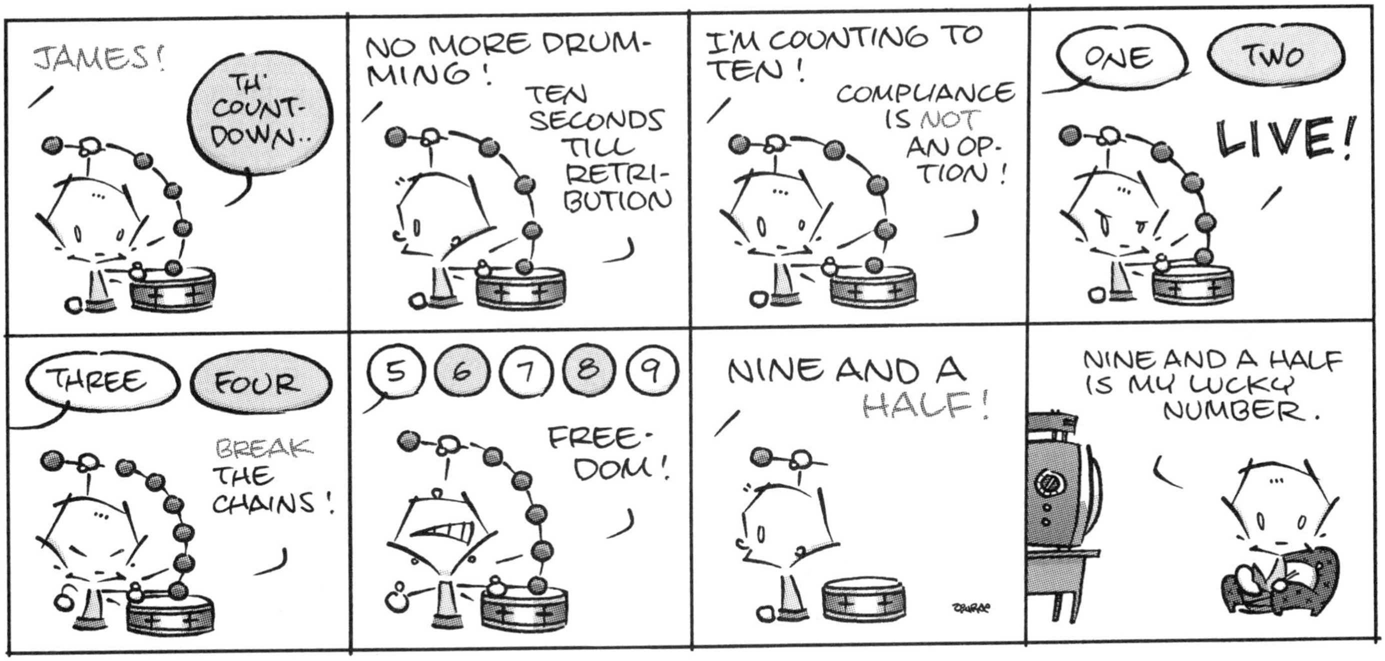
JAMES!
TH' COUNT-DOWN..
NO MORE DRUMMING!
TEN SECONDS TILL RETRIBUTION
I'M COUNTING TO TEN!
COMPLIANCE IS NOT AN OPTION!
ONE
TWO
LIVE!
THREE
FOUR
BREAK THE CHAINS!
5
6
7
8
9
FREEDOM!
NINE AND A HALF!
NINE AND A HALF IS MY LUCKY NUMBER.

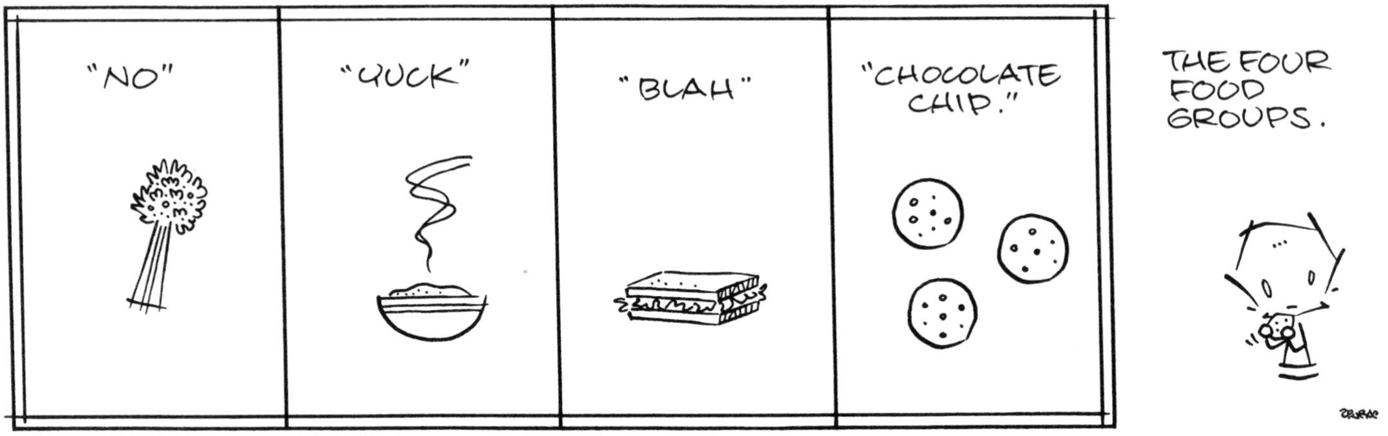
"NO"
"YUCK"
"BLAH"
"CHOCOLATE CHIP."
THE FOUR FOOD GROUPS.

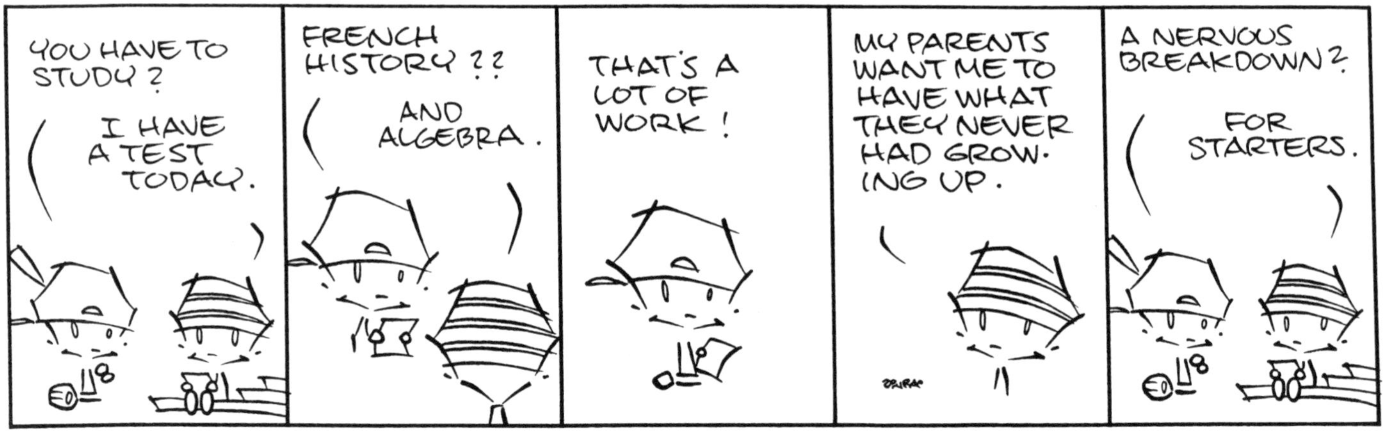
YOU HAVE TO STUDY?
I HAVE A TEST TODAY.
FRENCH HISTORY??
AND ALGEBRA.
THAT'S A LOT OF WORK!
MY PARENTS WANT ME TO HAVE WHAT THEY NEVER HAD GROWING UP.
A NERVOUS BREAKDOWN?
FOR STARTERS.

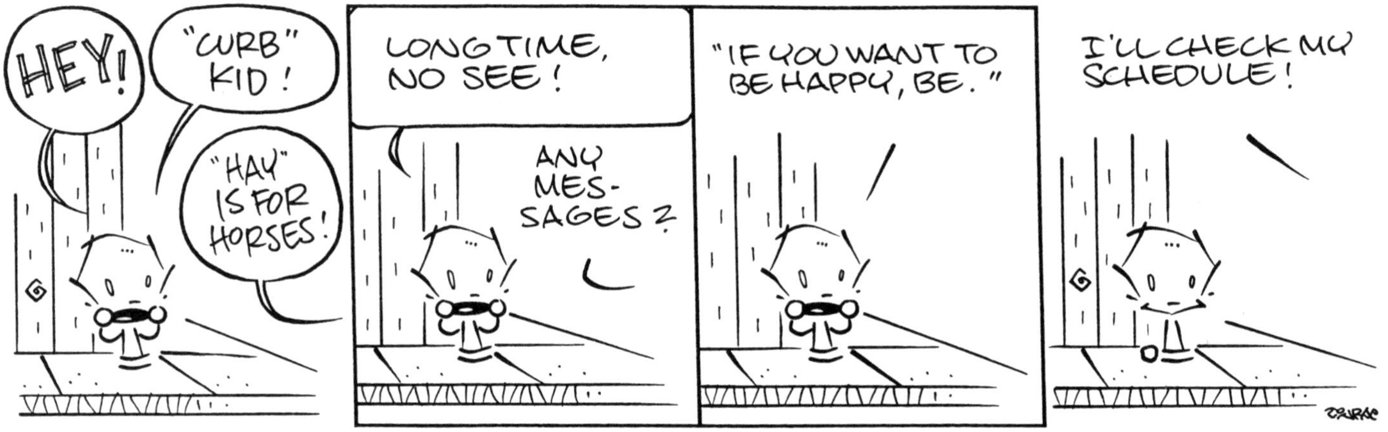
HEY!
"CURB" KID!
"HAY" IS FOR HORSES!
LONG TIME, NO SEE!
ANY MESSAGES?
"IF YOU WANT TO BE HAPPY, BE."
I'LL CHECK MY SCHEDULE!

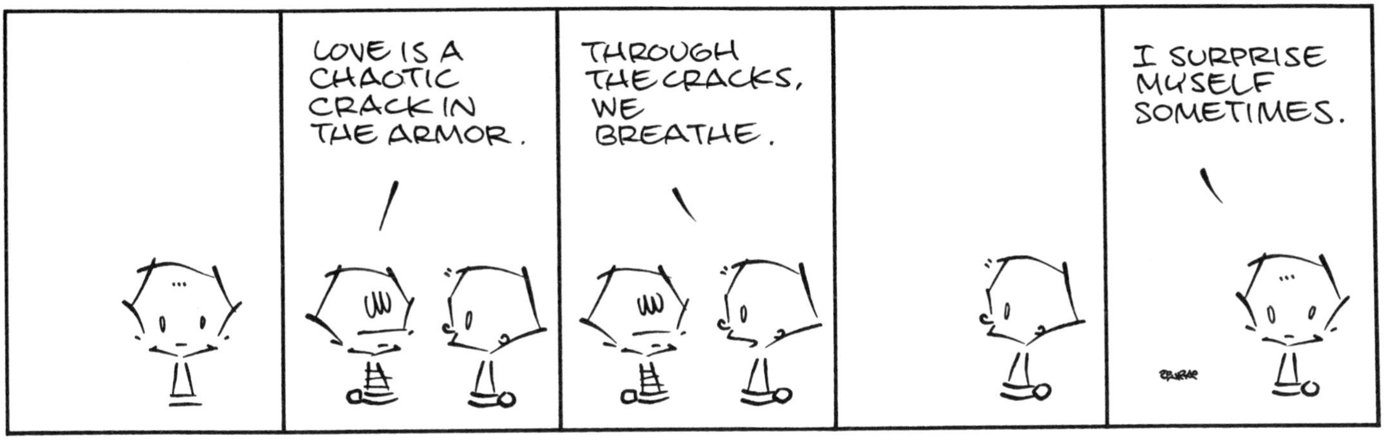
LOVE IS A CHAOTIC CRACK IN THE ARMOR.
THROUGH THE CRACKS, WE BREATHE.
I SURPRISE MYSELF SOMETIMES.

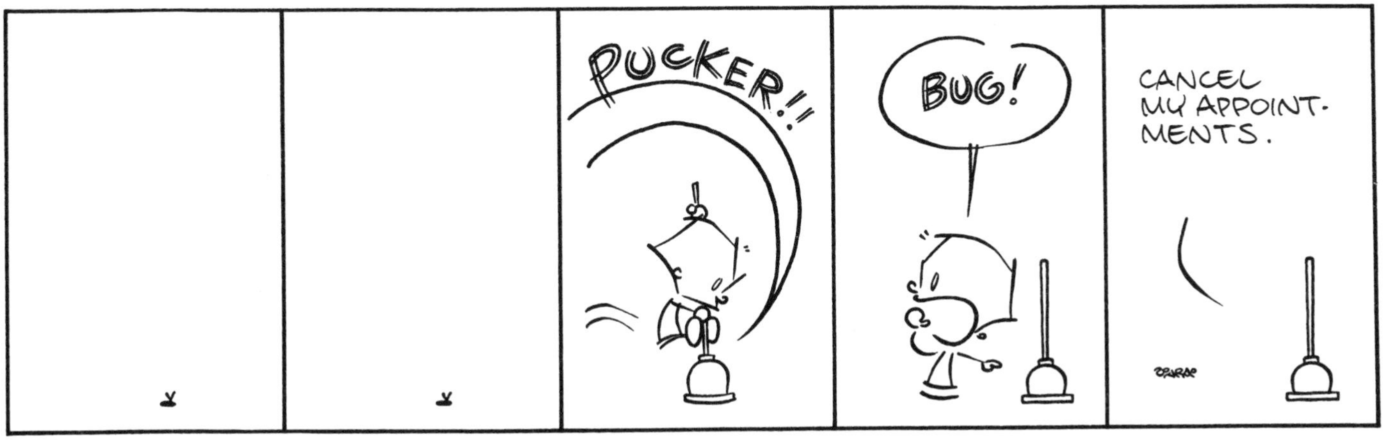
PUCKER!!
BUG!
CANCEL MY APPOINT-MENTS.

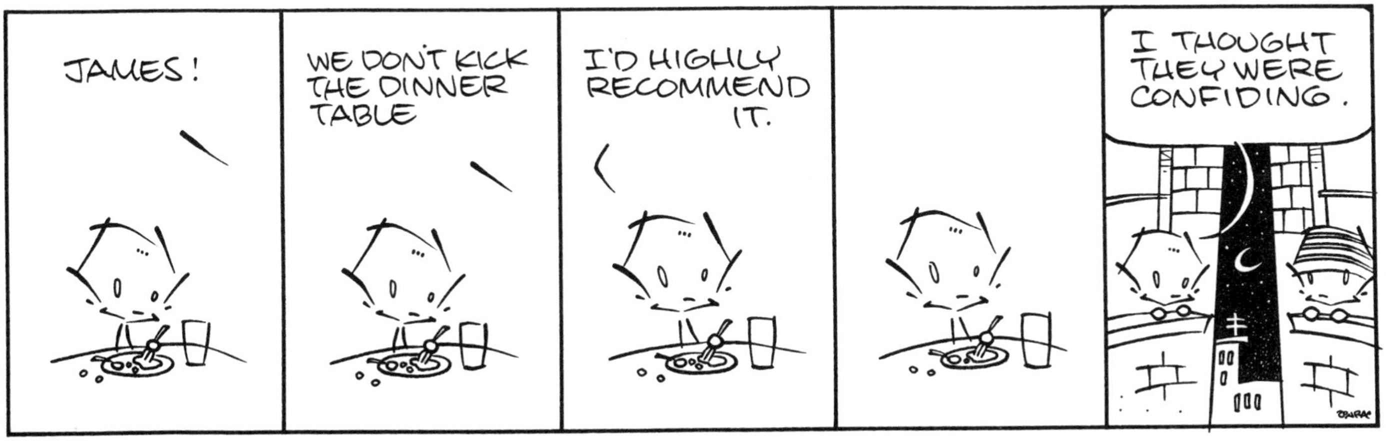
JAMES!
WE DON'T KICK THE DINNER TABLE
I'D HIGHLY RECOMMEND IT.
I THOUGHT THEY WERE CONFIDING.

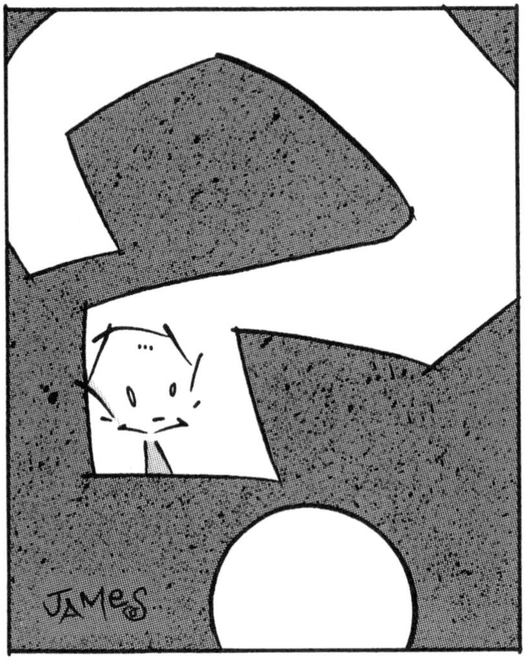
JAMES

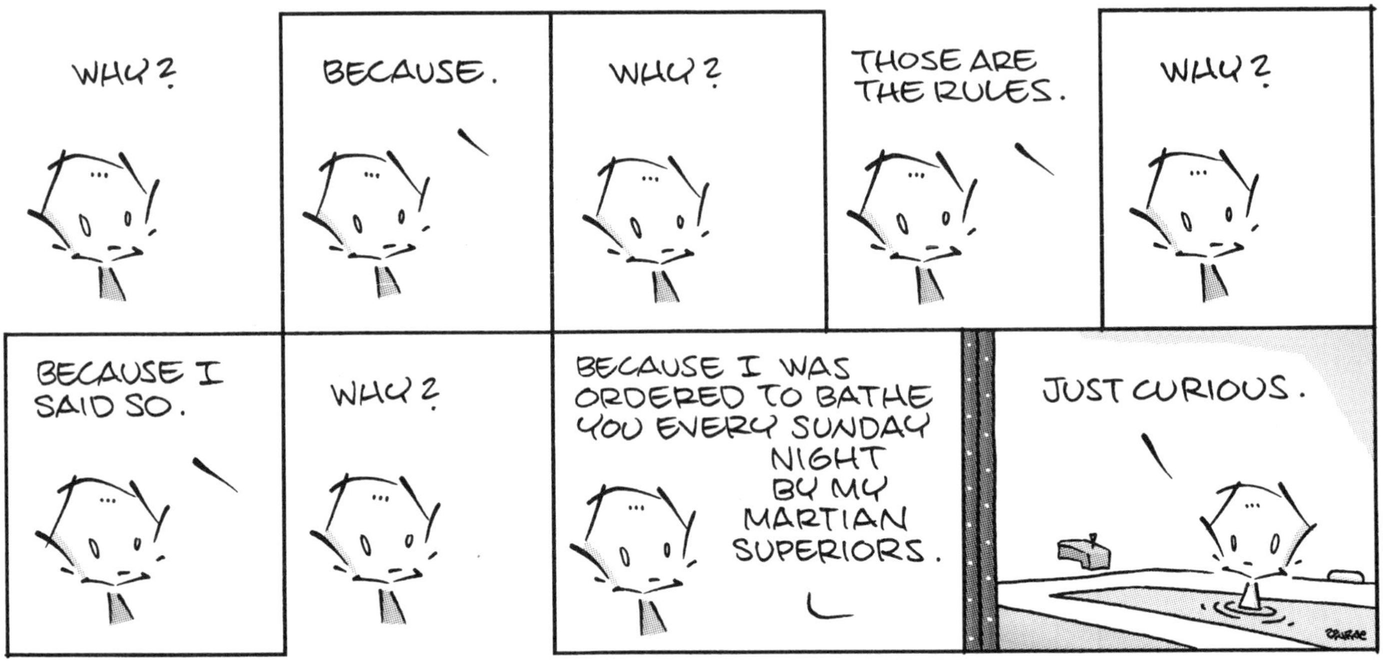
WHY?
BECAUSE.
WHY?
THOSE ARE THE RULES.
WHY?
BECAUSE I SAID SO.
WHY?
BECAUSE I WAS ORDERED TO BATHE YOU EVERY SUNDAY NIGHT BY MY MARTIAN SUPERIORS.
JUST CURIOUS.

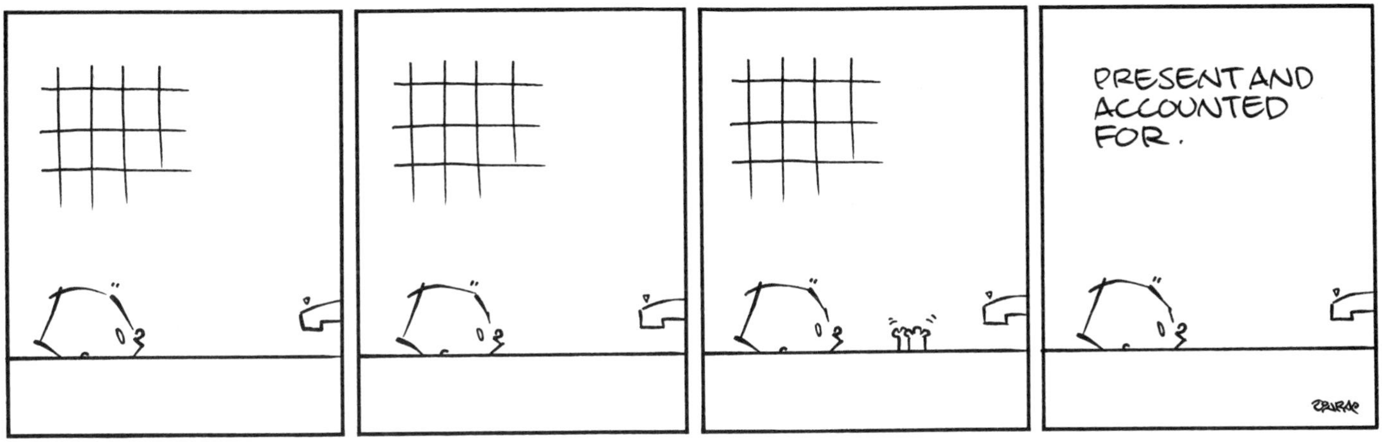
PRESENT AND ACCOUNTED FOR.

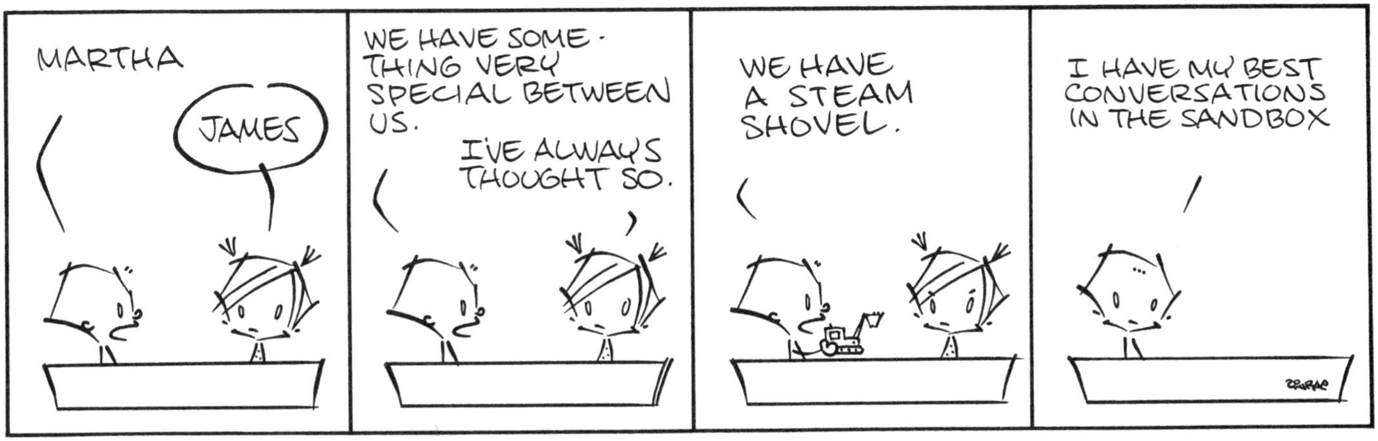
MARTHA
JAMES
WE HAVE SOME-THING VERY SPECIAL BETWEEN US.
I'VE ALWAYS THOUGHT SO.
WE HAVE A STEAM SHOVEL.
I HAVE MY BEST CONVERSATIONS IN THE SANDBOX

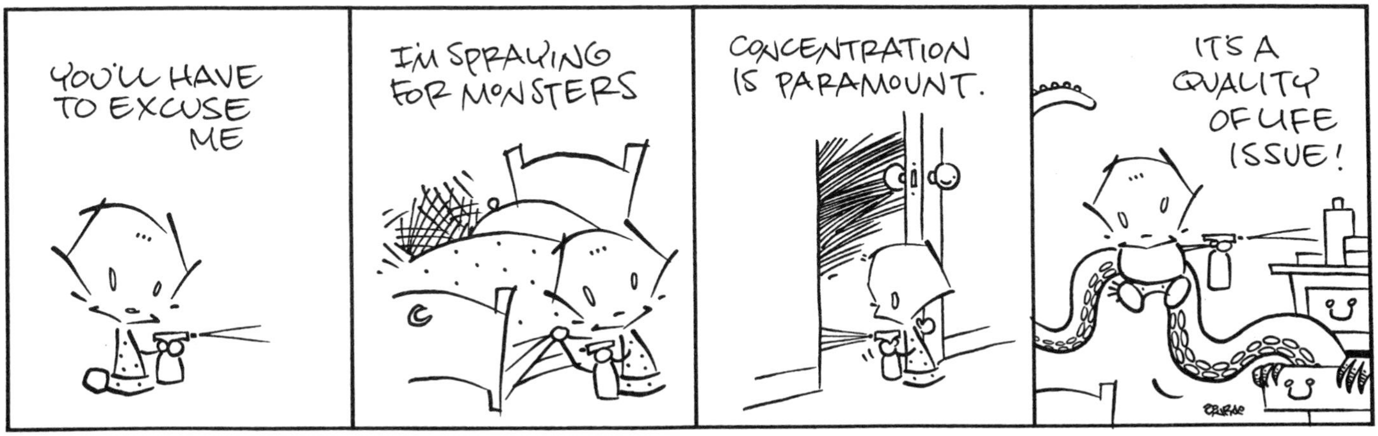
YOU'LL HAVE TO EXCUSE ME
I'M SPRAYING FOR MONSTERS
CONCENTRATION IS PARAMOUNT.
IT'S A QUALITY OF LIFE ISSUE!

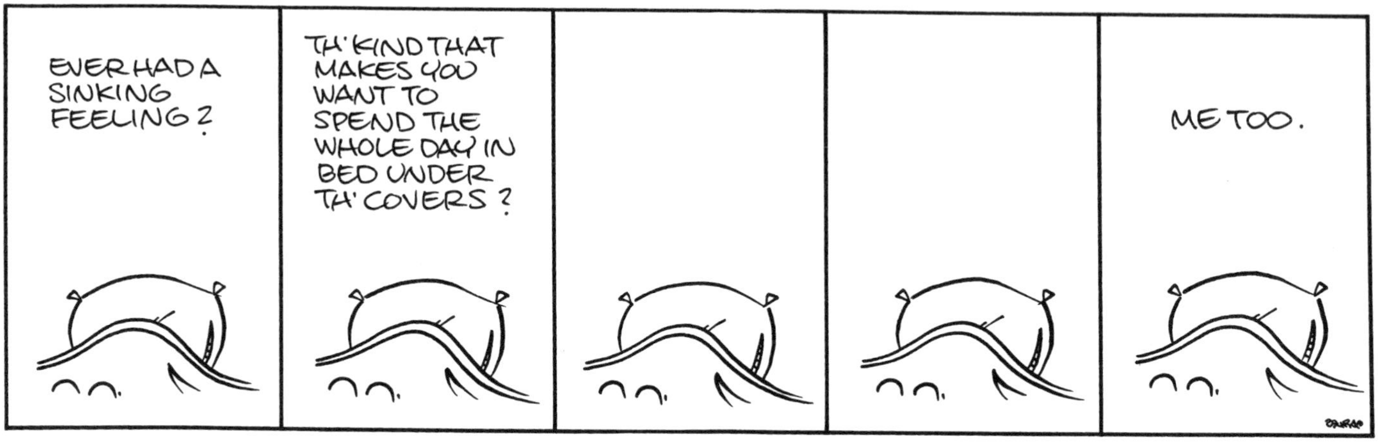
EVER HAD A SINKING FEELING?
TH' KIND THAT MAKES YOU WANT TO SPEND THE WHOLE DAY IN BED UNDER TH' COVERS?
ME TOO.

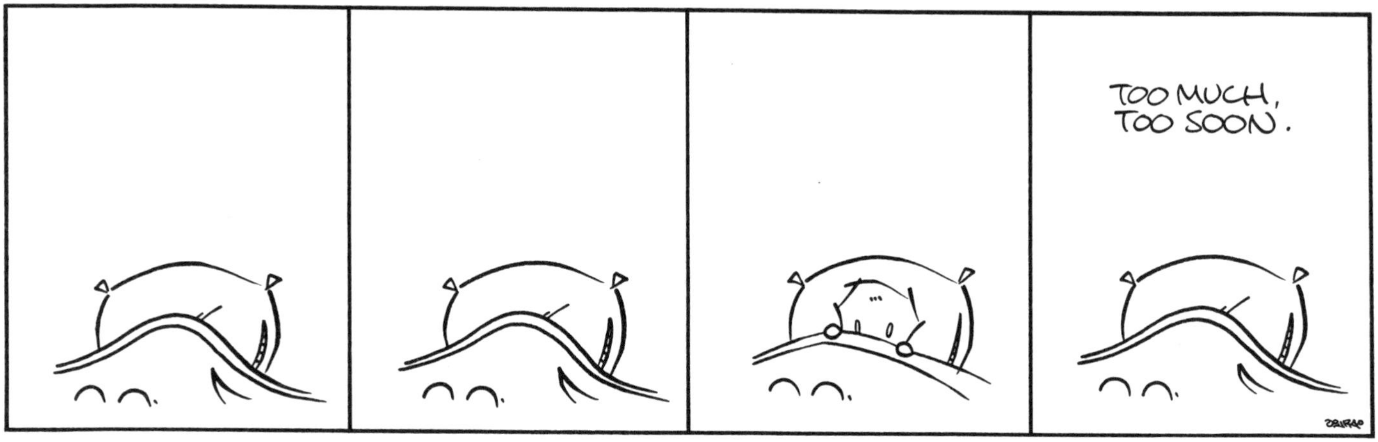
TOO MUCH, TOO SOON.

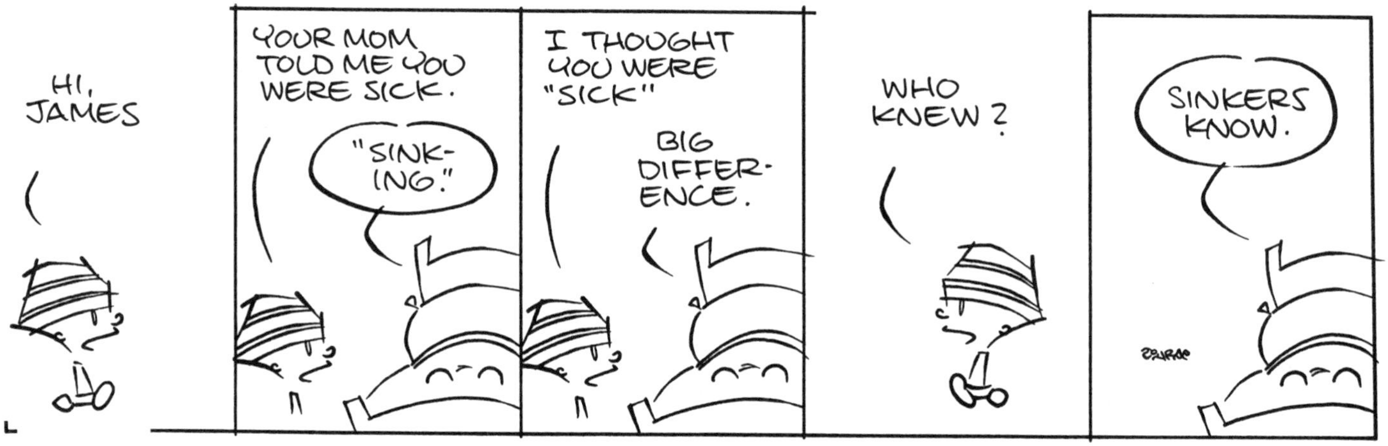
HI, JAMES
YOUR MOM TOLD ME YOU WERE SICK.
"SINK-ING."
I THOUGHT YOU WERE "SICK"
BIG DIFFER-ENCE.
WHO KNEW?
SINKERS KNOW.

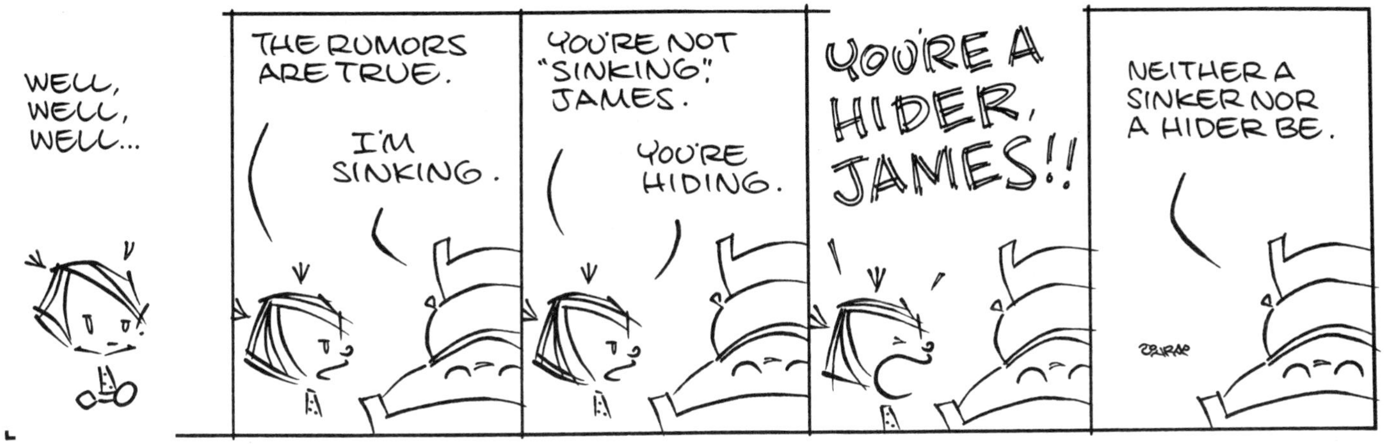
WELL, WELL, WELL...
THE RUMORS ARE TRUE.
I'M SINKING.
YOU'RE NOT "SINKING," JAMES.
YOU'RE HIDING.
YOU'RE A HIDER, JAMES!!
NEITHER A SINKER NOR A HIDER BE.

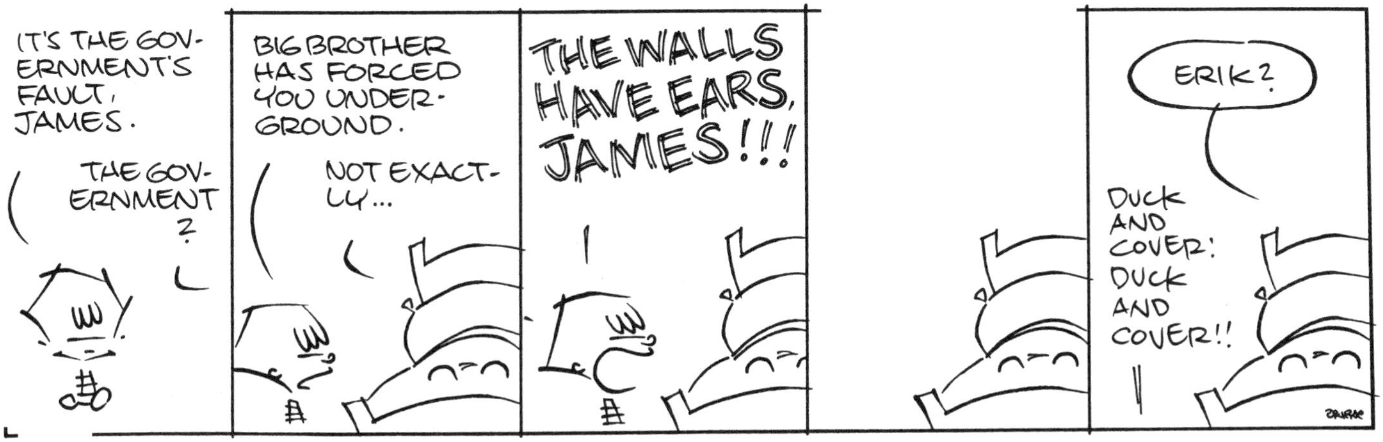
IT'S THE GOVERNMENT'S FAULT, JAMES.
THE GOVERNMENT?
BIG BROTHER HAS FORCED YOU UNDERGROUND.
NOT EXACTLY...
THE WALLS HAVE EARS, JAMES!!!
ERIK?
DUCK AND COVER! DUCK AND COVER!!

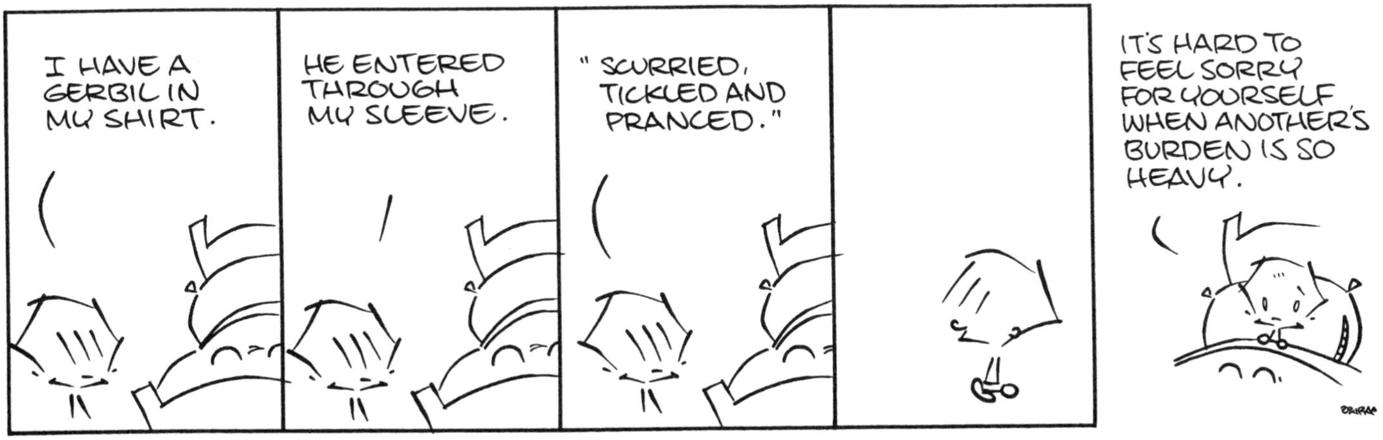
I HAVE A GERBIL IN MY SHIRT.
HE ENTERED THROUGH MY SLEEVE.
"SCURRIED, TICKLED AND PRANCED."
IT'S HARD TO FEEL SORRY FOR YOURSELF WHEN ANOTHER'S BURDEN IS SO HEAVY.

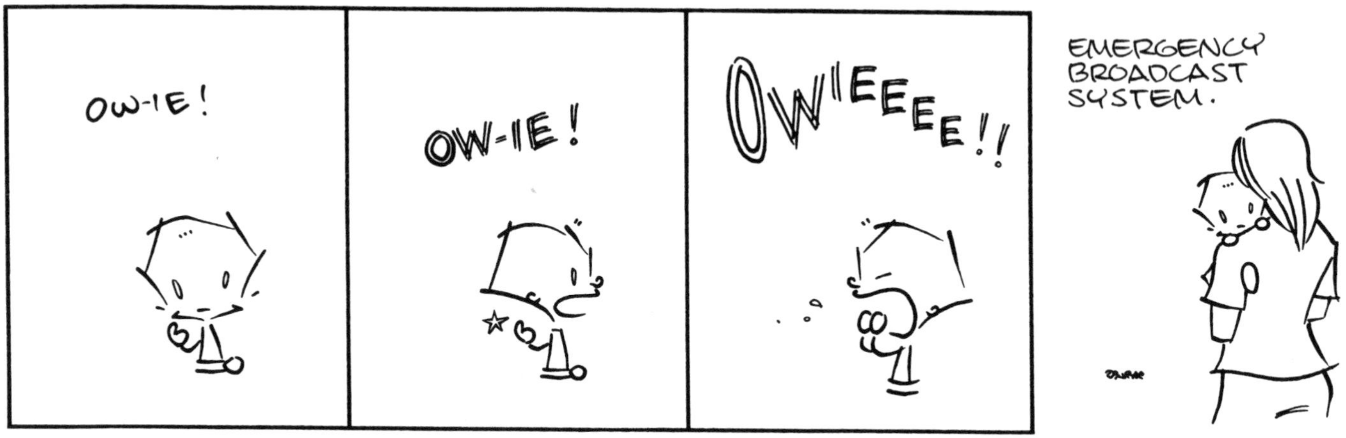
OW-IE!
OW-IE!
OWIEEEEE!!
EMERGENCY BROADCAST SYSTEM.

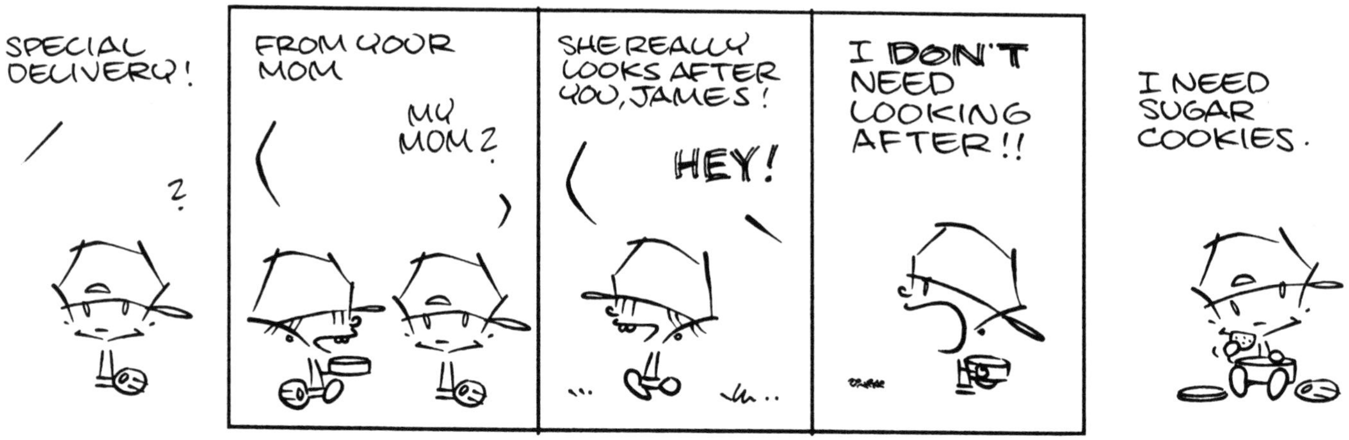
SPECIAL DELIVERY!
?
FROM YOUR MOM
MY MOM?
SHE REALLY LOOKS AFTER YOU, JAMES!
HEY!
I DON'T NEED LOOKING AFTER!!
I NEED SUGAR COOKIES.

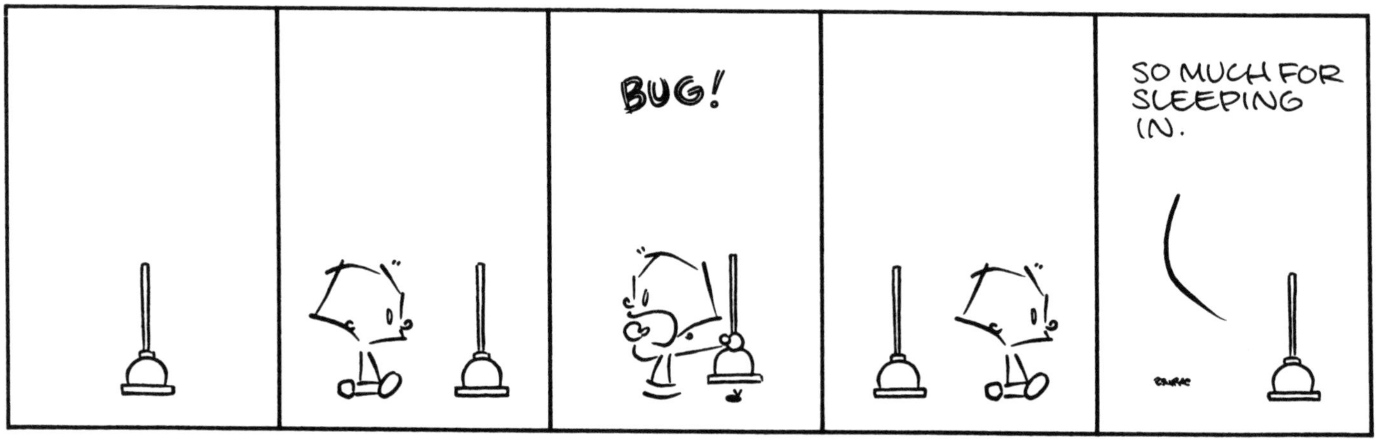
BUG!
SO MUCH FOR SLEEPING IN.

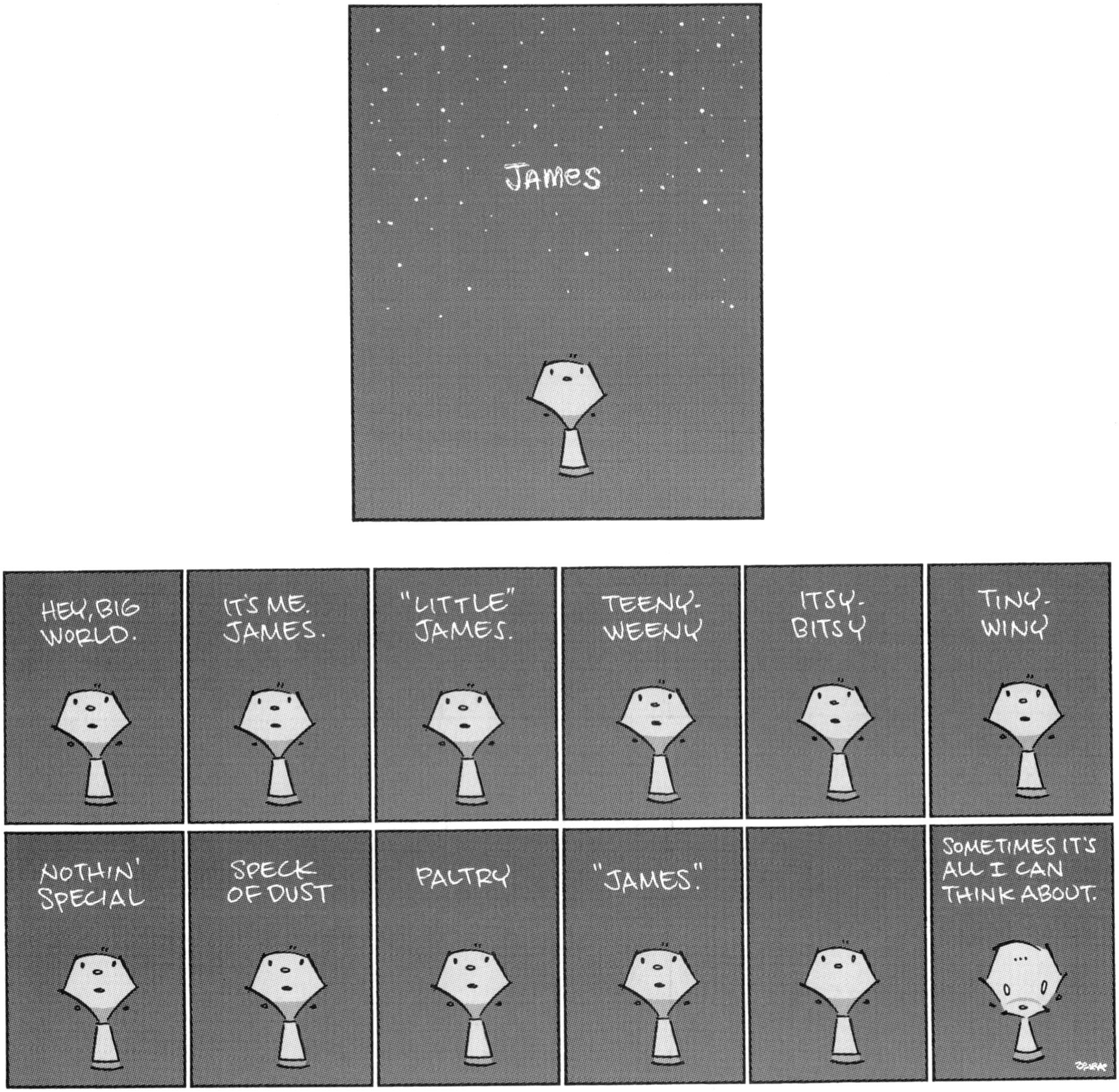
JAMES
HEY, BIG WORLD.
IT'S ME. JAMES.
"LITTLE" JAMES.
TEENY-WEENY
ITSY-BITSY
TINY-WINY
NOTHIN' SPECIAL
SPECK OF DUST
PALTRY
"JAMES."
SOMETIMES IT'S ALL I CAN THINK ABOUT.

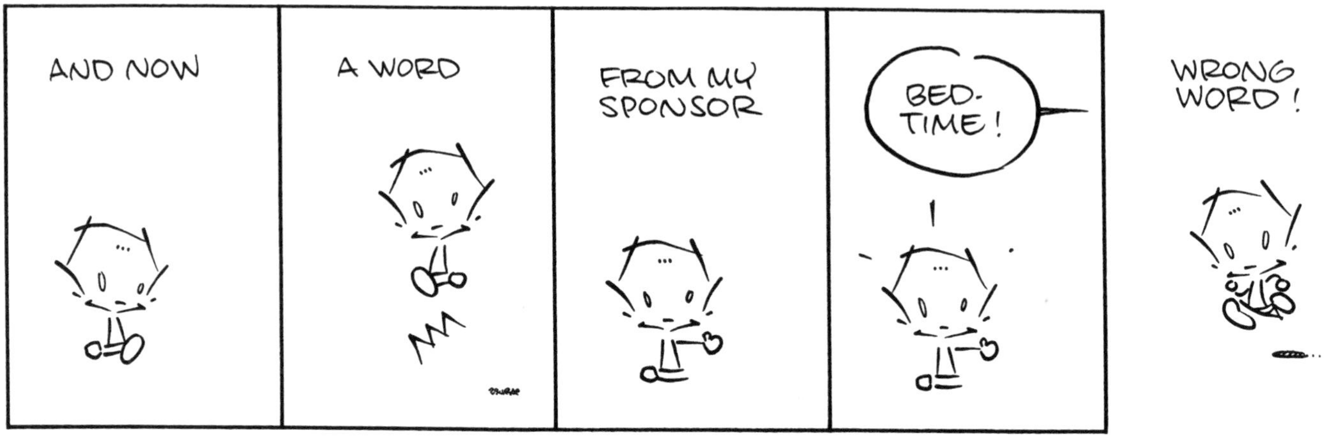
AND NOW
A WORD
FROM MY SPONSOR
BED-TIME!
WRONG WORD!

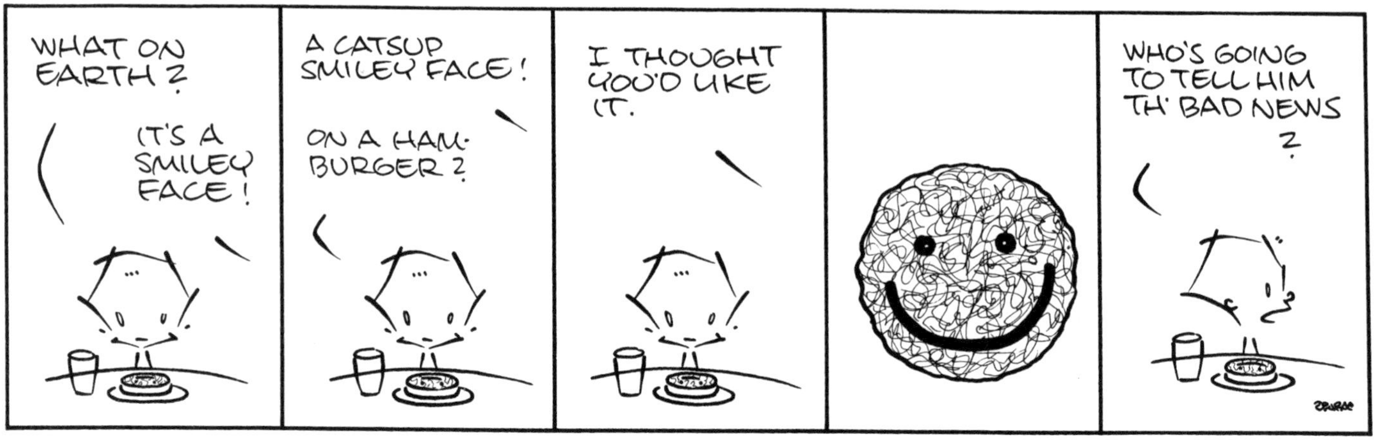
WHAT ON EARTH?
IT'S A SMILEY FACE!
A CATSUP SMILEY FACE!
ON A HAM-BURGER?
I THOUGHT YOU'D LIKE IT.
WHO'S GOING TO TELL HIM TH' BAD NEWS?

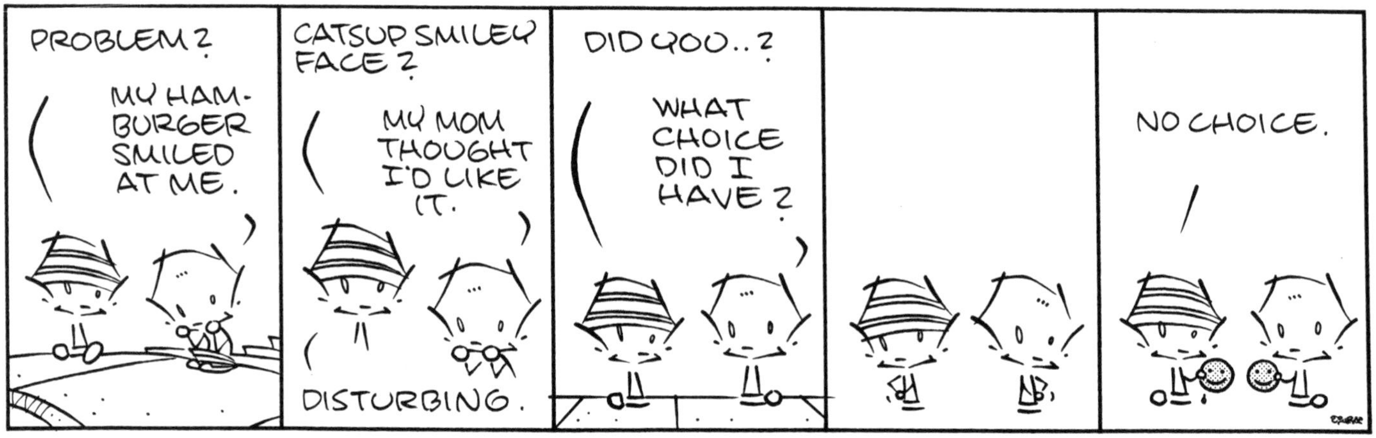
PROBLEM?
MY HAM-BURGER SMILED AT ME.
CATSUP SMILEY FACE?
MY MOM THOUGHT I'D LIKE IT.
DISTURBING.
DID YOU..?
WHAT CHOICE DID I HAVE?
NO CHOICE.

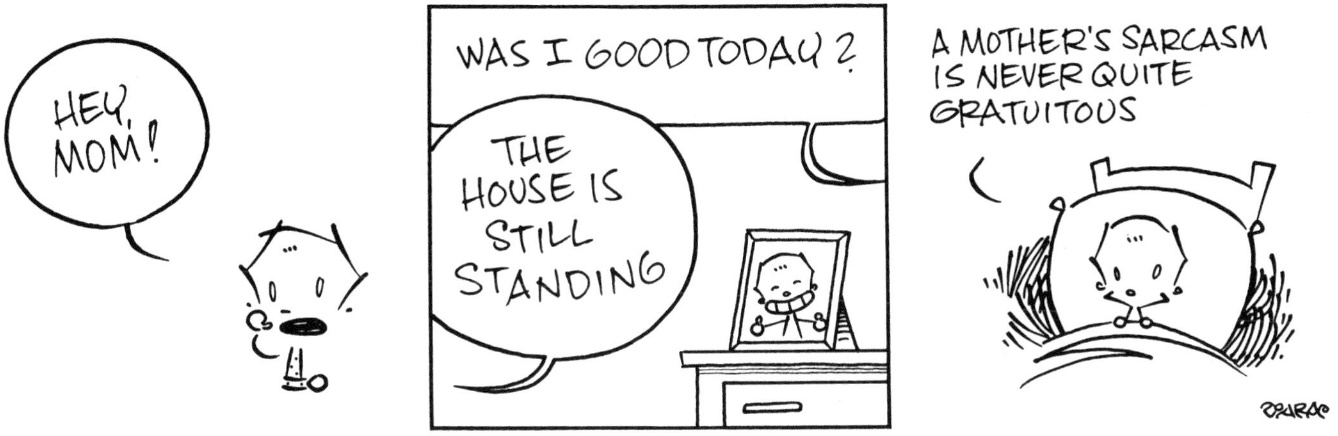
HEY, MOM!
WAS I GOOD TODAY?
THE HOUSE IS STILL STANDING
A MOTHER'S SARCASM IS NEVER QUITE GRATUITOUS

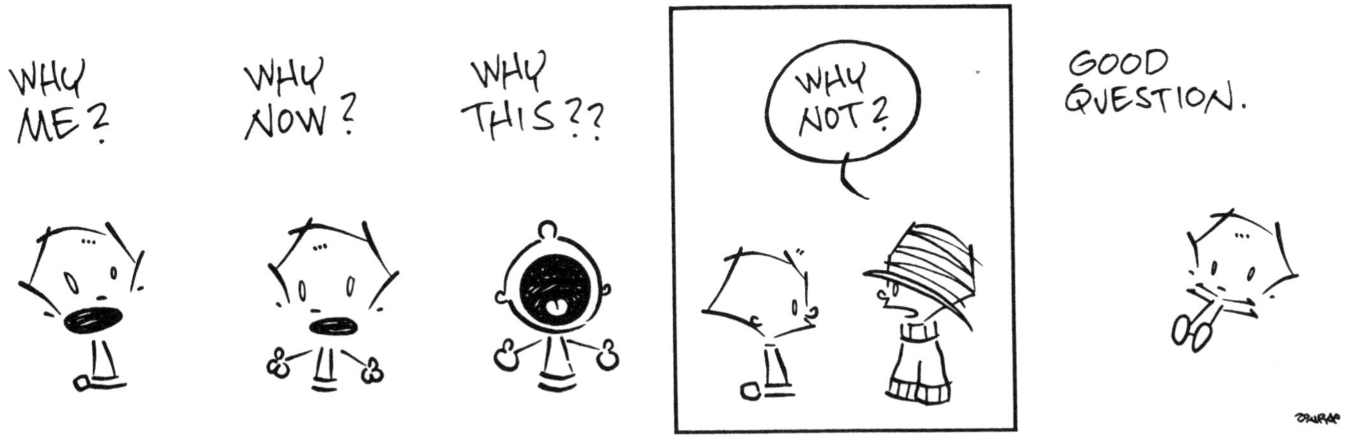
WHY ME?
WHY NOW?
WHY THIS??
WHY NOT?
GOOD QUESTION.

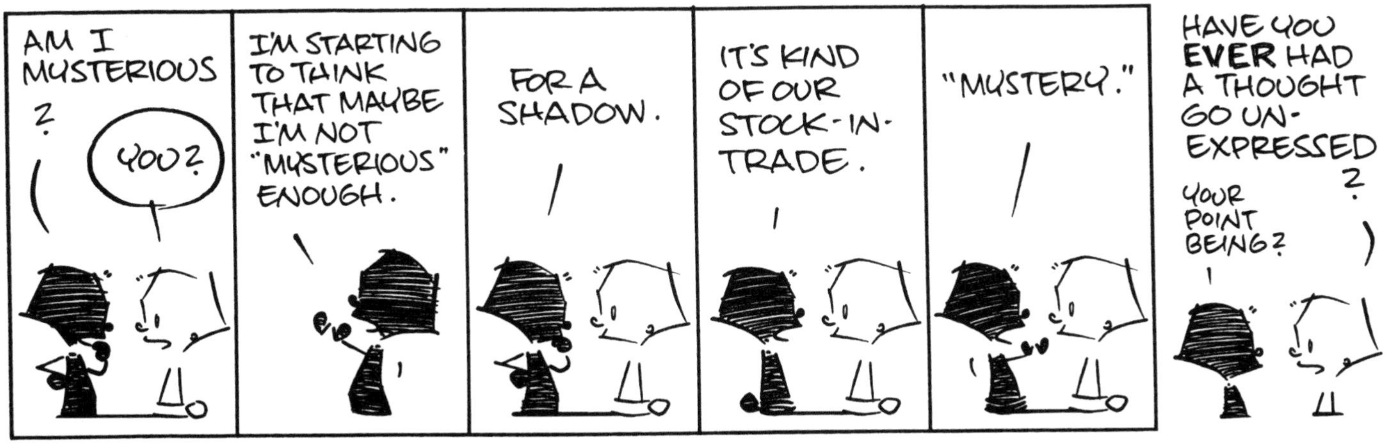
AM I MYSTERIOUS?
YOU?
I'M STARTING TO THINK THAT MAYBE I'M NOT "MYSTERIOUS" ENOUGH.
FOR A SHADOW.
IT'S KIND OF OUR STOCK-IN-TRADE.
"MYSTERY."
HAVE YOU **EVER** HAD A THOUGHT GO UN-EXPRESSED?
YOUR POINT BEING?

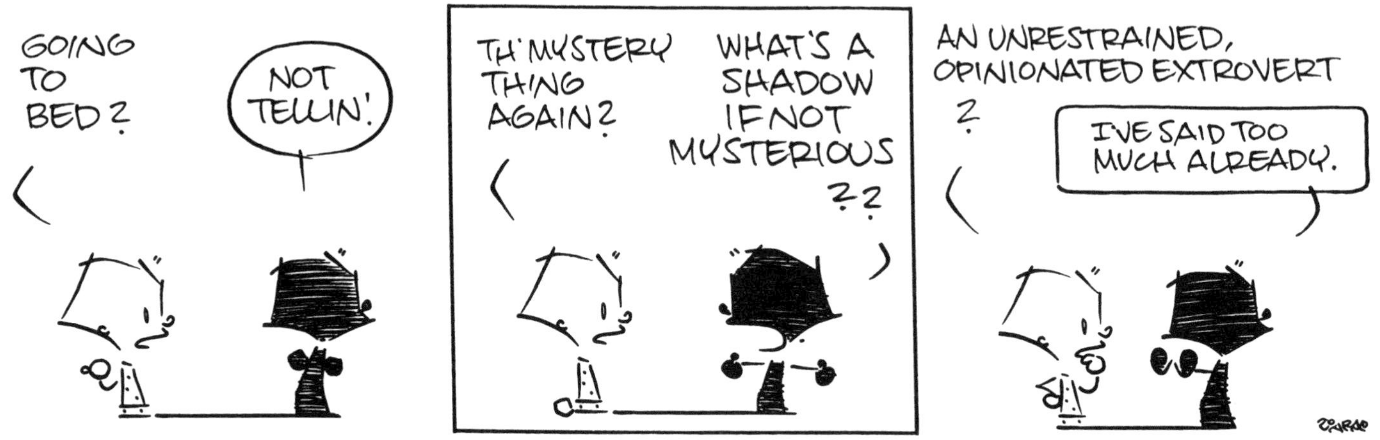
GOING TO BED?
NOT TELLIN'!
TH' MYSTERY THING AGAIN?
WHAT'S A SHADOW IF NOT MYSTERIOUS??
AN UNRESTRAINED, OPINIONATED EXTROVERT?
I'VE SAID TOO MUCH ALREADY.

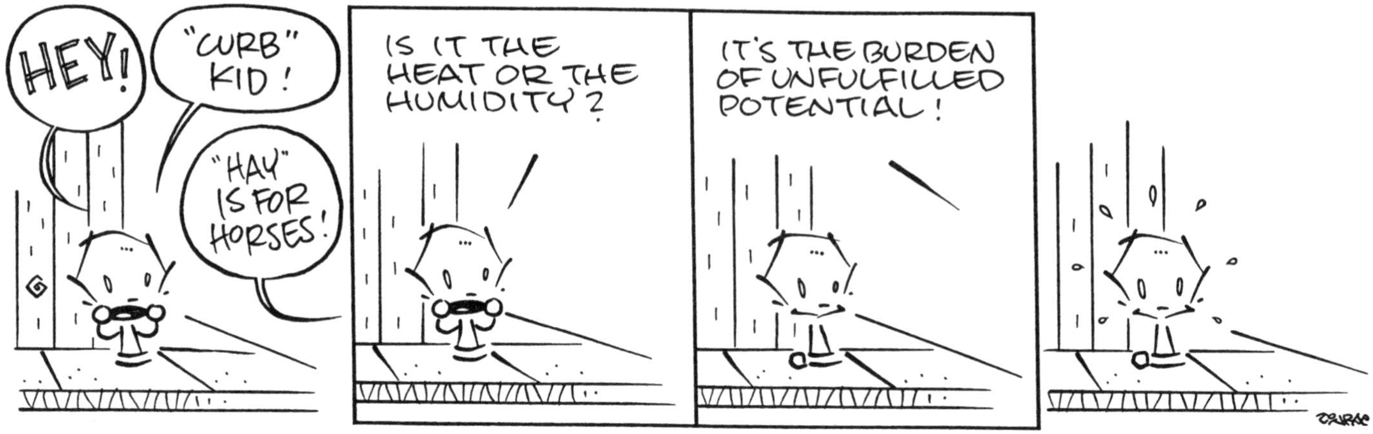
HEY!
"CURB" KID!
"HAY" IS FOR HORSES!
IS IT THE HEAT OR THE HUMIDITY?
IT'S THE BURDEN OF UNFULFILLED POTENTIAL!

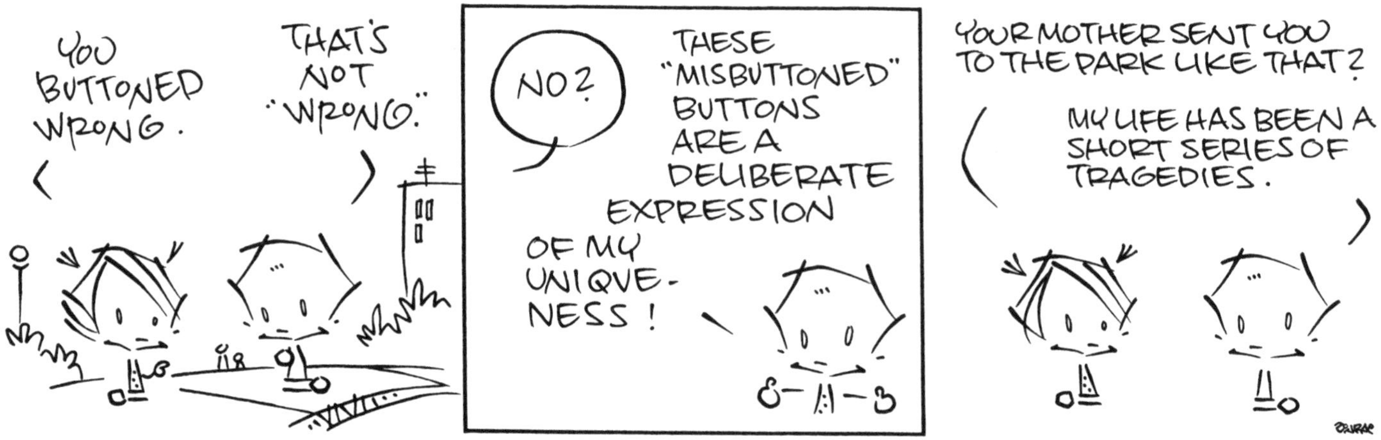
YOU BUTTONED WRONG.
THAT'S NOT "WRONG."
NO?
THESE "MISBUTTONED" BUTTONS ARE A DELIBERATE EXPRESSION OF MY UNIQUENESS!
YOUR MOTHER SENT YOU TO THE PARK LIKE THAT?
MY LIFE HAS BEEN A SHORT SERIES OF TRAGEDIES.

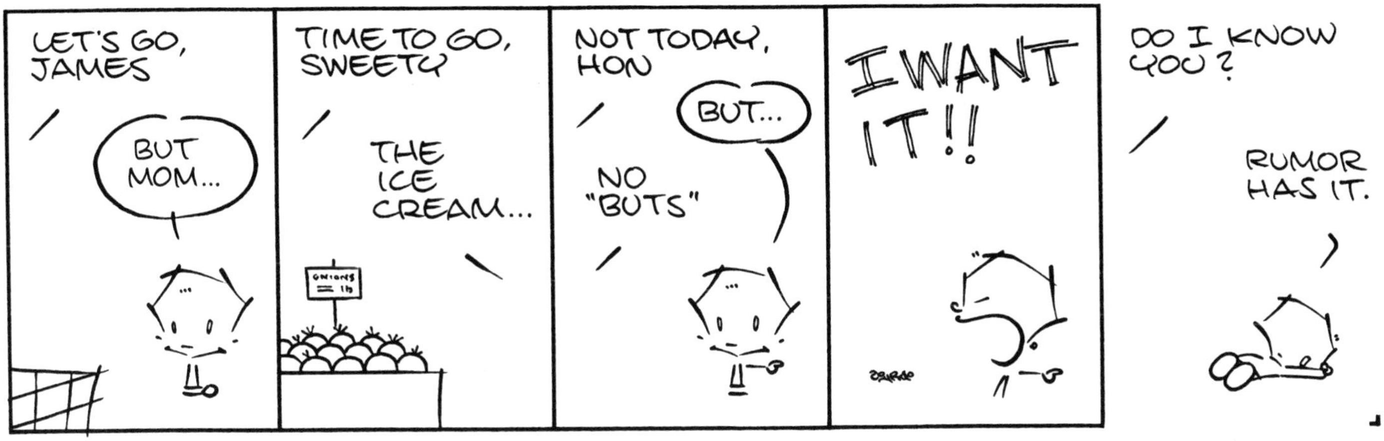
LET'S GO, JAMES
BUT MOM...
TIME TO GO, SWEETY
THE ICE CREAM...
ONIONS = 1lb
NOT TODAY, HON
BUT...
NO "BUTS"
I WANT IT!!
DO I KNOW YOU?
RUMOR HAS IT.

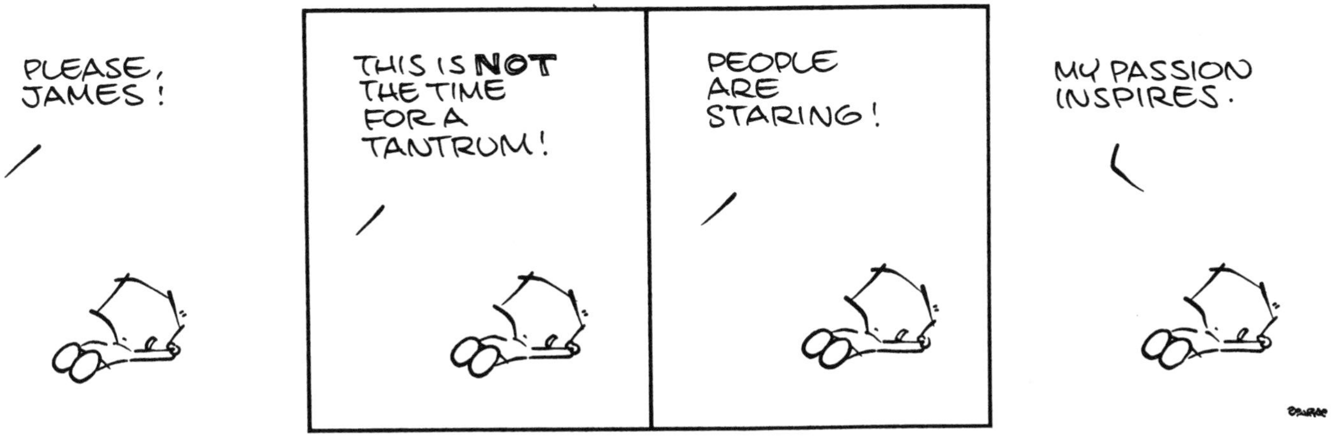
PLEASE, JAMES!
THIS IS NOT THE TIME FOR A TANTRUM!
PEOPLE ARE STARING!
MY PASSION INSPIRES.

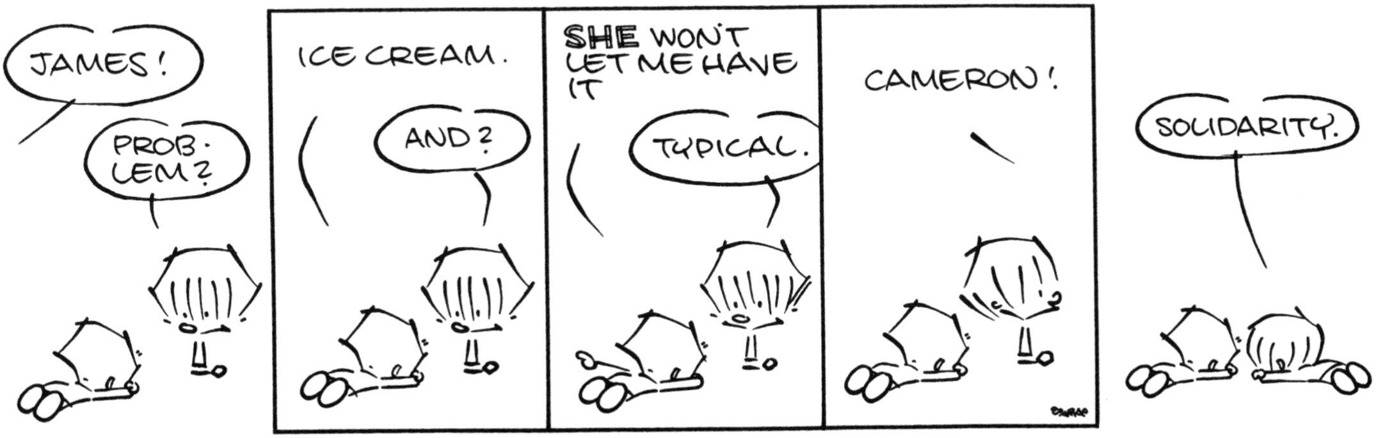
JAMES!
PROB-LEM?
ICE CREAM.
AND?
SHE WON'T LET ME HAVE IT
TYPICAL.
CAMERON!
SOLIDARITY.

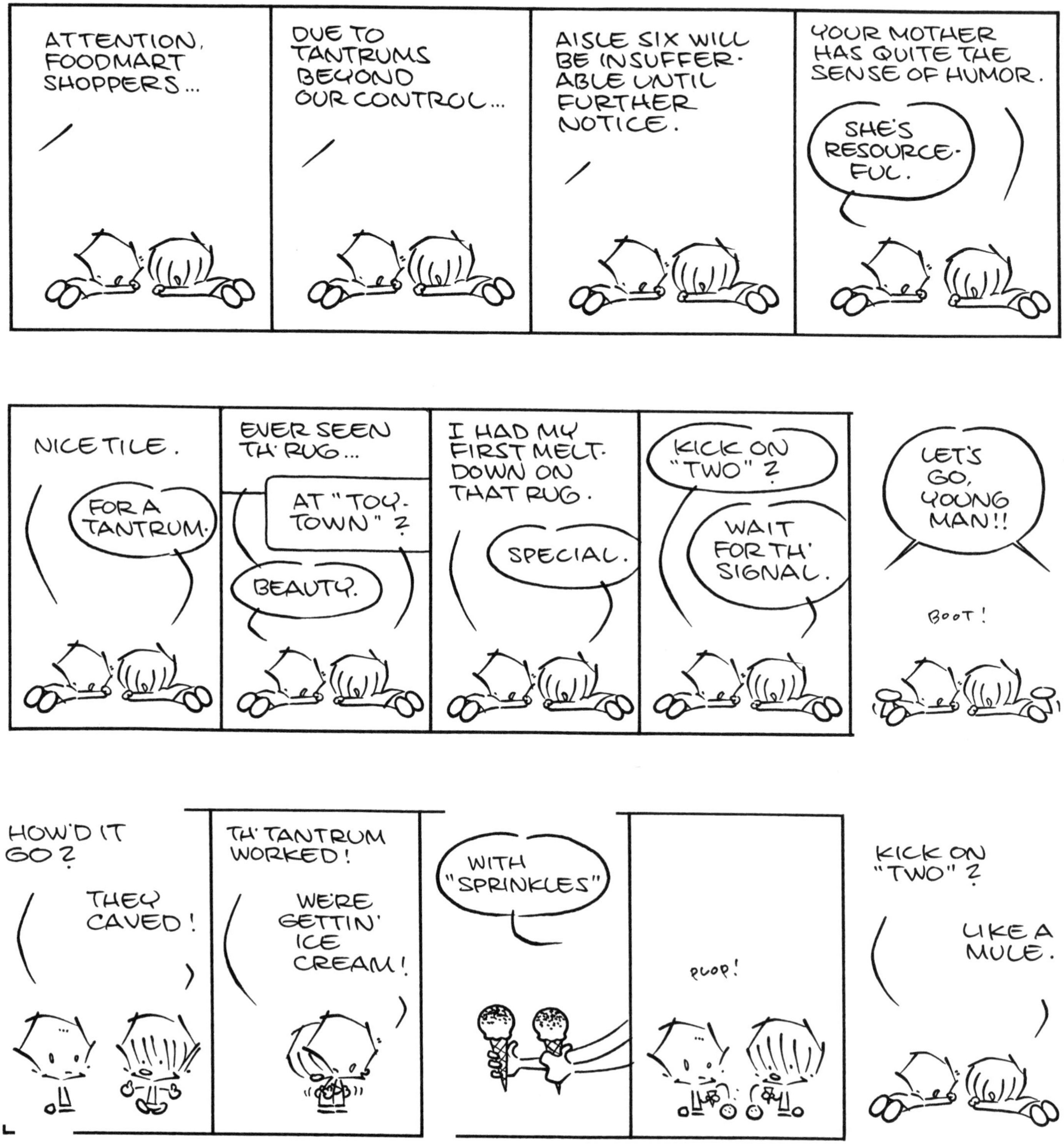
ATTENTION, FOODMART SHOPPERS...
DUE TO TANTRUMS BEYOND OUR CONTROL...
AISLE SIX WILL BE INSUFFER-ABLE UNTIL FURTHER NOTICE.
YOUR MOTHER HAS QUITE THE SENSE OF HUMOR.
SHE'S RESOURCE-FUL.
NICE TILE.
FOR A TANTRUM.
EVER SEEN TH' RUG...
AT "TOY-TOWN"?
BEAUTY.
I HAD MY FIRST MELT-DOWN ON THAT RUG.
SPECIAL.
KICK ON "TWO"?
WAIT FOR TH' SIGNAL.
LET'S GO, YOUNG MAN!!
BOOT!
HOW'D IT GO?
THEY CAVED!
TH' TANTRUM WORKED!
WE'RE GETTIN' ICE CREAM!
WITH "SPRINKLES"
PLOP!
KICK ON "TWO"?
LIKE A MULE.

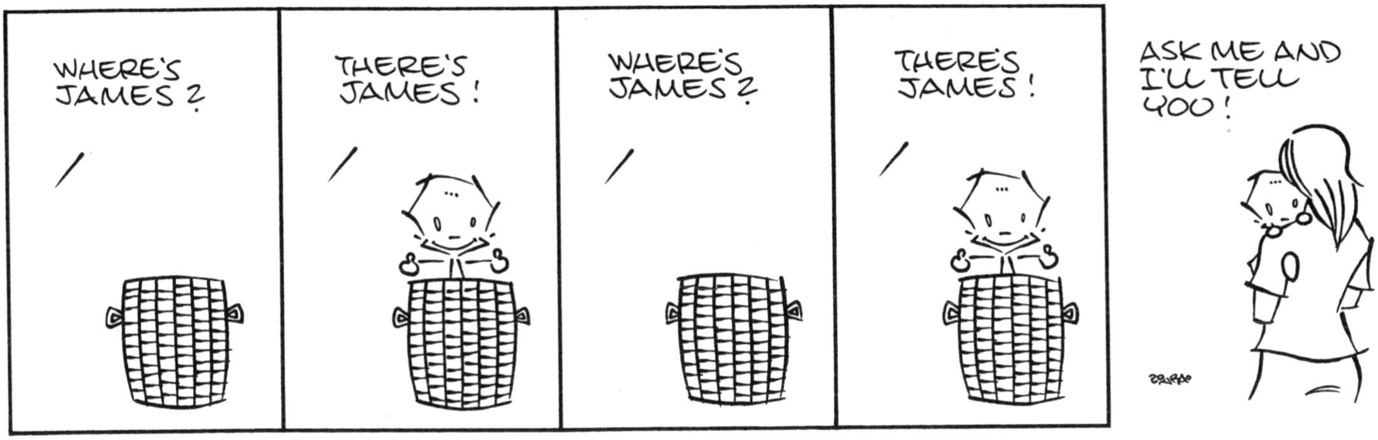
WHERE'S JAMES ?
THERE'S JAMES !
WHERE'S JAMES ?
THERE'S JAMES !
ASK ME AND I'LL TELL YOU !

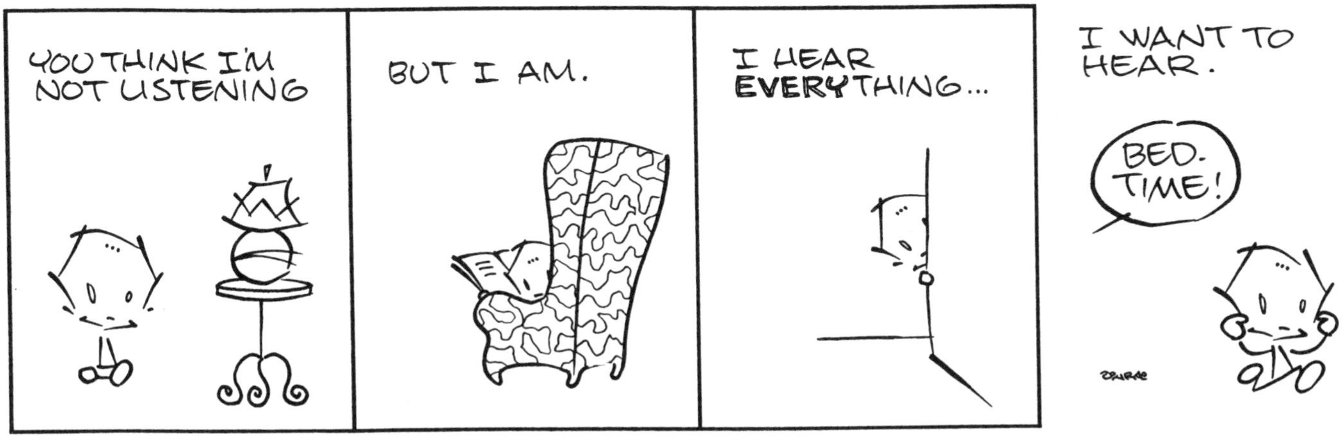
YOU THINK I'M NOT LISTENING
BUT I AM.
I HEAR EVERYTHING...
I WANT TO HEAR.
BED-TIME!

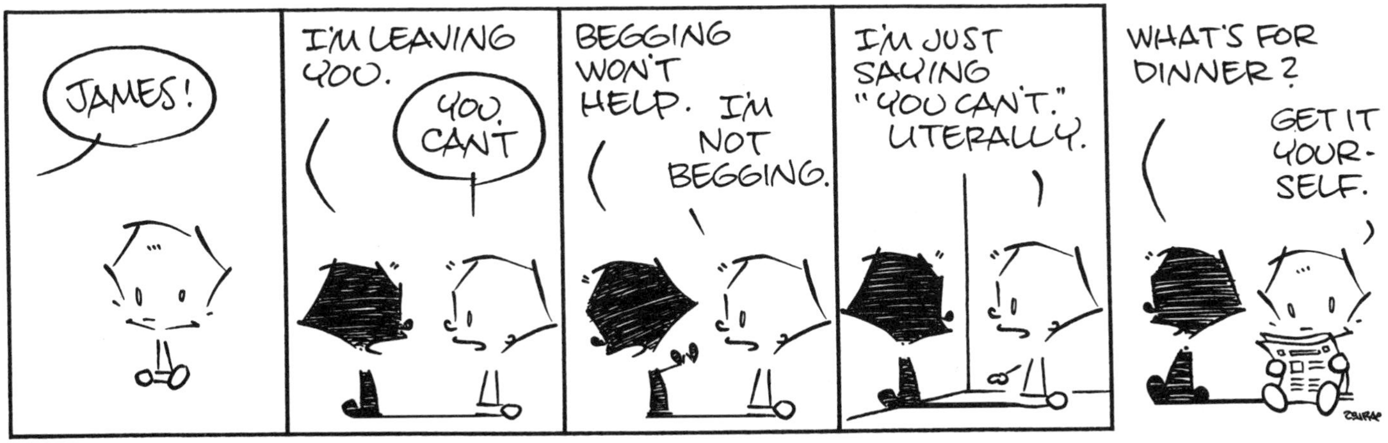
JAMES!
I'M LEAVING YOU.
YOU CAN'T
BEGGING WON'T HELP.
I'M NOT BEGGING.
I'M JUST SAYING "YOU CAN'T." LITERALLY.
WHAT'S FOR DINNER?
GET IT YOUR-SELF.

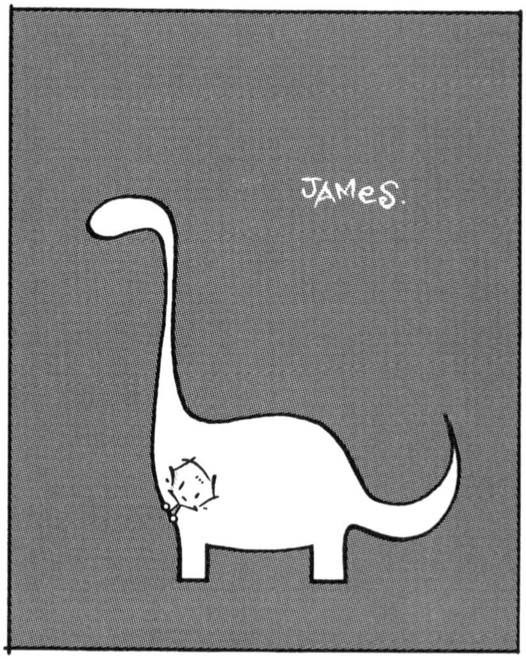
JAMES.

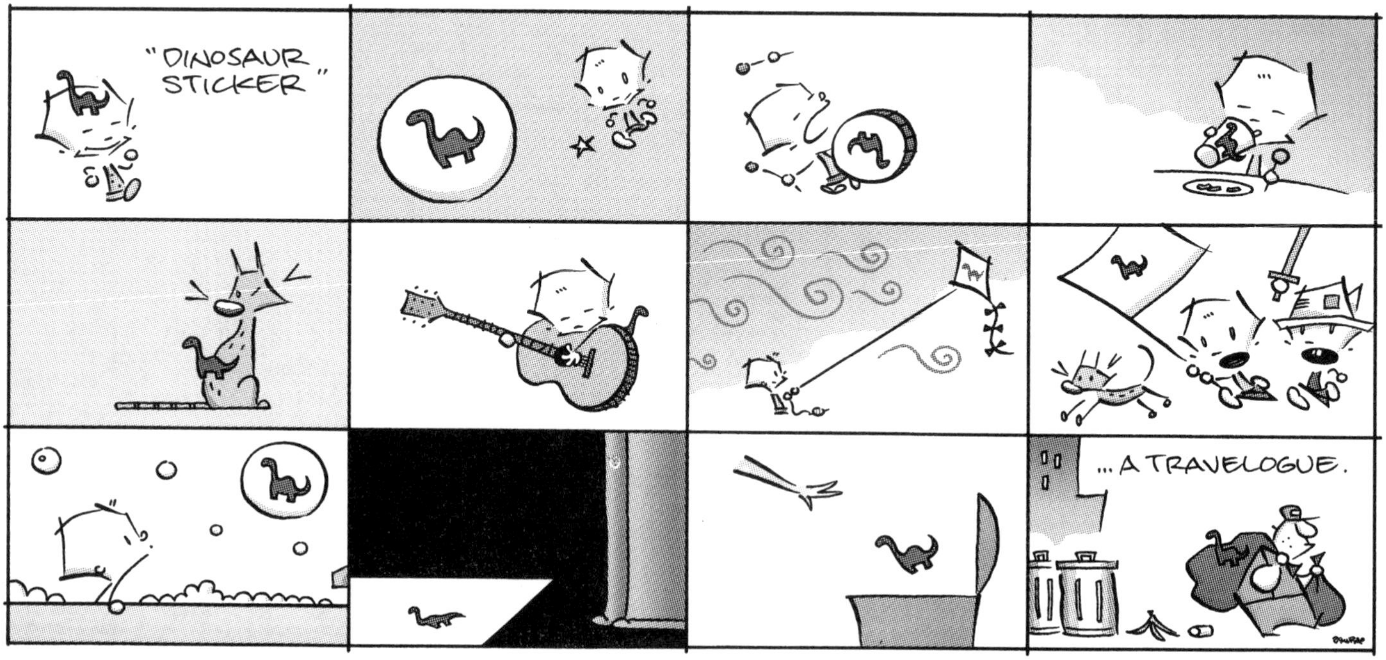
"DINOSAUR STICKER"
...A TRAVELOGUE.

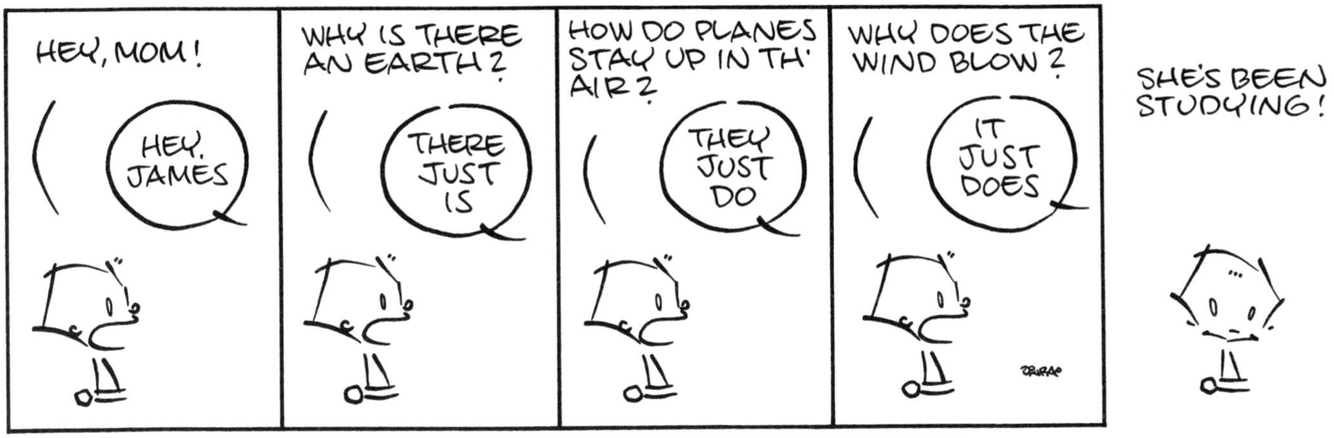
HEY, MOM!
HEY, JAMES
WHY IS THERE AN EARTH?
THERE JUST IS
HOW DO PLANES STAY UP IN TH' AIR?
THEY JUST DO
WHY DOES THE WIND BLOW?
IT JUST DOES
SHE'S BEEN STUDYING!

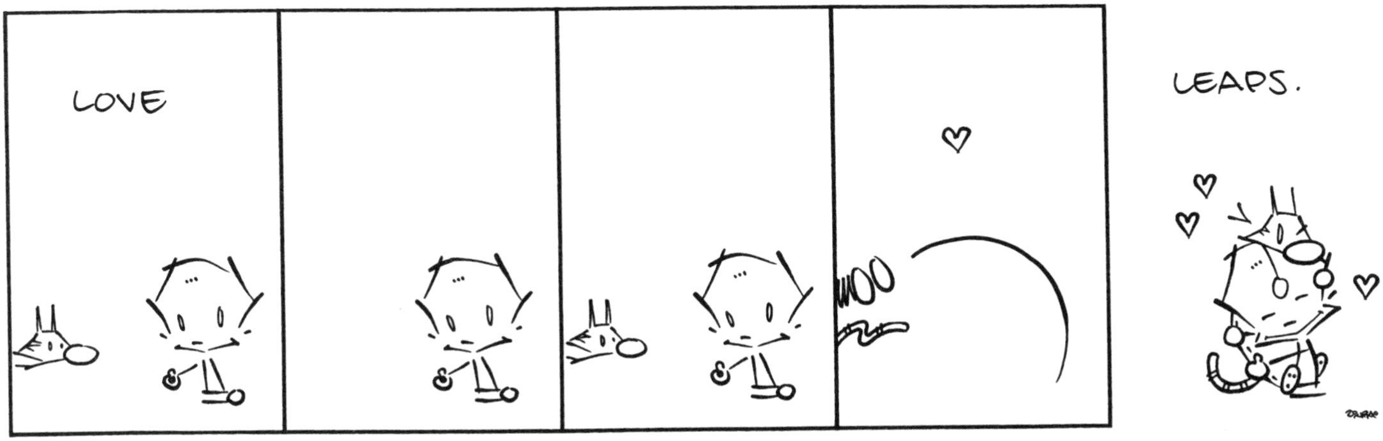
LOVE
WOO
LEAPS.

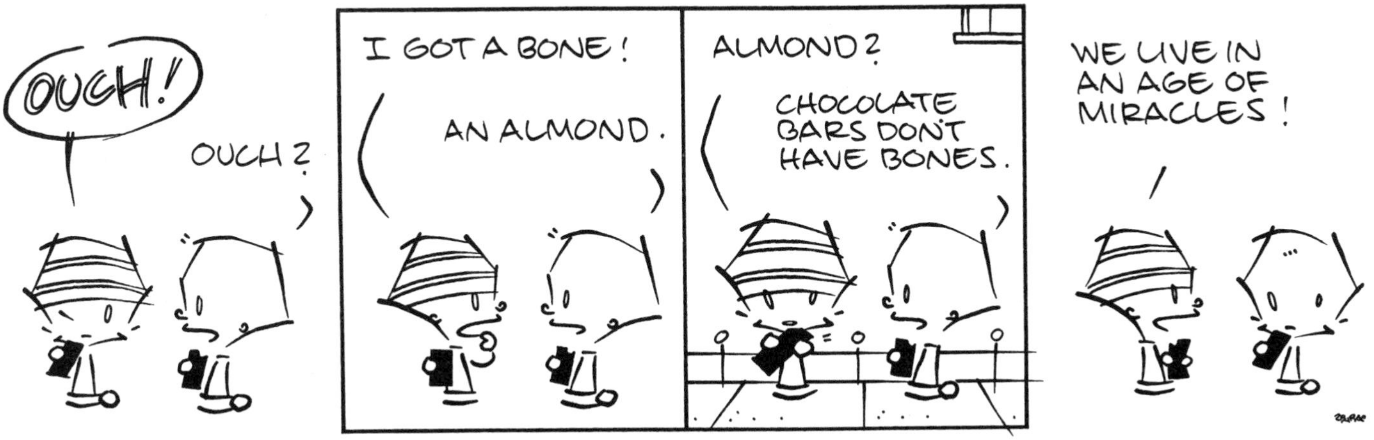
OUCH!
OUCH?
I GOT A BONE!
AN ALMOND.
ALMOND?
CHOCOLATE BARS DON'T HAVE BONES.
WE LIVE IN AN AGE OF MIRACLES!

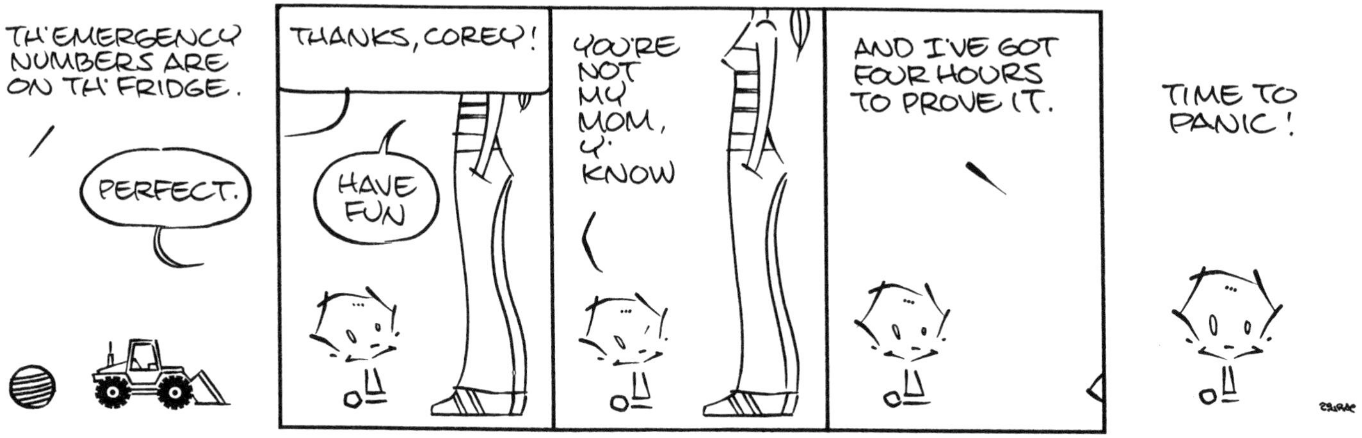
TH' EMERGENCY NUMBERS ARE ON TH' FRIDGE.
PERFECT.
THANKS, COREY!
HAVE FUN
YOU'RE NOT MY MOM, Y' KNOW
AND I'VE GOT FOUR HOURS TO PROVE IT.
TIME TO PANIC!

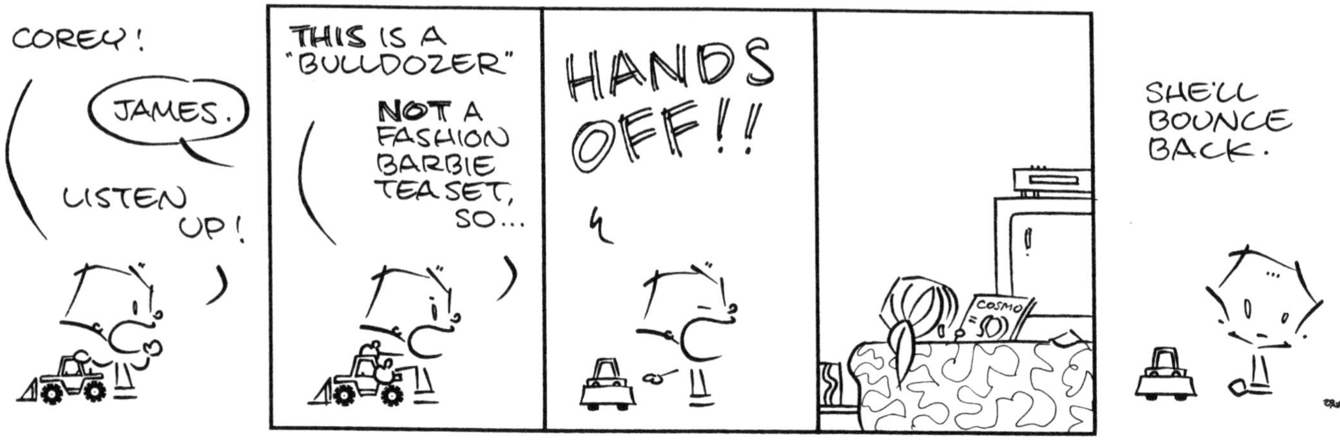
COREY!
JAMES.
LISTEN UP!
THIS IS A "BULLDOZER"
NOT A FASHION BARBIE TEA SET, SO...
HANDS OFF!!
COSMO
SHE'LL BOUNCE BACK.

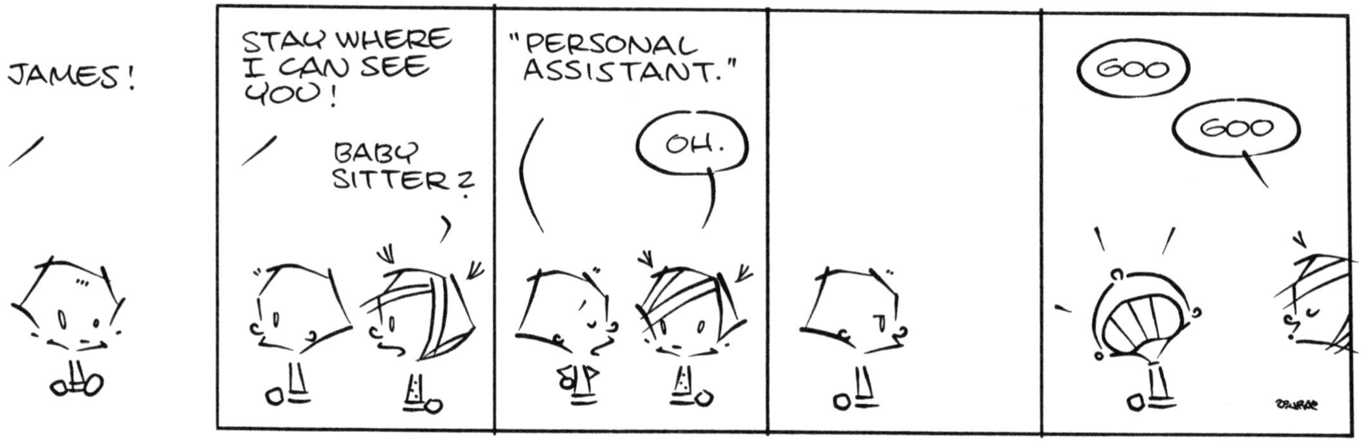
JAMES!
STAY WHERE I CAN SEE YOU!
BABY SITTER?
"PERSONAL ASSISTANT."
OH.
GOO
GOO

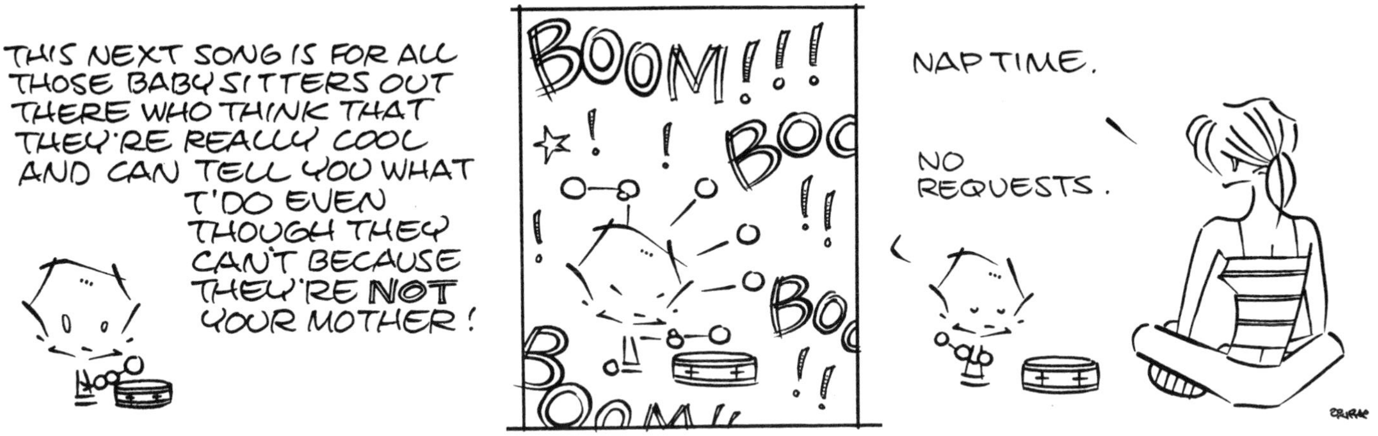
THIS NEXT SONG IS FOR ALL THOSE BABY SITTERS OUT THERE WHO THINK THAT THEY'RE REALLY COOL AND CAN TELL YOU WHAT T'DO EVEN THOUGH THEY CAN'T BECAUSE THEY'RE **NOT** YOUR MOTHER!
BOOM!!!
BOO
BOO
BOOM!!
NAP TIME.
NO REQUESTS.

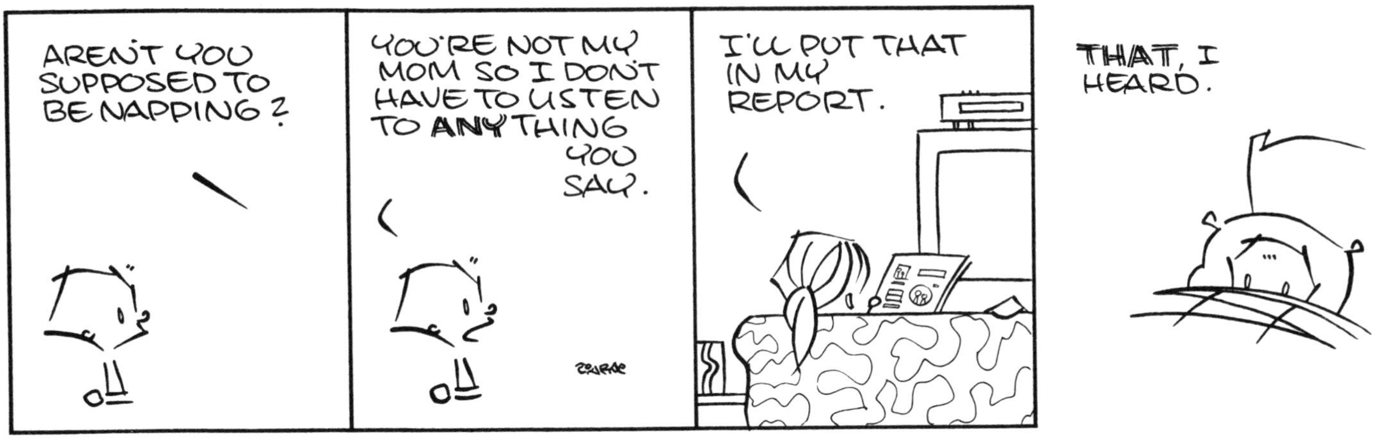
AREN'T YOU SUPPOSED TO BE NAPPING?
YOU'RE NOT MY MOM SO I DON'T HAVE TO LISTEN TO **ANY**THING YOU SAY.
I'LL PUT THAT IN MY REPORT.
THAT, I HEARD.

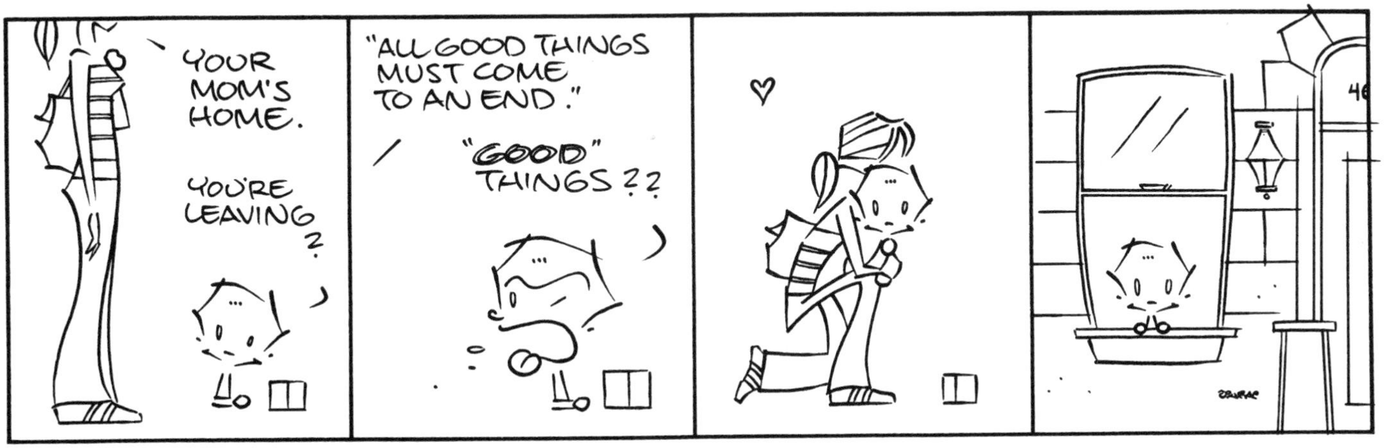
YOUR MOM'S HOME.
YOU'RE LEAVING?
"ALL GOOD THINGS MUST COME TO AN END."
"**GOOD**" THINGS??

Ceci n'est pas une tomate

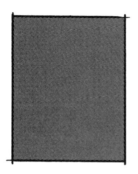

James

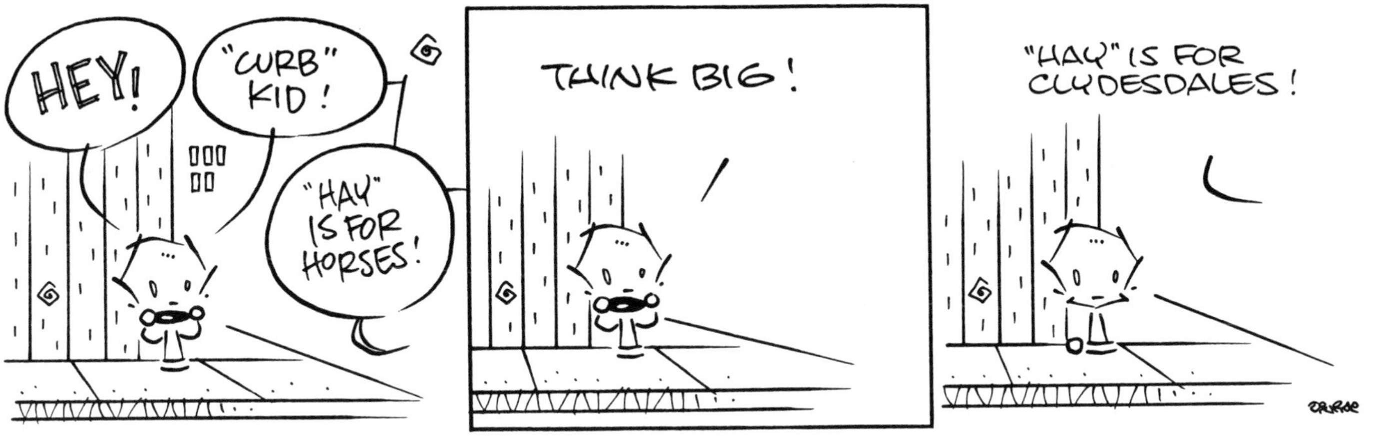
HEY!
"CURB" KID!
"HAY" IS FOR HORSES!
THINK BIG!
"HAY" IS FOR CLYDESDALES!

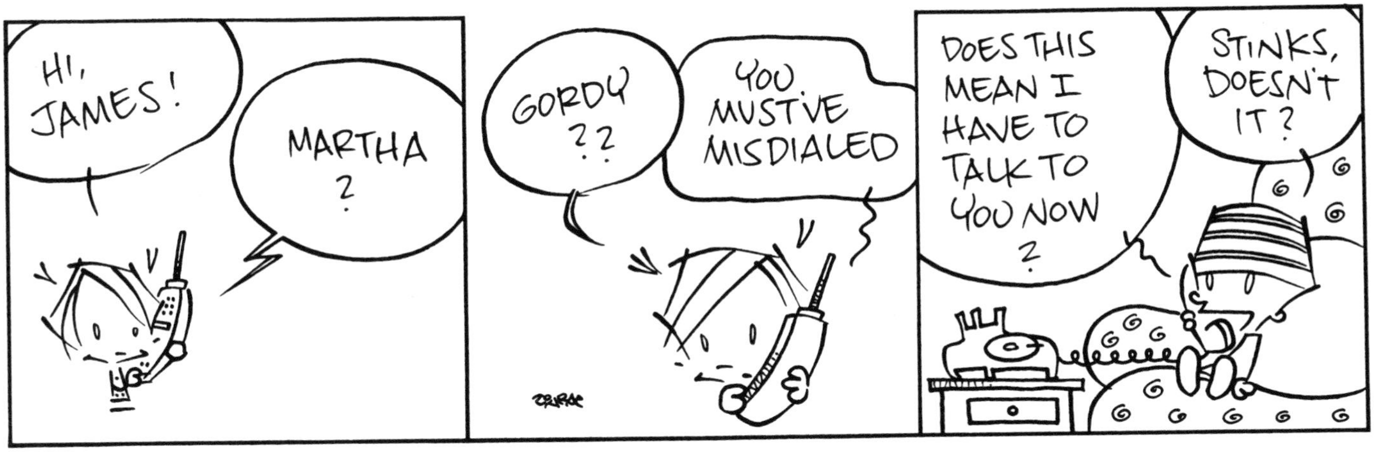
HI, JAMES!
MARTHA ?
GORDY ??
YOU MUSTVE MISDIALED
DOES THIS MEAN I HAVE TO TALK TO YOU NOW ?
STINKS, DOESN'T IT ?

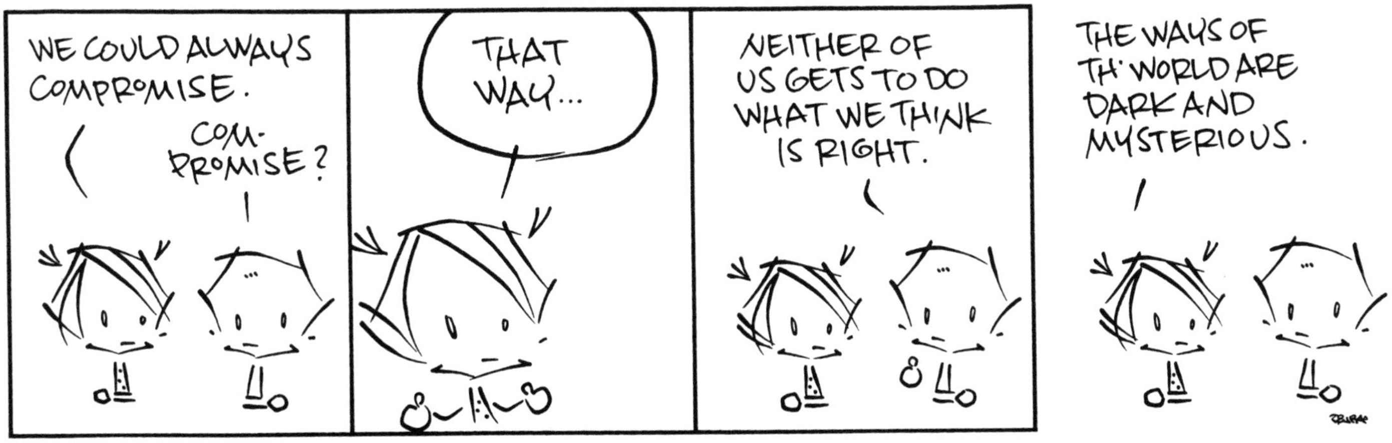
WE COULD ALWAYS COMPROMISE.
COM-PROMISE?
THAT WAY...
NEITHER OF US GETS TO DO WHAT WE THINK IS RIGHT.
THE WAYS OF TH' WORLD ARE DARK AND MYSTERIOUS.

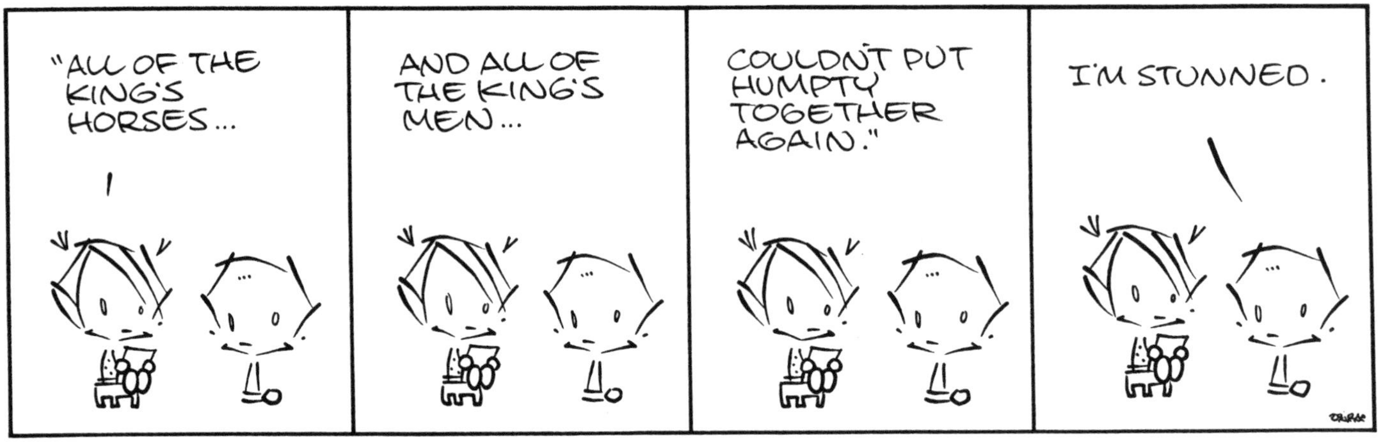
"ALL OF THE KING'S HORSES...
AND ALL OF THE KING'S MEN...
COULDN'T PUT HUMPTY TOGETHER AGAIN."
I'M STUNNED.

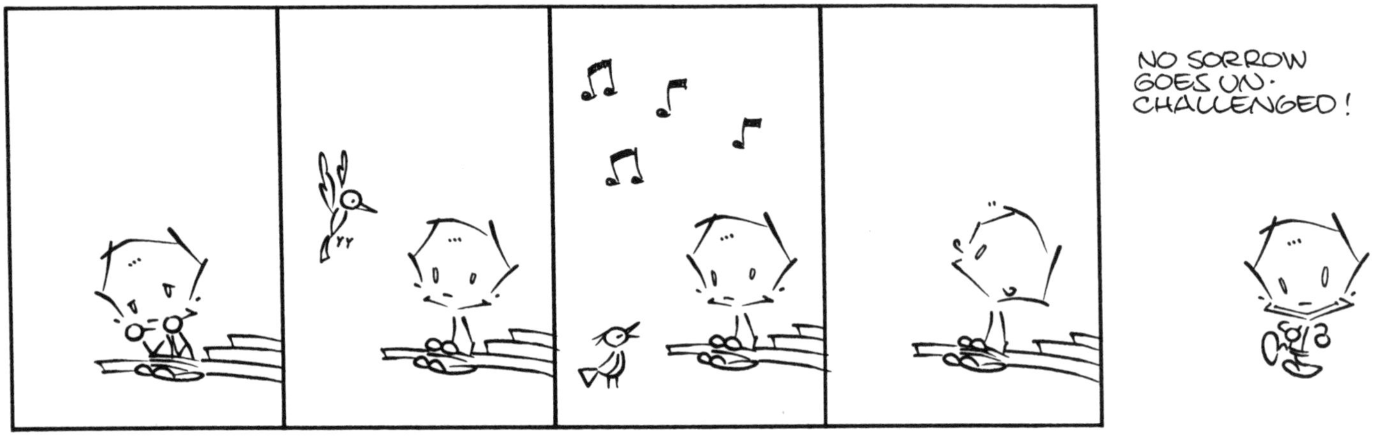
NO SORROW GOES UN-CHALLENGED!

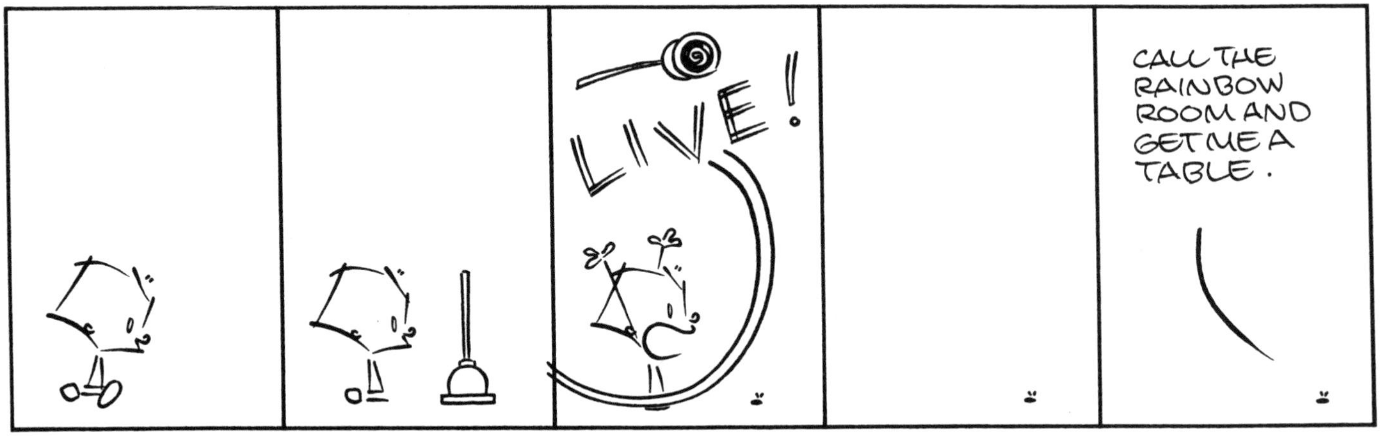
LIVE!
CALL THE RAINBOW ROOM AND GET ME A TABLE.

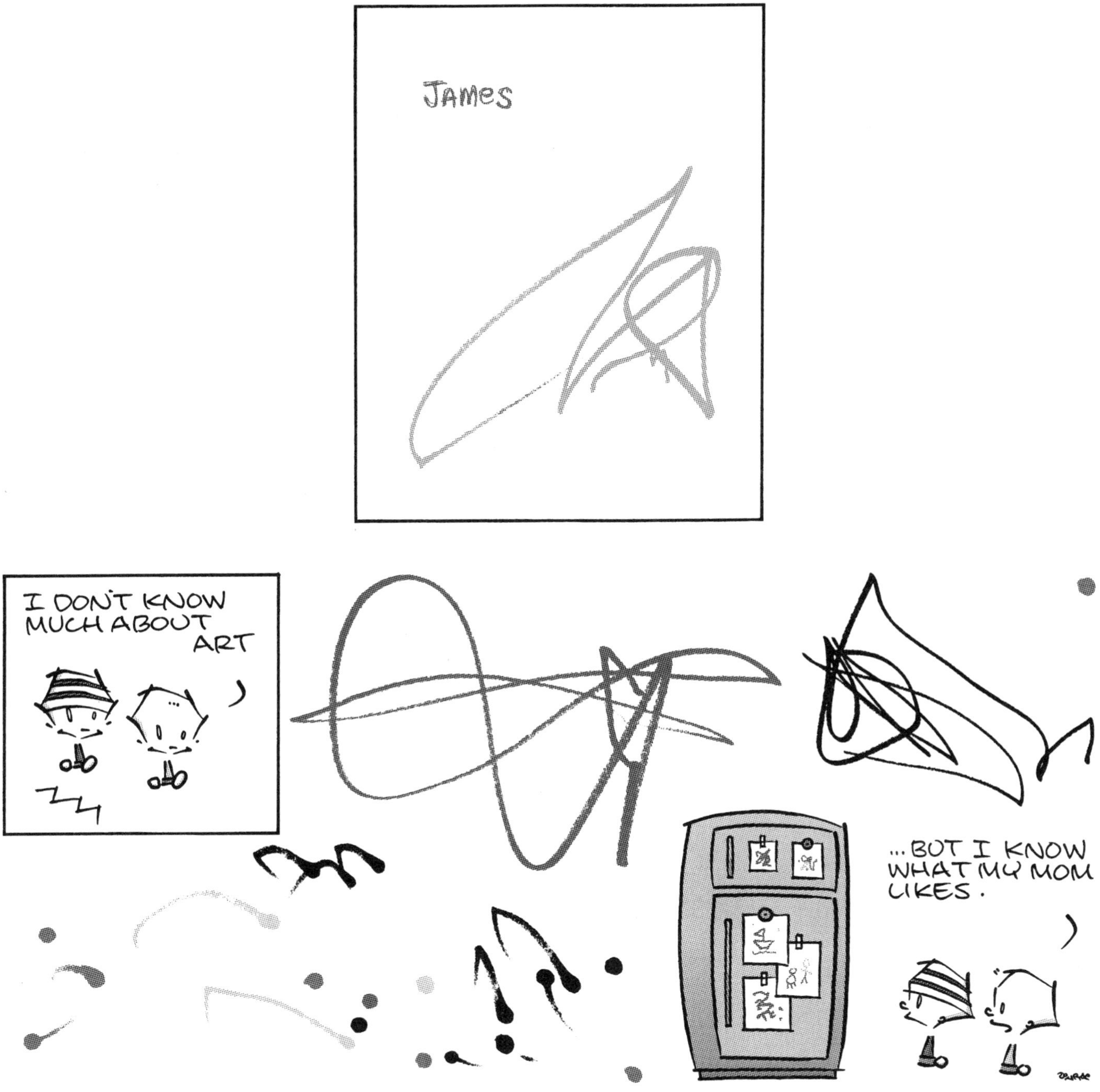
JAMES
I DON'T KNOW MUCH ABOUT ART
...BUT I KNOW WHAT MY MOM LIKES.

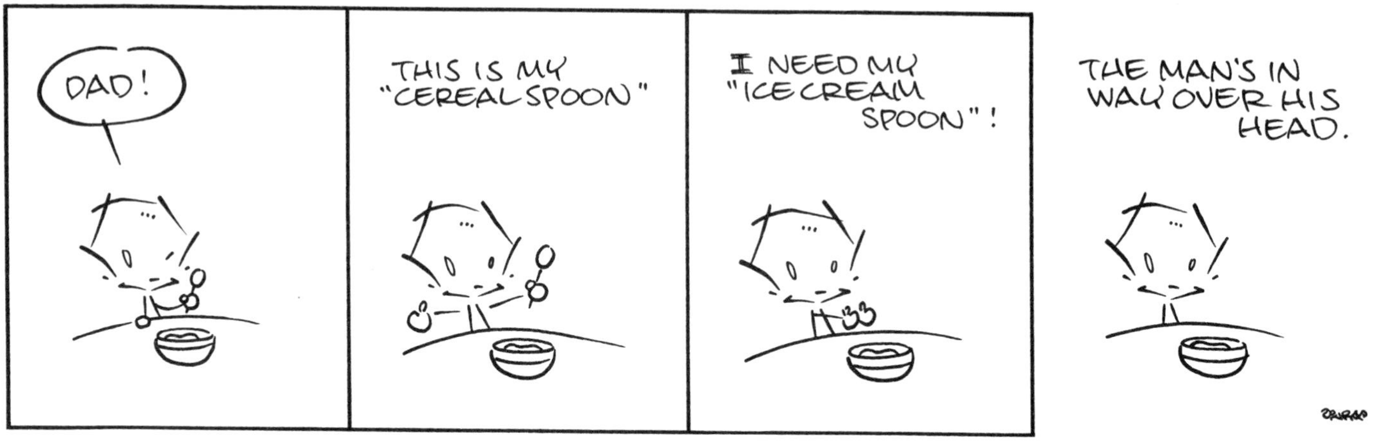
DAD!
THIS IS MY "CEREAL SPOON"
I NEED MY "ICE CREAM SPOON"!
THE MAN'S IN WAY OVER HIS HEAD.

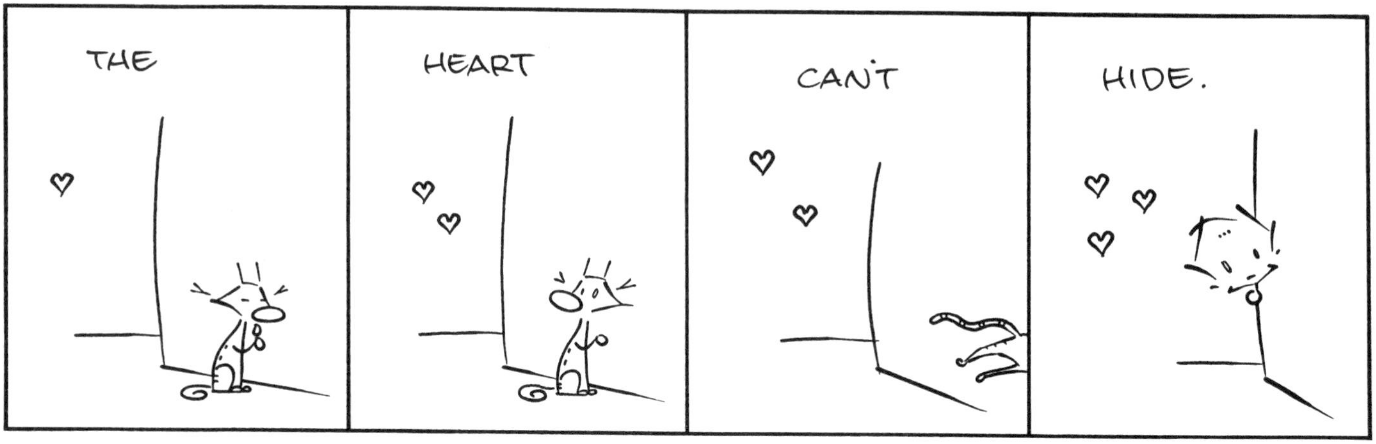
THE
HEART
CAN'T
HIDE.

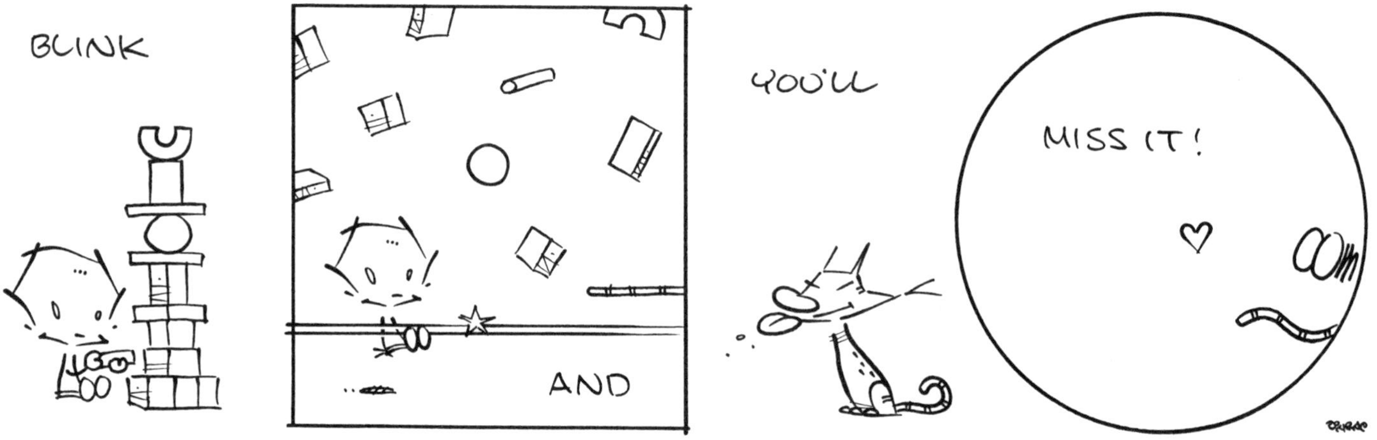
BLINK
AND
YOU'LL
MISS IT!

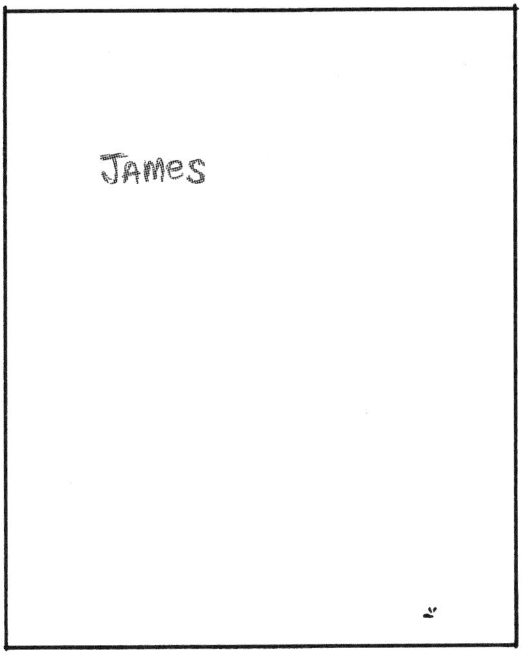
JAMES

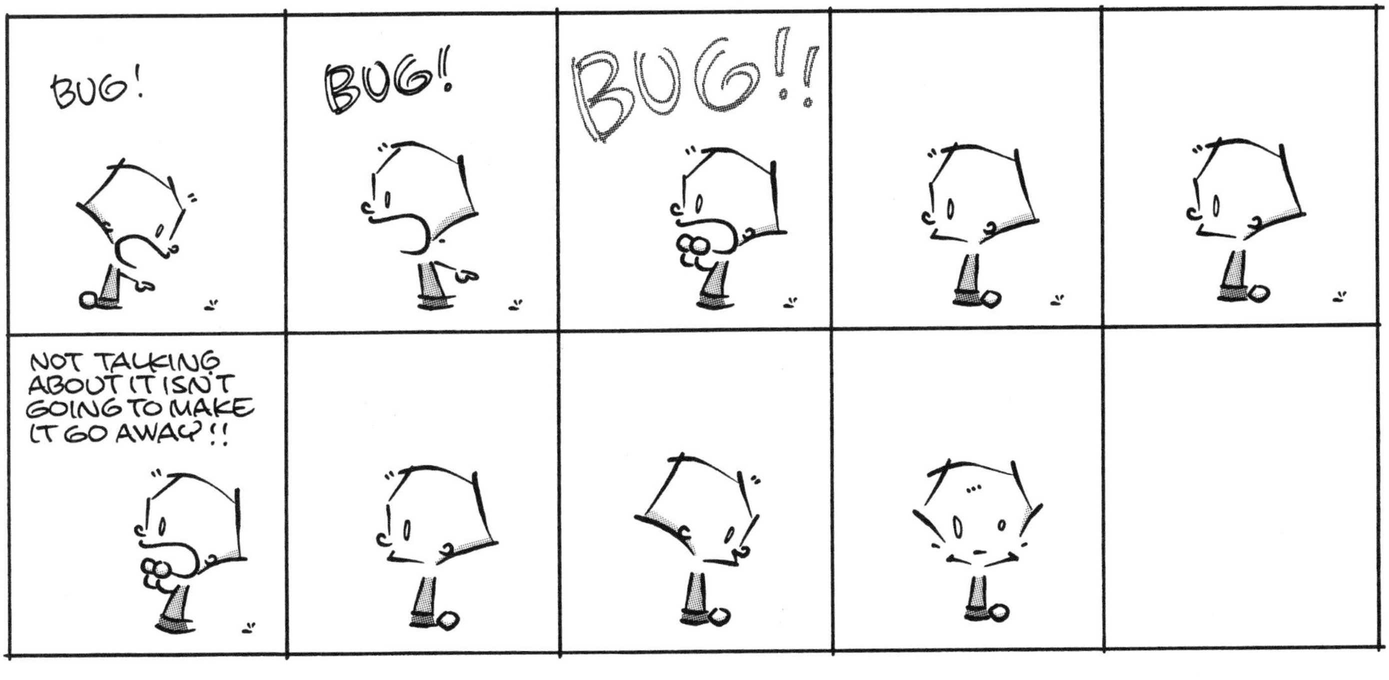
BUG!
BUG!
BUG!!
NOT TALKING ABOUT IT ISN'T GOING TO MAKE IT GO AWAY!!